Mathematics

Key Stage 4
incorporating GCSE

Volume 3

Higher tier (Levels 9 & 10)

R.C. Solomon

DP Publications Ltd
Aldine Place
LONDON W12 8AW

1992

Acknowledgements

We are grateful to the following for permission to reproduce illustrations:

The Royal Signals Museum

Yale Babylonian Collection

George Arthur Plimpton Collection, Rare Book and Manuscript Library, Columbia University

The Hulton Picture Library

The photograph on page 15 is reproduced by courtesy of the Trustees of the British Museum.

A CIP catalogue record for this book is available from the British Library

ISBN 1 873981 23 6

First edition 1992
Reprinted 1993

Typeset by
DP Publications Ltd

Printed in Great Britain by
Bath Press Ltd, Bath

Series preface

Volume 1 - Levels 4, 5 and 6

Volume 2 - Levels 7 and 8

Volume 3 - Levels 9 and 10

This is a totally new series written to meet all the requirements of the National Curriculum Key Stage 4, which also gives pupils the necessary preparation for the revised GCSE (1994).

The tests at the end of Key Stage 4, ie GCSE, mark the end of compulsory schooling. For very many pupils, these tests will be the evidence of their education that they will take with them into the adult world. It is important that during those last two years at school pupils acquire the following:

- Mathematical skills required for success in adult life.
- Recognition of the applications of Mathematics in everyday life.
- Appreciation of Mathematics as a source of interest in its own right.

How does the series work?

There are three books in the series, which cover the mathematical material for all but a small minority of the school population in this age group. There is some degree of overlap between the books, as it is important not to cater for too narrow an ability range. The books are in line with the achievement levels 4-10, though not rigidly: the National Curriculum stratification of the curriculum into levels is used as a framework round which to structure a course of study.

Each volume contains the following:

25 Chapters

The chapters cover the material specified by the National Curriculum. They are largely self-contained (ie it is not assumed that pupils will have covered all previous topics), thereby ensuring greater flexibility.

A variety of exercises

Many different types of exercise are included, to fulfil the National Curriculum criterion that pupils should become expert at a variety of tasks. The books of this series contain exercises of different lengths, as follows:

- Short questions in contexts *relevant to this age of pupil* (with answers at the back of the book – to be removed if desired).
- Longer, end of chapter questions, which may incorporate material from other parts of the syllabus. These questions might occupy *one or two class periods* and provide something for faster learners to do while the other pupils catch up.
- Guidelines for four extended tasks which could occupy *two or three weeks* and are concerned with the *use and application of mathematics*.
- Problems which can be solved using *spreadsheet programs*.
- *Puzzles* and *paradoxes* which demonstrate that mathematics is not as unambiguous as it may seem.

The extended tasks and many of the longer questions at chapter ends are open-ended, to give scope for exploration by pupils. A *balance* is maintained between questions which arise from *outside mathematics* and those which are part of the *internal development of mathematics*.

These tasks and questions have been taken from a wide variety of sources. One particularly fruitful source has been the history of mathematics, from Egypt, India, China, etc, as well as from Greece and modern Europe. It is hoped that pupils will learn to appreciate the long history and wide diffusion of mathematics.

Four consolidation sections

Spaced regularly throughout the books are consolidation sections containing the following:

A cross curriculum topic

This is taken from contexts from Science, Politics, History, etc. and is chosen to demonstrate the usefulness of mathematics across many subjects. They will serve as a useful basis for discussion, and provide interesting and readable interludes in the teaching text. The four topics between them touch upon much of the material of the book. By reference to the appropriate chapters they will help pupils see the application and source of the principles they are studying.

An extended task (as described above)

Exercises

There are miscellaneous exercises which are separated into Group A, containing questions *similar to those in the chapters*, Group B containing *challenge* questions, and Group C of *longer* questions.

Puzzles and paradoxes

These will demonstrate that mathematics is not as straightforward as it may seem!

Material on using computers

The National Curriculum Council stresses that every advantage should be taken of computers and calculators. Spreadsheets provide an ideal environment within which to explore mathematics, and each book includes a chapter containing problems which can be investigated with a spreadsheet.

Graded revision examples, test papers and GCSE examination papers

There are sets of *revision examples* and *revision tests* to ensure that students refresh and maintain their knowledge of previous material, and also *four examination papers* modelled on the new sample questions released by the *GCSE boards* in *April 1992*.

Free teachers' guide

There is a *free* Teachers' Guide to accompany each volume for teachers using the books as class texts. The guides contain *keys* to connect the material in the books with the *levels* of the National Curriculum. *Solutions* and *notes* on the longer exercises and the extended tasks are given, along with suggestions for how they could be developed by talented pupils.

What about the author?

Bob Solomon has spent many years teaching and writing mathematics at this level. His GCSE Mathematics book is widely recommended as a revision course text in sixth form colleges and colleges of further education; his 'Higher' level book for GCSE has been described as 'the very best practice by the very best teachers'. Theta said of his A-Level revision text that it was 'clearly the result of many years of teaching experience'.

Fits the National Curriculum and GCSE

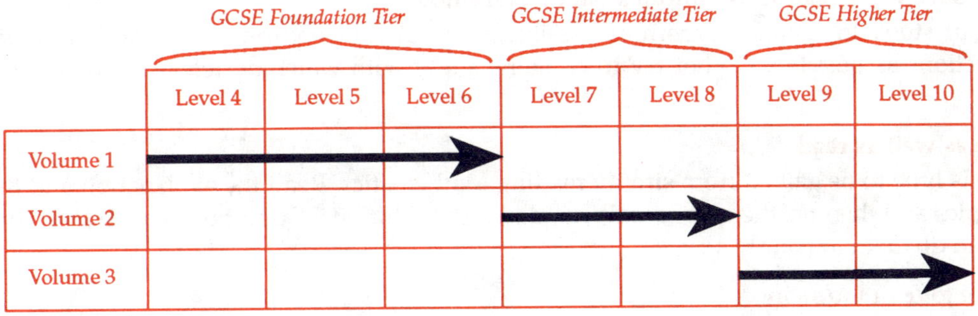

	GCSE Foundation Tier			*GCSE Intermediate Tier*		*GCSE Higher Tier*	
	Level 4	Level 5	Level 6	Level 7	Level 8	Level 9	Level 10
Volume 1	→	→	→				
Volume 2				→	→		
Volume 3						→	→

Preface for Volume III

This is the *third* book in the series, and covers Levels 9 and 10 of the Mathematics syllabus. It can be used to take the pupil up to the testing at Key Stage 4 at those levels, and as preparation for the further study of Mathematics.

RC Solomon
June 1992

Study and examination hints

1. Study hints

This book has been written to help you understand the material of Levels 9 and 10 of National Curriculum Mathematics. Of course it must be used in an efficient way. The following hints will help you make good use of your study time.

A good rule to follow is: ***Little but often***
An hour a day for seven days is more useful than seven hours of work on a single day.

Make sure you get a full 60 minutes out of every hour
Do your study in as quiet a room as possible, with all your equipment to hand, and with as few distractions as possible. Do not try to combine study with watching television or listening to the radio.

Write as well as read
There is little to be gained from simply reading Mathematics. Read the explanation and the worked examples and then try the exercises. Write down the solutions. Do not try to convince yourself that you can do them in your head.

Do not give in too soon
There are answers at the back of the book, but use them for checking that you are right, rather than for finding out how to do a problem.

At the end of the book are four exams and two mental tests. You are allowed a calculator for these exams. Make sure you are confident in its use. For the mental tests, get someone to read out the questions to you, repeating them once, and taking 20 minutes over each test. You are not allowed a calculator in these tests.

2. Examination hints

How well you do in an exam depends mainly on how well you have prepared for it. But many candidates do poorly because of bad examination technique. The following hints will help you make the most of your examination time.

Read the question carefully
Very many marks are lost by candidates who have misunderstood a question. Not only do they lose the marks for that question, but they also lose time because the question is made more complicated by their mistake.

Do not spend too much time on one question
There is little or no point in spending a third of the time on a question that carries a twentieth of the marks. Leave that question, and come back to it later if you have time at the end of the exam.

Show your working
If you obtain a wrong answer just because of a slight slip, then you will not lose many marks provided that you show all your working. If you put down a wrong answer without any explanation then you will get no marks at all.

Try to make your solutions neat

Use enough paper to ensure that your answer can be read easily. But do not spend too much time on this – there is no point in spending five minutes on a beautiful diagram for a question which is only worth 2 marks.

Recognise what each question is about

Many candidates find that they can answer a question when they are doing an exercise consisting of several similar problems, but cannot answer the same question when it occurs in a test paper surrounded by different questions. Read each question carefully, and identify the topic or topics of the question. The examiners are not trying to 'catch you out'. They are trying to test that you have studied each part of the syllabus and are able to answer questions on it.

Recognise combinations of topics

Many questions start with a problem in one area of mathematics, and then require you to apply your answer to another, related, area. Make sure you appreciate what the examiners are looking for.

Above all: ***Make good use of your time!***

During the months that you are preparing yourself for the examination make sure that each hour of learning or revision is well spent. During the actual examination, make the best use of the short time available.

Contents

Chapter 1

Numbers

When you divide 1 by 3 on a calculator, the result is a string of 3's, 0.33333333. When you multiply this by 3, what do you get? The result depends on the calculator.

Jane, with a scientific calculator, gets 1. Keith, with a non-scientific calculator, gets a string of 9's, 0.99999999.

Keith says: "If you continue the 9's for ever, these numbers are the same. 0.9999999... is equal to 1".

Jane says: "However many 9's you take, 0.9999999... is always less than 1. The numbers aren't the same, there's an infinitely small difference".

Who is right?

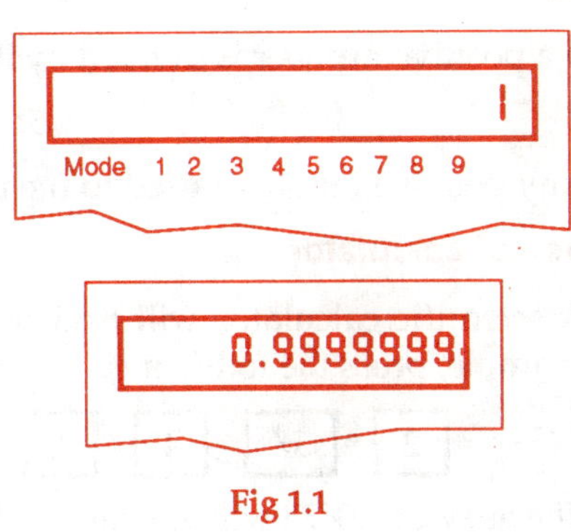

Fig 1.1

1.1 Integer powers

Composites and primes

When a number x is multiplied by itself n times, the result is the n'th power of the number x. The power n is also called the index.

x is also said to be raised to the n'th power. For example, 3 raised to the power 5 is:

$$3 \times 3 \times 3 \times 3 \times 3 = 3^5 = 243.$$

Multiplying

If 3 raised to the power 3 is multiplied by 3 raised to the power 4, the result is 3 raised to the power 7.

$$(3 \times 3 \times 3) \times (3 \times 3 \times 3 \times 3) = 3 \times 3 \times 3 \times 3 \times 3 \times 3 \times 3$$

We see that when powers are multiplied, the indices are added.

$$3^3 \times 3^4 = 3^7$$

Division

When 3 raised to the power 5 is divided by 3 raised to the power 3, the result is 3 raised to the power 2.

$$\frac{3 \times 3 \times 3 \times 3 \times 3}{3 \times 3 \times 3} = 3 \times 3 = 3^2$$

We see that, when powers are divided, the indices are subtracted.

$$3^5 \div 3^3 = 3^2$$

Negative powers

If the second power is greater than the first, the result is a negative index.

$$3^3 \div 3^5 = 3^{-2}.$$

This must be 1 over the previous result. It follows that the negative power of a number is 1 over the positive power.

$$3^{-2} = \frac{1}{3^2} = \frac{1}{9}$$

Zero

If a positive number is divided by itself, the result is always one. Applying this to powers:

$$5^4 \div 5^4 = 5^{4-4} = 5^0 = 1$$

Any positive number raised to the power 0 is 1.

Use of calculator

A scientific calculator will find negative powers. Press the ± button after the power. To find 2^{-4}, for example, press the following:

[2] [x^y] [4] [±] [=]

The answer 0.0625 will appear.

1.1.1 Examples

1) Evaluate: a) 2^5 b) 4^{-2}.

Solution Use the definition:

a) $2^5 = 2 \times 2 \times 2 \times 2 \times 2 = 32$

b) $4^{-2} = \frac{1}{4^2} = \frac{1}{16}$

2) Express $\frac{5^3 \times 5^5}{5^6}$ as a single power of 5.

Solution The indices are added along the top line of the fraction, and the bottom index is subtracted. This gives:

$5^{3+5-6} = 5^2$

1.1.2 Exercises

1) Evaluate the following:

a) 3^4 b) 4^4 c) 1^6 d) 2^{10}

e) $\left(\frac{1}{2}\right)^3$ f) 0.3^3 g) 1.5^3 h) $(-2)^3$

2) Evaluate the following:

a) 2^{-1} b) 3^{-3} c) 5^{-3} d) 4^{-3}

e) 1^{-7} f) $\left(\frac{1}{2}\right)^{-1}$ g) $\left(\frac{1}{3}\right)^{-2}$

3) Simplify the following:

a) $3^2 \times 3^4$ b) $2^4 \times 2^3$ c) $4^3 \times 4^2$

d) $3^5 \times 3^{-4}$ e) $7^6 \times 7^{-3}$

4) Simplify the following:

a) $4^6 \div 4^2$ b) $3^5 \div 3^3$ c) $4^5 \div 4^{-2}$ d) $5^{-6} \div 5^{-2}$ e) $5^{-3} \div 5^2$ f) $\left(\frac{1}{2}\right)^4 \div \left(\frac{1}{2}\right)^{-5}$

5) Express $\dfrac{2^5 \times 2^5}{2^3 \times 2^6}$ as a single power of 2.

6) Express $\dfrac{3^8}{3^7 \times 3^4}$ as a single power of 3.

7) Use your calculator to find the following, rounding your answers to 3 significant figures:

a) 1.2^{10} b) 6.5^8 c) 2.43^{13} d) 1.4^{-8} e) 0.27^{-10}

8) Replace the * by indices to make the following true:

a) $4 = 2^*$ b) $8 = 2^*$ c) $3^* = 81$ d) $100{,}000 = 10^*$ e) $\frac{1}{2} = 2^*$

f) $0.25 = 4^*$ g) $0.125 = 8^*$ h) $0.001 = 10^*$ i) $1 = 6^*$

1.2 Fractional indices and laws of indices

Fractional powers

When powers are multiplied, the indices are added. Apply this rule to fractional indices.

$$2^{\frac{1}{2}} \times 2^{\frac{1}{2}} = 2^{\frac{1}{2}+\frac{1}{2}} = 2^1 = 2$$

So when $2^{\frac{1}{2}}$ is squared, the result is 2. It follows that $2^{\frac{1}{2}}$ is the square root of 2. In general, a fractional index $\frac{1}{n}$ gives the n'th root.

$$2^{\frac{1}{n}} = \sqrt[n]{2}$$

Laws of indices

To summarize, indices obey the following rules:

Multiplying and dividing.

$$a^n \times a^m = a^{n+m} \qquad a^n \div a^m = a^{n-m} \qquad (ab)^n = a^n b^n$$

Negative, zero and fractional powers.

$$a^{-n} = \frac{1}{a^n} \qquad a^0 = 1 \qquad a^{\frac{1}{n}} = \sqrt[n]{a}$$

Successive powers.

$$(a^n)^m = a^{nm}$$

Use of calculator

The x^y button on your calculator will work for fractional indices. It can also find n'th roots, by pressing the inv button first. To find $\sqrt[8]{9}$, press the following:

9	inv	x^y	8	=

The answer 1.316074 will appear.

1.2.1 Examples

1) Evaluate: a) 3^0 b) $4^{\frac{1}{2}}$

Solution Use the definitions:

a) $3^0 = 1$ b) $4^{\frac{1}{2}} = \sqrt{4} = 2$

2) Simplify: a) $5^3 \times 25^2 \div 125^2$ b) $16^{\frac{3}{4}}$

Solution a) The numbers concerned here are all powers of 5. Re-write and simplify:

$5^3 \times (5^2)^2 \div (5^3)^2 = 5^3 \times 5^4 \div 5^6$

Add and subtract the indices:

$5^{3+4-6} = 5^1 = 5$

b) Re-write $16^{\frac{3}{4}}$ as $\left(16^{\frac{1}{4}}\right)^3$

The fourth root of 16 is 2. Cube this to give 8.

$16^{\frac{3}{4}} = 8$

1.2.2 Exercises

1) Evaluate the following:

a) $9^{\frac{1}{2}}$ b) $100^{\frac{1}{2}}$ c) $8^{\frac{1}{3}}$ d) $49^{-\frac{1}{2}}$ e) $64^{-\frac{1}{3}}$ f) $1000^{\frac{1}{3}}$

2) Evaluate the following:

a) $8^{\frac{2}{3}}$ b) $9^{\frac{3}{2}}$ c) $1000^{\frac{2}{3}}$ d) $\left(\frac{1}{4}\right)^{-2}$ e) $\left(\frac{1}{4}\right)^{-\frac{1}{2}}$ f) $0.01^{-\frac{1}{2}}$

3) Simplify the following:

a) $4^3 \times 2^6 \div 8^3$ b) $27^2 \times 9^2 \times 3^{-7}$ c) $10^{\frac{1}{2}} \times 100^{\frac{1}{4}}$

4) Simplify the following:

a) $x^{\frac{1}{2}} \times x^{\frac{1}{2}}$ b) $y^{\frac{1}{4}} \times y^{\frac{3}{4}}$ c) $3^x \times 9^x \div 27^x$

5) Use your calculator to find the following, rounding your answer to 3 significant figures:

a) $1.23^{3.24}$ b) $45.2^{0.12}$ c) $1.78^{-4.3}$ d) $\sqrt[10]{2.7}$ e) $\sqrt[7]{0.183}$

1.3 Rational and irrational numbers

Terminating and repeating decimals

Fractions can be converted to decimals. Sometimes the decimal corresponding to a fraction terminates, as in $\frac{3}{8} = 0.375$. Sometimes the decimal does not terminate, as in $\frac{5}{11} = 0.4545\ldots$, where the 45's go on for ever.

A decimal like 0.454545... is a recurring decimal. To show which numbers are repeated we often put dots on top, as in $\frac{5}{11} = 0.45454545\ldots = 0.\dot{4}\dot{5}$.

Irrational numbers

A fraction is sometimes called a rational number, because it is the ratio of two whole numbers. Any recurring or terminating decimal must be rational.

Numbers which cannot be represented as fractions are called irrational. Examples of irrational numbers are $\sqrt{2}$ and π . Any decimal which is neither terminating nor recurring must be irrational.

1.3.1 Example

Write 0.181818... using the dot notation. Convert it into a fraction.

Solution The 18 pattern is repeated. We can show this by putting dots above these numbers.

$0.181818... = 0.\dot{1}\dot{8}$

Because the 18 pattern is repeated the number must be rational. Call it x. When we multiply x by 100 the decimal point moves two places to the right.

$x = 0.181818...$ and $100x = 18.181818...$

When the first equation is subtracted from the second the recurring 18's cancel out.

$100x - x = (18.181818...) - (0.181818...) = 18$

This shows that $99x = 18$. We can now write x as a fraction.

$\mathbf{0.181818... = \frac{18}{99} = \frac{2}{11}}$

1.3.2 Exercises

1) Convert the following fractions to decimals, and show their recurring patterns by the dot symbol.

   a) $\frac{2}{3}$ b) $\frac{5}{9}$ c) $\frac{7}{11}$ d) $\frac{14}{111}$ e) $\frac{2}{7}$

2) Write out the first 7 decimal places of the following recurring decimals.

   a) $0.\dot{7}$ b) $0.\dot{1}\dot{2}$ c) $0.\dot{1}3\dot{5}$ d) $0.\dot{2}0\dot{7}$

3) Find the fractions corresponding to the following recurring decimals.

   a) 0.6666... b) 0.4444... c) 0.272727... d) 0.135135135...

4) Suppose that x and y are both rational numbers. So $x = \frac{a}{b}$ and $y = \frac{c}{d}$, where a, b, c, d are whole numbers.

   Show that the following are also rational numbers.

   a) $x \times y$ b) $x \div y$ c) $x + y$ d) $x - y$

5) Take the following terminating decimals, and square them. What is the connection between the number of decimal places before and after squaring?

   a) 1.4 b) 1.41 c) 1.414

6) From your results in (5), is it possible for $\sqrt{2}$ to be a terminating decimal?

7) What other square roots might be irrational?

8) When you find the sin or $\sin^{-1}$ of a number, is the result rational or irrational?

9) In the problem at the beginning of the chapter two people were arguing about whether 0.9999... is equal to 1. Use the techniques of this section to find the fraction corresponding to 0.9999...

1.4 Longer exercises

A. The irrationality of √2

Here you prove that √2 is irrational.

Suppose we could find whole numbers a and b, for which $\sqrt{2} = \frac{a}{b}$. We may assume that we have simplified the fraction as far as possible. *So a and b have no common factor.*

Square both sides. What do you get?

Multiply both sides by b^2. You should have $2b^2 = a^2$.

There are now two ways to proceed.

1) Is a^2 even or odd? Is a itself even or odd?

Replace a by $2c$. Put this into the equation. After simplifying you should get $b^2 = 2c^2$.

Is b^2 even or odd? Is b even or odd?

Does this tie up with the statement in italics above? What can you say about √2?

2) A second method is as follows.

Take several square numbers such as 36, 144, 81 and so on. How many times does 2 divide them? You should find that 2 always divides a square number an even number of times. Can you show why this is true?

Apply this result to a^2 and b^2.

How many times does 2 divide a^2? How many times does 2 divide b^2?

If $a^2 = 2b^2$, then 2 must divide a^2 one more time than it divides b^2. How does this fit in with the paragraph above? What can you say about √2?

B. Pouring water

You may have met problems like: *With a 5 pint jug and a 3 pint jug and a tap, how do you pour out a volume of 17 pints?*

The solution is to use the 5 pint jug once and the 3 pint jug four times.

The problem is equivalent to solving the equation $5x + 3y = 17$, where x and y must be whole numbers. The solution is $x = 1$ and $y = 4$.

Suppose now that you are allowed to pour from one jug to the other. How can you measure out a volume of 1 pint?

This is equivalent to solving the equation $5x + 3y = 1$, where x and y are whole numbers which may be negative.

1) Solve this equation, and hence give a way to measure out 1 pint.

2) How do you measure out 1 pint with a 4 pint jug and a 7 pint jug?

3) Now try with a 5 pint jug and a 7 pint jug.

4) Can you measure out 1 pint with a 4 pint jug and a 6 pint jug? Why not? What is the smallest [illegible]u can measure out?

5) Can you find a general rule, for when you can measure out exactly 1 pint, with two jugs of capacity n pints and m pints?

Multiple choice question *(Tick appropriate box)*

$3^2 \times 9^3$, expressed as a single power, is:

a) 3^8 ☐

b) 27^5 ☐

c) 3^{12} ☐

d) 162 ☐

e) 3^{11} ☐

Points to note

1) *Taking powers.*

Be careful not to confuse the power of a number with the product of the power and the number. For example:

$$a^2 \neq 2a.$$

Similarly, $\sqrt{a} \neq \frac{1}{2}a$.

2) *Arithmetic of indices*

There are very many points to note when calculating with indices. Usually these occur because taking powers has been confused with multiplying or dividing. Here are some things to watch out for:

$5^3 \times 5^2 \neq 5^6$ $\qquad$ $5^3 + 5^2 \neq 5^5$

$5^3 \times 4^2 \neq 20^5$ $\qquad$ $(3^5)^2 \neq 9^{10}$

Chapter 2

Further calculation

Every so often it is announced in the newspapers that a new large prime number has been found. In 1985 it was announced that the largest known prime is $2^{216091} - 1$.
Try to enter this number on a calculator. What happens? If the number was written out in full, how many digits would there be?

2.1 Standard form

Very large or very small numbers are often written in Standard Form. A number in standard form has only one digit before the decimal point, and is multiplied by a power of 10 to show how large or small it is.

$345{,}000 = 3.45 \times 10^5$

$0.0000000012 = 1.2 \times 10^{-9}$

Multiplication

When two numbers in standard form are multiplied, the number parts are multiplied and the powers of 10 are added.

$2 \times 10^5 \times 4 \times 10^7 = 8 \times 10^{12}$

Division

When two numbers in standard form are divided, the number parts are divided and the powers of 10 are subtracted.

$6 \times 10^7 \div 3 \times 10^4 = 2 \times 10^3$

Squares

When a number in standard form is squared, the number part is squared and the power of 10 is doubled. A similar principle applies to cubes, fourth powers and so on.

$(2.4 \times 10^3)^2 = 5.76 \times 10^6$

Negative powers of 10

In all these cases, be especially careful when the power of 10 is negative.

$6 \times 10^{-3} \div 3 \times 10^{-15} = 2 \times 10^{-3-(-15)} = 2 \times 10^{12}$

Adjustment

After arithmetic operations, there may no longer be exactly one digit before the decimal place. Then the number will not be in standard form. Adjust the number so that it is in standard form.

$23.4 \times 10^8 = 2.34 \times 10^9$

Use of calculator

You can use a calculator for numbers in standard form. The sequence to enter 3×10^5 is:

3	exp	5

If the power of 10 is negative, then press the ± button after the power. The sequence for 4×10^{-8} is:

4	exp	8	±

All the ordinary arithmetical operations can now be applied. But do not rely too much on your calculator. Any question will require you to show your working, so you must be able to handle numbers in standard form without the help of a calculator.

2.1.1 Example

There are 6.3×10^4 inches in a mile. How many cubic inches are there in a cubic mile? Give your answer in standard form.

Solution Cube the number above.

$(6.3 \times 10^4)^3 = 250.047 \times 10^{12}$

This is numerically correct, but it is not in standard form. Move the decimal point two places to the left, and increase the power of 10 by 2.

The number of cubic inches is 2.50047×10^{14}

2.1.2 Exercises

1) Convert the following to standard form:

a) 45,000 b) 100,100 c) 0.00003

d) 27×10^5 e) 432.1×10^7 f) 0.4×10^{12}

g) 53×10^{-4} h) 0.3×10^{-8} i) 0.005×10^{-12}

2) Write the following numbers in ordinary notation:

a) 2.7×10^4 b) 4.9732×10^3 c) 1.8×10^{-5}

3) Evaluate the following, leaving your answers in standard form:

a) $1.2 \times 10^8 \times 2.5 \times 10^4$ b) $3.2 \times 10^8 \times 4 \times 10^{-3}$

c) $2.5 \times 10^{-8} \times 8 \times 10^{-3}$ d) $5.9 \times 10^{12} \times 2.3 \times 10^{-12}$

4) Evaluate the following, leaving your answers in standard form:

a) $8 \times 10^{12} \div 5 \times 10^4$ b) $8 \times 10^{-6} \div 4 \times 10^4$

c) $7 \times 10^{-3} \div 8 \times 10^{-5}$ d) $6.3 \times 10^{-8} \div 9 \times 10^{-12}$

5) Evaluate the following, leaving your answers in standard form:

a) $(2.6 \times 10^5)^2$ b) $(3 \times 10^8)^3$

c) $(5 \times 10^{-3})^2$ d) $(4.2 \times 10^{-7})^3$

6) If there are 3.9×10^4 inches in a kilometre, how many square inches are there in a square kilometre?

7) The radius of the Earth is 6.4×10^6 metres. What is its volume?

8) The speed of light is 1.86×10^5 miles per second. How far does light travel in 10 years?

9) The speed of a glacier is 2×10^{-7} m.p.h. How far does it travel in a year?

10) If a hydrogen atom weighs 1.7×10^{-27} kg, how many atoms are there in 10 kg of hydrogen?

11) At the beginning of the chapter there was a problem about a large number. Use the fact that 2^{10} is approximately 10^3 to convert 2^{216091} to a power of 10. What is the approximate number of digits in the number?

2.2 Addition and subtraction of numbers in standard form

Suppose we want to add a length of 200 metres to a length of 3 kilometres. We cannot do this directly. Either convert the metres to kilometres or convert the kilometres to metres.

The same applies when adding or subtracting numbers in standard form. We must first convert one of the numbers so that it has the same power of 10 as the other.

2.2.1 Examples

1) A ship weighs 6×10^7 kg when fully laden. What is the weight after cargo of 9×10^6 kg has been taken off?

Solution Subtract 9×10^6 from 6×10^7. First ensure that they have the same power of 10.

$6 \times 10^7 - 9 \times 10^6 = 6 \times 10^7 - 0.9 \times 10^7$

The unladen weight is 5.1×10^7 kg

2) Evaluate $4.2 \times 10^{-8} + 7.5 \times 10^{-9}$.

Solution Convert the second number so that it has the same power of 10 as the first. Be careful with the negative power of 10.

$7.5 \times 10^{-9} = 0.75 \times 10^{-8}$

Now the numbers can be added.

$4.2 \times 10^{-8} + 0.75 \times 10^{-8} = 4.95 \times 10^{-8}$

2.2.2 Exercises

1) Evaluate the following, leaving your answers in standard form:

a) $4.3 \times 10^4 + 3.7 \times 10^3$
b) $7.5 \times 10^8 + 4.2 \times 10^9$
c) $8 \times 10^{12} + 9 \times 10^{10}$
d) $4 \times 10^{-6} + 3 \times 10^{-7}$
e) $9.6 \times 10^8 + 9 \times 10^7$
f) $9.3 \times 10^{-6} + 8.7 \times 10^{-7}$

2) Evaluate the following, leaving your answers in standard form:

a) $6.3 \times 10^4 - 4.7 \times 10^3$
b) $1.23 \times 10^{13} - 2.38 \times 10^{12}$
c) $8.4 \times 10^{32} - 9 \times 10^{30}$
d) $5.9 \times 10^{-4} - 5.8 \times 10^{-5}$
e) $8.7 \times 10^{-16} - 7.7 \times 10^{-18}$
f) $5.9 \times 10^4 - 6.3 \times 10^5$
g) $3.95 \times 10^{14} - 1.731 \times 10^{16}$
h) $3.2 \times 10^{-6} - 3.6 \times 10^{-5}$

3) The population of China is about 1.1×10^9, and the population of Japan is about 1.2×10^8. What is their combined population?

4) The Earth is 1.5×10^8 km from the Sun. The planet Saturn is 1.43×10^9 km from the Sun. What is the distance between Earth and Saturn,

   a) when they are on directly opposite sides of the Sun,

   b) when they are on the same side of the Sun?

5) An atom of hydrogen weighs about 1.7×10^{-27} kg, and an atom of oxygen about 2.7×10^{-26} kg. A molecule of water consists of two hydrogen atoms and one oxygen atom: what is its weight?

2.3 Compound interest

Suppose £1,000 is invested at 8%. If the interest is simple interest, then £80 is paid out each year and the sum invested remains at £1,000.

If the interest is compound interest, then it stays in the bank and the amount invested increases each year.

Problems of compound interest are best handled by means of a multiplying factor, as follows.

During each year, £100 increases to £108. So the sum of money is multiplied by a factor of $\frac{108}{100} = 1.08$.

Over a period of two years, this increase will have occurred twice. So the original sum of money will have been multiplied by 1.08 twice, i.e. it will have been multiplied by 1.08^2.

And so on. After n years the original sum of money will have been multiplied by 1.08^n.

Percentage decrease

The argument above applied to percentage increase. A similar principle applies to decrease.

Suppose a quantity is decreasing at 5% each year. Then after one year, the amount remaining will be 95% = 0.95 of the original amount.

After a second year, the amount will have been multiplied again by 0.95. So the amount remaining will be 0.95^2 of the original.

2.3.1 Example

Every year the value of a car decreases by 14%. If it was worth £5,500 when new, how much is it worth after 6 years?

Solution Every year the value is multiplied by $\frac{86}{100} = 0.86$. After 6 years it has been multiplied by this factor 6 times.

Value = £5,500 $\times$ 0.86^6 = £2,225

2.3.2 Exercises

1) Find the multiplying factors corresponding to the following percentage increases or decreases:

   a) 5% increase b) 30% increase c) 7% decrease d) 75% decrease

2) Find the percentage increase or decrease corresponding to the following multiplying factors:

   a) 1.06 b) 1.1 c) 1.7 d) 0.91 e) 0.4 f) 0.03

3) £2,000 is invested at 8%. How much is it after 12 years?

4) £4,500 is invested at 11%. How much is it after 9 years?

5) A population is increasing at 2% each year. If it is 30 million now, what will it be after 20 years?

6) The average price of a house in a certain town is increasing at 6% each year. If the average is £65,000 now, what will it be in 8 years time?

7) A radioactive material decays at 5% each year. If there is 1 kg now, how much will there be in 10 years time?

8) The value of a car decreases at 20% each year. If it was bought for £8,000, what will it be worth after 5 years?

9) In a certain country, the amount of forest is decreasing at 2% each year. If there is 400,000 square miles of forest now, how much will be left in 50 years time?

2.4 Reverse percentages

Suppose a sum of money is increased by 8%, and we are told the amount after the increase has taken place. To find the original sum, we must use a reverse percentage procedure.

The new sum can be found by multiplying the original sum by 1.08. So to go back from the new sum to the original we divide by 1.08.

2.4.1 Example

After a 9% salary increase, Julie is earning £17,440. How much was she earning before the increase?

Solution The salary increase has the effect of multiplying by $\frac{109}{100} = 1.09$. So to find the original salary divide by 1.09.

Salary before increase = £17,440 ÷ 1.09 = £16,000

2.4.2 Exercises

1) After an increase of 12%, a man's salary was £16,800. What was the salary before the increase?

2) A dealer sells a car for £2,760, making a profit of 15%. What did he buy the car for?

3) After a year of interest at 8%, Mandy has £129.60 in the bank. How much did she invest originally?

4) A man can invest money at 10%. How much should he invest now, to ensure that he has £2,200 in a years time?

5) A population is increasing at 2%. If it is 15,810,000 now, how much was it a year ago?

6) An antique dealer buys a picture, but has to sell at a loss of 10%. If she sold it for £450, how much did she pay for it?

7) The number of candidates for a certain exam has decreased by 5%. If 114,000 take it now, how many used to take it?

8) The value of a car depreciates at 25% each year. It it is worth £6,000 now, how much was it worth a year ago?

9) A radioactive material decreases at 16% each month. If there is 2.1 kg now, how much was there a month ago?

2.5 Longer exercises

A. Roots of numbers in standard form

The rule for finding the square root of a number in standard form might be: square root the number part, and halve the power of 10.

1) Apply this rule to $4{,}000{,}000 = 4 \times 10^6$. Is it correct?

2) How does the rule work when applied to $360{,}000 = 3.6 \times 10^5$? Why is the result not satisfactory?

   Amend the rule: if the power of 10 is odd we reduce the power by 1 to make it even, and move the decimal point one place to the right. So 3.6×10^5 becomes 36×10^4.

3) Apply the amended rule to find the square root of 3.6×10^5.

4) Without using the EXP button of your calculator, find the square roots of the following:

   a) 9×10^{12} b) 6.4×10^{11} c) 2.5×10^{23}

   d) 1.44×10^{-24} e) 3.6×10^{-5} f) 4.9×10^{-17}

5) See if you can find the cube roots of the following:

   a) 8×10^{15} b) 2.7×10^{43} c) 1.25×10^{38}

B. Present value

A thousand pounds that we are promised in a year's time is less valuable than a thousand pounds in our pockets now. (Because we do not have the use of the money throughout the year).

Suppose we are able to invest money at 10%. Then in order to have £1,000 in a year's time we would have to invest £1000 ÷ 1.1 = £909.09. This is called the present value of the promise.

Similarly the present value of a promise of £1,000 in two year's time is £1,000 ÷ 1.1^2 = £826.45.

The following problem involves present value.

A small firm is considering buying a photocopier for £12,000. It will be used for 5 years, and then will probably be sold for £5,000. Each year it will make a saving of £2,000, calculated at the end of the year.

1) Find the present value of the £2,000 saved in the first year.

2) Find the present value of all the money saved over the 5 years.

3) Find the present value of the secondhand price of the photocopier.

4) Is it worth buying the photocopier?

5) The same methods apply when we consider buying something by installments. Suppose we could buy a car, either by paying £6,500 now, or by paying £1,800 at the end of each year for the next 5 years. Which method is better?

Multiple choice question *(Tick appropriate box)*

In a sale, everything is reduced by 5%. What was the original cost of an item whose sale price is £798?

a) £1,596 ☐

b) £840 ☐

c) £837.9 ☐

d) £760 ☐

e) £399 ☐

Points to note

1) *Standard form*

   a) Do not try to add or subtract numbers in standard form without first making sure that they have the same power of 10.

   b) Be careful with negative powers of 10, especially when dividing numbers in standard form.

2) *Conversion*

   The conversion factor corresponding to an increase of 8% is 1.08, not 1.8.

3) *Reverse percentages*

   A percentage change is always a percentage of the original value, not of the changed value. Suppose you are told that an item is sold at £50 for a profit of 25%. To obtain the buying price you should divide £50 by 1.25, to obtain £40. Do not take 25% off the selling price.

Chapter 3
Proportion

In the British Museum there is an Egyptian manuscript dating from about 1650 BC. It contains 85 mathematical problems, one of which is as follows:

100 loaves of pesu*10 are exchanged for loaves of* pesu*15. How many loaves are there?*

The *pesu* was a measure of the size of a loaf. If one basket of grain made 10 loaves, then those loaves had *pesu* 10. The bigger the loaf the smaller the *pesu.*

How would you tackle this problem? The manuscript solves the problem as follows:

Reckon the amount of flour in these 100 loaves. It is 100 divided by 10, which is 10 baskets. The number of loaves of pesu *15 from 10 baskets is 15 times 10, which is 150. This is the number of loaves.*

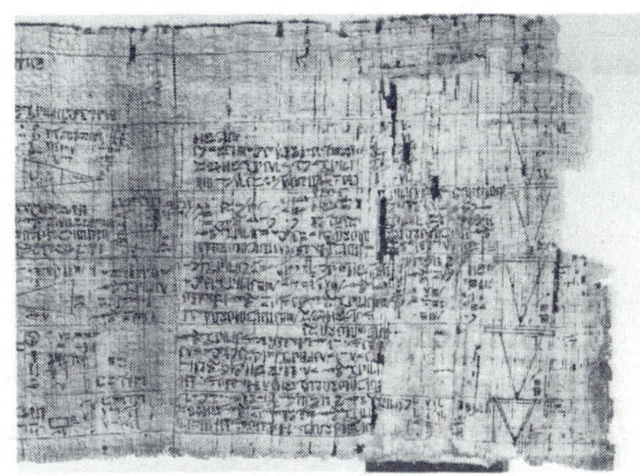

Fig 3.1

3.1 Proportion and inverse proportion

Direct proportion

If two quantities increase at the same rate, so that if one is doubled then the other is doubled, the quantities are proportional.

In this case there is a relationship of the form $y = kx$, where k is a constant.

Inverse proportion

If two quantities increase at opposite rates, so that if one is doubled then the other is halved, the quantities are inversely proportional.

In this case there is a relationship of the form $y = \frac{k}{x}$, where k is a constant.

Constant of proportionality

k is the constant of proportionality. It can be found from a pair of values of y and x. The relationship can then be written down exactly.

3.1.1 Examples

1) The extension E of a spring is proportional to the tension T. A tension of 2 N gives an extension of 4 cm. Find an equation giving E in terms of T, and use it to find the extension for a 7N load.

Solution E is proportional to T. So E is a multiple of T. Write $E = kT$.

To find the proportionality constant k, put $E = 4$, $T = 2$. This gives $4 = k \times 2$, so $k = 2$.

Thus the equation is $E = 2T$. Put $T = 7$ into this equation:

$\mathbf{E = 2 \times 7 = 14}$ **cm**

2) For a fixed voltage, the current I along a wire is inversely proportional to the resistance R. $I = 4$ amps when $R = 60$ ohms. Find an equation linking I and R, and find the resistance necessary for a current of 6 amps.

Solution Here the equation is of the form $I = \frac{k}{r}$.

Put in the values given, obtaining $4 = \frac{k}{60}$. So $k = 240$.

The equation is $I = \frac{240}{R}$.

Put $I = 6$ into this equation, obtaining $6 = \frac{240}{R}$.

$R = \frac{240}{6} = 40$ **ohms.**

3.1.2 Exercises

1) A car travels 34 miles on one gallon of petrol. How far will it get on a tankful of 8 gallons?

2) 40 cm^3 of a metal weigh 120 grams. What is the weight of 30 cm^3?

3) When a sum of money is divided between 8 children, each gets £3. If there were only four children, how much would each get?

4) It takes 3 men 4 days to complete the painting of a house. How long should it take 6 men?

5) After a motorway is completed, the average speed increases from 40 m.p.h. to 60 m.p.h. A certain journey took 3 hours before. How long does it take now?

6) y is proportional to x. $y = 30$ when $x = 10$. Find y in terms of x, and find y when $x = 5$.

7) R is proportional to S. When $S = 6$, $R = 18$. Find: a) R when $S = 24$, b) S when $R = 90$.

8) For a wire of fixed resistance, the current I is proportional to the voltage V. $I = 7$ amps for $V = 12$ volts.

   a) Find the current if $V = 6$ volts.

   b) Find the voltage necessary to transmit a current of 70 amps.

9) Distances on a map are proportional to distances on the ground. If 5 cm corresponds to 20 km, what does 25 cm correspond to?

10) p is inversely proportional to q. For $p = 7$, $q = 10$. Find an equation linking p and q. Find q when $p = 14$.

11) F and G are inversely proportional, and F is 6 when $G = 8$.

    a) Find F when $G = 12$. b) Find G when $F = 3$.

12) The pressure P of a fixed mass of gas is inversely proportional to the volume V. $P = 50$ kg/m^2 when $V = 4$ m^3. Find the equation which gives V in terms of P. Find the volume of the gas when the pressure is 40 kg/m^2.

13) The wavelength L of certain waves is inversely proportional to the frequency f. When $f = 250{,}000$ cycles per second the wave length is 1000 metres.

a) Find the frequency of waves with length 5,000 m.

b) Find the length of waves with frequency 1,000,000 cycles per second.

14) In the problem at the beginning of the chapter there is a relationship between the number of loaves and the *pesu*. What is the relationship? Solve the problem using proportionality.

3.2 Proportionality to powers

The ∝ symbol

The statement "y is proportional to x" is often written as:

$$y \propto x$$

Direct proportion

More complicated cases of proportion occur when y is proportional to a power of x. For example, y might be proportional to the square of x. This could be written as:

$$y \propto x^2$$

As in 3.1, this is equivalent to an equation of the form $y = kx^2$, where k is a constant. k can be found from a pair of values of y and x.

Inverse proportion

If y is inversely proportional to the cube of x, then we can write

$$y \propto \frac{1}{x^3} \text{ or } y = \frac{k}{x^3}$$

and then proceed as in 3.1.

3.2.1 Example

The mass M of a metal sphere is proportional to the cube of the radius r. If the mass of a sphere radius 2 cm is 120 grams, find an equation giving M in terms of r. Find the radius of a sphere whose mass is 960 grams.

Solution The formula is $M \propto r^3$, which is equivalent to the equation $M = kr^3$.

Put $M = 120$ and $r = 2$, to obtain $120 = k \times 8$. So $k = 15$.

The equation is $M = 15r^3$

Put $M = 960$ into the equation, obtaining $960 = 15r^3$

$r^3 = 64$

The radius is 4 cm

3.2.2 Exercises

1) y is proportional to the square of x. $y = 16$ when $x = 2$.

a) Find y in terms of x. b) Find y when $x = 3$. c) Find x when $y = 4$.

2) T is proportional to the square of S. When S is 3 then T is 18.

a) Find the equation linking T and S. b) Find T when S is 6.

c) Find S when T is 32.

3) z is proportional to the cube of w. $z = 4$ when $w = 2$. Find z when $w = 5$.

4) P is proportional to the cube of Q. $P = 16$ when $Q = 2$. Find the equation linking P and Q. Find Q when P is 432.

5) The mass M of a cube is proportional to the cube of the length L of the side. A cube of side 4 cm^3 has mass 256 grams. Find M in terms of L. Find the mass of a cube side 3 cm, and the side of a cube which has mass 13.5 grams.

6) The energy of a moving body is proportional to the square of the speed. A body moving at 5 m/sec has 50 Nm of energy. Express the energy E in terms of the speed V. If the body has energy 200 Nm, how fast is it moving?

7) The energy E stored in a spring is proportional to the square of the extension e. Express this fact using the symbol $\propto$. If the extension is 3 for an energy of 45, find an equation linking e and E. Find E when $e = 2$.

8) B is inversely proportional to the square of C. $B = \frac{1}{2}$ for $C = 2$. Find the expression linking B and C. Find B when $C = \frac{1}{2}$, and find C when $B = 32$.

9) The illumination from a light source is inversely proportional to the square of the distance from that light source. If a light gives 9 candle–power at a distance of 4 m, find the illumination at a distance of 6 metres.

10) The resistance R of a fixed length of wire is inversely proportional to the square of the radius r. When the radius is $\frac{1}{2}$ mm, the resistance is 12 ohms. Find R in terms of r. Find the resistance if the radius is $\frac{1}{4}$ mm. What radius should be chosen to give a resistance of $\frac{3}{4}$ ohms?

3.3 Finding the power

Sometimes we do not know which power of x is involved. Then we need two pairs of values of x and y, to find the power as well as the constant of proportionality.

Suppose that x has doubled between the two pairs of values. Look to see what has happened to y.

If y has also doubled, then y is directly proportional to x.

If y has halved, then y is inversely proportional to x.

If y has increased by a factor of $4 = 2^2$, then y is proportional to the square of x.

If y has decreased by a factor of 4, then y is inversely proportional to the square of x.

Once the power has been found, then we can proceed as in the previous sections.

3.3.1 Example

It is known that there is a proportionality relationship between x and y. It is found that $y = 40$ when $x = 2$, and that $y = 360$ when $x = 6$. Find an equation linking x and y.

Solution x has gone from 2 to 6, up by a factor of 3. y has gone from 40 to 360, up by a factor of $\frac{360}{40} = 9$.

Note that $9 = 3^2$. Hence y must be proportional to the square of x.

Because $y = 40$ when $x = 2$, the constant of proportionality is 10.

The equation is $y = 10x^2$

3.3.2 Exercises

In Questions 1 to 5 there is a proportionality relationship between x and y. Find the equations linking y to x.

1) $y = 4$ when $x = 2$, and $y = 16$ when $x = 4$.
2) $y = 12$ when $x = 3$, and $y = 6$ when $x = 6$.
3) $y = 40$ when $x = 2$, and $y = 320$ when $x = 4$.
4) $y = 60$ when $x = 2$, and $y = 15$ when $x = 4$.
5) $y = 36$ when $x = 4$, and $y = 4$ when $x = 12$.
6) y is proportional to a power of x. The following table gives various values of y and x. Find the power, and find y when $x = 6$.

x	2	3	4
y	12	27	48

7) It is thought that T is proportional to a power of S. When S is doubled T increases by a factor of 8.

   What is the power? If S is divided by 3, what is T divided by?
8) The product of x and y is constant. What is the proportionality relationship between x and y?
9) The ratio of P and Q is constant. What is the proportionality relationship between P and Q?

3.4 Longer exercises

A. Pressure, volume, temperature

In 1666 a proportionality relationship was found between pressure and volume. Boyles' Law says:

> **The pressure of a given mass of gas at a constant temperature is inversely proportional to its volume.**

If we squeeze a quantity of gas, for example in a bicycle pump, the pressure goes up and the volume goes down.

1) If 5 m^3 of gas has pressure 2 atmospheres, what is the pressure when the gas has been contracted to 2 m^3?

   If temperature varies, the full law is:

   For a given mass of gas,

$$\frac{PV}{T} = k$$

   where P is the pressure, V the volume, T the temperature.
2) If the pressure P is held constant, what is the relationship between V and T?
3) If the volume V is held constant, what is the relationship between P and T?

   The temperature T must be measured in absolute degrees, not in Celsius or Fahrenheit. The temperature at which $T = 0$ is called absolute zero. To find absolute zero in Celsius the following experiment was performed:

A fixed mass of gas was contained in a fixed volume. It was heated up, and its pressure and temperature in Celsius were measured.

The results were:

P	3.7	4.4	5.1	5.8	6.5
t	0	50	100	150	200

4) Plot P against t, taking P from 0 to 7 and t from –300 to 200. What is absolute zero in Celsius?

B. Log-log paper

In 3.3 we saw how to find the relationship between x and y from two pairs of values. But in experimental situations, the values of x and y are only approximate. We need more than two pairs of values to get a good estimate for the power.

Suppose we know that y and x are related by $y = kx^n$, where both k and n are unknown. Experimental values are as follows:

x	1.5	1.7	2	2.2	2.5	2.7
y	2.7	3.5	4.7	5.8	7.5	8.7

If we plotted y against x on ordinary paper, the result would be a curve. We could not guess what n was. On the right is "stretched" graph paper, called log-log paper.

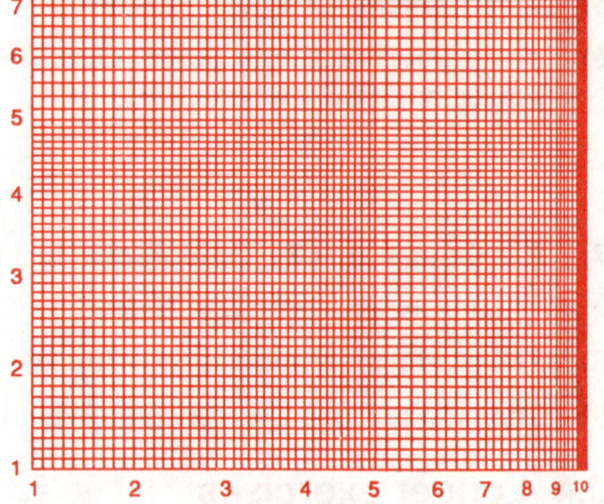

Fig 3.2

1) Plot y against x on this paper. Draw a straight line through your points.
2) What is the gradient of this line? (This is the value of n.)
3) Where does the line cross $x = 1$? (This is k.)
4) Write down the law in the form $y = kx^n$. Check your formula with the original figures

Multiple choice question *(Tick appropriate box)*

There is a relationship of proportionality between x and y. $y = 18$ when $x = 3$ and $y = 2$ when $x = 9$. The relationship is best expressed by:

a) $y \propto x^2$ ☐

b) $x \propto \frac{1}{y^2}$ ☐

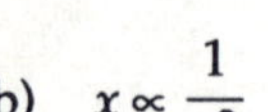

c) $y \propto \frac{1}{x^2}$ ☐

d) $y = \frac{1}{x^2}$ ☐

e) $y \propto \frac{k}{x^2}$ ☐

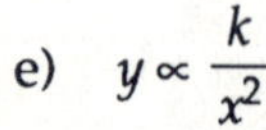

Points to note

1) *Arithmetic*

Watch out for arithmetic errors. Be sure that you do the correct operation when finding the constant k. For example:

From $4 = k2$ we get $k = 2$. (Not $k = \frac{1}{2}$ or $k = 8$)

From $4 = \frac{k}{2}$ we get $k = 8$. (Not $k = 2$ or $k = \frac{1}{2}$)

2) *Proportion*

The $\propto$ symbol is often misused. The statement $y \propto x$ is not an equation. It can be made into an equation, as $y = kx$.

Similarly, it is unnecessary to write $y \propto kx$. Either write $y \propto x$ or $y = kx$.

Chapter 4

Error and accuracy

"Check in time for the car-ferry is 10 p.m., but we'd better allow between 30 and 40 minutes to buy the tickets and so on."

"It's 60 miles to the port –"

"Give or take 5 miles –"

"We can average a speed of 40 m.p.h. to get there –"

"We don't know the traffic conditions; say 40 m.p.h. to the nearest 10 m.p.h. –"

The Jones family have been discussing when they should leave to go on holiday. When should they set off to catch the ferry?

Fig 4.1

4.1 Error

The ± symbol

When a quantity is measured, the answer given may not be correct. The difference between the measurement and the true value is the error. We can use the ± symbol to show how big the error is.

Suppose a weight is given as 53 ± 3 kg. This means that the measurement is 53 kg, but that the true value of the weight could be 3 kg on either side. So the true weight must lie between 50 and 56 kg.

Error in rounding

When a number is rounded, then a possible error is involved.

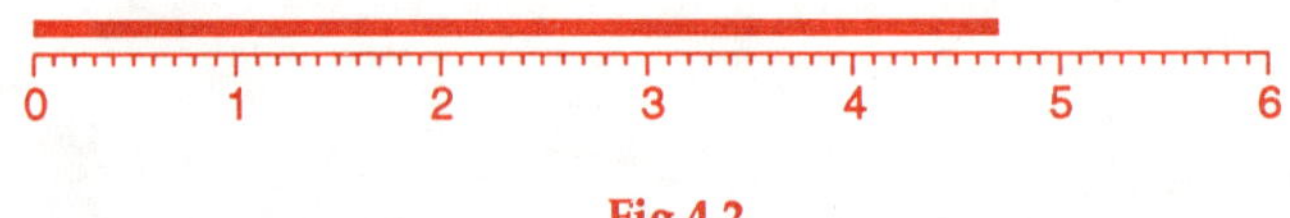

Fig 4.2

In the figure above the length is given as 4.7 cm, to 1 decimal place. Then the length cannot be bigger than 4.75, otherwise it would be closer to 4.8. Similarly the length cannot be less than 4.65, otherwise it would be closer to 4.6. The length lies between 4.65 and 4.75. We could also write the length as 4.7± 0.05.

4.1.1 Example

The distance between two towns is given as 90 miles to the nearest 10 miles. What are the limits between which the distance lies?

Solution A distance over 95 miles would have been rounded to 100 miles or more. A distance less than 85 miles would have been rounded to 80 miles or less.

The distance lies between 85 and 95 miles

4.1.2 Exercises

1) The following measurements were given. In each case find the greatest and least values of the true figure.

   a) 11 ± 3 b) 3.56 ± 0.02 c) -0.015 ± 0.006

2) Express the following ranges using the ± symbol.

   a) 33 to 37 b) 22.1 to 22.2 c) –0.1 to 0.7

3) The weight of a car is given as 910 kg, to the nearest 10 kg. What is the least possible weight of the car?

4) The population of a town is given as 80,000, to the nearest 10,000. Between what limits must the population lie?

5) The weight of a book is given as 0.54, rounded to 2 decimal places. Between which values must the true weight lie?

6) The distance between two cities is given as 320 miles, to 2 significant figures. Between which values must the distance lie?

7) The weight of a cake is given as 600 grams, to the nearest 10 grams. Express this using the ± symbol.

8) A temperature is given as –32.4, to one decimal place. Express this using the ± symbol.

9) In a country there are two political parties, the Blue Party and the Green Party. An opinion poll measures support for the Blue party at 52%.

   a) If the margin of error is 3%, is the Blue Party supported by the majority of the population?

   b) If the figure is given correct to the nearest 2%, is the Blue Party supported by a majority of the population?

4.2 Addition and subtraction of measurements

Suppose that two sticks were measured at 12 ± 1 cm and 7 ± 2 cm. Suppose they are laid end to end as shown below.

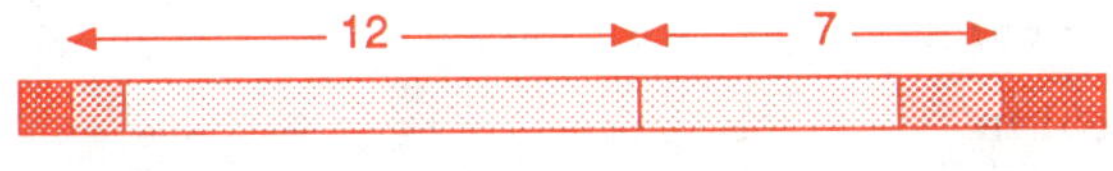

Fig 4.3

The total length could be as high as $13 + 9 = 22$ cm, if both lengths have been underestimated. The total length could be as low as $11 + 5 = 16$ cm, if both lengths have been overestimated.

So the total length is 19 ± 3 cm. Notice that the errors have been added.

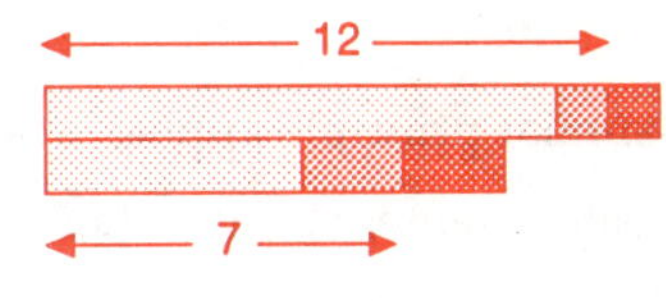

Fig 4.4

Suppose instead the sticks are laid alongside, and we want to find the "overhang".

If the first stick is overestimated and the second underestimated, then the overhang could be as low as $11 - 9 = 2$ cm. If the first is underestimated and the second overestimated, the overhang could be as high as $13 - 5 = 8$ cm.

So the overhang is 5 ± 3 cm. Note that again the errors have been added.

The general rule is: When two quantities are added or subtracted, the errors are added.

4.2.1 Example

A packet of flour contains 1.2 kg, and I take out 0.4 kg. Both weights are given to 1 decimal place. How much is left?

Solution The maximum error in measuring the original weight is 0.05 kg. The error in measuring the amount taken out is also 0.05 kg. Add these to find the error in the amount left.

The amount left is 0.8 ± 0.1 kg

4.2.2 Exercises

1) Evaluate the following, leaving the ± symbol in your answers:
   a) $7 \pm 2 + 5 \pm 1$ b) $3.1 \pm 0.1 - 4.7 \pm 0.1$ c) $4 \pm 1 + 6 \pm 1 - 7 \pm 1$
2) Cream weighing 100 grams is added to a cake weighing 500 grams, both figures being given to the nearest 10 grams. What is the final weight?
3) The temperature of a liquid was 30.5°, and then it rose to 48.8°, both figures being given to 1 decimal place. What was the rise in temperature?
4) Two adjacent buildings are 250 and 340 feet high, both heights to the nearest 10 feet. What is the difference between the heights?
5) In a relay race the four runners take 11.23 secs, 12.42 secs, 10.56 secs and 9.96 secs, all times being given to 2 decimal places. What was the total time for the race?

4.3 Multiplication and division of measurements

Multiplying

Suppose a field is 20 m by 30 m, where both figures could be inaccurate by up to 1 m. To find the area of the field, we multiply the sides together: the error can be found by taking the greatest and least possible values of the sides.

Greatest value of area = $21 \times 31 = 651$ m^2

Least value of area = $19 \times 29 = 551$ m^2

So the area is 600 ± 51 m^2.

Dividing

A similar principle applies when dividing. The extreme possible values of $30 \pm 1 \div 20 \pm 1$ are:

Greatest value: $31 \div 19 = 1.63$

(Notice that we take the greatest value of the first number and the least value of the second.)

Least value: $29 \div 21 = 1.38$

So $30 \pm 1 \div 20 \pm 1 = 1.5 \pm 0.13$

4.3.1 Examples

1) The base of a triangle is 13.5 cm and its height is 26.7 cm, where both figures are given to 1 decimal place. What is the area of the triangle? Give your answer to an appropriate degree of accuracy.

Solution The base of the triangle could be as high as 13.55, and the height 26.75. The greatest possible area is then:

$\frac{1}{2} \times 13.55 \pm 26.75 = 181.23125$

Similarly the least possible area is:

$\frac{1}{2} \times 13.45 \times 26.65 = 179.22125$

These values agree on the first two significant figures.

The area is 180 cm²

2) Evaluate $(4.08 \times 5.74) \div 2.99$, showing the accuracy of your answer. All figures are given to 2 decimal places.

Solution The greatest value of the expression will be:

$(4.085 \times 5.745) \div 2.985 = 7.862$

The least value is:

$(4.075 \times 5.735) \div 2.995 = 7.803$

These values are about 0.03 on either side of 7.83.

$\mathbf{(4.08 \times 5.74) \div 2.99 = 7.83 \pm 0.03}$

4.3.2 Exercises

1) Give the ranges within which the results of the following must lie:

a) $3 \pm 1 \times 5 \pm 1$ b) $3.1 \pm 0.1 \times 2.4 \pm 0.1$ c) $10 \pm 1 \div 2 \pm 0.5$

2) Evaluate the expressions in Question 1, showing the accuracy of your answer with the ± symbol.

3) In the following, each number is given to 1 decimal place. In each case evaluate the expression, showing the accuracy of your answer.

a) 3.1×4.2 b) 7.3×4.1 c) 2.2^2

d) $100.1 \div 0.4$ e) 66.7×0.3 f) 0.4^3

4) A rectangle is 12 cm by 23 cm, both figures being rounded to the nearest whole number. What is the area of the rectangle?

5) To 1 decimal place, the radius of a circle is 4.2 cm. What is its area?

6) The volume of a block of metal is 44.8 cm^3, and the density of the metal is 7.5 g/cm^3, both figures being given to 1 decimal place. What is the weight of the metal?

7) What is the weight of 93 ball bearings, each of which weighs 3.23 grams to 2 decimal places?

8) A distance is 120 miles, to the nearest 10 miles, and a car travels at 45 m.p.h., to the nearest 5 m.p.h. How long does it take to travel the distance?

9) The area of a rectangle is 37.3 cm^2, to 1 decimal place, and its base is 12.12 cm, to 2 decimal places. What is its height?

10) The Pound Sterling is worth 2100 Italian Lire, to the nearest 100. How much is 200,000 Italian Lire worth in Pounds Sterling?

11) To the nearest £5, the average wage in a factory is £205. Wages are increased by 8%, to the nearest 1%. What is the new average wage?

12) In the problem at the beginning of the chapter, the Jones family were discussing when to leave on their holiday. What is the very latest they can leave to be sure of catching the ferry?

4.4 Longer exercises

A. In the supermarket

When you buy a lot of items at the supermarket, it is a good idea to make a rough estimate of what the total will be.

1) Find the exact total of the list on the right.

2) Round each number to the nearest 10 p, then try to find the total mentally. How close was your rough answer to the correct one?

3) If you find it hard to add the numbers mentally, round the numbers to the nearest £1 and add. Why is your answer so inaccurate?

4) Find another shopping list to test your ability to estimate the total by rounding each price to the nearest 10 p.

Chilli Beans	0.45
Spring Water	1.45
Chopped Toms	0.26
Potatoes	0.20
Broad Beans	0.32
Grlc Baguette	1.15
Ntrl Yoghourt	0.75
White Cabbage	0.29
Satsumas	1.35
Oven Chips	1.09
Baby Red Cabbage	0.29
Tomatoes Small	0.99
Unsmk middle	2.75
D/Gloucester	0.78
Bananas	0.93
Whole Cucumber	0.49
TOTAL	

B. Percentage error

The percentage error of a measurement is the error expressed as a percentage of the measurement. So if the measurement is 10 ± 0.2, the percentage error is $0.2/10 \times 100 = 2\%$.

1) Find the percentage errors in the following measurements:
   a) 12 ± 3 b) 20 ± 0.1 c) 5.32 ± 0.01

2) The sides of a rectangle are 10 ± 0.1 cm and 20 ± 0.1 cm. Find the percentage errors in these measurements.

3) Use the methods of section 4.3 to find the error in the area of the rectangle. What is the percentage error?

4) What is the connection between your answers to (2) and (3)?

5) If you have found a connection, test it with some other measurements.

6) Find the percentage error in the calculation of $20 \pm 0.1 \div 10 \pm 0.1$. Is this connected to your answers to (2) above?

Multiple choice question *(Tick appropriate box)*

A bottle contains 0.51 litres, to 2 decimal places. An amount of 0.25 ± 0.01 litres is poured out. The amount left is:

a) 0.26 ± 0.015 ☐

b) 0.26 ± 0.005 ☐

c) 0.26 ± 0.02 ☐

d) 0.76 ± 0.015 ☐

Points to note

1) *Rounding*

   If a quantity is given as 240 to the nearest 10, then the least value it could have is 235, not 230.

2) *Subtracting Measurements*

   When measurements are subtracted, the errors are added.

3) *Division of Quantities*

   When a measurement x is divided by a measurement y, then the greatest value of the result is obtained by taking the greatest value of x and the least value of y.

Chapter 5
Sequences

A famous paradox goes as follows. Achilles and a tortoise have a race. Achilles can run 10 times as fast as the tortoise, so the tortoise is given a start of 1000 paces.

The race starts. By the time that Achilles has reached the tortoise's starting point, the tortoise is 100 paces ahead. By the time that Achilles has made up the difference of 100 paces, the tortoise is 10 paces ahead. And so on – the tortoise will always be ahead of Achilles.

Is this correct? Will the tortoise win the race?

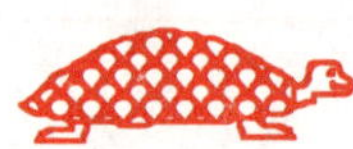

Fig 5.1

5.1 Constant difference

Consider the sequence 2, 5, 8, 11, 14, ... The difference between successive terms is always 3. The sequence has a constant difference. This sort of sequence is called an Arithmetic Progression.

If the constant difference is 3, the general term of the sequence is of the form $3n + k$, where k depends on the starting point. For the sequence above the general term is $3n - 1$.

5.1.1 Example

Describe the sequence 5, 9, 13, 17, 21, ... Find an expression for the n'th term.

Solution The terms are going up in steps of 4.

The sequence begins with 5 and has constant difference 4

By the n'th term, 4 will have been added $n - 1$ times. Hence the general n'th term is:

$\mathbf{5 + (n-1)4 = 1 + 4n}$

5.1.2 Exercises

1) Describe the following sequences, and find expressions for their n'th terms.

   a) 1, 4, 7, 10, 13, ... b) 13, 18, 23, 28, 33, ...

   c) $2, 2\frac{1}{2}, 3, 3\frac{1}{2}, 4, \ldots$ d) 7, 5, 3, 1, –1, ...

2) A salary starts at £10,000 and increases at £1,000 each year. Find an expression for the salary after n years.

3) £1,000 is invested at 8% simple interest. How much is gained each year? How much is there after n years?

4) An insurance salesman is paid a basic £6,000 and a commission of £200 for each policy he sells. What is his salary if he sells n policies?

5) The n'th term of a sequence is $7n - 1$. By putting $n = 1$ and $n = 2$ find the first term and the constant difference.

6) In the following, the n'th terms are given. Find the first term and the constant difference.

a) $5n+1$ b) $1+\frac{1}{2}n$ c) $7-2n$

7) The following expressions give the n'th term for sequences. Which of them have a constant difference? Find the constant different for those that do.

a) $5+\frac{n}{2}$ b) $n(n-1)$ c) $\frac{24}{n}$ d) $6-(n+3)$

5.2 Exponential sequences

Consider the sequence 3, 6, 12, 24, 48, ... Each term is twice the one before. This sequence has a constant ratio of 2. It is called a Geometric Progression, and is said to be increasing exponentially.

Suppose a sequence starts at a, and that the constant ratio is k. Then the n'th term will be ak^{n-1}.

Compound interest

A example of a quantity increasing exponentially is given by compound interest. If £1,000 is invested at 8%, then every year the money is multiplied by 1.08. After n years the original sum will have been multiplied by 1.08, n times. It will amount to 1000×1.08^n.

Exponential functions

A function of the form $y = ak^x$, where a and k are constants, is an exponential function.

5.2.1 Examples

1) Describe the series 2, 6, 18, 54, 162 ... Give an expression for the n'th term.

Solution Each term is 3 times the previous term.

The first term is 2 and the constant ratio is 3

To reach the n'th term we must multiply by 3, $n-1$ times. So the n'th term has been multiplied by 3^{n-1}.

The n'th term is $2 \times 3^{n-1}$

2) A radioactive material decays so that it halves every year. If we start with 2 kilograms, find an expression for the amount left after x years. Plot a graph of this expression, and estimate when there will be 0.1 kg left.

Solution After x years, the original amount will have been halved x times. So it will have been multiplied by $\left(\frac{1}{2}\right)^x$

The amount left is $2 \times \left(\frac{1}{2}\right)^x$

The graph of this function is shown. Read off where it reaches 0.1:

After 4 years there will be 0.1 kg

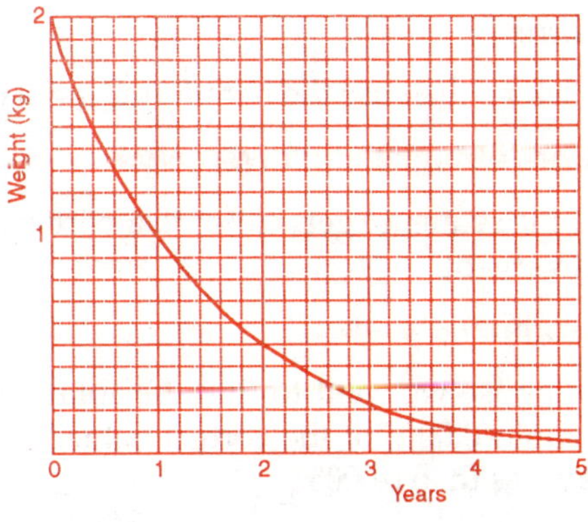

Fig 5.2

5.2.2 Exercises

1) For each of the following, describe the sequence and find an expression for the n'th term.

    a) $1, 2, 4, 8, 16, \ldots$ b) $5, 15, 45, 135, 405, \ldots$

    c) $2, 1, \frac{1}{2}, \frac{1}{4}, \frac{1}{8}, \ldots$ d) $2, -6, 18, -54, 162, \ldots$

2) The following are the n'th terms of exponential sequences. Find the first term and the common ratio.

    a) 2^n b) 5×3^n c) $6 \times \left(\frac{1}{3}\right)^n$

3) The population of a country is increasing at 2% each year. What will it be multiplied by each year? If it starts at 12 million, what will it be after x years? Plot a graph of this function, and find how long it takes for the population to double.

4) £10,000 is invested at 9% compound interest. How much is there after x years? By plotting a graph of the amount against time find when there will be £30,000.

5) A car is bought for £6,000. Every year its value decreases by 25%. How much is it worth after x years? By plotting a graph of value against time find when it will be worth £1,000.

6) The half life of a radioactive material is 1 year. If we have 4 g now, how much will there be after n years? How much was there n years ago?

7) The half life of a radioactive material is 4 years. If we have 2 g now, how much will there be after n years? How much was there n years ago?

8) An investment trust claims that it can double money in 6 years. If £10,000 is invested with it, how much will there be after n years?

9) Look at the example at the beginning of this chapter. Write down the successive gaps between Achilles and the Tortoise. What sort of sequence is this? By adding these terms find how far Achilles runs before he overtakes the Tortoise.

5.3 Iteration

Many equations cannot be solved exactly. Often very close approximations can be found by finding a sequence which gets closer to the solution. This process is called iteration.

The successive approximations are written $x_1, x_2, x_3, \ldots, x_n$. The method of approximation is often of the form:

Pick x_1, then use the iteration $x_{n+1} = f(x_n)$.

Convergence and divergence

If the sequence gets closer to a particular number, then it is convergent. If the process does not work, it is divergent.

Decimal places

Suppose we want to find the solution to 3 decimal places. That means that the value we give must be within 0.0005 of the correct value. So continue the iteration until two successive approximations differ by less than 0.0005.

5.3.1 Examples

1) The following flow-chart evaluates $\sqrt{2}$. Use it to fill in the table of values. How would you find $\sqrt{2}$ to a greater degree of accuracy?

x	y	z
1	2	1.5
1.5	1.333	

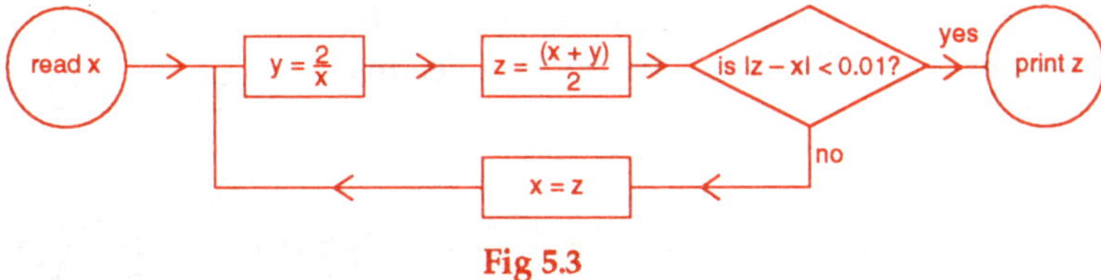

Fig 5.3

Solution Fill in the table as shown:

x	y	z
1	2	1.5
1.5	1.333	1.417
1.417	1.412	1.414

The answer 1.414 will be printed.

To get a greater degree of accuracy change the entry in the diamond shaped box. Changing it to $|z - x| < 0.00005$ will make the answer accurate to 4 decimal places.

2) To solve the equation $x^3 + x - 1 = 0$, we start with the approximation $x_1 = \frac{1}{2}$, and then use the iteration: $x_{n+1} = \sqrt[3]{1 - x_n}$.

Find the next three approximations. Write a flow chart which will find the solution to 2 decimal places.

Solution Put $x_1 = \frac{1}{2} = 0.5$ into the iteration formula. This gives x_2.

$$x_2 = \sqrt[3]{1 - 0.5} = 0.794.$$

Repeat this procedure to find x_3 in terms of x_2.

$$x_3 = \sqrt[3]{1 - 0.794} = 0.591$$

$$x_4 = \sqrt[3]{1 - 0.591} = 0.742.$$

The next three approximations are 0.794, 0.591, 0.742

The flow chart is shown on the next page. Note that after each iteration x takes over from y. The iteration is stopped once x and y differ by less than 0.005.

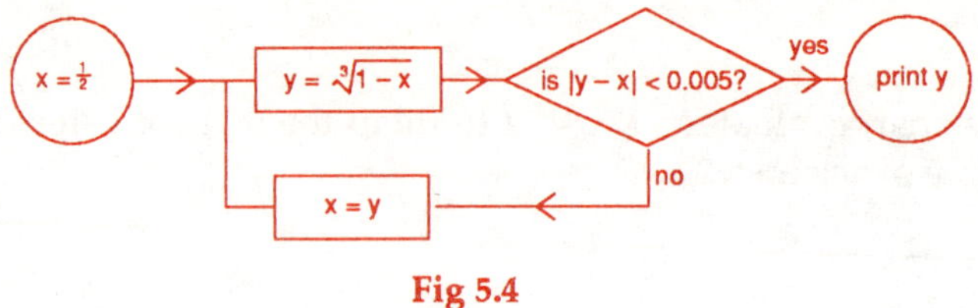

Fig 5.4

5.3.2 Exercises

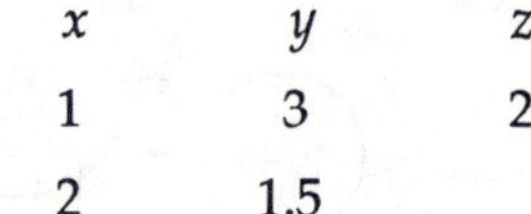

x	y	z
1	3	2
2	1.5	

1) The following flow chart (Fig 5.4) evaluates √3. Use it to fill in the table on the right, and hence to find √3 to 3 decimal places.

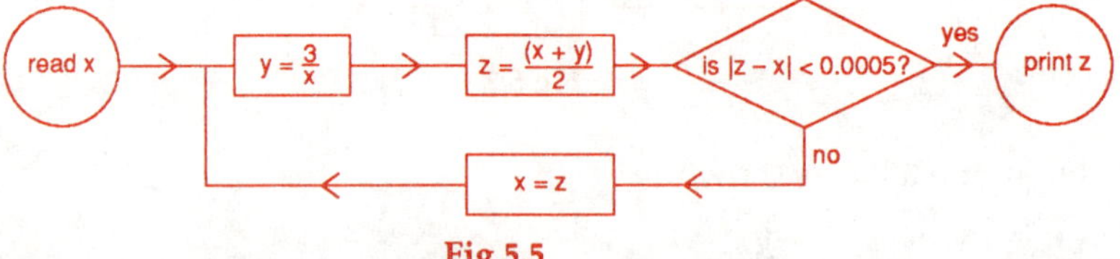

Fig 5.5

2) Write a flow-chart which will evaluate √10. Use it to find √10 to 3 decimal places.

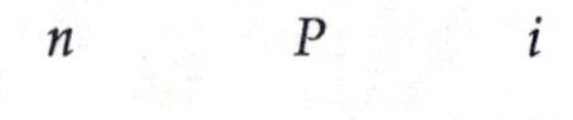

n	P	i

3) If n is a positive integer, $n!$ is the product of all the numbers up to and including n. The following flow-chart evaluates $n!$ Use it to find 4!, 6!.

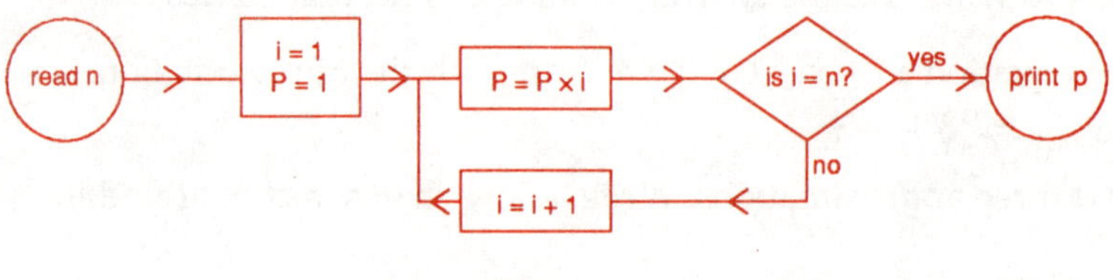

Fig 5.6

4) The following flow-chart evaluates the sum of all the numbers up to and including n. Fill in the empty boxes.

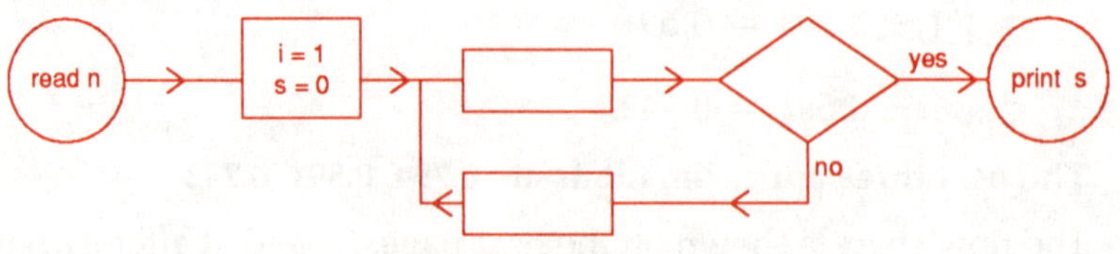

Fig 5.7

5) Solve the equation $x^4 = x + 1$, by taking 1 as your first approximation and using the iteration:

$$x_{n+1} = \sqrt[4]{x_n + 1}.$$

Continue to 3 decimal place accuracy. Write a flow chart to describe the iteration.

6) Solve the following equations by means of the iterations suggested, to 3 significant figures.

a) $x^3 + 2x - 5 = 0$. (Put $x_1 = 1$, and use $x_{n+1} = \sqrt[3]{5-2x_n}$)

b) $x^2 + 5x - 1 = 0$. (Put $x_1 = 1$, and use $x_{n+1} = \frac{1}{x_n} - 5$)

c) $\cos x = \frac{x}{100}$. (Put $x_1 = 50$, and use $x_{n+1} = \cos^{-1}\left(\frac{x_n}{100}\right)$)

7) Write flow charts to describe the iterations of Question 6.

8) Find whether the following sequences converge or diverge. If they converge find the number which they converge to.

a) $x_1 = 2,\ x_{n+1} = \sqrt{x_n + 1}$

b) $x_1 = 3,\ x_{n+1} = \frac{1}{2}\left(x_n - \frac{2}{x_n}\right)$

c) $x_1 = 1,\ x_{n+1} = x_n^{\ 3} + 1$

d) $x_1 = 5,\ x_{n+1} = \sqrt[3]{x_n - 1}$

5.4 Longer exercises

A. Water out of a tank

Suppose a tank contains 1,000 litres of water. There is a tap at the bottom, through which water drains at 100 litres per minute. If this flow is constant, then the tank will be empty in 10 minutes.

In practice, the rate of flow depends on the depth of the water. The rate of flow might be proportional to the depth of the water left in the tank. Let us say that when the depth is h metres, the rate of flow is $100h$ litres per minute. Initially the depth of water is 1 m.

1) Approximately, how much water drains out in the first minute? (Assume that throughout this minute the rate of flow is constant.) How much is left behind? What is the new depth?

2) After 1 minute, what is the new rate of flow? How much water drains out in the second minute? How much is left behind? What is the new depth?

3) Repeat this process for the first 12 minutes. Fill in the table below:

Time t	0	1	2	3	4	5	6	7	8	9	10	11	12
Depth h	1	0.9											

4) Plot the graph of h against t. Does the tank ever empty?

5) On the same paper plot the graph of $h = 0.905^t$ What do you notice?

B. Equations and sequences

Finding the sequence

Suppose you are given an equation to solve. It may be a cubic (involving x^3) equation, for which you do not know any formula. How can you find the root? Take the equation $x^3 - x = 1$.

1) Rearrange the equation, so that the x which occurs by itself is the subject of the equation. Starting with 1, use an iteration similar to those in this chapter. Does the sequence converge?

2) Rearrange the equation, so that the x which occurs in the x^3 term is the subject of the equation. Starting with 1, use an iteration similar to those in this chapter. Does the sequence converge?

3) Write down another equation which you cannot solve by exact means. There will be at least two occurrences of x in your equation. Rearrange the equation in two different ways, giving two different iteration schemes. Which one of them works?

Finding the equation

Suppose you have investigated a sequence, and found that it converges to a particular value α. What equation does α obey?

4) Take the sequence defined by

$$x_1 = 1, x_{n+1} = \frac{1}{2}\left(x_n + \frac{3}{x_n}\right).$$

Find the first few terms of this sequence. What is it converging to?

5) Say it converges to α. Then when it is very close to α, both x_{n+1} and x_n must be virtually equal to α. So α must obey the equation

$$\alpha = \frac{1}{2}\left(\alpha + \frac{3}{\alpha}\right).$$

Solve this equation to find α. Compare your answer with the answer to (4).

6) Take the sequence defined by:

$$x_1 = 1, x_{n+1} = \frac{2}{3}\left(x_n + \frac{1}{{x_n}^2}\right)$$

What does it converge to?

7) Why does the sequence defined by:

$$x_1 = 1, x_{n+1} = \frac{1}{2}\left(x_n - \frac{2}{x_n}\right)$$

not converge?

Multiple choice question *(Tick appropriate box)*

The first term of a sequence is 100. Each subsequent term is 20% less than the one before. The n'th term is:

a) 100×0.8^n ☐

b) $100 \times 1.2^{n-1}$ ☐

c) $100 \times 0.2^{n-1}$ ☐

d) 125×0.8^n ☐

e) 80^n ☐

Points to note

1) *Common difference*

   At the n'th term of sequences with a common difference, the common difference will have been applied $n - 1$ times, not n times.

2) *Exponential functions*

   a) The comment above applies also to sequences with a common ratio.

   b) In the expression 2×3^x, only the 3 is raised to the power x, not the 2. It is different from $(2 \times 3)^x$.

3) *Iteration*

   a) Do not confuse x_2 with x^2.

   b) When drawing a flow chart for an iteration, make sure that you do not reset the value of x back to the original value.

   c) When a number is going through a flow-chart, its value may be changing. Be careful that you do not use the wrong value of the number.

   d) If an approximation is accurate to 3 decimal places, then successive values must differ by less than 0.0005, not by 0.001.

Chapter 6

Spreadsheets

When Mike and Tom start their game of tennis, they are equally likely to win the first point. But if Mike wins a point then he is encouraged, and has probability 0.6 of winning the next point. If Mike loses a point, he gets discouraged and his chance of winning the next goes down to 0.3.

Who will win in the long run? By what margin?

Fig 6.1

A spreadsheet provides a rich environment within which to do mathematics. This chapter contains some of the many situations which can be investigated with the aid of a spreadsheet. They involve material which occurs throughout the book.

Types of spreadsheet

There are many different spreadsheets available. In this chapter the instructions are given for Lotus 1-2-3 and for Excel. It is hoped that they will work for many other spreadsheets. Some differences are as follows:

Formulas. A formula like A1+A2 must start with + in Lotus, as +A1+A2. In Excel it can be either +A1+A2 or =A1+A2.

If a formula begins with a number, then in Excel an = or a + sign must be put first, as in =3*A1.

Functions. A function begins with @ in Lotus, and either @ or = in Excel. If a range of values is given, it is defined using a . sign (Lotus) or a : sign (Excel). So for finding the sum of a range of numbers, we write @SUM(A1.A10) in Lotus and =SUM(A1:A10) in Excel.

In this chapter the Lotus notation will mainly be used.

Spreadsheet techniques

It is assumed that you are familiar with the entering of items into a spreadsheet, and with copying formulas from one group of cells to another. You should be familiar with the notion of relative addresses. The use of macros will help in many examples, but they are not essential.

6.1 Convergence and divergence

The terms of a sequence can be worked out on a spreadsheet. If the terms get closer to a particular value, then the sequence converges.

6.1.1 Example

We wish to solve the equation $x^3 + 3x^2 - 2x - 4 = 0$. Rewrite the equation in three ways, making each of the occurrences of x the subject of the formula. Use a spreadsheet to see whether the corresponding sequence, starting from 1, converges to a solution for the equation.

Solution If the first occurrence of x is made the subject, we obtain

$$x = \sqrt[3]{4 + 2x - 3x^2}$$

This corresponds to the iteration:

$$x_0 = 1,\ x_{n+1} = \sqrt[3]{4 + 2x_n - 3x_n^2}$$

Similarly, the other iterations are:

$$x_{n+1} = \tfrac{1}{3}\sqrt{4 + 2x_n - x_n^3} \text{ and } x_{n+1} = \tfrac{1}{2}(x_n^3 + 3x_n^2 - 4)$$

Set up a spreadsheet, with 1 in A1, B1, C1. The three formulas in A2, B2, C2 are:

```
+(4+2*A1-3*A1^2)^(1/3)
+(@SQRT(4+2*B1-B1^3))/3
+(C1^3+3*C1^2-4)/2
```

When you copy this down the columns the spreadsheet will be as shown below. Note that the A and C columns fluctuate, but that the B column reaches a fixed value.

	A	B	C
1	1	1	1
2	1.442249	0.745355	0
3	0.863676	0.751045	–2
4	1.516780	0.751180	0
5	0.508764	0.751183	–2
6	1.618662	0.751183	0

The second sequence converges to 0.751183

6.1.2 Exercises

1) Rewrite the following equations in different ways corresponding to the occurrences of x. Write down the equivalent sequences. Use a spreadsheet to find which sequence converges, for different starting points.

   a) $x^3 + x - 3 = 0$ b) $3x^4 - 3x^2 + x + 1 = 0$

   c) $\cos x = \dfrac{x}{50}$ d) $\tan x = 5 - \dfrac{x}{50}$

2) Use a spreadsheet to see what happens to the following functions as n gets bigger and bigger.

   a) $\dfrac{n^2+1}{n^2-1}$ b) $\dfrac{5n^2+8}{n^3-3}$ c) $n \times \sin\left(\dfrac{1}{n}\right)$

d) $n^{\frac{1}{n}}$ e) $\left(1+\frac{1}{n}\right)^n$ f) $\left(1-\frac{1}{n}\right)^n$

6.2 Areas under curves

The trapezium rule of Chapter 11 enables us to approximate the area under curved graphs, by representing it as trapeziums stacked together.

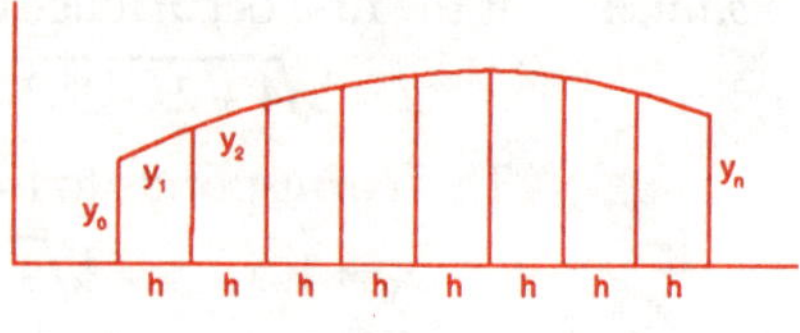

Fig 6.2

Split the interval into equal sub-intervals of length h. The successive values of y are $y_0, y_1, y_2, \ldots, y_n$. The area of the trapeziums, i.e. the approximate area under the graph, is:

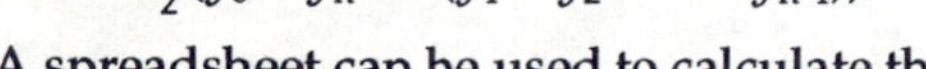

Area $\approx \frac{h}{2}(y_0 + y_n + 2(y_1 + y_2 + \ldots + y_{n-1}))$

A spreadsheet can be used to calculate this formula.

6.2.1 Example

Use a spreadsheet to approximate the area under the curve $y = 4 - x^2$, from $x = -2$ to $x = 2$, taking 40 trapeziums.

Solution The width of the interval is 4, so the value of h is $\frac{4}{40} = 0.1$.

Use 41 rows of the first column to put in the values of x, from -2 to 2, in steps of 0.1. In the B column put in the values of the function, by putting 4-A1^2 in B1 and copying it down to B41. In C1 put @SUM(B2.B40), to add up all the middle values. In C2 put +B1+B41+2*C1. Finally, in C3 put (0.1/2)*C2. This will contain the approximation to the area.

The area is approximately 10.66

6.2.2 Exercises

1) Use a spreadsheet to estimate the areas under the following curves.

   a) $y = x^2$, for $x = 1$ to $x = 2$, taking $h = 0.05$.

   b) $y = x^2 + x^3$, for $x = -1$ to $x = 2$, taking $h = 0.1$.

   c) $y = 2^x$, for $x = 0$ to $x = 1$, taking $h = 0.1$.

2) A more accurate rule for finding area is Simpson's rule. The area is given by:

   $$\frac{h}{3}(y_0 + y_n + 4(y_1 + y_3 + \ldots) + 2(y_2 + y_4 + \ldots))$$

   (Note that n, the number of intervals, must be an even number).

   Set up a spreadsheet to use Simpson's rule to find the area under some curves.

3) The graph of $y = \sqrt{1-x^2}$ is a semicircle of radius 1. So the area under the curve from $x = -1$ to $x = 1$ is $\frac{1}{2}\pi$. Test the accuracy of the Trapezium rule and Simpson's rule by applying them to this area.

4) If you are expert in the use of spreadsheets, set up a general spreadsheet which will use the Trapezium rule to find areas for different curves and different values of h.

6.3 Matrices for simultaneous equations

Consider the simultaneous equations $3x + 4y = 2$ and $2x - 5y = 8$. This can be written as a single equation in matrices.

$$\begin{pmatrix} 3 & 4 \\ 2 & -5 \end{pmatrix} \cdot \begin{pmatrix} x \\ y \end{pmatrix} = \begin{pmatrix} 2 \\ 8 \end{pmatrix}$$

The arithmetic of matrices appears in Chapters 20 and 23. A spreadsheet may contain facilities to deal with matrices. In this case the equation can be multiplied by the inverse of the matrix, to obtain:

$$\begin{pmatrix} x \\ y \end{pmatrix} = \begin{pmatrix} 3 & 4 \\ 2 & -5 \end{pmatrix}^{-1} \cdot \begin{pmatrix} 2 \\ 8 \end{pmatrix}$$

The spreadsheet will work out the inverse and multiply the matrices together, so that the values of x and y can be read off.

6.3.1 Example

Use a spreadsheet to solve the simultaneous equations $3x - y = 2$ and $4x + 2y = 18$.

Solution In matrix form the equation becomes:

$$\begin{pmatrix} 3 & -1 \\ 4 & 2 \end{pmatrix} \cdot \begin{pmatrix} x \\ y \end{pmatrix} = \begin{pmatrix} 2 \\ 18 \end{pmatrix}$$

Enter the terms of the matrix in A1, B1, A2, B2. Enter the right hand side of the equation in D1 and D2.

Use the matrix facilities of the spreadsheet to put the inverse in cells A4, B4, A5, B5. Multiply this inverse matrix with the matrix in D1, D2. Place the result in cells D4 and D5.

The spreadsheet should be as below. Read off the values of x and y.

	A	B	C	D	E
1	3	-1		2	
2	4	2		18	
3					
4	0.2	0.1		2.2	
5	-0.4	0.3		4.6	

$x = 2.2$ and $y = 4.6$

6.3.2 Exercises

1) Use a spreadsheet to solve the following simultaneous equations:

a) $2x + 3y = 8$
$5x - y = 3$

b) $4x - 3y = 18$
$5x + 2y = 34$

c) $x + 5y = 8$
$2x - 3y = 29$

2) A spreadsheet can also be used to solve three simultaneous equations in three unknowns and so on. Solve the following:

a)
$$2x + 3y + 4z = 7$$
$$3x - y + 5z = -5$$
$$x + 8y - 3z = 28$$

b)
$$2w + x - 3y + 5z = 14$$
$$3w - 3x + 2y - 4z = -1$$
$$5w + 4x - 3y + 2z = 5$$
$$3w + 3x + 6y - 5z = 1$$

3) Set up some other systems of simultaneous equations and solve them on a spreadsheet. Is there a limit to the size of the matrix which it can handle?

6.4 Matrices for probability

If the probabilities of one event depend on another event, a matrix can be used to express the dependence.

6.4.1 Example

If a day is dry, the probability that the next day will also be dry is 0.8. If a day is rainy, the probability that the next day will be dry is 0.4.

Write this information in matrix form. If Monday is dry, use a spreadsheet to find the probability that Wednesday will be rainy.

Solution Let p and q be the probabilities of a dry and wet day respectively, and P and Q the corresponding probabilities for the next day. The information gives the equations:

$P = 0.8p + 0.4q$ and $Q = 0.2p + 0.6q$.

Write this in matrix form.

$$\begin{pmatrix} P \\ Q \end{pmatrix} = \begin{pmatrix} 0.8 & 0.4 \\ 0.2 & 0.6 \end{pmatrix} \cdot \begin{pmatrix} p \\ q \end{pmatrix}$$

Enter the values of the matrix in cells A1, B1, A2, B2. If Monday is dry, then for Monday $p = 1$ and $q = 0$. Enter these values in cells D1 and D2.

Use the matrix facilities of the spreadsheet to multiply the matrices. Place the result in cells F1 and F2. This will be the probabilities for Tuesday. Repeat, placing the result in H1 and H2. These are the probabilities for Wednesday. The spreadsheet will look as below.

	A	B	C	D	E	F	G	H
1	0.8	0.4		1		0.8		0.72
2	0.2	0.6		0		0.2		0.28

The probability that Wednesday is dry is 0.72

6.4.2 Exercises

1) Continue the example above, to find the probabilities that Thursday and Friday will be dry.

2) Max is answering a series of questions in a quiz. If he gets a question right, the probability that he will get the next one right is 0.5. If he gets it wrong, the probability that the next one will be right is 0.4. Write this in matrix form as in the example above. If he gets the first question wrong, find the probabilities that he gets the second, third and fourth questions wrong.

3) A maze contains a succession of forks. A rat enters the maze: if it turns right at one fork, the probability that it will turn right at the next is 0.3. If it turns left at a fork, the probability that it will turn right at the next fork is 0.6. Write this in matrix form as in the example above. If the rat is equally likely to turn right or left at the first fork, find the probabilities that it will turn right at the second, third and fourth forks.

4) As the matrix multiplication is continued, the probabilities approach fixed values. Use a spreadsheet to repeat the multiplication and answer the following. (Note: if you are expert at spreadsheets, then write a macro to perform the repeated multiplication).

   a) In Question 1, what proportion of days are dry, in the long run?

   b) In Question 2, what proportion of questions will Max get wrong, in the long run?

   c) In Question 3, at what proportion of forks will the rat turn right, in the long run?

5) Look again at the problem at the beginning of the chapter. Write the information in matrix form, and use a spreadsheet to find the proportion of points that Mike wins, in the long run.

6.5 Simulating probability

A spreadsheet contains a function which takes random values between 0 and 1. This can be used for probability experiments.

In Lotus the function is @RAND, and in Excel it is =RAND(). Below the Lotus notation is used.

6.5.1 Example

A fair coin is spun three times, and the number of Heads is counted. This is repeated 100 times. Use a spreadsheet to simulate this experiment, and record the proportion of times that 0 heads, 1 head, 2 heads and 3 heads were obtained.

Solution The function @INT(@RAND*2) will be 0 or 1 with equal probability. So this can represent whether Tails or Heads is obtained.

Use the first 3 columns for the three spins. Put @INT(@RAND*2) into A1, and copy this across and down to C100. Let the D column represent the number of Heads, by putting +A1+B1+C1 in D1 and copying it down to D100.

We need to record the number of times 0 heads were obtained. The function @IF(D1=0,1,0) will be 1 if D1 contains 0, and 0 if D1 contains 1, 2, or 3. Enter this in E1. Similarly put @IF(D1=1,1,0) in F1, @IF(D1=2,1,0) in G1 and @IF(D1=3,1,0) in H1. Copy these down to row 100.

In E101 add these up, by the formula @SUM(E1.E100), Copy this across to H101. The bottom bit of the spreadsheet might look like what follows on the next page.

	A	B	C	D	E	F	G	H
97	1	0	0	1	0	1	0	0
98	1	0	1	2	0	0	1	0
99	0	0	0	0	1	0	0	0
100	1	1	0	2	0	0	1	0
101					12	34	38	16

The proportions of 0, 1, 2, 3 heads are 0.12, 0.34, 0.38, 0.16 respectively

6.5.2 Exercises

1) Two four-sided dice are rolled and the total is recorded. This is repeated 100 times. Use a spreadsheet to simulate this, and record the proportion of times each total is obtained.

2) A fair coin is spun 20 times and the total of Heads is recorded. This is repeated 100 times. Amend the spreadsheet of the example above to simulate this experiment, and record the frequency of each score.

3) Draw a histogram of the results of Question 2. (The graph-drawing facility of the spreadsheet can be used for this). You should find that the curve has the same shape as the normal curve of Chapter 22.

4) Suppose the coin of Question 2 is biased, so that the probability of Tails is $\frac{2}{3}$. A function which will take the value 0 with probability $\frac{2}{3}$ and 1 with probability $\frac{1}{3}$ is @INT(@RAND*1.5). Repeat Questions 2 and 3 for this bent coin.

5) The Monte-Carlo method for finding area involves picking points at random and counting the proportion which fall within the area. In the diagram the quarter circle has radius 1, and it is enclosed within a square of side 1. So the proportion of points which fall within the circle should be:

$$\frac{\pi.1^2}{4} = 0.785$$

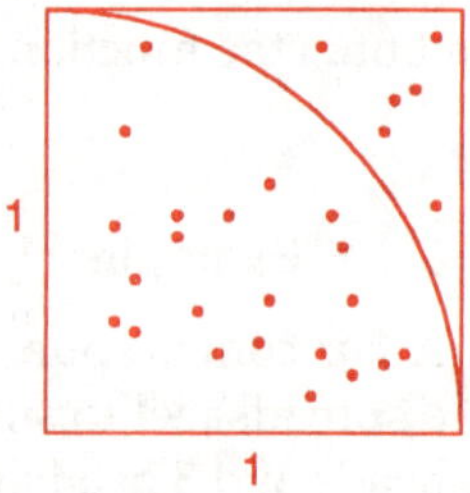

1

1

Fig 6.3

This can be simulated on a spreadsheet as follows. Put @RAND in A1 and B1. These represent the x and y coordinates. The point is within the circle if $x^2 + y^2 < 1$, so put @IF(A1^2+B1^2<1,1,0) in C1. So C1 will contain 1 if the point is within the circle, and 0 if it is outside. Copy this row down for 100 rows. Add the total of the C column and divide by 100. This should be close to 0.785.

Points to note

1) *Notation*

Make sure you are familiar with the notation of your spreadsheet, in particular with the way in which formulas and functions should be written. Don't forget the + or the = or the @.

2) *Multiplication*

If a formula contains a multiplication, don't forget the *. Put 3*A1, not 3A1.

Cross-curriculum topic

The musical scale

Sound

The sense of hearing was the latest to evolve, and in some ways it is the most sensitive. What causes sound is a variation in air-pressure, and the ear has evolved to detect this. The ear can register extraordinarily small changes in air pressure, as small as 10^{-10} of atmospheric pressure. Even the tiny alteration in air-pressure caused by the rustling of leaves can be picked up by the human ear.

Unlike sight or touch, the sense of hearing registers only one thing at a time, the variation in air pressure. But hearing is so complex that this variation can be split up and analyzed so that we can detect the different causes of the variation. We can distinguish between the songs made by different birds. We can analyse the sounds that other people make to us, and understand each other's speech: not only can we make sense of spoken words but we can tell whether the speaker is from Bristol or Liverpool, and whether he or she is speaking angrily or with sympathy.

Sound, or noise, will in general have no pattern. The making of sounds with a regular structure, designed to give pleasure to the hearer, is music.

Notes

If the air pressure is varying in a regular pattern, then a note is heard. Suppose we draw the graph of the air pressure against time, then a curve like that on the right is found.

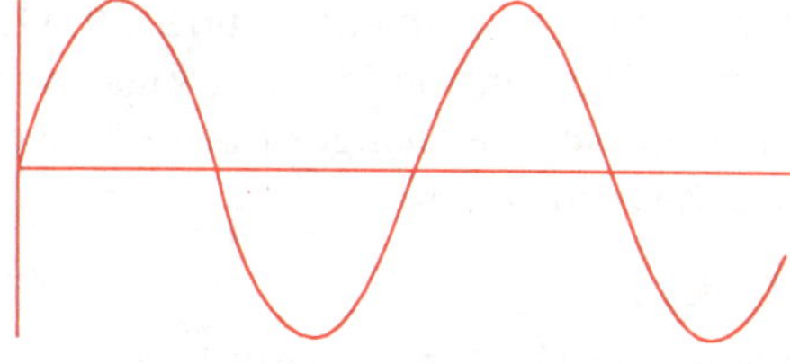

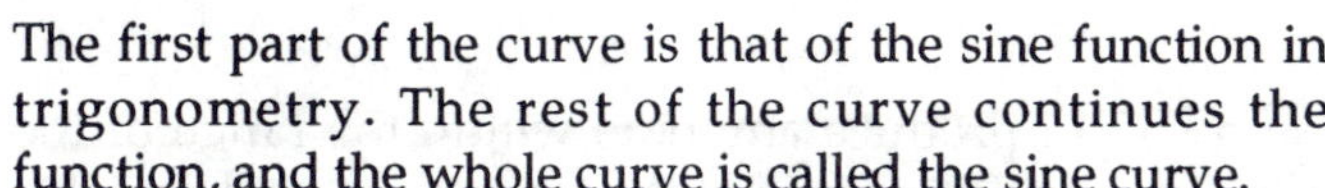

The first part of the curve is that of the sine function in trigonometry. The rest of the curve continues the function, and the whole curve is called the sine curve.

We can see that the curve goes up and down, and then repeats itself. The number of repetitions per second is called the Frequency. Middle c on a piano has a frequency of about 260 cycles per second. The greater the frequency the higher the note.

The sound curve of middle c will have a graph of the form $y = \sin(260 \times 360t)$, so that in 1 second it will have gone through 360° (a full circle) 260 times.

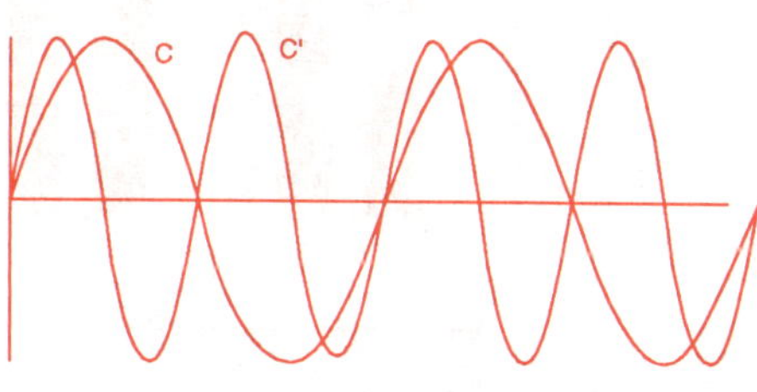

The sound curve of c′ (an octave above middle c) will have graph of the form $y = \sin(2 \times 260 \times 360t)$, so that it will make 2×260 cycles every second. In general, if a note has frequency k times that of middle c, then its graph is like $y = \sin(k \times 260 \times 360t)$. The graphs of c and c′ are shown on the right. Note that the c′ graph can be obtained by "squashing" the c graph.

Changing notes

Musical instruments can produce different notes. Many instruments use strings to produce the note – guitars, pianos, harpsichords, violins etc. Let us see how different notes are obtained.

There are three factors about a stretched string which affect the note it produces. Its length, its tension and its weight per unit length. Let us change each of these in turn.

Length

Suppose we halve the length of the string. Then the note gets higher. In fact its frequency exactly doubles, causing the note to rise by one octave. The mathematical way to express this is by saying:

The frequency is inversely proportional to the length

Tension

Suppose we increase the tension in the string. Then the note gets higher. The relationship is not quite as simple as the one above. In order to double the frequency, i.e. to raise the note by one octave, it is not enough to double the tension. We must quadruple the tension. In general, the increase in frequency is the square root of the increase of the tension. The Mathematical phrase is:

The frequency is proportional to the square root of the tension

Weight per unit length

If the string is made thicker or heavier, then the note decreases. It is not a simple relationship – in order to halve the frequency, taking the note down by one octave, we have to make the string four times as heavy. The Mathematical relationship is:

The frequency is inversely proportional to the square root of the density

When a stringed instrument is tuned, the length and thickness of each string cannot be changed. So the tuner adjusts the tension in the strings so that the right notes are produced. While a violinist is actually playing, however, he changes the note by moving his finger down the string to alter the length, so as to produce the correct note.

The scale

A violinist can shorten a string to any length, and so can produce any note within the range of the instrument. Similarly the trombone plays different notes by sliding part of the instrument, and can also achieve a continuous range of notes. Singers can produce any note within their range.

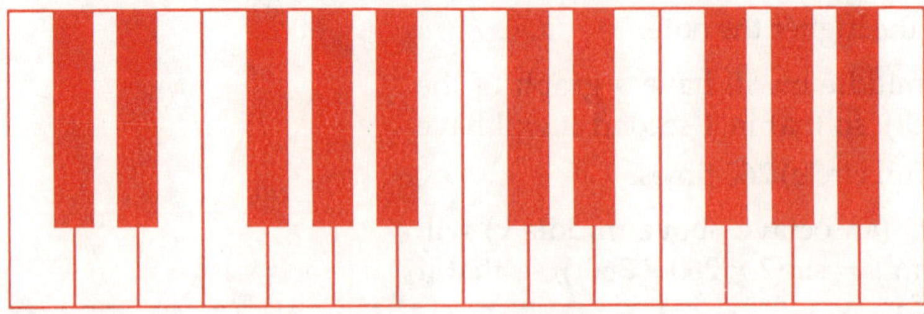

But the piano, for example, has a finite number of strings, and the pianist is restricted to a finite number of notes. The piano keyboard is shown above – the pianist can only play the notes given. Similarly the clarinet is limited by the number of stops to the notes it can play. What should these notes be, so that a wide range of harmonious music can be played using them?

The basic scales of Western music are based on the musical theory invented by Pythagoras and his followers, 2,500 years ago. (The Theorem about right-angled triangles is named after the same Pythagoras.)

Two notes will combine harmoniously if the frequency of one is a multiple of the frequency of the other. So certainly our scale must contain c, c′, c″ and so on.

Notes will also combine harmoniously if their frequencies are in any simple number ratio, and the smaller the numbers involved the more harmonious it will be. In particular, if frequencies are in the ratio 2:3 then they form a pleasing combination. This pair of notes is called a fifth. If we start with c, then a fifth above is g. This note will have a frequency $\frac{3}{2} = 1.5$ that of c. Or we could start at c′, and go down a fifth to a frequency of $2 \div 1.5 = 1.33333$. This note is f.

We can go on, to find a note which sounds well with g. A fifth above g will have frequency 1.5 that of g, or $1.5^2 = 2.25$ that of c. This note is d′: it is outside the c-c′ octave, so divide by 2 to have a frequency relative to c of 1.125. This note is d.

The next note, a fifth above d, is a with frequency of 1.6875. Then comes e, with a frequency of 1.2656. (This also involves halving to get back within the c-c′ octave.) The next is b, at 1.8984375. A table of our notes, in order of frequency, is as follows:

c: 1	d: 1.125	e: 1.2656	f: 1.3333
g: 1.5	a: 1.6875	b: 1.8984	c′: 2

This range of notes is known as the Pythagorean scale. If the strings of a harp are tuned to these notes, then there are many pleasing combinations of sounds that can be played.

But the scale is limited: we are confined to these 8 notes, and cannot shift a tune up or down to accommodate singers with different ranges. Also this scale is incomplete.
We have not gone down a fifth from f, or up a fifth from b.

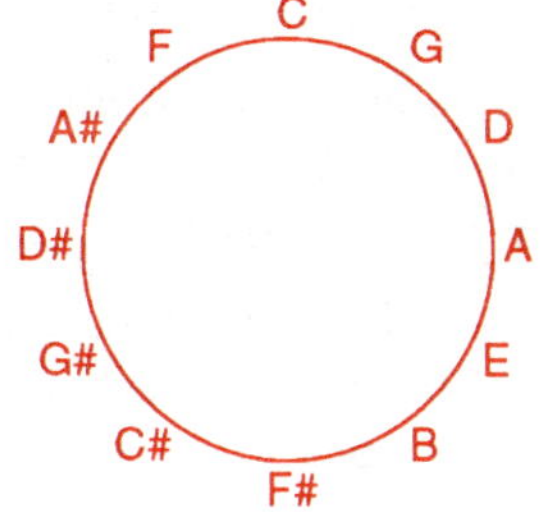

When we keep going up and down by fifths we introduce the flats and sharps. We get a circle of notes, as shown on the right.

This circle has been obtained by successively multiplying by 1.5, and then if necessary dividing by 2 to remain within the c-c′ octave. We see that after 12 operations we seem to get back to c again, and so the circle is complete.

We almost get back to c, but not quite. Twelve multiplications by 1.5 gives us $1.5^{12} = 129.7$. Divide by 2 seven times, and we get 1.014. This is not quite c, it is 1.4% greater. So the twelve tone scale will not quite join up.

There are two ways of coping with this. The first is to stick with the Pythagorean scale or some variant of it, so that we do have perfect ratios between notes. The disadvantage of this is that when we change scale, if for example a tune is to be sung by a soprano instead of a tenor, the whole character of the tune might change because the ratios become different. The other way of coping is by equal temperament.

Equal temperament

By tradition there are 12 intervals between notes in the full scale from c to c′. If we wish to be able to play the same tune in different keys, then all the intervals must be made equal. This dates from about the time of J S Bach, whose *Well Tempered Clavier* shows how equal intervals between notes enables music to be played in many different keys.

Suppose the ratio between successive intervals is k. Then after 12 of these intervals we have gone from c to c′, which is a doubling of frequencies. This gives the equation:

$$k^{12} = 2.$$

We can turn this equation round, to obtain $k = \sqrt[12]{2}$, which is approximately 1.0595. This gives us the relative frequency of c# , the first note above c. The next note up is d, and it has relative frequency $1.0595^2 = 1.1224$. Repeat this procedure, to find the frequencies relative to c of all the other notes as follows:

c: 1	c#: 1.0595	d: 1.1225	d#: 1.1892
e: 1.2599	f: 1.3348	f#: 1.4142	g: 1.4983
g#: 1.5874	a: 1.6818	a#: 1.7818	b: 1.8877
c′: 2			

Compare this with the Pythagorean scale: the ratio of g to c is 1.4983, which is very close to 1.5. The ratio of f to c is 1.3348, which is close to 1.3333. The price for a uniform scale is that the intervals are no longer exact, and perhaps do not sound quite as harmonious as they should.

Other scales

We have seen that in setting up the musical scale of 12 notes we have to choose between essentially two imperfections; either the scale is limited to one particular range of notes, or the ratios within the scale are not perfectly harmonious.

If we had a different number of notes in the octave, would we be able to have perfect ratios and at the same time perfectly equal intervals? Suppose there were n notes between c and c′, and the ratio between notes was always k. Then:

$$k^n = 2, \quad \text{i.e. } k = \sqrt[n]{2}$$

For any value of n the n'th root of 2 cannot be written as a simple fraction. These roots are called irrational, because they are not the ratio of whole numbers. The ratios between notes will never be simple, whole number ratios.

So whatever the number of notes in the scale, we have to make a compromise. If we always have the same ratio k, then it must be irrational. If we insist on whole number ratios between successive notes, then these ratios must vary.

There will always be imperfections in harmonious music. This is not caused by our musical instruments, or by the human ear, or even by the air that conveys sound. It is not a fault in Music, it is a fault in Mathematics.

The mathematics of music

There has always been a close connection between mathematics and music. Here material from Chapters 1, 3, 4, 5, 8, 10 and 15 has been touched upon.

Extended task. Babylonian mathematics

One of the places in which civilization began was round the rivers Tigris and Euphrates, in present day Iraq. There were many cities there – Ur, Sumer, Babylon, Nineveh, but for convenience the whole civilization is referred to as Babylonian.

Quite a lot of evidence about this civilization has survived, because of their writing material. Instead of writing on perishable paper or parchment or wood, they wrote on clay tablets which were then baked hard. About 300 of the tablets which have survived are directly mathematical, and they reveal a sophisticated tradition. Indeed, one feature of Babylonian mathematics is still used today, 4,000 years later.

1) **Number system**

There were only two symbols for numbers. represented 1, and 10.

These symbols could be repeated, to show  = 3, or = 43.

a) Change to ordinary numbers.

Change 42 and 17 to Babylonian numbers.

Evaluate + and -

There was no special symbol for 100, or for 1,000 etc, yet Babylonian mathematics was capable of expressing very large numbers. They used a system based on 60, called a sexagesimal system. When numbers exceed 60, then the first set of symbols would represent the number of 60's. So for example:

$= 2 \times 60 + 35 = 155.$

This system worked up to 3599, after which the first set of digits would represent the $60^2 = 3600$'s, the next set the 60's, the final set the digits.

b) Change to ordinary numbers.

Change 73 and 4,000 to Babylonian numbers.

2) **Fractions**

The system worked just as well in the other direction, for numbers less than 1 as well as for numbers bigger than 1. 1 was divided into 60 equal parts, called first minute parts. Using a semicolon ; as a "sexadecimal point" we can write ;30 to mean $\frac{30}{60} = \frac{1}{2}$ and so on.

Each of these first minute parts was divided into 60 second minute parts. There are $60^2 = 3600$ second minute parts in 1. For example ;15 27 would mean $\frac{15}{60} + \frac{27}{3600} = 0.2575$

The process was repeated, with third minute parts, fourth minute parts and so on.

a) Where do we still use this way of writing numbers smaller than 1?

b) Convert ;30 9 and ;6 54 to ordinary decimals.

The way to find sexagesimals fractions is by repeated division into 60. To find $\frac{1}{45}$ proceed as follows:

60 divided by 45 is 1, remainder 15. 15 minutes is $15 \times 60 = 900$ seconds, and when this is divided by 45 we get 20 exactly. So the sexagesimal form of $\frac{1}{45}$ is ; 1 20

c) Express $\frac{1}{2}, \frac{1}{3}, \frac{1}{4}, \frac{1}{5}, \frac{1}{6}, \frac{1}{7}, \frac{1}{8}, \frac{1}{9}$ in sexagesimal notation. Which of these sexagesimals terminate? Can you find a condition on n for $\frac{1}{n}$ to terminate when it is written in sexagesimal notation?

d) $\frac{1}{14}$ does not terminate when written in this way. Can you write it as a repeating sexagesimal?

3) **The square root of 2**

The tablet on the right is in the museum of Yale University. It shows a square with its diagonal. The lengths of the side and the diagonal are given, and the ratio of these lengths. Amongst other things, this tablet shows that the Babylonians were aware of Pythagoras's Theorem 1,500 years before Pythagoras was born.

The ratio of diagonal to side is given as 1;24 51 10.

a) Convert this to an ordinary decimal.

b) What is the exact ratio between the diagonal and side of a square? How accurate is the Babylonian value?

Obviously the value was not achieved by measurement. Probably they used a principle like the following:
If x is an approximation to $\sqrt{2}$, then $\frac{1}{2}x + \frac{1}{x}$ is a better approximation.

c) Starting with $x = 1\frac{1}{2}$ as your first approximation, use this principle twice to find a close value for $\sqrt{2}$. If you work in sexagesimal notation, what value will you get?

4) **Plimpton 322**

The tablet shown below is in the Plimpton collection in New York.

It is the most interesting example of Babylonian Mathematics that has survived. A bit has been chipped off, and there are mistakes, but once these have been corrected the numbers are as follows. They have been written in modern notation.

A	B	C	D
28561/14400	119	169	1
23280625/11943936	3367	4825	2
44209201/23040000	4601	6649	3
343768681/182250000	12709	18541	4
9409/5184	65	97	5
231361/129600	319	481	6
12538681/7290000	2291	3541	7
1560001/921600	799	1249	8
591361/360000	481	769	9
66601921/41990400	4961	8161	10
5625/3600	45	75	11
8579041/5760000	1679	2929	12
83521/57600	161	289	13
10426441/7290000	1771	3229	14
11236/8100	56	106	15

Column D just numbers the others. See if you can find connections and patterns between the columns.

Suggestions:

(i) Add B and C and halve.

(ii) Subtract B from C and halve.

(iii) Square B and C and subtract.

What might have been the purpose of the tablet?

Miscellaneous exercises

Group A

1) Evaluate the following:

a) 2^9 b) 3^{-2} c) $\left(\frac{1}{2}\right)^3$ d) $\left(\frac{1}{5}\right)^{-2}$

e) $16^{\frac{1}{2}}$ f) $27^{\frac{1}{3}}$ g) $27^{-\frac{1}{3}}$ h) $100^{\frac{3}{2}}$

2) Express the following as single powers:

a) $2^3 \times 2^8 \times 2^7$ b) $3^8 \div 9^2$ c) $3^{\frac{1}{2}} \times 27^{\frac{1}{2}}$

3) Use a calculator to evaluate the following, giving your answers to 3 significant figures:

a) 1.3^8 b) 0.275^{-3} c) $1.8^{2.73}$

4) Express the following with the dot notation, then convert them to fractions.

a) 0.888888.... b) 0.757575757575.....

5) Evaluate the following, leaving your answers in Standard Form.

a) $3.2 \times 10^8 \times 8 \times 10^{-5}$ b) $8.1 \times 10^{-8} \div 3 \times 10^{-12}$

c) $4.7 \times 10^{12} + 8.1 \times 10^{14}$ d) $6.1 \times 10^{-5} - 7.2 \times 10^{-6}$

6) A grain of rice weighs 5×10^{-6} kg. How many grains are there in 1,200 kg?

7) What is the value of an investment of £12,000 after 10 years of interest at 9%?

8) What must you invest now at 9%, so that in a year's time you will have £1,308?

9) A car was sold for £4,600 at a profit of 15%. What was the original price?

10) After depreciating 5%, the pound is worth 1.862 dollars. What was it worth before?

11) The power generated by an electrical circuit is proportional to the square of the current. When the current is 3 amps the power is 36 Watts. Find an expression for the power P in terms of the current I. Use your expression to find P when I = 5 amps.

12) There is a proportionality relationship between X and *Y*. When X = 2 then *Y* = 60, and when X = 4 then *Y* = 15. Find the relationship, and evaluate *Y* when X = 1.

13) a) A measurement is given as 73 ± 2. Write down the greatest and least values of the measurement.

b) A measurement must lie between 12.1 and 12.7. Express this using the ± symbol.

c) A quantity is given as 8.13, correct to 3 significant figures. Between which values must it lie?

14) Evaluate the following, showing the accuracy of your answers.

a) $7.3 \pm 0.1 + 8.1 \pm 0.2$

b) 12.05 – 6.97 (both being given to 2 decimal places.)

c) $73 \pm 2 \times 8 \pm 1$

d) 12.1 + 1.3 (both being given to 1 decimal place.)

15) The population of a city is 410,000, to the nearest 10,000. Its area is 100 square miles, to the nearest 10 square miles. What is the density of the population? Show the accuracy of your answer.

16) Find the next two terms of the following sequences:

a) $-\frac{1}{3}, -1, -1\frac{2}{3}, -2\frac{1}{3}, \ldots$ b) 0, 3, 8, 15, 24, ...

c) 4, 12, 36, 108, ... d) 256, 192, 144, 108, ...

17) The following give the n'th terms of sequences. Write down the first 4 terms of each. Describe the sequences.

a) $3n + 2$ b) $5 - n$ c) $\left(\frac{1}{3}\right)^n$ d) $8 \times (-2)^n$

18) Solve the following equation by the suggested iteration:

$x^5 + x = 1.$ (Put $x_0 = \frac{1}{2}$, $x_{n+1} = \sqrt[5]{1-x}$)

Group B. Challenge questions

19) Suppose x and y are digits between 2 and 9. Simplify:

a) $x \times 10^8 + y \times 10^7$ b) $x \times 10^8 + y \times 10^6$

20) The number of bacteria on a plate doubles every hour. At the moment there are 64,000.
   a) How many bacteria will there be in 2 hours time?
   b) How many bacteria were there an hour ago?
   c) How many bacteria will there be in $\frac{1}{2}$ hour's time?
21) If X is proportional to the square of Y, and Y is proportional to the cube of Z, what is the relationship between X and Z?
22) The period P of a simple pendulum is proportional to the square root of the length L. A pendulum of length 3.24 m has period 6.3 seconds. Find the period of a pendulum of length 25 cm. Find how long a pendulum should be if its period is to be 4.2 seconds.
23) The radius of a circle was measured with a percentage error of 1%. What was the percentage error in its area?
24) Space is divided by 4 planes, none of which are parallel and no three of which intersect in the same line. How many separate regions do these planes divide space into?
25) To solve $x^4 + 5x = 10$, two iterations are suggested. Which one works?

   a) $x_{n+1} = \sqrt[4]{10 - 5x_n}$ b) $x_{n+1} = \dfrac{(10 - x_n^{\,4})}{5}$

26) An old-fashioned way of teaching negative numbers was to say:

   "Minus times minus equals a plus,
   The reason for this we need not discuss."

   Suppose a speed of +5 m/sec represents moving due North at 5 m/sec. What is a speed of –5 m/sec?

   A time of +10 seconds represents 10 seconds in the future. What is a time of –10 seconds?

   What happens after moving at –5 m/sec for –10 seconds? Does this justify the rule above?
27) Suppose the HCF of a and b is a. What can you say about a and b?
28) Suppose the LCM of a and b is a. What can you say about a and b?
29) Every number has at least two factors, 1 and itself.
   a) What numbers have exactly 2 factors?
   b) What numbers have exactly 3 factors?
   c) Describe the numbers which have an odd number of factors.
30) With several values of A write down tan A and tan $(90° - A)$. What is the relationship between them? Can you show why this is so?
31) For what numbers are the square root and the cube root both whole numbers?
32) Find $\sqrt{12345678987654321}$

Group C. Longer exercises

33) **Accuracy and roots**

   Square and square-root are opposite operations. So if you start with a number, square it then square-root it, you should get back to where you started. But some accuracy might have been lost.

a) Start with a number. Press the √ button 10 times. Then press the x^2 ten times. Do you get back to the original number? What is the percentage error?

b) What is the least number of times you must press the √ and x^2 button before you get an error? Does it depend on the number you started with?

c) Fill in the following table:

Number of √'s	1	5	10	20	50
Percentage Error					

d) Sin and $\sin^{-1}$ are also inverse functions. Repeat (a), (b) and (c) with these functions.

34) **Wythoff's game**

a) Take two piles of matches, 10 in the first and 7 in the second. The two players move alternately. Each player can remove either any number of matches from one pile or equal numbers of matches from both piles. So two possible first moves could be:

Take 5 from the first pile, leaving 5 and 7

Take 2 from both piles, leaving 8 and 5

The loser is the person who takes the last match.

Play this game several times. Does the first or second player have the advantage?

b) Try the game with different numbers of matches as the starting position. Who wins?

c) Compile a list of the starting positions from which the first player can always win, for example 1–2, or 2–3. Is there a pattern?

Revision exercises

1) Find the HCF and LCM for the pairs of numbers:

a) 30 and 29 b) 8 and 72

2) A £ used to be divided into 20 shillings. A guinea consisted of 21 shillings. What is the least sum that is both a whole number of pounds and a whole number of guineas?

3) Evaluate the following to 4 significant figures, without writing anything down except the final answer.

a) $(1.273 + 9.148)^2 \times (1.426 + 3.745)$ b) $(8.17+8.39)\times\dfrac{2.345}{1.123+6.342}$

4) Make rough estimates for the following calculations. Then perform them giving your answers to 3 decimal places.

a) $\dfrac{31.1-19.3}{12.2+8.12}$ b) $(12.3 + 8.4)^2$

5) Evaluate mentally: a) $2{,}000 \times 0.7$ b) $4{,}000 \div 0.02$

6) Evaluate the following, giving your answers in Standard Form to 3 significant figures when relevant:

a) $5.1 \times 10^{12} \times 3 \times 10^4$ b) $2 \times 10^8 \div 3 \times 10^3$

7) Work out the following using pencil and paper:

a) $1017 + 323$ b) 394×1001 c) $47824 \div 56$

8) Use a calculator to check your answers to Question 7.

9) At the end of their holiday in Spain, Nigel has 3125 pesetas and Fiona has 6673. How many pounds can they get, at 213 pesetas per £?

10) I travel 100 miles on 3.2 gallons of petrol.

 a) How many miles per gallon did I get?

 b) How many gallons per mile were used?

11) Write:

 a) $\frac{15}{65}$ in its simplest form

 b) $\frac{100}{7}$ as a mixed number

 c) $3\frac{7}{12}$ as a vulgar fraction.

12) Evaluate the following:

 a) $3\frac{1}{4}\times 1\frac{2}{7}$ b) $\frac{9}{11}\div 1\frac{1}{8}$

 c) $1\frac{7}{10}+2\frac{2}{3}+\frac{4}{7}$

13) $\frac{1}{2}$lb is divided in the ratio 3:5. What are the shares?

14) $\frac{4}{3}$ is divided in the ratio 3:2:5. What is the largest share?

15) A population of 12 million increases by 3%. What is the new population?

16) A man buys 500 shares at £5 each. The price falls by 12%. What is the new value of the shares?

17) Out of 128 people, 16 are over 65. What percentage are over 65?

18) Round to the nearest whole number: a) –12.8 b) 12.5

19) Find $2.7^{3.7}$, giving your answer to 3 significant figures.

20) Make rough estimates of a) $3^{2.1}$ b) $\sqrt{56}$.

21) Make a rough guess of a salary of £15,870 after a 9% rise.

22) Find:

 a) The fourth power of 1.2 b) the cube root of 21 c) the reciprocal of $5\frac{3}{4}$.

23) Continue the sequences below for two more terms:

 a) $1, \frac{1}{2}, 0, -\frac{1}{2}, ..$ b) $1, -\frac{1}{2}, \frac{1}{4}, -\frac{1}{8}, ...$

24) A current is given as 5.30 amps, to 2 decimal places. Between what limits does the current lie?

25) p, q represent lengths, A, B areas. Which of the following expressions must be incorrect?

 a) $pq + A$ b) $p^2q + B$ c) $\frac{AB}{q}+p^2$

Puzzles and Paradoxes

1) You have a pair of scales, and need to weigh items in whole numbers of ounces up to 40 ounces. You can do this with only 4 weights. What are they?

2) The *Josephus* problem occurs in many countries and at many different times. The version following (on the next page) comes from Japan.

A widow with 15 children married a widower, also with 15 children. There was only enough money to leave to 15 of the 30 children, so they were arranged in a circle and every 9th one was disinherited. The widow ordered the children so that none of hers were chosen. How did she arrange this?

3) What is wrong with the following?

$$\frac{-1}{1} = \frac{1}{-1}, \text{ so } \sqrt{\frac{-1}{1}} = \sqrt{\frac{1}{-1}}$$

Multiplying across we get:

$$\sqrt{-1} \times \sqrt{-1} = \sqrt{1} \times \sqrt{1}. \text{ i.e. } -1 = 1.$$

4) No cat has two tails, you will agree. What is wrong with the following arithmetic?

1 cat has 1 tail

0 cat has 2 tails

(adding) 1 cat has 3 tails

5) Here are two famous puzzles about weighing coins. The second was very popular during the Second World War. So many people wasted time trying to solve the puzzle that it was suggested that the enemy should be told of it, in order to hamper their war effort.

a) You have 2 red coins, 2 blue, 2 green. Of each pair of coins, one is heavy and one is light, though they are identical in appearance. All the 3 heavy coins weigh the same, as do the light coins. With just two weighings on a balance, how can you find which coins are heavy?

b) You have 12 coins, of which one is either heavier than the others or lighter, you don't know which. How can you identify this coin, with just three weighings on a balance?

Chapter 7

Quadratic expressions

From a height of 2 m, a ball is thrown upwards at 30 m/sec. t seconds later, its height above the ground is $2 + 30t - 5t^2$.
How high will it reach? Will it strike a point 45 m above the ground?

Fig 7.1

7.1 Expansion

A quadratic expression is something like $x^2 + 3x + 2$, in which there is an x^2 term as well as an x term and a number term.

Quadratic expressions often occur when two simpler expressions are multiplied together. The example above is obtained when $x + 1$ is multiplied by $x + 2$.

$$(x + 1)(x + 2) = x^2 + 3x + 2$$

The procedure of multiplying brackets together is called expansion.

7.1.1 Example

Expand and simplify the following as far as possible:

a) $(x + y)(x - y)$ b) $(3x + 2)(4x - 7)$ c) $(x + y)(p + q)$.

Solution a) Multiply through, to obtain $x^2 + xy - yx - y^2$

The xy and yx terms cancel, giving:

$\mathbf{(x + y)(x - y) = x^2 - y^2}$

b) Multiply through, to obtain $12x^2 + 8x - 21x - 14$

Collect the x terms, to obtain:

$\mathbf{(3x + 2)(4x - 7) = 12x^2 - 13x - 14}$

c) Multiply through, making sure that you get all the terms.

$\mathbf{(x + y)(p + q) = xp + xq + yp + yq}$

7.1.2 Exercises

Expand the following, simplifying your answers as far as possible.

1) $(x + 3)(x - 2)$ 2) $(x + 1)(x - 9)$ 3) $(x - 4)(x - 8)$

4) $(p + q)(p - q)$ 5) $(x + 3)(x - 3)$ 6) $(2x - 1)(2x + 1)$

7) $(x + 1)^2$ 8) $(x + 7)^2$ 9) $(2x - 1)^2$

10) $(3x - 1)(2x + 1)$ 11) $(4x + 3)(2x - 3)$ 12) $(2x + 3y)(x - 4y)$

13) $(m + n)(r + s)$ 14) $(p - q)(r - s)$ 15) $(2x + y)(3w - z)$

7.2 Factorization

In the previous section we considered the expansion of pairs of brackets.

Factorization is the opposite procedure, of writing an expression as simpler expressions multiplied together.

Consider the following expansions:

a) $(x-5)(x+8) = x^2 + 3x - 40$

b) $(a+b)(a-b) = a^2 - b^2$

c) $(2x-3)(3x-5) = 6x^2 - 19x + 15$

d) $(p+q)(r+s) = pr + ps + qr + qs$

Each of these expansions corresponds to a factorization.

7.2.1 Examples

1) Factorize $y^2 + 5y + 6$.

Solution This expression is similar to the right-hand side of a) above. To match the left-hand side of a) the factorization must be:

$(y+a)(y+b)$

Here a and b are numbers whose product ab is 6 and whose sum $(a+b)$ is 5. Try the factors of 6 until you find the pair whose sum is 5. The factors must be 2 and 3:

$\mathbf{y^2 + 5y + 6 = (y+2)(y+3)}$

2) Factorize $4t^2 - s^2$

Solution This expression consists of one square subtracted from another. It matches the right-hand side of b) above. Hence it can be factorized to the left-hand side of b). The a term corresponds to $2t$, and the b term corresponds to s.

$\mathbf{4t^2 - s^2 = (2t+s)(2t-s)}$

3) Factorize $6x^2 - x - 2$.

Solution This is similar to the right-hand side of c). When it is factorized it must be:

$(ax+b)(cx+d)$

Here a, b, c and d are numbers such that $ac = 6$ and $bd = -2$. The first pair could be 6×1 or 3×2, and the second pair could be 2 and -1 or -2 and $+1$.

Try the possible arrangements until the correct values are found:

$\mathbf{6x^2 - x - 2 = (2x+1)(3x-2)}$

4) Factorize $wx - zy - wy + zx$.

Solution This is similar to the right hand side of d). Link together the terms with a w and the terms with a z. Factorize by w and by z.

$(wx - wy) + (zx - zy) = w(x-y) + z(x-y)$

Now factorize through by $(x-y)$.

$\mathbf{wx - zy - wy + zx = (x-y)(w+z)}$

7.2.2 Exercises

Factorize the following as far as possible:

1) $x^2 + 3x + 2$ 2) $x^2 + 4x + 4$ 3) $x^2 + 7x + 12$

4) $x^2 - 11x + 24$ 5) $x^2 + x - 6$ 6) $y^2 - y - 12$

7) $z^2 + 5z - 6$ 8) $w^2 - 4w - 12$ 9) $x^2 - 5x - 24$

10) $p^2 + 7p - 30$ 11) $p^2 - q^2$ 12) $t^2 - 1$

13) $4 - n^2$ 14) $q^2 - 9$ 15) $9 - s^2$

16) $7 - 7s^2$ 17) $2 - 8x^2$ 18) $9 - 81a^2$

19) $49t^2 - 9s^2$ 20) $16m^2 - 25n^2$ 21) $y^2 - \frac{1}{4}$

22) $\frac{1}{9} - z^2$ 23) $2x^2 + 5x - 3$ 24) $3x^2 - 10x - 8$

25) $5y^2 + 9y + 4$ 26) $6x^2 + 35x - 6$ 27) $6a^2 + 11a + 5$

28) $6p^2 - 5p - 6$ 29) $st - sq + rt - rq$ 30) $ax + by - ay - bx$

31) $6st - 4s + 3t - 2$ 32) $xy + 6 + 2y + 3x$ 33) $2zw - 3 + w - 6z$

7.3 Solving quadratic equations

Suppose the quadratic expression $x^2 - 7x + 12$ is put equal to 0. Then it becomes the quadratic equation $x^2 - 7x + 12 = 0$.

The expression above can be factorized, to $(x - 3)(x - 4) = 0$.

The product of $(x - 3)$ and $(x - 4)$ is 0. So one of these factors must be 0. From this we obtain two solutions to the equation.

7.3.1 Example

Solve the equation $x^2 + 2x - 15 = 0$.

Solution Factorize the quadratic, to obtain $(x + 5)(x - 3) = 0$.

Either $x + 5 = 0$ or $x - 3 = 0$.

Either $x = -5$ or $x = 3$

7.3.2 Exercises

Solve the following equations:

1) $x^2 - 3x + 2 = 0$ 2) $x^2 - 5x + 6 = 0$ 3) $x^2 - 19x + 60 = 0$

4) $x^2 + 6x + 5 = 0$ 5) $x^2 + 11x + 30 = 0$ 6) $x^2 - x - 6 = 0$

7) $x^2 + 2x - 15 = 0$ 8) $x^2 - 6x + 9 = 0$ 9) $x^2 + 4x + 4 = 0$

10) $2x^2 - 5x + 2 = 0$ 11) $3x^2 - 7x - 6 = 0$ 12) $4x^2 - 4x + 1 = 0$

7.4 Completing the square

Some expansions and factorizations have been of the form $x^2 + 6x + 9 = (x + 3)^2$. This expression is a perfect square.

The quadratic expression $x^2 + 6x + 11$ can be recognized as 2 greater than the perfect square above. So we have:

$x^2 + 6x + 11 = x^2 + 6x + 9 + 2 = (x + 3)^2 + 2$

This process is known as *completing the square.*

Note that 3 is half of 6. In general, when completing the square of $x^2 + bx + c$ we consider the expansion of $(x + \frac{1}{2}b)^2$.

Finding the minimum of a quadratic

We know that $(x + 3)^2$ cannot be negative. It is always positive, except when x is equal to -3. Hence $(x + 3)^2 + 2$ is greater or equal to 2.

The minimum value of $x^2 + 6x + 11$ is 2, reached at $x = -3$

Graphs of quadratics

The graph of $y = x^2 + 6x + 11$ is shown on the right. Notice that the line of symmetry is $x = -3$, and that the lowest point is (–3,2).

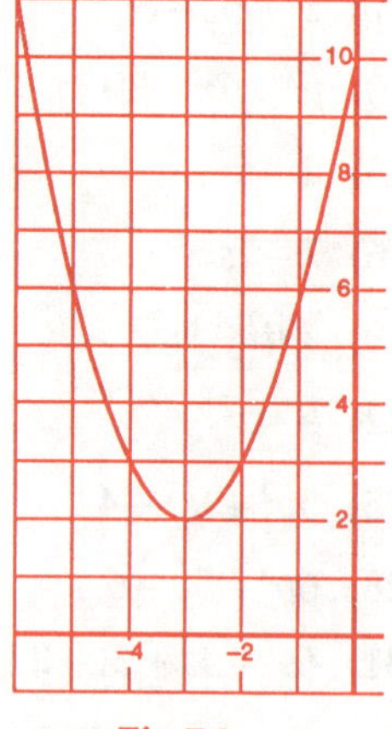

Fig 7.2

7.4.1 Example

Complete the square of the quadratic expression $x^2 - 4x + 3$. Hence find the minimum value of $x^2 - 4x + 3$, and where it is reached.

Solution The coefficient of x is -4. Half of this is -2. Consider the expansion of $(x - 2)^2$.

$(x - 2)^2 = x^2 - 4x + 4$

This is 1 greater than the original expression. Hence we can complete the square to obtain:

$\mathbf{x^2 - 4x + 3 = (x - 2)^2 - 1}$

$(x - 2)^2$ is always greater than 0, except at $x = 2$. So we have:

The minimum of $x^2 - 4x + 3$ is -1, reached at $x = 2$

7.4.2 Exercises

1) Complete the square of the following quadratic expressions:

a) $x^2 + 4x + 6$ b) $x^2 - 8x - 9$ c) $x^2 + 4x + 8$

d) $x^2 - 10x + 1$ e) $x^2 - 3x + 5$ f) $x^2 + x - 3$

2) Find the least values of the quadratic expressions in Question 1, and where they are reached.

3) Sketch the graphs of the expressions in Question 1, showing the lines of symmetry and the lowest points.

4) By writing $2x^2 - 4x + 12$ as $2(x^2 - 2x + 6)$, find its minimum.

5) Complete the squares of the following and find their minimums.

a) $2x^2 + 4x + 8$ b) $3x^2 - 6x + 12$ c) $5x^2 + 20x - 30$

6) By writing $5 - 4x - x^2$ as $-(x^2 + 4x - 5)$, find its maximum.

7) Find the maximums of the following, and where they are reached:

a) $2 + 4x - x^2$ b) $6 - 6x - x^2$ c) $1 + x - x^2$ d) $2x + 1 - x^2$

8) The problem at the beginning of the chapter involved a ball thrown in the air. Complete the square of the expression for its height, and hence find the greatest height reached.

7.5 Longer exercises

A. Completing the square geometrically

"Completing the square" was known long before the invention of modern algebra. The process was described in terms of areas of squares and rectangles.

For $x^2 + 4x + 7$, consider the diagram on the right.

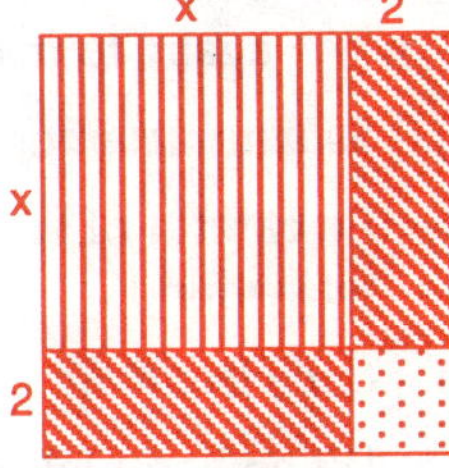

Fig 7.3

1) What is the area of the region shaded vertically?

2) What is the total area of the regions shaded diagonally?

3) What is the dotted area?

4) How much more area is needed to reach $x^2 + 4x + 7$?

5) Write $x^2 + 4x + 7$ in completed square form.

6) Draw the diagrams which show how to complete the square for

a) $x^2 + 6x + 12$ b) $x^2 + 3x - 1$ c) $x^2 - 4x + 5$.

B. Maximum and minimum problems

The technique of completing the square can solve practical problems, as the example below shows.

A farmer has 100 m of fence to enclose a rectangular field. One side of the field is a stone wall.

Fig 7.4

1) If he uses x m for the sides perpendicular to the wall, how much is left for the side parallel to the wall?

2) What is the area of the field?

3) The expression you obtain in (2) should be a quadratic. Complete the square of this expression.

4) What is the maximum area of the field?

Multiple choice question *(Tick appropriate box)*

$2x^2 - 4x - 30$, factorized as fully as possible, is:

a) $2(x^2 - 2x - 15)$ 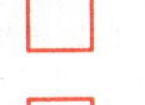

b) $2(x - 5)(x + 3)$ ☐

c) $2(x - 5x)(x + 3x)$ ☐

d) $2(x - 5)(x - 3)$ ☐

e) $2(x + 5)(x - 3)$ ☐

Points to note

1) *Factorization*

   a) Make sure you take out as many factors as you can.

   b) Watch out for the following when factorizing:

   $$49x^2 - 1 \neq (49x - 1)(49x + 1)$$

   $$x^2 + 5x + 6 \neq (x + 2x)(x + 3x)$$

   c) $x^2 + a^2$ is not the difference of two squares. It cannot be factorized at all.

   d) Be careful of signs when factorizing. If in doubt, after you have factorized expand out again, to make sure that you have the correct figures.

2) *Solving quadratics*

   Be careful of signs when solving. If $(x + 3)(x - 4) = 0$, then x is either -3 or $+4$, not the other way round.

3) *Completing the square*

   When completing the square of say $x^2 - 4x + 5$, write down the expansion of $(x - 2)^2$, not of $(x - 4)^2$ or of $(x + 2)^2$. In other words, do not forget to halve and do not ignore the minus sign.

Chapter 8

Algebraic techniques

With your calculator, you can show that

$$\frac{1}{\sqrt{2}-1} = \sqrt{2}+1$$

to as many decimal places as your calculator has. Are they exactly equal?

See if you can show why the two expressions are the same. Some other ones you could try are:

$$\frac{1}{2-\sqrt{3}} = 2+\sqrt{3} : \quad \frac{2}{\sqrt{7}+\sqrt{5}} = \sqrt{7}-\sqrt{5} : \quad \sqrt{22-12\sqrt{2}} = 3\sqrt{2}-2$$

8.1 Changing the subject of a formula

The subject of a formula is the letter which is expressed in terms of the other letters. Often we want to rearrange a formula so that a different letter is the subject. There are two cases to be distinguished:

If the new subject occurs once

Suppose there is only one occurrence of the new subject. Rearrange the formula until the new subject is by itself on one side of the equation.

If the new subject occurs more than once

Suppose the new subject occurs more than once. Then all the occurrences of the new subject must be collected together on one side of the equation. Factorize to obtain a single occurrence of the new subject.

8.1.1 Example

1) Make r the subject of the equation $V = \frac{1}{4}r^3$.

Solution To get rid of the fraction, first multiply both sides by 4.

$4V = r^3$

Now cube-root both sides, to obtain:

$$r = \sqrt[3]{4V}$$

2) Make x the subject of the equation $ax + b = cx - d$.

Solution Add d to both sides, and subtract ax from both sides.

The equation is now: $b + d = cx - ax$.

Write this as: $b + d = (c - a)x$.

Now divide both sides by $(c - a)$. The final answer is:

$$x = \frac{b+d}{c-a}$$

8.1.2 Exercises

In each of the following equations, change the subject to the letter in brackets.

1) $A = 3x + B$ (x)
2) $4y - 2 = z$ (y)
3) $a(z + 3) = b$ (z)
4) $k(m + n) = 3$ (k)
5) $A = 4\pi r^2$ (r)
6) $s = u + at^2$ (t)
7) $ax + cx = T$ (x)
8) $y + b = ay$ (y)
9) $mg - T = ma$ (m)
10) $x - 5a = 3x + 2b$ (x)
11) $ap + bq = cp + dq$ (q)
12) $a(x + 3) = b(7 - x)$ (x)
13) $m = \dfrac{R}{R+r}$ (R)
14) $y = \dfrac{x+1}{x-3}$ (x)
15) $ax + bx = cx + 3$ (x)
16) $a(y + 1) + b(y - 3) + c(y - 8) = 0$ (y)

8.2 Algebraic fractions

An algebraic fraction is a fraction in which some of the terms are expressed as unknown letters. The rules for numerical fractions apply also to algebraic fractions.

Simplifying

The value of a fraction is unchanged if both top and bottom are multiplied by the same amount, or are both divided by the same amount. This amount could be an actual number or an algebraic expression.

$$\frac{15x}{30y} = \frac{x}{2y} \quad \text{and} \quad \frac{x+1}{(x+1)^2} = \frac{1}{x+1}$$

Multiplying and dividing

When fractions are multiplied, their numerators are multiplied and their denominators are multiplied.

$$\frac{x}{y} \times \frac{a}{b} = \frac{xa}{yb}$$

When a fraction is divided by another, then invert the second fraction and multiply.

$$\frac{x}{y} \div \frac{a}{b} = \frac{xb}{ya}$$

8.2.1 Examples

1) Simplify the following fractions:

a) $\dfrac{a}{a^2+a}$ b) $\dfrac{x^2-3x+2}{x^2-1}$ c) $\dfrac{p-1}{1-\frac{1}{p}}$

Solution a) Divide top and bottom by a:

$$\frac{a}{a^2+a} = \frac{1}{a+1}$$

b) Factorize top and bottom:

$$\frac{(x-1)(x-2)}{(x-1)(x+1)}$$

Divide top and bottom by $x - 1$:

$$\frac{x^2-3x+2}{x^2-1} = \frac{x-2}{x+1}$$

c) Multiply top and bottom by p:

$$\frac{p(p-1)}{p-1}$$

Divide top and bottom by $p - 1$:

$$\frac{p-1}{1-\frac{1}{p}} = p$$

2) Express as a single fraction: $\frac{2a}{5} \times \frac{3}{x}$

Solution Multiply together the tops and bottoms, to obtain:

$$\frac{2a}{5} \times \frac{3}{x} = \frac{6a}{5x}$$

3) Simplify $\frac{2a^2}{3} \div \frac{4a}{9}$

Solution Turn the second fraction upside down, and then multiply the tops and bottoms.

$$\frac{2a^2}{3} \div \frac{4a}{9} = \frac{2a^2}{3} \times \frac{9}{4a} = \frac{18a^2}{12a}$$

$6a$ divides both top and bottom. Cancel to obtain:

$$\frac{2a^2}{3} \div \frac{4a}{9} = \frac{3a}{2}$$

8.2.2 Exercises

Simplify the following:

1) $\frac{2x}{2y}$

2) $\frac{4x}{2z}$

3) $\frac{3x+6}{3}$

4) $\frac{4x+2}{6y+8}$

5) $\frac{px}{qx}$

6) $\frac{ay^2}{by}$

7) $\frac{4y^2+6y}{2y}$ 8) $\frac{x+y}{5x+5y}$ 9) $\frac{a}{ab+ac}$

10) $\frac{2x+y}{2ax+ay}$ 11) $\frac{(x+1)^2}{x^2-1}$ 12) $\frac{x^2+6x+5}{x^2+8x+7}$

13) $\frac{4y^2-25}{2y+5}$ 14) $\frac{x^2-3x-10}{x^2-4}$ 15) $\frac{x}{\frac{1}{2}}$

16) $\frac{1/x}{1/y}$ 17) $\frac{\frac{1}{a}+1}{a+1}$ 18) $\frac{\frac{1}{x}+\frac{1}{y}}{x+y}$

Express the following as single fractions, simplifying your answers as much as possible:

19) $\frac{a}{b} \times \frac{c}{d}$ 20) $\frac{3x}{5} \times \frac{4x}{6}$ 21) $\frac{2x}{3y} \div \frac{y}{2x}$

22) $\frac{x}{y} \div \frac{z}{w}$ 23) $\frac{7ab}{4c} \times \frac{2c}{ab}$ 24) $\frac{5pq}{r} \div \frac{10p}{qr}$

25) $\frac{1}{3x} \times \frac{1}{x-1}$ 26) $\frac{3z}{z-1} \times \frac{2z}{z+1}$ 27) $\frac{x+2}{3} \div \frac{x-1}{2}$

28) The problem at the beginning of the chapter asked you to prove an identity involving $\sqrt{2}$. Show it to be true by multiplying top and bottom of the fraction by $\sqrt{2} + 1$.

8.3 Addition and subtraction of algebraic fractions

When fractions are added or subtracted, they must first be put over a common denominator. This denominator is often the product of the original denominators.

$$\frac{a}{b} + \frac{x}{y} = \frac{ay}{by} + \frac{bx}{by} = \frac{ay+bx}{by}$$

8.3.1 Examples

1) Simplify $\frac{2p}{3} + \frac{5p}{2}$

Solution Here both terms must be put over a common denominator of 6.

$$\frac{4p}{6} + \frac{15p}{6} = \frac{4p+15p}{6}$$

$$\frac{2p}{3} + \frac{5p}{2} = \frac{19p}{6}$$

2) Express as a single fraction: $\dfrac{1}{x-1} - \dfrac{2}{x+3}$

Solution The common denominator of this fraction is $(x-1)(x+3)$. Put both terms over this:

$$\frac{(x+3)-2(x-1)}{(x-1)(x+3)}$$

$$\frac{1}{x-1} - \frac{2}{x+3} = \frac{5-x}{(x-1)(x+3)}$$

8.3.2 Exercises

Express the following as single fractions, simplifying your answers as far as possible.

1) $\dfrac{x}{3} + \dfrac{2x}{5}$

2) $\dfrac{3a}{2} - \dfrac{a}{4}$

3) $\dfrac{r}{4} + \dfrac{r-1}{3}$

4) $\dfrac{3(x-2)}{4} - \dfrac{5x}{3}$

5) $\dfrac{7b-1}{2} + \dfrac{3b+1}{3}$

6) $\dfrac{4(c-1)}{3} - \dfrac{3(c+1)}{4}$

7) $\dfrac{2}{x} + \dfrac{3}{xy}$

8) $\dfrac{3}{a} + \dfrac{4}{bc}$

9) $\dfrac{3}{x} + \dfrac{4}{x+1}$

10) $\dfrac{5}{z} - \dfrac{2}{1-z}$

11) $\dfrac{z}{3} + \dfrac{2}{z+1}$

12) $\dfrac{5}{3y+2} + \dfrac{4}{y}$

13) $\dfrac{2}{y-1} + \dfrac{1}{y+3}$

14) $\dfrac{1}{3w+1} - \dfrac{1}{w+2}$

15) $\dfrac{3}{2p-1} + \dfrac{5}{2p+3}$

16) $\dfrac{7}{3-2q} - \dfrac{2}{1-q}$

8.4 Longer exercise

Rowing against the current

You can row a boat at 5 km/hr in still water. There is a current in the river. When you are rowing upstream the current is hindering you, and when you are rowing downstream it is helping you. Do the effects cancel out?

1) Suppose you want to go 10 km upstream and back. How long would it take:

   a) with a current of 3 km/hr   b) with no current at all?

2) You want to go upstream against a 3 km/hr current. The journey takes 30 minutes longer than if there was no current. How far upstream are you going?

3) You want to go 20 km upstream, and the current changes to v km/hr. The journey takes 1 hour longer than if there was no current. Form an equation in v and solve it.

4) You want to row 15 km upstream and back again. If the whole journey takes 8 hours, how fast is the current?

5) Is it possible to row upstream and back, and take less time than if there was no current?

Multiple choice question *(Tick appropriate box)*

Make x the subject of the formula $ax = bx + c$. The answer is:

a) $x = \frac{bx}{a} + \frac{c}{a}$ ☐

b) $x = \frac{c}{a + b}$ ☐

c) $x = \frac{a - b}{c}$ ☐

d) $x = \frac{\frac{1}{2}c}{a - b}$ ☐

e) $x = \frac{c}{a - b}$ ☐

Points to note

1) *Algebra for changing the subject*

Be careful that you do not make basic algebraic mistakes. In particular, be sure that you obey the rule of: *Do to the left what you do to the right.*

2) *When the new subject occurs more than once*

If x is to be made the subject of the formula, then it must occur by itself on one side of the equation. If your answer is something like $x = ax + 3$, then x has not been made the subject.

3) *Simplification of fractions*

A fraction remains unchanged if the top and bottom are both multiplied by the same quantity. But it changes if the same quantity is added or subtracted from top and bottom.

$$\frac{a}{b} = \frac{2a}{2b}, \text{ but } \frac{a}{b} \neq \frac{a+2}{b+2}$$

4) *Multiplication and division*

When multiplying a fraction by a term, don't multiply both top and bottom by the term.

$$5 \times \frac{a}{b} \neq \frac{5a}{5b}$$

It may be helpful to think of 5 as $\frac{5}{1}$, which gives the correct expression:

$$\frac{5}{1} \times \frac{a}{b} = \frac{5 \times a}{1 \times b} = \frac{5a}{b}$$

5) *Addition and subtraction*

When adding fractions, do not add the tops and bottoms.

$$\frac{a}{b} + \frac{c}{d} \neq \frac{a+c}{b+d}$$

Sums of fractions cannot be inverted.

From $\frac{1}{f} = \frac{1}{h} + \frac{1}{k}$ it does not follow that $f = h + k$

Chapter 9

Equations

One of the inventors of algebra was a Greek called Diophantus, who lived about 1,700 years ago. Nothing is known about him, apart from his age when he died. On his tomb was written the following riddle:

This tomb holds Diophantus. He was a boy for a sixth of his life, a youth for a further twelfth, he married after a further seventh. After 5 years a son was born, who died at half his father's total age. Four years later Diophantus died.

How old was Diophantus when he died?

9.1 Equations

An equation states that one mathematical expression is equal to another. Examples of equations are:

$$2y = 5y - 8: \qquad x^2 + 3x = 2: \qquad 2^{3x} = 4^{2x+1}$$

Usually an equation contains an unknown. To solve the equation is to find the value or values of this unknown.

There is one basic rule to obey when solving equations.

Do to the left what you do to the right.

So if 5 is subtracted from the left hand side of an equation, 5 must be subtracted from the right also. If the left is divided by 4, the right also must be divided by 4.

Once an equation has been solved, the result can be checked by putting the answer into the original equation.

If the unknown occurs once

Suppose we are given an equation in which there is only one unknown, which occurs just once in the equation. Then we re-arrange the equation until the unknown is by itself on one side of the equation.

If the unknown occurs twice

Suppose we are given an equation in which the unknown occurs more than once. Then collect together all the occurrences of the unknown on one side of the equation. If these are like terms, they can be simplified to a single term

Problems which lead to equations

We do not study equations just for their own sake. Equations can be used to solve problems about money, measurements and so on.

Suppose we are asked to find a quantity. (Which might be a sum of money, or a distance, or an age.) Call this unknown quantity x, and then write down the facts about the quantity. This will be an equation in x which we can then try to solve.

9.1.1 Examples

1) Solve the equation $3x + 13 = 40$

Solution Subtract 13 from both sides, to obtain $3x = 27$.

Divide both sides by 3:

$\mathbf{x = 9}$

2) Solve the equation $5y - 4 = 2y + 5$, checking your answer.

Solution Subtract $2y$ from both sides, to obtain $5y - 2y - 4 = 5$.

The y terms can be simplified, to $3y - 4 = 5$

Add 4 to both sides, obtaining $3y = 5 + 4 = 9$

Divide both sides by 3,

$\mathbf{y = 3}$

Check the answer by putting $y = 3$ in the original equation.

Left hand side $= 5 \times 3 - 4 = 11$

Right hand side $= 2 \times 3 + 5 = 11$

3) Solve the equation $\frac{p}{3} + \frac{p-1}{5} = 11$.

Solution Multiply both sides by 15, the least common multiple of 3 and 5.

$5p + 3(p - 1) = 165$

Multiply out the bracket, to obtain $5p + 3p - 3 = 165$.

Collect together terms, to get $8p = 168$

$\mathbf{p = 21}$

4) A man is three times as old as his son. In 12 years time he will be twice as old. Let the son be aged y years. Find an equation in y and solve it.

Solution The father is $3y$ years. In 12 years time the son will be $y + 12$, and the father will be $3y + 12$.

The father will then be twice as old. This gives the equation:

$3y + 12 = 2(y + 12)$

Expand out and solve to obtain **$y = 12$ years**

9.1.2 Exercises

Solve the following equations:

1) $2x + 5 = 11$
2) $5z - 3 = 7$
3) $5 - 3a = 2$
4) $7 + 3b = 10$
5) $5(x - 2) = 15$
6) $4(b + 3) = 16$
7) $\frac{z}{7} = 21$
8) $\frac{12}{y} = 4$
9) $\frac{1}{2}x + 3 = 1$
10) $\frac{1}{4}(x - 3) = 5$
11) $2x - 10 = x + 18$
12) $\frac{3}{4}y + y = 28$

13) $5m + 1 = 19 - 4m$
14) $\frac{1}{5}n - \frac{1}{7}n = 4$
15) $3z + 5 = z - 7$
16) $8(2 - x) = 64 - 5x$
17) $5g = 4(18 - g)$
18) $\frac{1}{2}x + \frac{1}{3}x + \frac{1}{4}x = 26$
19) $3(x + 4) = 5(x - 2)$
20) $\frac{1}{4}w - \frac{2}{5}w = 9$
21) $\frac{1}{2}y + \frac{1}{3}(y + 1) = 7$
22) $\frac{1}{4}(z - 3) = \frac{1}{3}(2 + z)$
23) $\frac{1}{5}(t + 7) = \frac{1}{3}(9 - t)$
24) $\frac{3q+6}{8} - \frac{2q-5}{4} = 6$
25) $\frac{p+1}{2} + \frac{p+3}{5} = 13$

26) I think of a number x, double it and then add 5. If the result is 37, what was the original number?

27) The three angles of a triangle are $x°$, $3x° - 30°$, $60° - x°$. Find x.

28) A car is driven at x mph for $1\frac{1}{2}$ hours, then at $x + 20$ mph for $\frac{1}{2}$ hour. The total distance covered is 90 miles. Find x.

29) A woman is six times as old as her daughter. 3 years ago she was 11 times as old. Let the daughter's age be x years. Form an equation in x.

Solve the equation to find how old the woman is.

30) The sum of three consecutive numbers is 441. Letting n be the smallest of the three, write down the other numbers in terms of n. Find an equation in terms of n, and solve it.

31) A girl buys x magazines at 50p each and $x - 3$ magazines at 40p each. She spends £6 in all. Find x.

32) Money is left in a will, so that Anne gets twice as much as Brian, and Brian gets three times as much as Christine. If Christine gets £ x, express the amounts received by Brian and Anne in terms of x. If the total amount left was £1800, find how much each received.

33) Adrian takes a holiday job at £ x per week. After 4 weeks his pay increases by £10 per week. He then works for 5 more weeks. Write in terms of x the total amount he has earned.

If the total is £833, find x.

34) The manager of a shoe shop spends £S on shoes at £10 a pair, and £$(S + 100)$ on boots at £15 a pair. If she obtains 50 pairs in all, find S.

35) A train runs for $x + 10$ miles at 40 m.p.h., then for $x - 60$ miles at 60 m.p.h. The total time for the run was 3 hours. Find x.

36) Look at the problem at the beginning of the chapter. Let x be Diophantus' age. Write down an equation in x and solve it.

9.2 The quadratic formula

If an equation contains the square of the unknown then it is called a quadratic equation.

Sometimes a quadratic expression can be factorized. Then it can be solved by the methods of Chapter 7.

Sometimes the equation does not factorize. In this case the formula must be used.

For $ax^2 + bx + c = 0$,

$$x = \frac{-b \pm \sqrt{b^2 - 4ac}}{2a}$$

The formula method is more powerful than the factorization method. If a quadratic equation can be solved, then it can be solved by use of the formula. In particular, if the equation can be factorized, then the $b^2 - 4ac$ term will be a perfect square.

9.2.1 Examples

1) Solve the equation $z^2 + 13z + 2 = 0$, giving your answer to 3 decimal places.

Solution This equation does not factorize. So the formula must be used. Here $a = 1$, $b = 13$, $c = 2$. Substitute these values in to obtain:

$$z = \frac{-13 \pm \sqrt{13^2 - 4\times 1\times 2}}{2\times 1}$$

$$z = \frac{-13 \pm \sqrt{161}}{2}$$

So we have either $z = \frac{1}{2}(-13 + \sqrt{161})$ or $z = \frac{1}{2}(-13 - \sqrt{161})$

$z = -0.156$ or $z = -12.844$

2) A rectangle is 3 cm longer than it is wide. The area is 110 cm^2. Find the width.

Solution Let the width be x cm. The length must be $x + 3$ cm. The area is 110, which gives the equation:

$x(x + 3) = 110$

Expand and re-arrange to get:

$x^2 + 3x - 110 = 0$

This does not factorize. We must use the formula. Here $a = 1$, $b = 3$, $c = -110$. Be careful with the negative value of c.

$$x = \frac{-3 \pm \sqrt{3^2 - 4\times 1\times(-110)}}{2\times 1} = \frac{-3 \pm \sqrt{449}}{2}$$

So either $x = 9.095$ or $x = -12.095$. The negative answer is not meaningful here.

The width is 9.095 cm

9.2.2 Exercises

Solve the following equations, giving your answers to 3 significant figures:

1) $4x^2 + 10x + 3 = 0$ 2) $y^2 - 5y + 2 = 0$ 3) $z^2 + 3z - 5 = 0$

4) $q^2 - q - 3 = 0$ 5) $x^2 + 2x = 11$ 6) $x + 5 = 3x^2$

7) $x(x + 1) = 3$ 8) $(y + 1)(y + 2) = 28$ 9) $z(z - 3) = z + 1$

10) $p + 1 = \frac{3}{p}$ 11) $\frac{1}{1+x} = x$ 12) $\frac{x}{x+3} = \frac{5}{x}$

13) A positive number x is 100 less than its square. Find the number.

14) The area of a circle is 5π greater than the perimeter. Find the radius.

15) The sides of a right-angled triangle are x cm, $x + 2$ cm, and $5x$ cm, which is the hypoteneuse. Find x.

16) A rectangle has area 100 and perimeter 52. Find the length and the breadth.

17) A cylinder has height 7 cm, and its surface area is 28 cm^2. Use the formula $A = 2\pi r^2 + 2\pi rh$ for the area of a cylinder to find the base radius r of the cylinder.

18) The sum of the area of a square in cm^2 and its perimeter in cm is 43. Find the side of the square.

9.3 Index equations

In some equations the unknown is the index. If two powers of a number (except 0 or 1) are equal, then the indices must be equal.

If $a^x = a^y$, then $x = y$.

In order to reduce an equation to this form we may have to use the following rules for indices.

$a^n \times a^m = a^{n+m}$ $\quad$ $a^n \div a^m = a^{n-m}$ $\quad$ $(a^n)^m = a^{n \times m}$:

$a^{-n} = 1 \div a^n$ $\quad$ $a^{\frac{1}{n}} = \sqrt[n]{a}$ $\quad$ $(ab)^n = a^n b^n$

9.3.1 Example

Express 9^x as a power of 3. Hence solve the equation $9^x = 3^{3x-1}$.

Solution Write 9 as 3^2, and use the appropriate rule above.

$9^x = (3^2)^x = 3^{2x}$

Putting this in the equation we get $3^{2x} = 3^{3x-1}$.

It follows that $2x = 3x - 1$. Solve this equation.

$x = 1$

9.3.2 Exercises

Solve the following equations.

1) $2^x = 16$ $\quad$ 2) $2^{3x} = 64$ $\quad$ 3) $3^{2x} = 81$

4) $2^{x+7} = 2^{2x+1}$ $\quad$ 5) $2^{3x} = 4^{x+3}$ $\quad$ 6) $3^{1-x} = 9^{x-4}$

7) $25^{2x+1} = 125^{x+2}$ $\quad$ 8) $8^x = 128$ $\quad$ 9) $4^{3x} = 8^{x+9}$

9.4 Longer exercise

Designing problems

In Mathematics lessons you have spent a lot of time solving the problems other people have set for you. In this exercise you set your own problems.

"Think of a number"

1) A problem of this sort was Questión 26 of 9.1.2. Devise one of these problems, work out the formula for it and then test it by asking a friend to "Think of a Number".

A variant on this sort of problem is where the answer is always the same, regardless of the original number chosen. In a very simple form it could be: "Think of a number, add 1, take away the number you first thought of ... " of course the result will always be 1.

2) Devise one of these problems, trying to disguise it so that the way it works is not so obvious.

"My father is 3 times as old as me, but ..."

Example 4 of 9.1.1 was a problem about different ages.

3) Think of someone older than you, whose age is a multiple of yours. A few years ago the multiple was different. Set a question of the form: "My uncle is three times as old as me, but 5 years ago he was … "

4) Think of someone younger than you. Set a question of the form: "My sister is a quarter my age, but in ten years time she … "

Multiple choice question *(Tick appropriate box)*

When we solve the equation $2x^2 - 9x + 1 = 5$ we obtain:

a) 23.9 or - 23.9 ☐

b) 4 or $\frac{1}{2}$ ☐

c) 6.34 or 11.66 ☐

d) 0.41 or -4.91 ☐

e) 4.91 or -0.41 ☐

Points to note

1) *Algebra*

Be very careful when multiplying out brackets, or when multiplying two negative numbers together.

2) *Solving equations*

a) Remember the basic rule of: *Do to the left what you do to the right.* If you perform an operation to one side of an equation then you must be fair and do it to the other side as well.

b) Do the correct operations when solving equations.

For $x + 3 = 5$, *subtract* 3 from both sides.

For $y - 4 = 7$, *add* 4 to both sides.

For $3z = 9$, *divide* by 3.

For $\frac{w}{8} = 10$, *multiply* by 8

3) *Equations in which the unknown appears twice*

The unknown cannot appear on both the sides of the answer. If your solution is of the form $x = 3 - 2x$ then you have not solved the equation at all, you have merely re-written it in another form. The solution of the equation must be a statement which gives us the numerical value of the unknown.

4) *Use of quadratic formula*

a) If you have the equation $x^2 - 2x + 2 = 0$, then $a = 1$ (not 0) and $b = -2$ (not 2).

b) The expression $m \pm n$ means that we take either $m + n$ or $m - n$. Either n is added or it is subtracted. Do not multiply.

c) Be careful when b or c are negative. Remember that "minus times minus is plus". For the equation $x^2 - 3x - 8 = 0$, both b and c are negative.

d) When using the formula for a quadratic, remember that the $2a$ term must divide the whole of the top line. So press the = button on your calculator before you divide by $2a$.

5) *Indices*

Watch out for the following:

$$a^n \neq an \qquad \sqrt{a} \neq \tfrac{1}{2}a \qquad ab^2 \neq (ab)^2$$

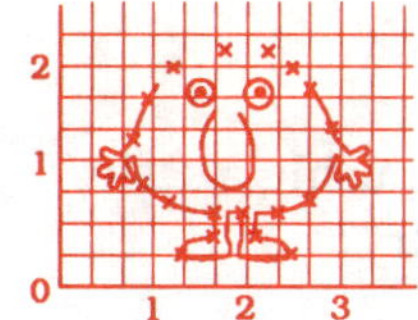

Chapter 10
Graphs

During an exam you spend a long time drawing a graph. In the last couple of minutes you notice that you have misread the question – the question asked for $y = x^2 - 2x - 1$ and you have drawn $y = x^2 - 2x + 1$.

How can you correct the graph without having to redraw it completely?

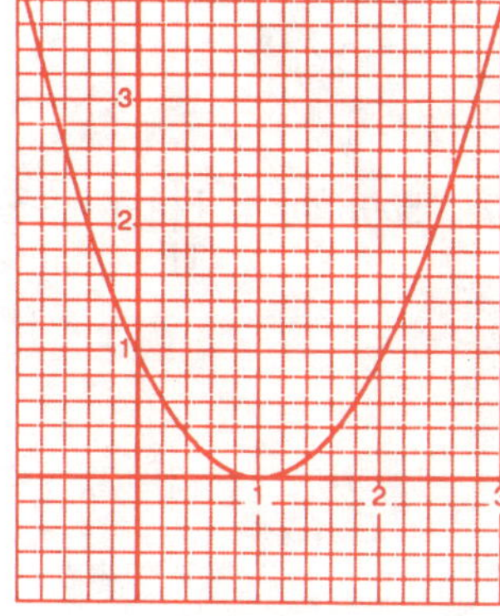

Fig 10.1

10.1 Quadratic and inverse graphs

Quadratic graphs

The graph of a function like $y = x^2 + 3x - 1$ is a quadratic graph. These graphs have the following features:

If the x^2 term is positive the graph has a lowest point. This is called a minimum.

If the x^2 term is negative the graph reaches a highest point. This is called a maximum.

The graph will have a line of symmetry. This line goes through the maximum or minimum. (See Fig 10.2).

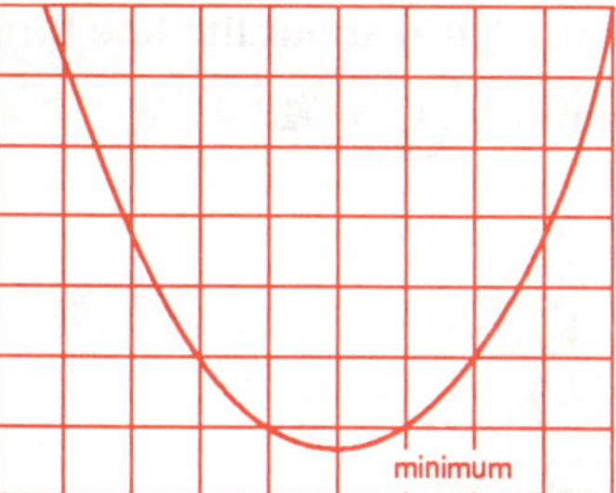

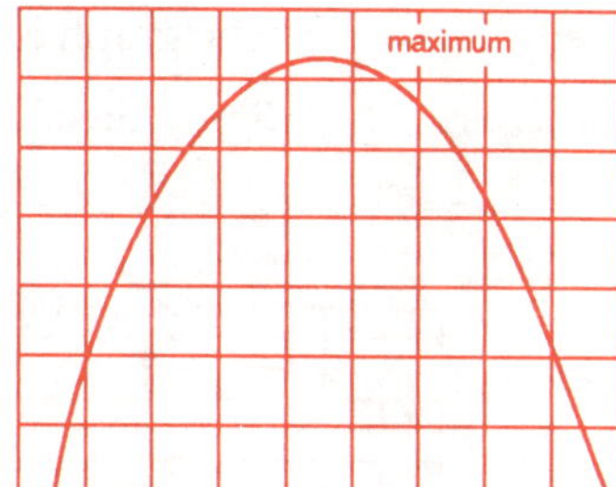

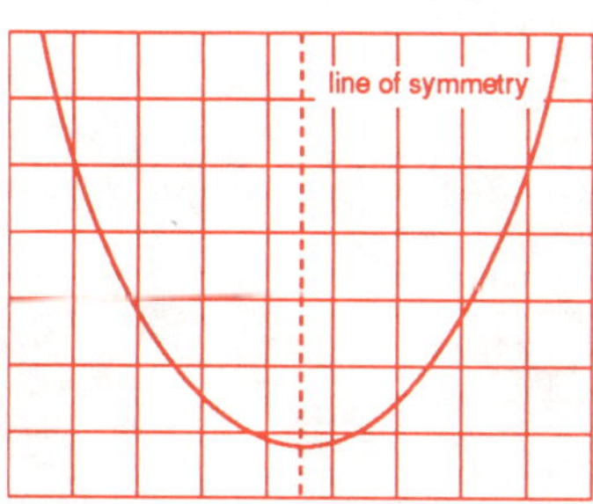

Fig 10.2

Inverse graphs

The graph of a function like $y = \frac{2}{x}$ is an inverse graph. This function is not defined at $x = 0$. The graph never crosses the y - axis.

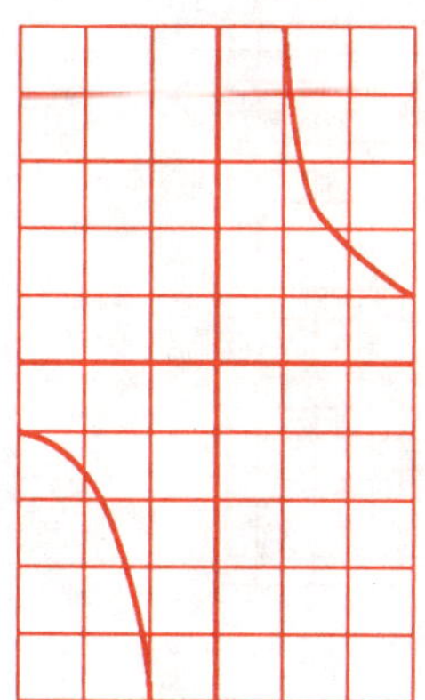

Fig 10.3

10.1.1 Examples

1) Complete the table for the function $y = x^2 + 3x - 1$. Draw a graph of the function using a scale of 1 cm per unit. What is the maximum or minimum? What is the line of symmetry?

x	–3	–2	–1.5	–1	0	1
x^2						
$3x$						
y						

Solution For $x = -3$, $x^2 = 9$ and $3x = -9$. So $y = -1$. Complete the rest of the table similarly. The final result is:

x	–3	–2	–1.5	–1	0	1
x^2	9	4	2.25	1	0	1
$3x$	–9	–6	–4.5	–3	0	3
y	–1	–3	–3.25	–3	–1	3

The graph is shown in Fig 10.4 below.

The lowest point is –3.25.

There is a minimum of –3.25

The graph is symmetrical about the line through the minimum.

The line of symmetry is $x = -1.5$

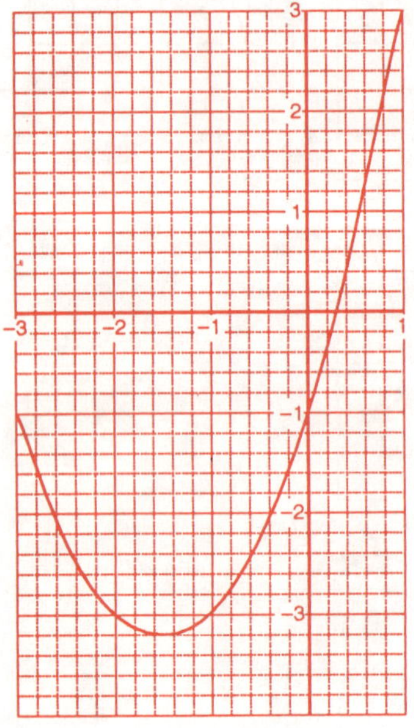

Fig 10.4

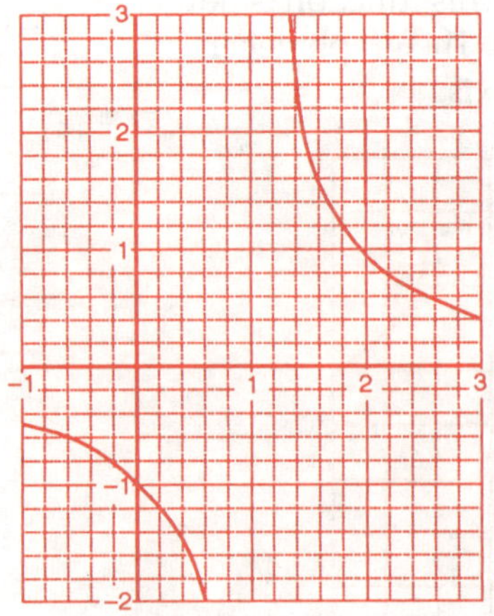

Fig 10.5

2) Let $y = \frac{1}{x-1}$.

Plot the graph of this function, taking x-values of –1, 0, 0.5, 0.75, 1.25, 1.5, 2. When is $y = 3$? For what value of x is the function not defined?

Solution For $x = 0.75$, $y = \frac{1}{0.75-1} = \frac{1}{-0.25} = -4$.

Find the rest of the values similarly. Fill up a table as follows:

x	–1	0	0.5	0.75	1.25	1.5	2
y	–0.5	–1	–2	–4	4	2	1

The graph is shown in Fig 10.5 (at the bottom of the previous page). Read off the value of x when $y = 3$:

$y = 3$ for $x = 1.3$

The graph never crosses the line $x = 1$.

The function is not defined for $x = 1$

10.1.2 Exercises

1) Complete the following table for the function $y = x^2 - 2x + 3$.

x	–1	0	0.5	1	1.5	2	3
y							

Draw a graph of the function, using a scale of 1 cm per unit. Find the line of symmetry of the graph, and its maximum or minimum.

2) Complete the table for the function $y = 1 + \frac{2}{x}$.

Draw a graph of the function. What value of x is excluded?

x	0.25	0.5	0.75	1	1.5	2	3
y							

3) Complete the following table for the function $y = x^2 + 2x - 1$.

x	–3	–2	–1.5	–1	–0.5	0	1
y							

Draw the graph of your function. What is the minimum of the function? What is the line of symmetry of the graph?

4) Complete the following table for the function $y = x + \frac{1}{x}$.

x	0.1	0.2	0.4	0.5	0.8	1	1.5	2	3
y									

Draw a graph of the function. What is the minimum of the function? What value of x is excluded?

5) Plot the following graphs, giving their maximums or minimums and their lines of symmetry:

a) $y = x^2 - 1$ b) $y = x^2 + 2x + 3$ c) $y = x^2 + 3x - 2$ d) $y = 1 + x - x^2$

6) What is the line of symmetry of the graph of $y = x^2 + bx + c$? (Here b and c are constant.)

7) Does the graph of $y = ax^2 + bx + c$ have a maximum or a minimum? (Here a, b and c are constant.)

8) Plot the following graphs, stating where the functions are not defined.

a) $y = \frac{4}{x}$ b) $y = 3 - \frac{2}{x}$ c) $y = \frac{3}{x-2}$ d) $y = 1 + \frac{1}{x+3}$

9) For what value of x is the function $y = \frac{1}{x+a}$ not defined? (Here a is a constant.)

10.2 Solving equations with graphs

Suppose we draw two graphs on the same paper. Say they are $y = x + 1$ and $y = x^2$.

Where the graphs cross both equations will be true.

$y = x + 1$ and $y = x^2$.

Hence at the intersection points, the x coordinate will obey the equation:

$x + 1 = x^2$

So an equation can often be solved by drawing two graphs and seeing where they cross.

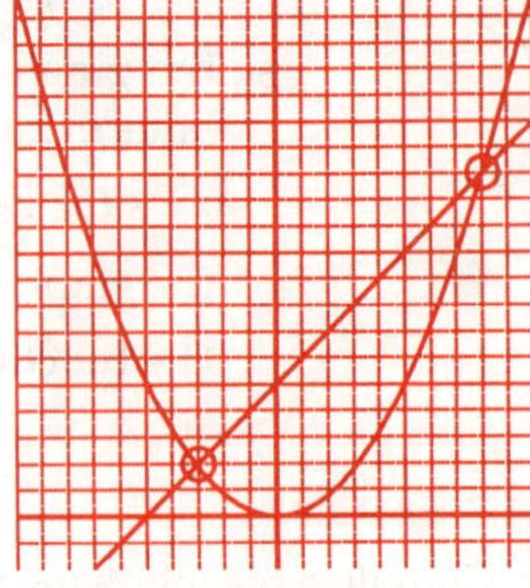

Fig 10.6

10.2.1 Example

A function f is given by $f(x) = x^3 - 2x + 1$. Complete the following table:

x	−2	−1	−0.5	0	0.5	1	1.5	2
$f(x)$								

Draw a graph of the function, using a scale of 1 cm per unit. By drawing a suitable line find the solutions of the equation:

$x^3 - 2x + 1 = x + 1$

Solution Put $x = -2$ into the formula:

$y = (-2)^3 - 2(-2) + 1 = -8 + 4 + 1 = -3.$

The other values are found similarly. The complete table is:

x	−2	−1	−0.5	0	0.5	1	1.5	2
$f(x)$	−3	2	1.875	1	0.125	0	1.375	5

The graph is shown in Fig 10.7.

Draw the line $y = x + 1$. Notice that it crosses the graph at 3 places.

The solutions are $x = -1.7, 0, 1.7$

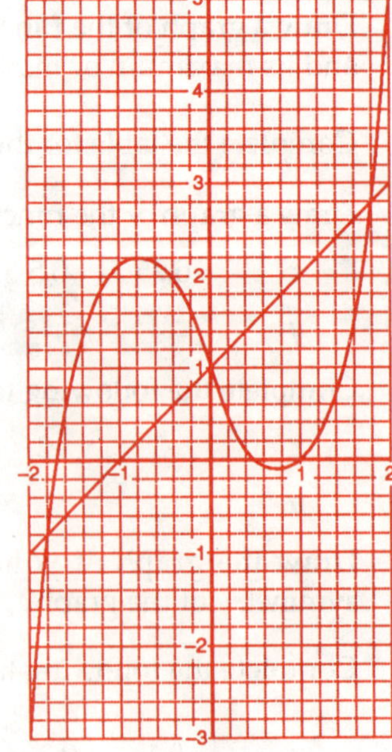

Fig 10.7

10.2.2 Exercises

1) Complete the following table for the function $y = x^2 - 3x + 1$. Draw a graph of the function using a scale of 1 cm per unit.

x	0	1	1.5	2	3
y	1			−1	

Use your graph to solve the equation $x^2 - 3x + 1 = 0$. By drawing a suitable line solve the equation

$x^2 - 3x + 1 = x$.

2) Draw a graph of the function $y = 3 - x^2$, using the x-values −2, −1, −0.5, 0, 0.5, 1, 2.

Use your graph to solve the equation $3 - x^2 = 1$, and by drawing a suitable line solve $3 - x^2 = x + 1$.

3) Complete the table of values for the function $f(x) = x^3 - x$:

x	−2	−1	−0.5	0	0.5	1	1.5	2
$f(x)$								

Draw the graph of this function. By drawing an appropriate line solve the equation:

$x^3 - x = \frac{1}{2}x - 1$.

4) Complete the table of values for the function $f(x) = x^3 - 2x^2$:

x	−1	−0.5	0	0.5	1	1.5	2
$f(x)$							

Draw a graph of this function. By drawing an appropriate line solve the equation:

$x^3 - 2x^2 = x - 2$.

5) Complete the table of values for the function $y = x^2 - \frac{1}{x}$.

x	0.25	0.5	0.75	1	1.5	2
y						

Draw the graph of this function. On the same paper draw the graph of the line $y = x - \frac{1}{2}$.

Show that where the graphs cross x obeys the equation

$x^3 - x^2 + \frac{1}{2}x - 1 = 0$.

Write down the solutions to this equation.

6) Complete the table of values for the function $f(x) = x + \frac{1}{x^2}$:

x	0.25	0.5	0.75	1	1.5	2	3
$f(x)$							

Draw the graph of this function, taking 1 cm to be 1 unit along the x-axis and 1 cm to be 4 units up the y-axis.

On the same paper draw the line $g(x) = \frac{1}{2}x + 3$. Show that where the lines cross x obeys the equation:

$x^3 - 6x^2 + 2 = 0$.

Write down the solution to this equation.

7) Draw the graph of $y = x - \frac{1}{2}x^3$, taking x-values of −2, −1, −0.5, 0, 0.5, 1, 2. Use your graph to solve

$x - \frac{1}{2}x^3 = 2 + x.$

10.3 Moving graphs

Shifting

Often two graphs have the same shape, and can be obtained from each other by a simple shifting process, as follows.

Suppose we have a graph of $y = f(x)$. Let k be a constant.

The graph of $y = f(x) + k$ is obtained by shifting the original graph up by k units. Of course, if k is negative then the graph will be shifted down. See Fig 10.8.

The graph of $y = f(x - k)$ is obtained by shifting the original graph to the right by k units. (Because everything happens k units later.) Of course, if k is negative then the graph will be shifted to the left.

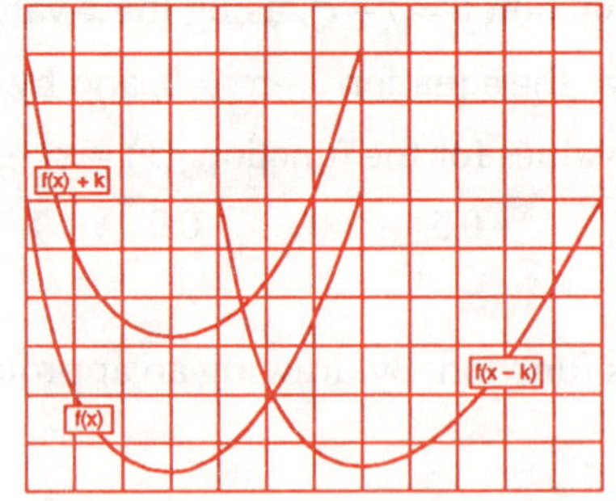

Fig 10.8

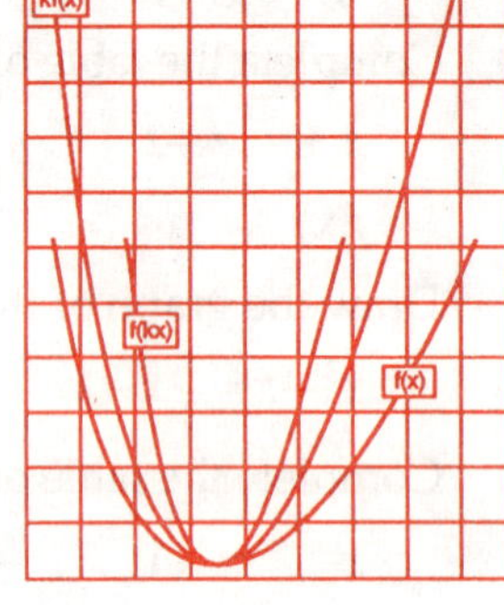

Fig 10.9

Stretching and squashing

Often one graph can be obtained from another by stretching or squashing one of the axes.

The graph of $y = kf(x)$ is obtained by stretching the y-axis by a factor of k. (Because each y-value has been multiplied by k). See Fig 10.9.

The graph of $y = f(kx)$ is obtained by squashing the x-axis by a factor of k. (Because everything happens k times as quickly.)

10.3.1 Examples

1) The graph shown in Fig 10.10 is $y = \frac{1}{x}$

On the same paper sketch a) $y = \frac{1}{x} - 2$ and b) $y = \frac{1}{2x}$

Solution a) $y = \frac{1}{x} - 2$ is obtained by shifting the original down by 2 units.

b) $y = \frac{1}{2x}$ is obtained by squashing the original by 2, along the x-axis.

Both graphs are shown illustrated in Fig 10.11.

2) In Fig 10.12, the graphs are a) $y = x^2$ b) $y = x^2 + k$ and c) $y = (x + m)^2$.

Find k and m.

Solution The graphs have the same shape. (a) has been shifted down by 3 units to (b). (a) has been shifted to the left by 4 units to (c).

$k = -3$ and $m = 4$

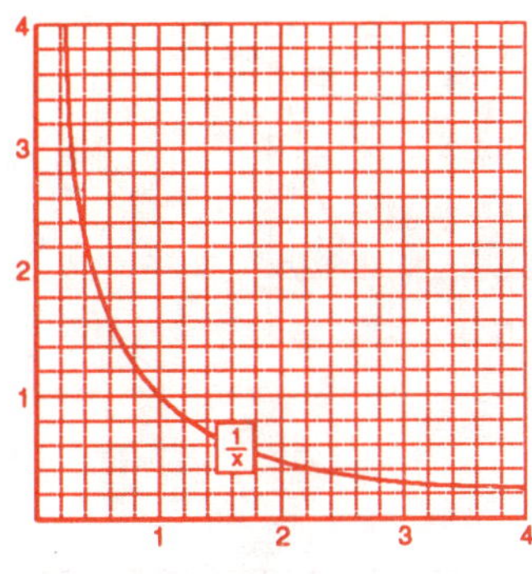

Fig 10.10

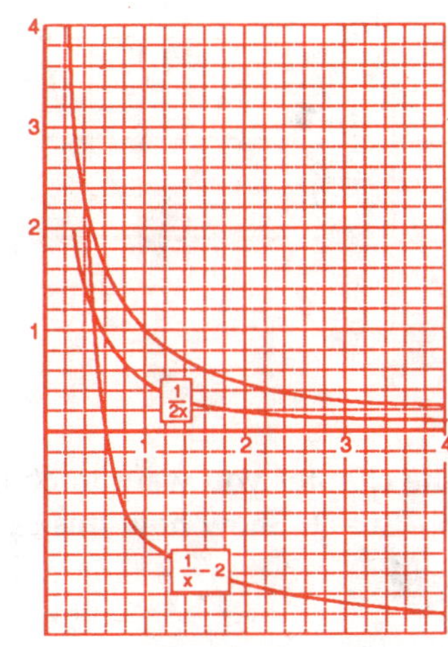

Fig 10.11

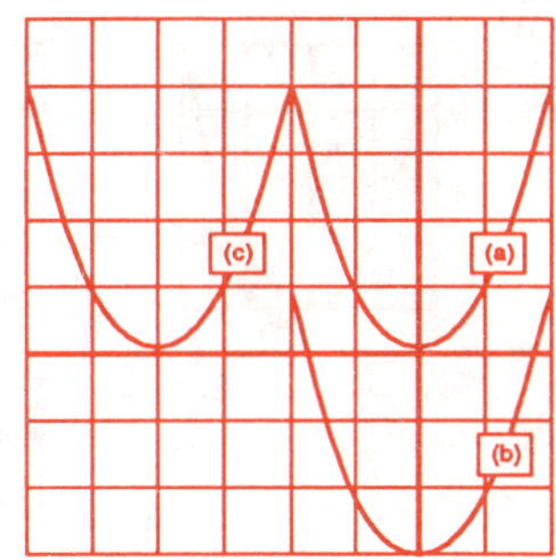

Fig 10.12

10.3.2 Exercises

1) Use the graph of $y = x^2$ to sketch the graph of a) $y = x^2 + 3$ b) $y = (x - 2)^2$ c) $y = (2x)^2$

2) Use the graph of $y = \frac{1}{x}$ to sketch the graphs of

a) $y = \frac{1}{x} - 2$ b) $y = \frac{1}{x+3}$ c) $y = \frac{1}{3x}$

3) The graphs shown are of

a) $y = \frac{1}{x}$ b) $y = \frac{1}{x} + k$ c) $y = \frac{1}{x+m}$

a) 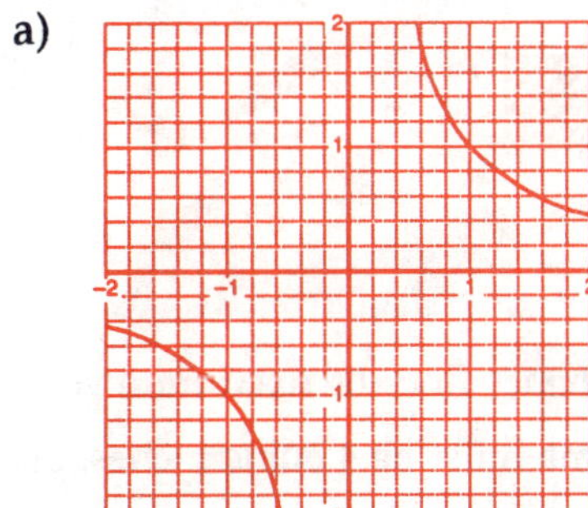

b) 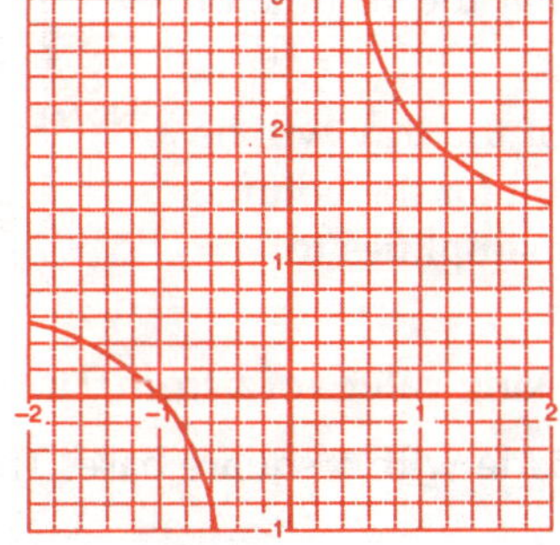

c) 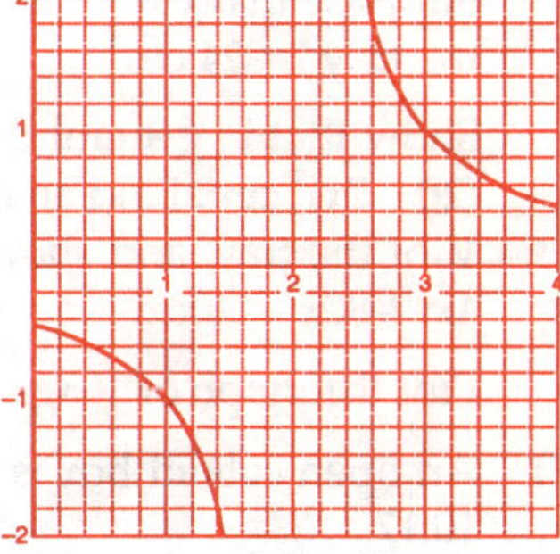

Fig 10.13

Find k and m.

4) The graphs in Fig 10.14 are of

a) $y = x^2$ b) $y = x^2 + p$ c) $y = (x + q)^2$ d) $y = (x + r)^2 + s$.

Find p, q, r and s.

5) Fig 10.15 shows the graph of $y = f(x)$. Sketch the graphs of

a) $y = f(x) - 2$ b) $y = f(x + 2)$ c) $y = 2f(x)$.

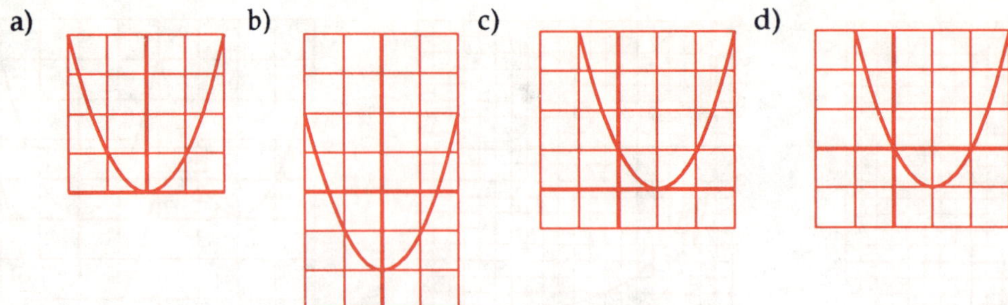

Fig 10.14

6) In the problem at the beginning of the chapter you want to convert the graph of $y = x^2 - 2x + 1$ to $y = x^2 - 2x - 1$. Show how this can be done by shifting the x-axis.

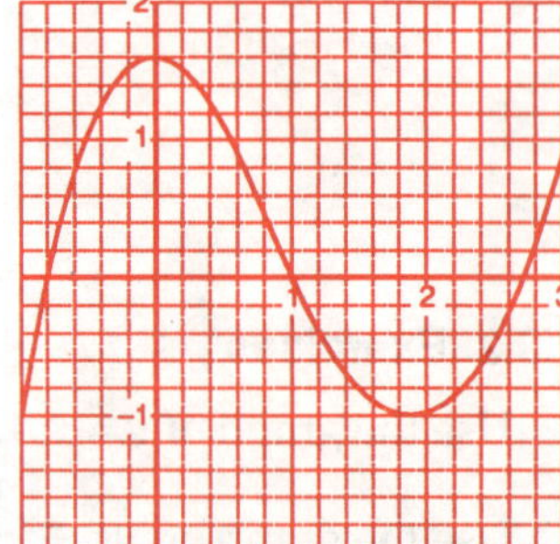

Fig 10.15

10.4 Longer exercise

Maximizing and minimizing

In 10.1 we looked at several graphs to find their minimum or maximum. There are many cases in real life in which something should be minimized or maximized – a firm will want to maximize profit, car-designers will want to minimize fuel consumption. The following are some basic examples on this.

1) A tray is to be made from a square cardboard sheet, of side 20 cm. Little squares (shown shaded in Fig 10.16) of side x are to be cut off and the cardboard is then folded along the dotted lines.

   Suppose that $x = 1$ cm. Show that the volume of the tray is 324 cm^3.

   Show that in general the base of the tray will be $(20 - 2x)^2$ cm^2. Find an expression for the volume V of the tray, and show that it simplifies to $V = 4x^3 - 80x^2 + 400x$.

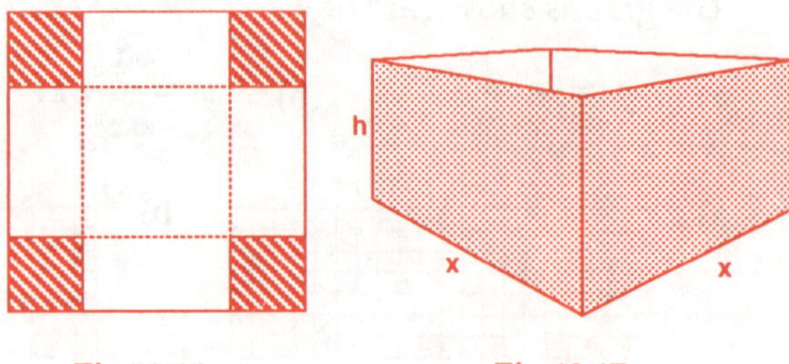

Fig 10.16 Fig 10.17

   Plot the graph of V against x, taking values of x from 0 to 10, and hence find the maximum volume.

2) An open cuboid box is to be made with a square base. The volume must be 4 cubic inches. See Fig 10.17.

   Let the height be h inches, and let the square base have side x inches. Show that $hx^2 = 4$.

   Show that the surface area A of the box is given by $A = x^2 + 4xh$. Show that this can be re-written as

   $$A = x^2 + \frac{16}{x}$$

   Plot a graph of A against x, taking values of x from $\frac{1}{2}$ to 3. Hence find the least possible surface area of the box.

Multiple choice question *(Tick appropriate box)*

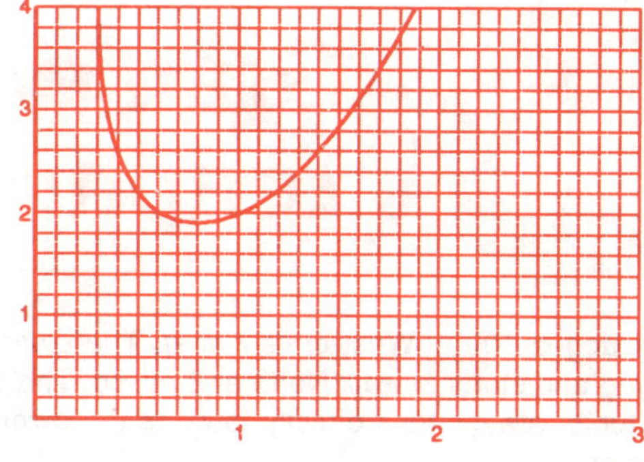

Fig 10.18

The graph shown is of the function $y = x^2 + \frac{1}{x}$

The solution of the equation $3 - x = x^2 + \frac{1}{x}$ in this region is:

a) $x = 1$ ☐

b) $x = 1$ or 0.4, $y = 2$ or 2.6 ☐

c) $x = 0.35$ or 1.5 ☐

d) $x = 0.4$ or 1 ☐

e) None of these ☐

Points to note

1) *Graphs of functions*

Algebraic mistakes are very frequent when working out tables of values. Be very careful when negative numbers are involved. For example, it is easy to get the wrong sign when working out $1 - 2x^2$ for $x = -1$.

Be careful also when dividing. When $x = 0.5$, $\frac{1}{x}$ is equal to 2, not 0.5.

Do not divide by 0.

$1 - \frac{1}{x}$ has no meaning when $x = 0$.

2) *Solving equations by graphs*

a) If you are solving an equation in x by the graph method, then you need only give the x-value of the crossing point. The y-value is unnecessary.

b) If a line and a curve cross at more than one point, then give the x-values of all the points where they cross. They are all solutions of the equation.

3) *Shifting graphs*

The graph of $y = f(x - k)$ is obtained by shifting the original graph of $y = f(x)$ to the right, not to the left.

Chapter 11

Gradients and areas of graphs

A dog is 100 m West of its owner. The owner whistles to the dog and starts to walk North at 2 m/sec. The dog, being rather stupid, always runs directly towards the owner. Its speed is 3 m/sec.

Sketch the curve which the dog follows. When does it overtake its owner?

Fig 11.1

11.1 Straight line graphs

Gradient

The gradient or slope of a straight line is the ratio of its y-change to its x-change. So if a line goes 3 up vertically, and 4 along horizontally, then its gradient is $\frac{3}{4}$.

If the line makes P° with the x-axis, then its slope is tan P°.

Equation of straight lines

The equation of a straight line graph is of the form $y = mx + c$, where m and c are constants.

The gradient of the line is m, and the line crosses the y-axis at $(0,c)$.

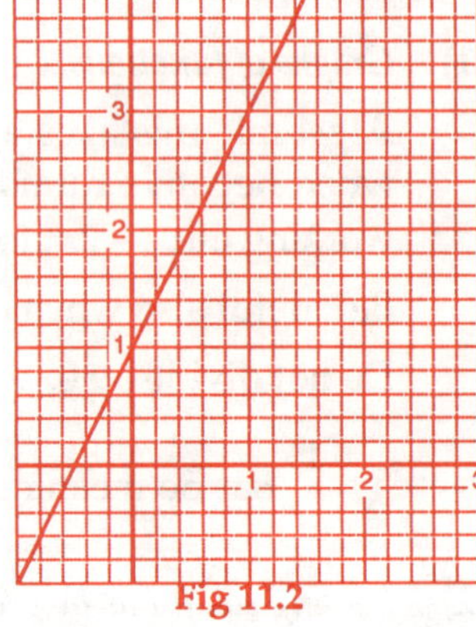

Fig 11.2

The gradient of the line of Fig 11.2 is 2, and it crosses the y-axis at (0,1). So its equation is $y = 2x + 1$.

11.1.1 Examples

1) Find three pairs (x,y) such that $y = 2x + 1$. Plot these points on a graph, and join them up with a straight line.

   Repeat this process with the equation $y = 3 - 2x$, plotting the points on the same graph.

   Use your graph to solve the simultaneous equations:

$$y - 2x = 1$$
$$y + 2x = 3$$

Solution 3 points which satisfy $y = 2x + 1$ are $(-1,-1)$, $(0,1)$, $(1,3)$. They are plotted on the graph of Fig 11.3.

3 points which obey $y = 3 - 2x$ are $(-1,5)$, $(0,3)$, $(1,1)$. They are also plotted on Fig 11.3.

The two equations are both true at the crossing point of the two lines. Read off the co-ordinates of this point:

$x = \frac{1}{2} : y = 2$

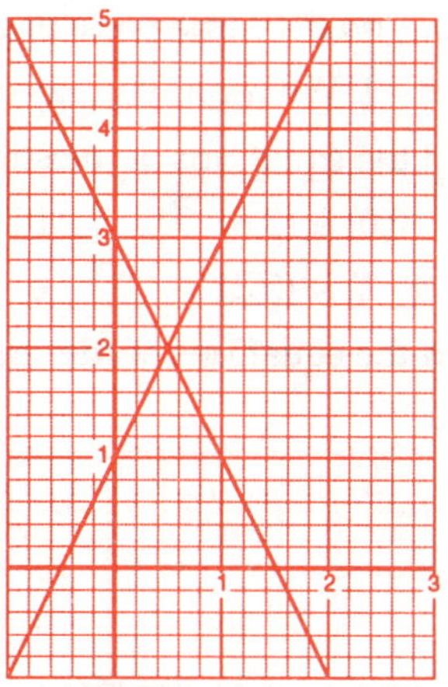

Fig 11.3

2) Find the equation of the straight line which passes through (1,5) and (3,9)

Solution The y-change between these points is $9 - 5 = 4$. The x-change is $3 - 1 = 2$. Hence the gradient of the line is $\frac{4}{2} = 2$.

So the equation of the line is $y = 2x + c$, where c is a constant. The line goes through (1,5), so put in $x = 1$ and $y = 5$, to obtain $5 = 2 \times 1 + c$.

This gives $c = 3$. The equation can be written down:

The equation is $y = 2x + 3$

11.1.2 Exercises

1) Find the gradient of the line segments in Fig 11.4.

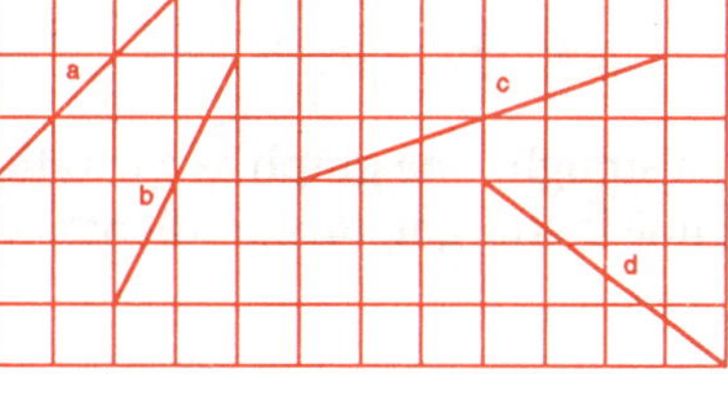

Fig 11.4

2) Find three points of the form (x,y) which satisfy the equation:

$y = 3x + 1.$

Plot these points on the graph of Fig 11.5. Find the gradient of the line.

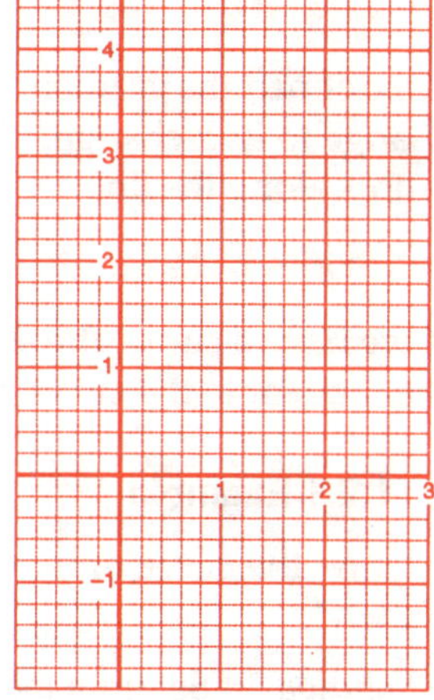

Fig 11.5

3) Repeat Question 2, using the same graph paper, for the equation:

$2y = x + 7.$

Hence solve the simultaneous equations:

$$y = 3x + 1$$
$$2y = x + 7$$

4) Use the method of Question 2 to find the gradients of the lines given by the equations:

a) $y = 4x - 3$ b) $y = x + 1$ c) $y = \frac{1}{2}x + 3$ d) $4y + 3x = 2.$

5) Solve the following pairs of simultaneous equations, by means of drawing lines on graph paper and finding the point of intersection:

a) $y = x + 1$, $y = 3x - 5$

b) $y = 2x - 4$, $y = 11 - 3x$

c) $2y + 3x = 12$, $x + 3y = 11$

d) $y = \frac{1}{2}x - 1$, $4y = 3x - 8$

6) Draw, on the same piece of graph paper, the lines corresponding to the equations $y = x$, $y = x + 3$, $y = x - 1$. What can you say about the lines?

7) Find the equations of the straight lines which go through the following pairs of points:

a) (0,0) & (2,6) b) (1,2) & (4,5) c) (2,1) & (3,–2)

d) (3,2) & (5,3) e) (–1,–2) & (2,4) f) (–2,3) & (2,–5)

8) Find the equations of the straight lines shown in Fig 11.6.

a)

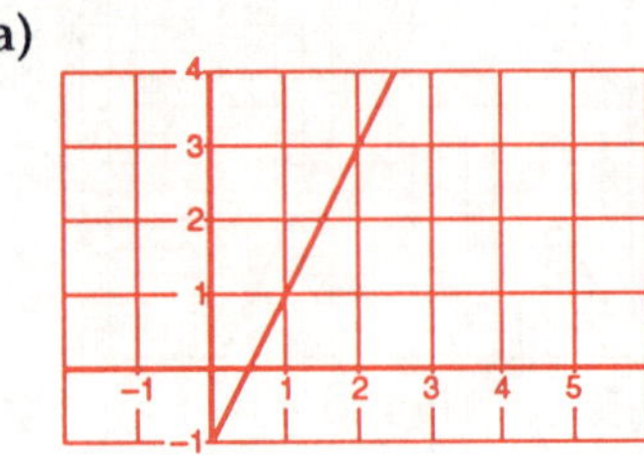

b)

c)

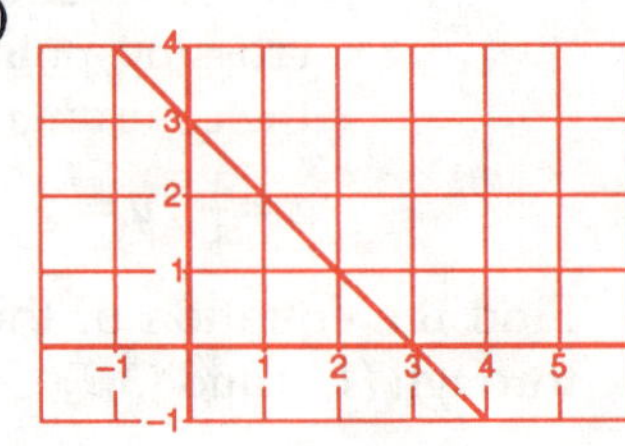

Fig 11.6

9) A plumber has a call-out charge, and a fixed charge per hour for his work. 3 hours work costs £50, and 5 hours work costs £74. What is the call-out charge and the hourly rate? If he works for x hours, what is the charge?

10) A money changer charges a commission for changing pounds to dollars, then a fixed exchange rate of dollars per pound. £100 will buy \$152, and £150 will get \$232. What is the commission and the exchange rate? How many dollars do you get for £x?

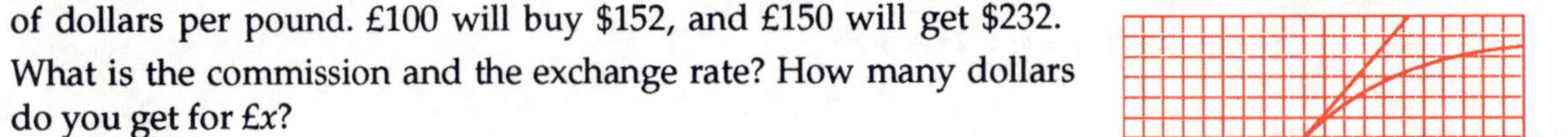

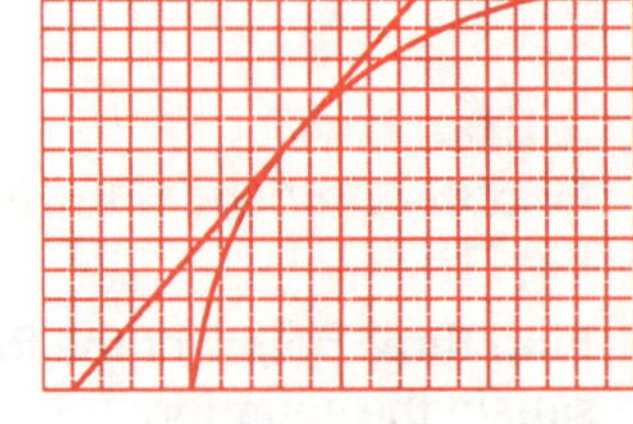

Fig 11.7

11.2 Gradients of curved graphs

We defined the gradient of a straight line graph as the ratio of its y-change to its x-change. If a line is straight, this gradient is constant for all points along the line.

Gradients of tangents

If we have a curve, the slope is constantly changing. We find the gradient of the curve as follows. Draw the tangent to the curve at a point and find the gradient of the tangent.

11.2.1 Example

Draw the curve of $y = 4 - x^2$, taking values of x between –2 and 2. Find the gradient of the curve at $x = -1$.

Solution Set up a table of values as below:

x	–2	–1	–.5	0	.5	1	2
y	0	3	3.75	4	3.75	3	0

Draw the curve as shown in Fig 11.8 (on next page). Draw a tangent at the point (–1,3). The tangent also goes through (–2.5,0), and hence its gradient is $\frac{3}{1.5}$.

The gradient is 2

11.2.2 Exercises

1) Set up a table of values of the function $y = x^2 - 1$, for x equal to -2, -1, -0.5, 0, 0.5, 1, 2. Draw the graph of the function. Find the gradient when $x = -1$ and when $x = 2$.
2) Let $y = 2^x$ Plot the graph of y, taking $0, \frac{1}{2}, 1, 1\frac{1}{2}, 2$ as your x-values. Find the gradient at $x = 1$ and $x = 2$.
3) Let y be given in terms of x by $y = x + \frac{1}{x}$. Draw the graph of y against x, taking as your x-values 1, 2, 3, 4, 5. Find the gradient at $x = 2$ and at $x = 3$.
4) Set up a table of values of the function $y = \frac{1}{x}$, for x equal to $\frac{1}{4}, \frac{1}{3}, \frac{1}{2}, 1, 1\frac{1}{2}, 2$. Draw the graph of the function. Find the gradient when $x = \frac{1}{2}$ and when $x = 1$.
5) Set up a table of values of the function $y = \cos x$, for x equal to 0°, 10°, 20°, 30°, 40°, 50°, 60°. Draw the graph of the function, and find its gradient at $x = 20°$ and at $x = 50°$.

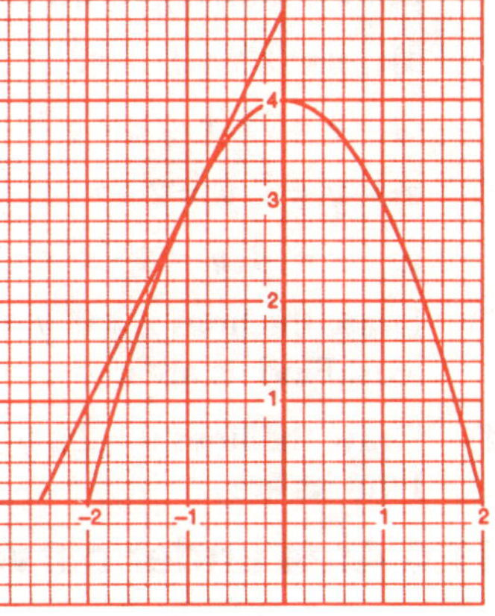

Fig 11.8

11.3 Areas under straight line graphs

Suppose a graph is made up of straight lines as shown. Then the area underneath it can be split up into triangles and trapezia. The area can then be found as follows:

Triangle A: The height of the triangle is 2, and the base is 1. The area is then $\frac{1}{2} \times 1 \times 2 = 1$.

Trapezium B: The two parallel sides have lengths 2 and 3. The distance apart of these sides is 2. Using the formula for a trapezium, the area is $\frac{1}{2} \times (2 + 3) \times 2 = 5$.

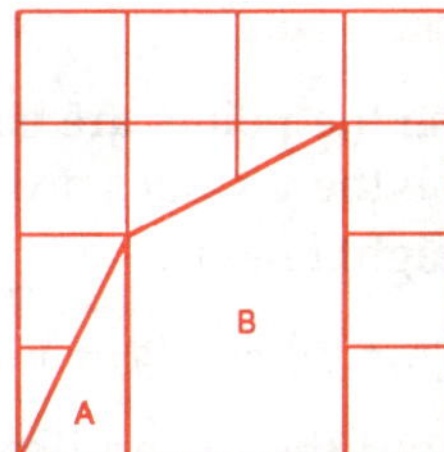

Fig 11.9

11.3.1 Example

A graph is bounded by straight lines as shown. Find the area underneath it.

Solution There is one triangle and two trapezia. Using the formulas for the areas we obtain:

Total area $= \frac{1}{2} \times 1 \times 2 + \frac{1}{2} \times 2(2 + 3) + \frac{1}{2} \times 2(3 + 1) = 10$

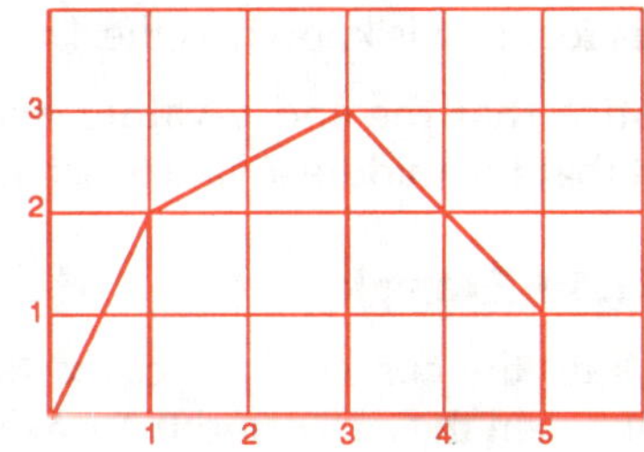

Fig 11.10

11.3.2 Exercises

1) Find the areas under the graphs shown below.

a)

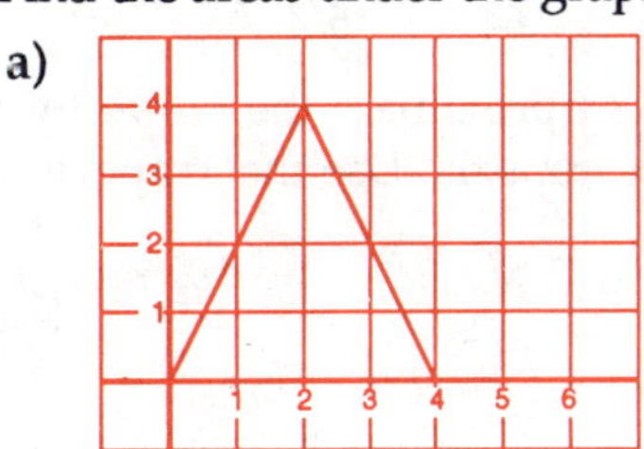

b)

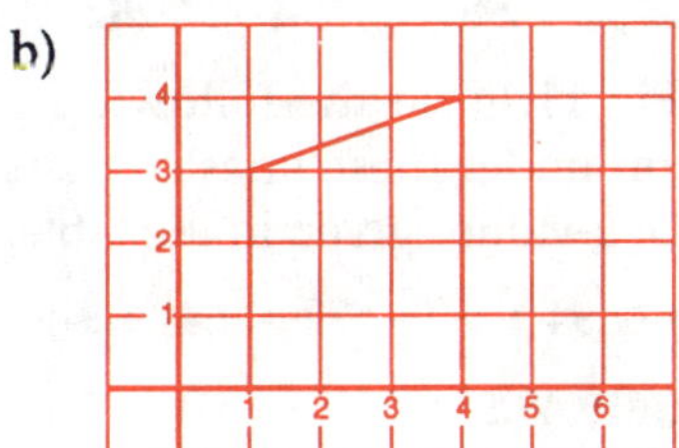

c)

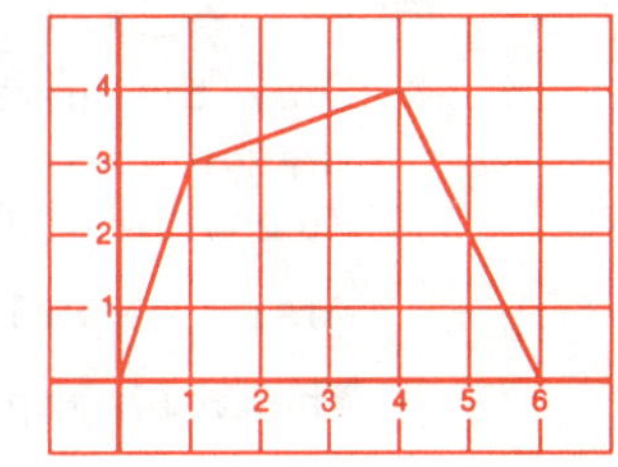

Fig 11.11

2) In the following, draw the lines and find the areas between them and the x-axis.

a) $y = 3, x = 1, x = 3$ b) $x = 1, x = 3, y = x$

c) $y = 2x, x = 1, x = 2$ d) $x = 0, x = 2, y = 2x + 1$

e) $y = x, y = 2 - x$ f) $y = x + 1, y = 3 - x$

g) $x = -1, y = 4 - x, x = 1$ h) $x = -1, y = 2x + 3, x = 2$

3) Draw the lines $x = 0$, $y = 2x + 1$, $y = 4 - x$, $x = 3$. Shade the region enclosed by these lines and the x-axis. Find its area.

4) Draw the lines $y = 2x$, $y = x + 1$, $y = 10 - 2x$. Shade the region enclosed by these lines and the x-axis. Find its area.

11.4 Area under curves

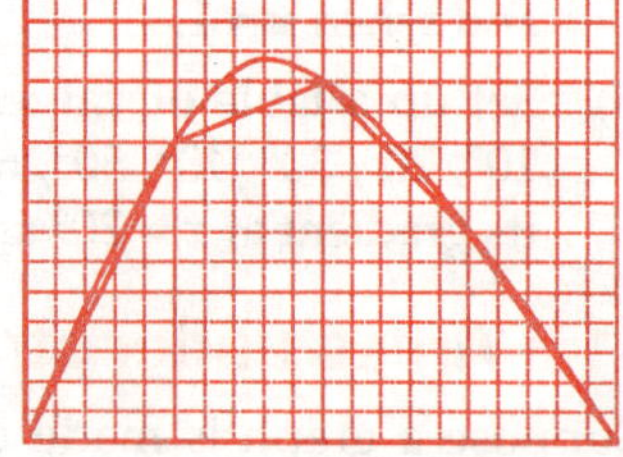

Fig 11.12

In the previous section, we found the area under a straight line graph. If the graph is curved, then this method has to be modified.

Join points on the curve by straight lines, and then the area under the original curve is approximately the area under the straight lines.

Trapezium rule

Suppose the points are equally spaced along the x-axis at a distance of h. Suppose the y values are $y_1, y_2, y_3, \ldots, y_n$. (See Fig 11.13). The area under the straight lines is:

$$\frac{1}{2}h(y_1 + y_2) + \frac{1}{2}h(y_2 + y_3) + \ldots + \frac{1}{2}h(y_{n-1} + y_n)$$

Factor out the $\frac{1}{2}h$, and collect terms to give the following:

$$\frac{1}{2}h(y_1 + 2(y_2 + y_3 + \ldots + y_{n-1}) + y_n)$$

This formula is known as the Trapezium Rule

Notice that the end y-values occur once each, but that the middle y-values occur twice each.

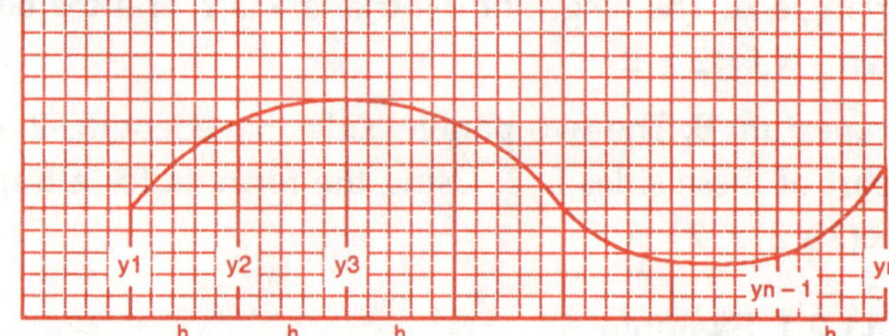

Fig 11.13

11.4.1 Example

Draw the curve of $y = \cos x$, taking values of x between 0° and 60°. Estimate the area enclosed between the curve and the x-axis.

Solution Set up a table of values as below:

x	0	10	20	30	40	50	60
y	1	.98	.94	.87	.77	.64	.5

Draw the curve (See Fig 11.14 on the following page). Approximate the curve by 6 straight lines. The region under these lines consists of six trapezia. Use the Trapezium Rule with $h = 10$ and the y-values given in the table.

Area $\approx \frac{1}{2} \times 10(1 + 2(.98 + .94 + .87 + .77 + .64) + .5)$

The area is approximately 49.5

11.4.2 Exercises

1) Complete the following table for the function $y = \sin x$. Hence estimate the area under this curve for x between 30° and 60°.

x	30	35	40	45	50	55	60
y							

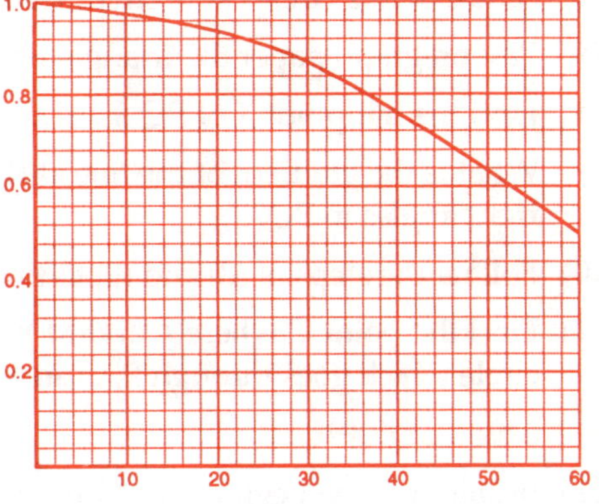

Fig 11.14

2) Complete the following table for the function $y = \sqrt{x}$. Hence estimate the area under this curve for x between 1 and 4.

x	1	1.5	2	2.5	3	3.5	4
y							

Questions 3 – 6 involve the same functions as Questions 1 – 4 of 11.2.2. The same table and graph can be used.

3) Set up a table of values of the function $y = x^2 - 1$, for x equal to $-2, -1, -\frac{1}{2}, 0, \frac{1}{2}, 1, 2$. Draw the graph of the function. Estimate the area between the curve and the x-axis, for x between -1 and 1.

4) Let $y = 2^x$. Plot the graph of y, taking $0, \frac{1}{2}, 1, 1\frac{1}{2}, 2$ as your x-values. Find the area under the graph from $x = 0$ to $x = 2$.

5) Let y be given in terms of x by $y = x + \frac{1}{x}$. Draw the graph of y against x, taking as your x-values 1, 2, 3, 4, 5. Find the area under the graph between $x = 1$ and $x = 5$.

6) Set up a table of values of the function $y = \frac{1}{x}$, for x equal to $\frac{1}{4}, \frac{1}{3}, \frac{1}{2}, 1, 1\frac{1}{2}, 2$. Draw the graph of the function. Estimate the area under the graph from $x = 1$ to $x = 2$.

7) Three sides of a field are straight, but the fourth is bounded by a river. In Fig 11.15 the field is shown dotted. Each square is 10 m by 10 m. Estimate the area of the field.

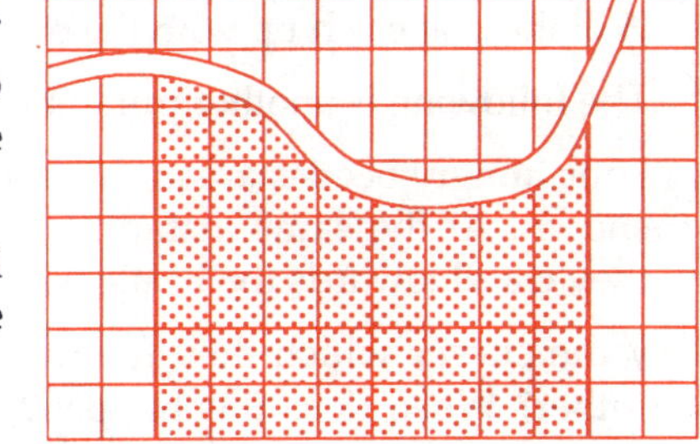

Fig 11.15

11.5 Longer exercises

A. Gradients and angles

1) On graph paper plot the quadrilateral with vertices at A(1,1), B(0,3), C(2,4), D(3,2). The shape should look like a square.

We could prove that it is indeed a square by measurement of lengths and angles. But it is more accurate and in the long run quicker to do it by calculation.

2) Use Pythagoras' Theorem to find the lengths AB, BC, CD, DA. Are they equal?

3) Use Trigonometry to find the angles made by AD and AB with the x-axis. What can you say about $D\hat{A}B$?

We can tell whether two straight lines are at right-angles or not without having to use trigonometry.

4) Write down the gradients of AB, AD, AC, BD.

5) What is the connection between the gradients of AB and AD, and between AC and BD?

6) Try some other pairs of straight lines, until you have found the condition on their gradients for them to be at right-angles.

If we have a triangle PQR, the circumcircle is the circle which goes through P, Q and R. The centre of this circle is the circumcentre.

7) Plot on graph paper the triangle with vertices P(2,–2), Q(–2,6), R(6,6).

8) Find the midpoint X of PQ. Find the gradient of PQ.

9) What is the gradient of the line at right-angles to PQ? What is the equation of the line L through X at right angles to PQ?

10) Follow the steps of (8) and (9) to find the line M through the midpoint of PR at right-angles to PR.

11) Find the point C where L and M meet. Verify, by drawing or calculation, that C is the centre of the circle which goes through P, Q and R .

B. Curves of pursuit

The problem at the beginning of this chapter was an example of a curve of pursuit. It is difficult to find the equation of the curve, but it can be drawn approximately.

1) Mark the original positions of dog and owner on graph paper. During the first second the owner walks 2 m North, and the dog runs 3 m East (approximately). Mark the new positions. In the next second the owner walks 2 m North, and the dog runs 3 m towards the new position of the owner. Mark in the new positions. Repeat, until the dog has caught up with the owner. When has this happened?

2) Suppose the dog and the owner walk at equal speeds. Will the dog catch up with the owner?

The following is another pursuit problem.

3) Four hungry beetles are at the four corners of a square as shown. At the same instant, and with the same speed, they crawl towards the beetle which they are facing.

Draw the curves which they follow. Do they catch up with each other? When does this happen? How many times have they gone round the centre of the circle?

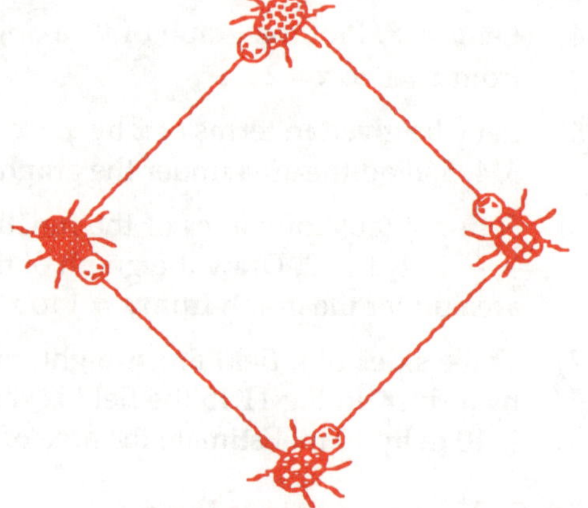

Fig 11.16

Multiple choice question *(Tick appropriate box)*

The equation of the line through (–1, 3) and (3, 1) is:

a) $y = -2x + 1$ ☐

b) $y = -\frac{1}{2}x + 2\frac{1}{2}$ ☐

c) $y = \frac{1}{2}x + 3\frac{1}{2}$ ☐

d) $y = -3x$ ☐

e) $y = \frac{1}{3}x$ ☐

Points to note

1) *Straight Line Graphs*

   a) If you know that the line $y = mx + c$ goes through (2,3) say, then that means that x and y are equal to 2 and 3 respectively. So the equation you obtain is:

   $$3 = 2m + c$$

   Do not put $m = 2$ and $c = 3$, to obtain $y = 2x + 3$

   b) Make sure that you get the gradient the correct way up. It must be the y-change over the x-change, not the other way round.

   c) The gradient is the y-change over the x-change. It is not the y-value over the x-value.

2) *Tangents*

   A tangent should just touch a curve. It does not necessarily go through the origin (0,0).

3) *Trapezium Rule*

   You can only use the trapezium rule if the intervals all have the same width.

Chapter 12

Travel graphs

From your own sensations, you can experience acceleration but not speed. For example, inside a train, you cannot tell how fast it is moving without looking outside.

Suppose you get into a lift at the bottom of a tall building. It accelerates at 2 m s^{-2} for 5 seconds, then continues at a steady speed for 10 seconds, then brakes to a halt in 3 seconds.

What was the maximum speed reached? How high has the lift risen?

Fig 12.1

12.1 Distance-time graphs

Suppose a body is moving. Let t represent the time that has elapsed, and let d represent the distance the body has moved. Then a graph with t along the horizontal axis and d up the vertical axis is a distance-time graph.

The gradient of a distance-time graph represents the rate of change of the distance. This is the speed.

If the graph is a straight line then its gradient can be found directly. The speed in Fig 12.2 is $2 \div 4 = \frac{1}{2}$ m/sec.

If the graph is curved then the speed can be found by drawing a tangent to the curve and measuring its gradient, as in Section 2, Chapter 11.

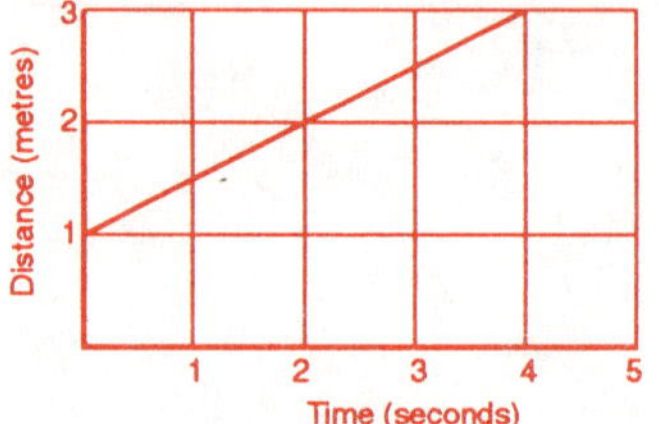

Fig 12.2

Fig 12.3

The gradient of a tangent to a distance-time curve gives the instantaneous speed at that time. The speed shown in Fig 12.3 at 1 second is $\frac{2}{2} = 1$ m/sec.

12.1.1 Example

Maurice enters a marathon race. He starts off at a steady rate, then as he gets tired he slows down. The graph of distance against time is shown in Fig 12.4 (on next page).

Find: a) his starting speed b) his speed 2 hours after the start.

Solution a) For the first hour the graph has a constant gradient. The y change is 6 miles, and the x change is 1 hour.

He starts off at 6 m.p.h.

b) Draw a tangent to the curve at $x = 2$, and complete the triangle in Fig 12.5 (on next page).

The y change of the tangent is 6 miles, and the x change is 2 hours.

After 2 hours his speed is $\frac{6}{2} = 3$ m.p.h.

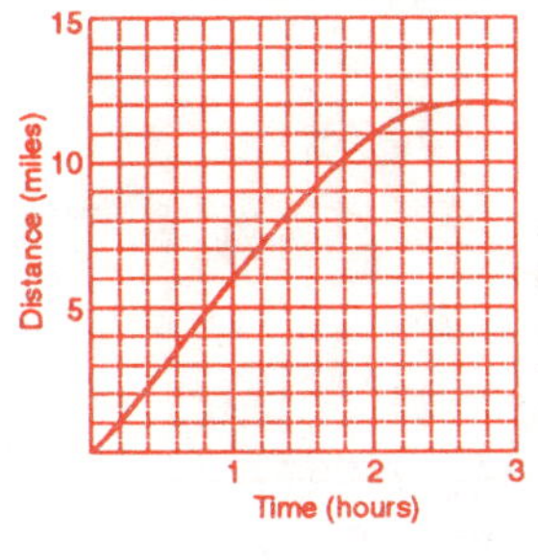

Fig 12.4

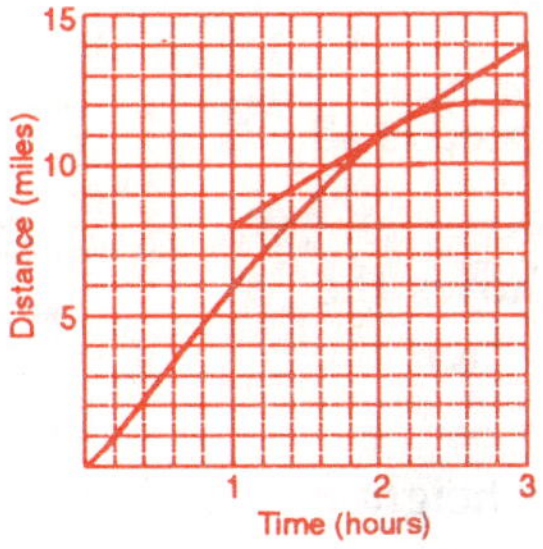

Fig 12.5

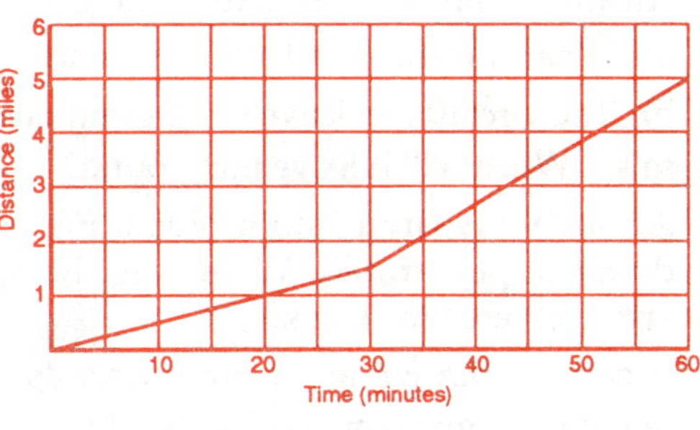

Fig 12.6

12.1.2 Exercises

1) Michael sets off for school, then realises that he might be late and starts to run. The graph of his distance against time is shown in Fig 12.6.

   a) What was his walking speed?

   b) What was his running speed?

2) Jan rides her moped to the shops, spends 10 minutes shopping, then rides home again. Fig 12.7 shows a graph of distance against time. What were the speeds of the two parts of the journey?

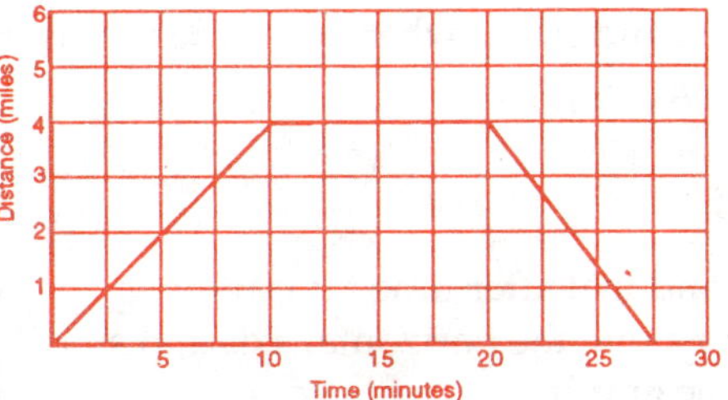

Fig 12.7

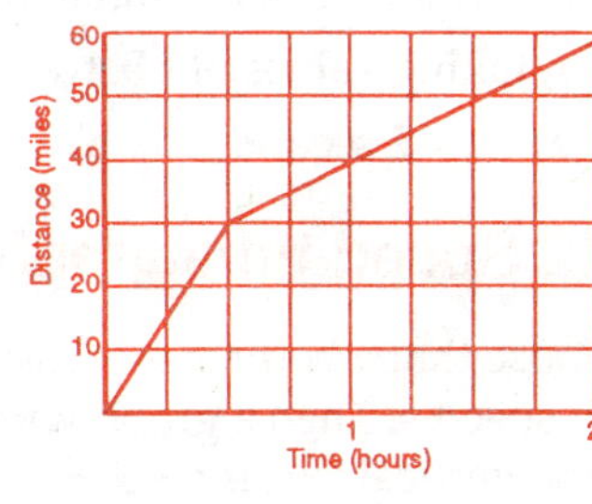

Fig 12.8

3) A car is travelling in the open country, then has to slow down when entering a built-up zone. Fig 12.8 shows a graph of distance against time. What are the speeds of the two parts of the journey?

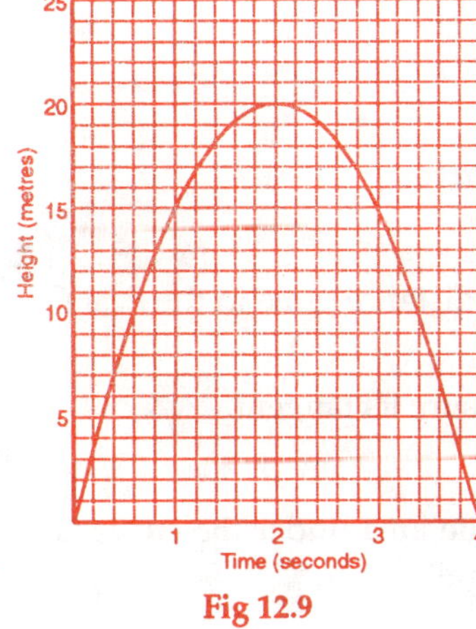

Fig 12.9

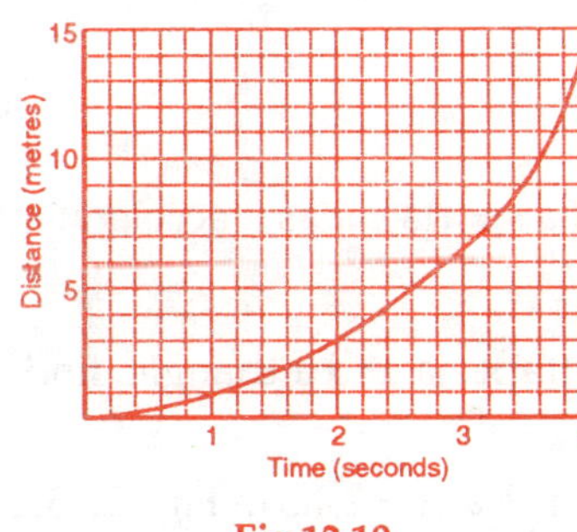

Fig 12.10

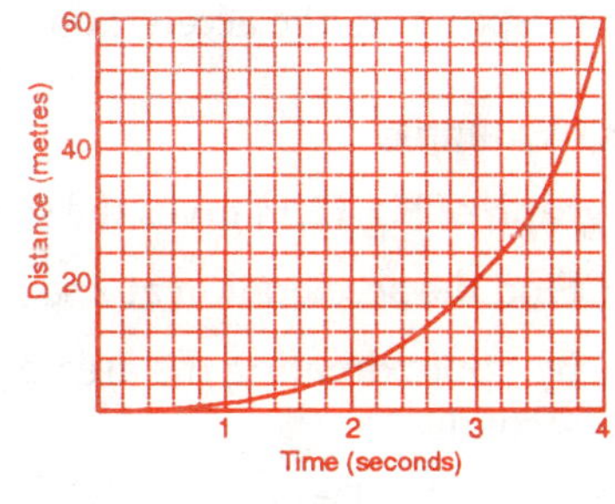

Fig 12.11

4) Fig 12.9 shows the graph of the height of a stone against time. By drawing suitable tangents find the speeds at 1 sec and at 3 secs.

5) A car starts from rest. The graph in Fig 12.10 shows the distance travelled against time. By drawing tangents find the speeds at 2 seconds and 3 seconds.

6) An aircraft takes off from rest. The graph in Fig 12.11 shows distance travelled against time.
   a) What was the speed after 2 seconds?
   b) The aircraft can leave the ground once its speed is 40 m s^{-1}. When will it leave the ground?
7) An arrow is fired into a block. Fig 12.12 shows the distance penetrated. What was the speed when the arrow entered the block?
8) A stone is thrown in the air. t seconds later its height h in metres is given by $h = 2 + 20t - 5t^2$.
   Draw a graph of h, taking values of t between 0 and 3.
   a) What was the starting speed? What was the speed after 1 second?
   b) What was the greatest height reached? When was this height reached?

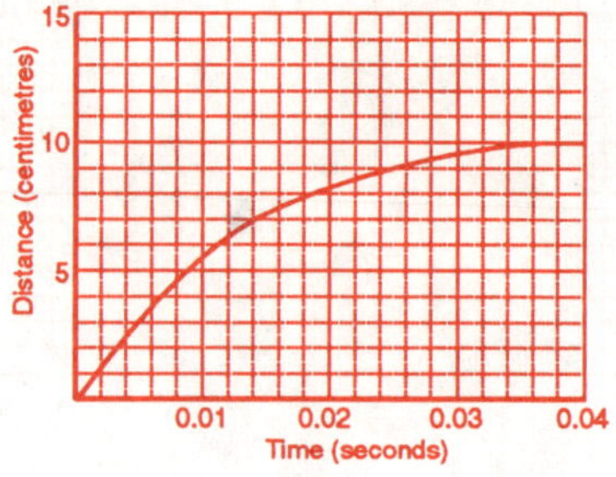

Fig 12.12

9) A car accelerates from rest. t seconds after starting its distance d in metres is given by $10\sqrt{t^3}$. Draw a graph of d, taking values of t between 0 and 6. What is the speed after
   a) 1 second b) 3 seconds?
10) A balloon is being inflated. After t seconds its radius r in cm is given by $r = 5\sqrt[3]{t}$. Draw a graph of r, taking values of t between 0 and 10. At what rate is the radius increasing when
   a) $t = 2$ seconds b) $t = 6$ seconds?

12.2 Speed-time graphs

Suppose that a body is moving, and that after time t it is moving with speed s. Then a graph with t along the horizontal axis and s up the vertical axis is a speed-time graph.

The area under a speed-time curve corresponds to the distance.

If the graph is curved its area can be approximated by triangles and trapezia, as in Section 4 of Chapter 11.

The gradient of a speed-time curve is the rate of change of speed. This corresponds to the acceleration.

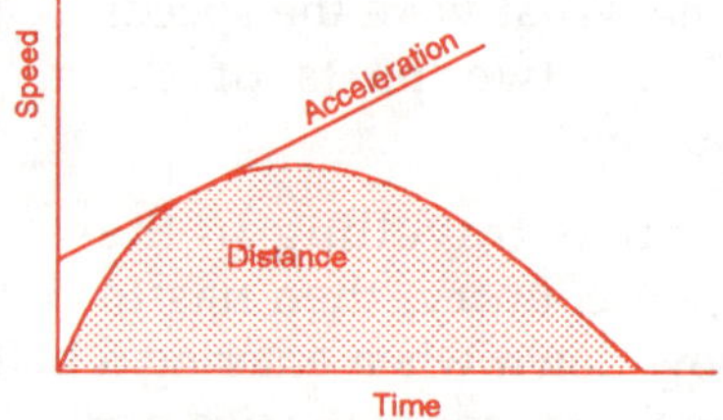

Fig 12.13

12.2.1 Example

The graph of Fig 12.14 gives the speed of a sports-car as it accelerates from rest.

a) Find the acceleration at 2 secs.

b) By approximating the area by two trapezia and a triangle, find the distance gone in the first 6 seconds.

Solution a) Draw a tangent to the curve at $x = 2$, as in Fig 12.15. Measure its tangent.

Acceleration $= \frac{24}{4} = 6$ **m. sec**$^{-2}$

b) Draw vertical lines at $x = 2$ and $x = 4$, as in Fig 12.16. The area under the curve is approximately the area in the two trapezia and the triangle.

Area $= \frac{1}{2} \times 16 \times 2 + \frac{1}{2} \times (16 + 25) \times 2 + \frac{1}{2} \times (25 + 30) \times 2$

The distance is approximately 112 m

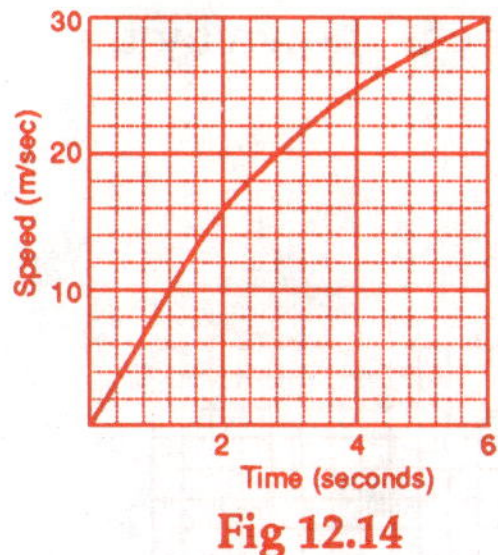

Fig 12.14

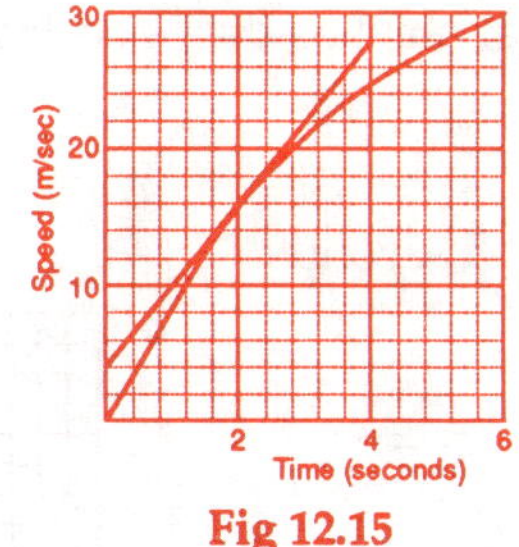

Fig 12.15

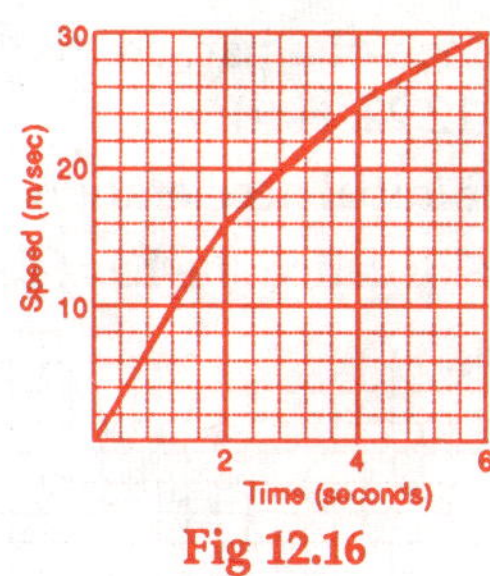

Fig 12.16

12.2.2 Exercises

1) The speed of a tube train between successive stations is given by Fig 12.17.

   a) Find the acceleration when it starts and the deceleration when it stops.

   b) Find the distance between the stations.

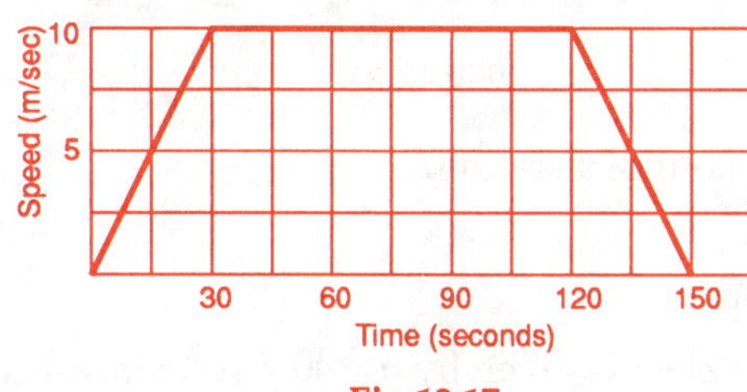

Fig 12.17

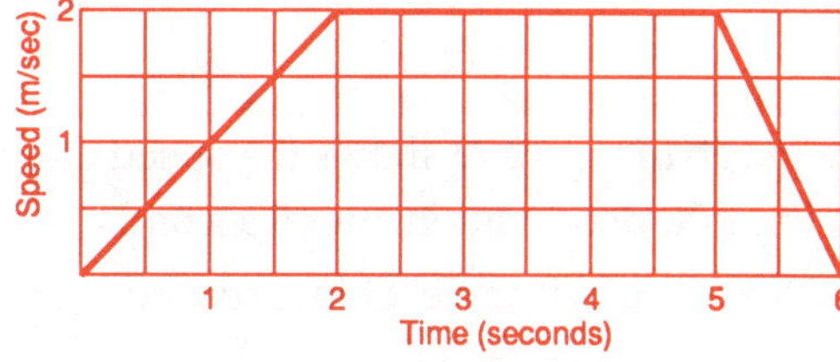

Fig 12.18

2) The speed of a lift is shown in Fig 12.18.

   a) What is the acceleration when it starts to rise?

   b) What is the total height it rises?

3) A car travels in the open country, then enters a built-up area. The graph of speed against time is shown in Fig 12.19.

   a) What was the deceleration of the car?

   b) What was the distance travelled over these 6 seconds?

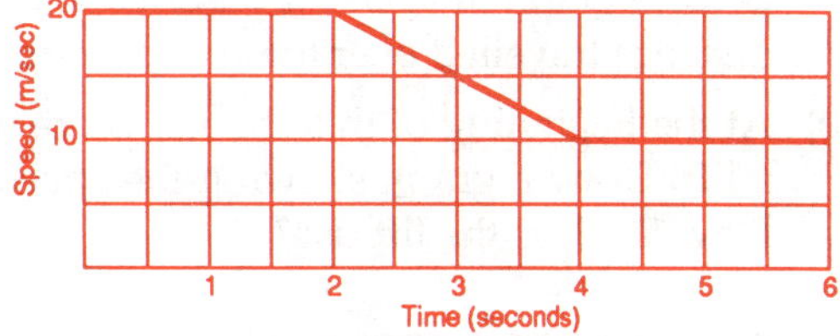

Fig 12.19

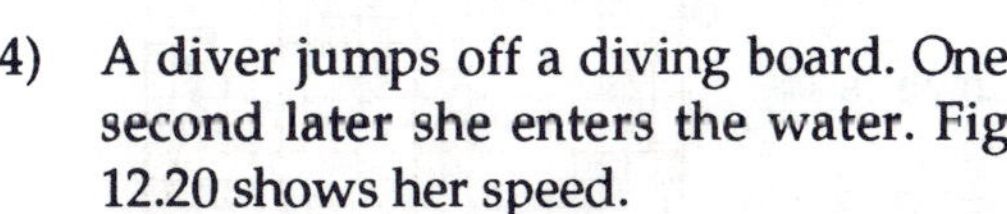

4) A diver jumps off a diving board. One second later she enters the water. Fig 12.20 shows her speed.

   a) What were the accelerations in the air and in the water?

   b) How high is the diving board above the water?

   c) How deeply did she dive into the water?

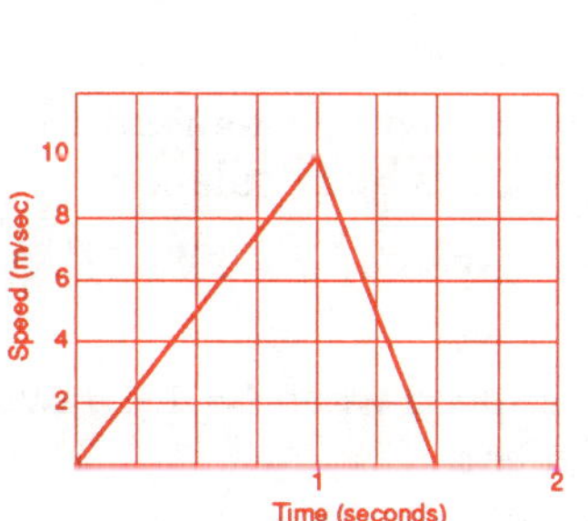

Fig 12.20

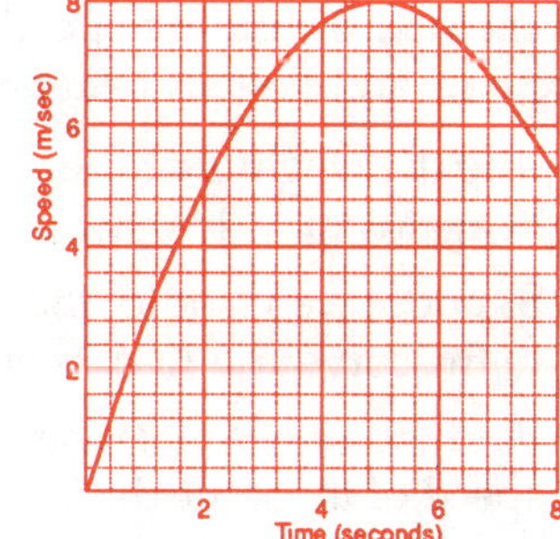

Fig 12.21

5) The speed of a runner during a sprint race is shown in Fig 12.21.

   a) Find the acceleration of the runner after 2 seconds.

   b) By splitting the region into 3 trapezia and a triangle estimate the total distance of the race.

6) The speed of a parachutist t seconds after she has dropped from the airplane is shown by the graph of Fig 12.22. Find
   a) her initial acceleration
   b) the distance she has fallen in the first 5 seconds.

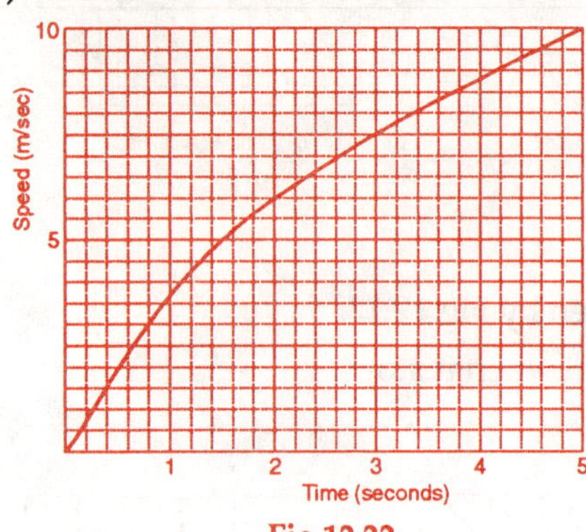

Fig 12.22

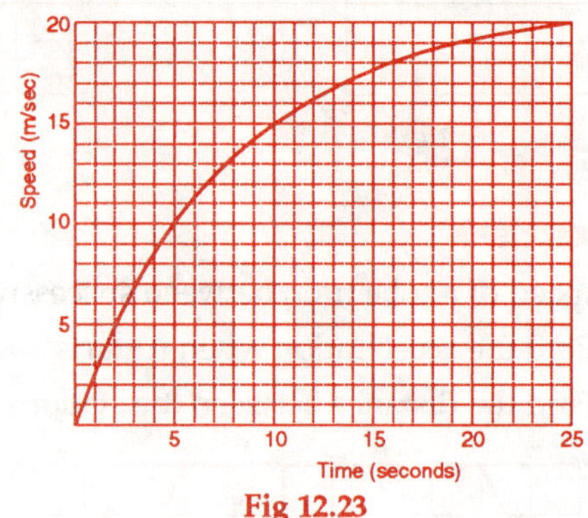

Fig 12.23

7) The graph in Fig 12.23 shows the speed of a train pulling out of a station.
   a) Find the acceleration after 5 seconds.
   b) How far did it travel before reaching a speed of 20 m s^{-1}?

8) A stone is thrown upwards. t seconds later its speed v in $m\ s^{-1}$ is given by $v = 40 - 10t$. Draw a graph of v, taking t between 0 and 4. What is the acceleration of the stone? How far does it travel over these 4 seconds?

9) The speed v in m s^{-1} of a particle is given by $v = 5 \sin 10t$, where t is the time measured in seconds. Draw a graph of v, taking t from 0 to 6. Find the acceleration of the particle when $t = 3$. Estimate the distance travelled over these 6 seconds.

10) At the beginning of this chapter there was a problem involving a lift. Draw a graph showing the speed of the lift against time. How far does the lift rise?

12.3. Longer exercises

A. Calculating speed

The method of finding speed by drawing a tangent to a curve is inaccurate and slow. A better method is by calculation.

Suppose the height h of a stone is given by $h = 20t - 5t^2$. A graph of height against time is shown.

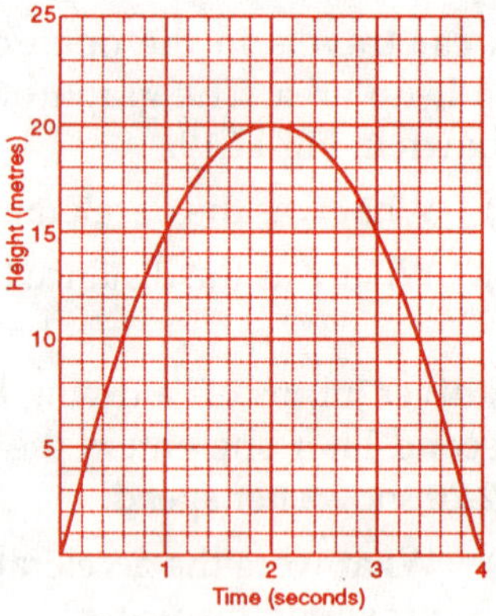

Fig 12.24

1) Suppose we want to find the speed when $t = 1$. Draw a tangent to the curve and find its gradient.

2) Find the values of h when $t = 1$ and $t = 2$. How far has it travelled over this second? Find the average speed of the stone during this second.

3) Use the formula to find the values of h when $t = 1$ and $t = 1.1$. Find the average speed of the stone over this 0.1 second.

4) Repeat (3), taking smaller time intervals. What value are these speeds approaching? What is the speed at $t = 1$? How close was your answer in (1)?

5) Use the methods of (2) – (4) to find the speeds when $t = 2$, $t = 3$ and $t = 1.5$. Can you guess what the general rule is?

B. Distance, speed, time

Journeys have been described in terms of distance-time graphs and speed-time graphs. How do you describe them in words? How do you convert from one to the other?

1) Below are two distance-time graphs. Describe the journeys in words. Sketch the speed-time graphs.

a)

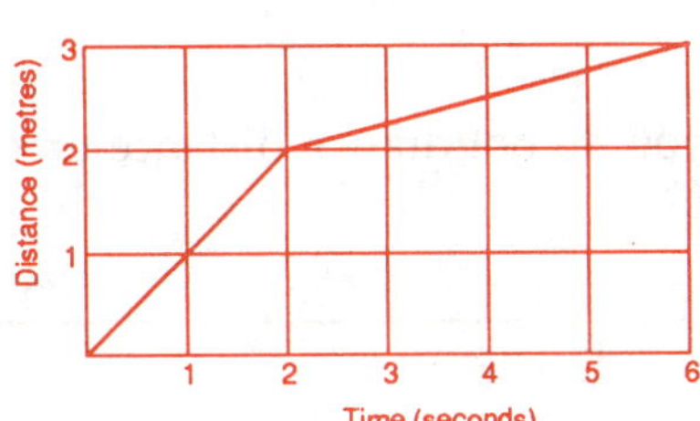

b)

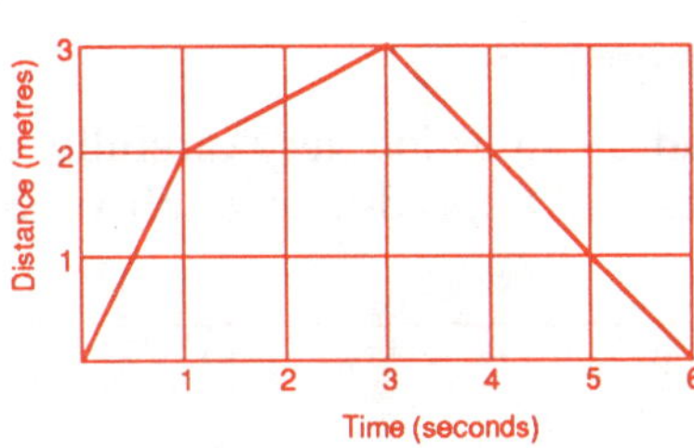

Fig 12.25

2) Below are two speed-time graphs. Describe the journeys in words. Sketch the distance-time graphs.

a)

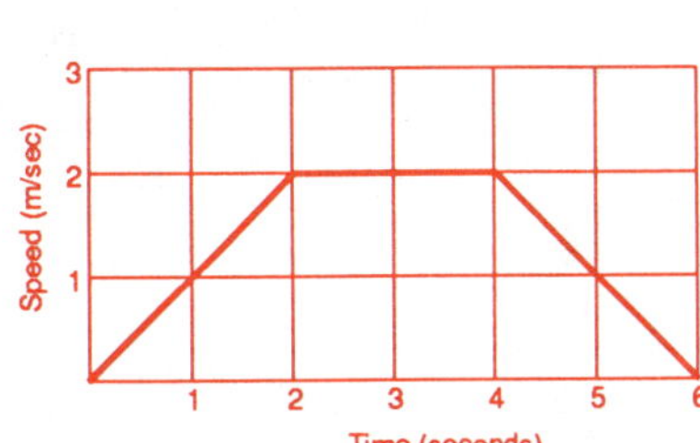

b)

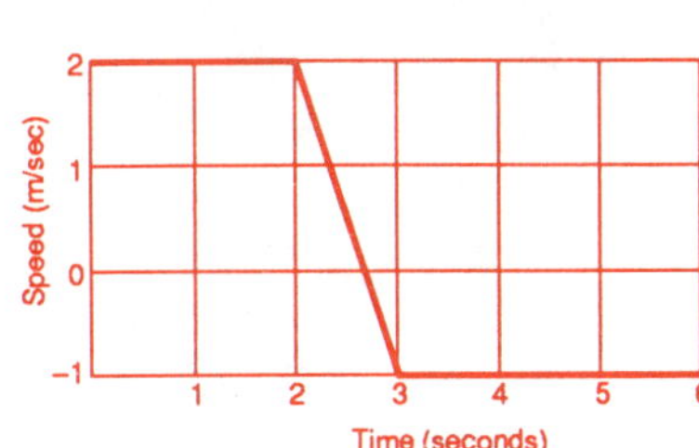

Fig 12.26

3) Sketch the distance-time and speed-time graphs for some journey that you do regularly, for example your journey to school.

Multiple choice question *(Tick appropriate box)*

The graph shows the distance travelled by a car after starting from rest. The speed after 2 seconds is:

a) 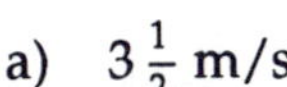 $3\frac{1}{2}$ m/s ☐

b) 11 m/s ☐

c) 5 m/s ☐

d) 10 m/s ☐

e) None of these. ☐

Distance (metres)

Time (seconds)

Fig 12.27

Points to note

1) *Speed*

   a) When working out the speed, make sure you take the distance-change over the time-change. It is not the distance over the time.

   b) When finding the speed from a curved graph, find the gradient of the tangent. Do not find the gradient of the line from the origin.

2) *Interpretation*

   Read the question very carefully, to make sure that you do not draw a distance-time graph instead of a speed-time graph, or the other way round.

Cross-curriculum topic

Eclipses

An eclipse occurs when the Earth, sun and moon are in a straight line. If the moon is between the Earth and the sun, then we have a solar eclipse. If the Earth is between the moon and the sun, then we have a lunar eclipse.

A total solar eclipse, in which the sun is completely blotted out by the moon, is an awe-inspiring event. Even animals and birds react with fear. It is a very rare event, so that when it occurred in primitive times it would be unlikely that even the oldest person had seen one before. Primitive men were terrified by these eclipses, and regarded them as omens of disaster. Eclipses were important events, and were recorded. From these records of eclipses we are often able to date events in the past.

Gradually it was found that eclipses are natural phenomena. People learned how to explain eclipses, and eventually to predict them. A great deal of knowledge was gained by the astronomical studies connected with eclipses.

Total and partial eclipses

If the moon is between the sun and the Earth it will block off at least part of the sunlight. We can also think of the moon's shadow reaching part of the Earth.

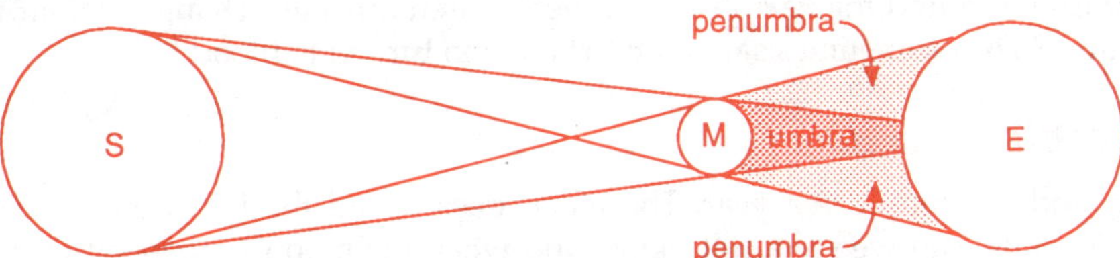

The part of the Earth completely within the shadow of the moon is called the umbra. From points within the umbra a total eclipse will be seen. The region partly covered by the shadow is the penumbra. From points in this region a partial eclipse will be seen. Because the sun is so bright a partial eclipse often goes unobserved.

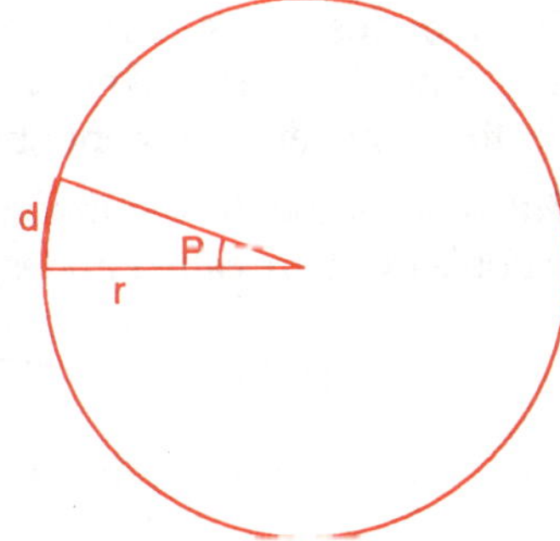

The apparent size of an object is given by the angle it subtends at the eye. This can be found by considering the object as part of the arc of a circle. The ratio of the arc to the circumference will be the same as the ratio of the angle to 360°.

$$\frac{d}{2\pi r} = \frac{P}{360°}$$

The sun is, on average, 149,600,000 km from the Earth and 1,392,000 km in diameter. The figures for the moon are 384,400 km and 3,476 km. From these we can calculate the angles that each body subtends on Earth. Changing the subject of the formula above, and putting the large numbers in standard form:

$$\text{Angle for sun} = \frac{1.392 \times 10^6}{1.496 \times 10^8} \times \frac{360}{2\pi} = 0.533°$$

$$\text{Angle for moon} = \frac{3.476 \times 10^3}{3.84 \times 10^5} \times \frac{360}{2\pi} = 0.518°$$

So from these figures it seems that the moon will always seem smaller than the sun. Even when the Moon's path goes straight past the centre of the sun, usually it never covers the sun completely. An annular eclipse occurs when the moon is in front of the sun, but there is a ring of fire showing round it.

But the orbits of Earth and moon are not perfectly round. The paths are oval shapes called ellipses, and the distances from moon to Earth and from Earth to sun vary throughout the year. The greatest distance of the sun from the Earth is 152,600,000 km, and the least distance of the moon is 363,300.

$$\text{Least angle for sun} = \frac{1.392 \times 10^6}{1.526 \times 10^8} \times \frac{360}{2\pi} = 0.523°$$

$$\text{Greatest angle for moon} = \frac{3.476 \times 10^3}{3.633 \times 10^5} \times \frac{360}{2\pi} = 0.548°$$

So it is possible for total eclipses to occur, though they do not last very long. If the Moon is as close as possible to the Earth, and the Earth is as far as possible from the sun, then a point in the centre of the umbra will experience a total eclipse for a bit over 7 minutes.

Total eclipses are very rare. For each spot on Earth, a total eclipse occurs every 250 years or so. The next one in the UK will be on August 11th 1999, and it will last for only 2 minutes!

Because the Earth is bigger than the moon, a total lunar eclipse happens more frequently, once every two or so years. Often the total eclipse can be seen from everywhere on the Earth, and it can continue for over an hour. A lunar eclipse is less dramatic than a solar eclipse. The moon is never completely blotted out, because light is bent round the Earth's atmosphere. Often this light changes colour towards the red end of the spectrum. So it is sometimes said that: "The moon turned to blood".

The moon's orbit

The Earth goes round the sun once a year. The moon goes round the Earth once a month. When the moon is furthest from the sun we see a full moon, and when the moon is nearest the sun we see a new moon. Why do we not have a lunar eclipse at every full moon, and a solar eclipse at every new moon?

The motions of the Earth around the sun and the moon around the Earth do not lie in the same plane. The moon's orbit makes an angle with the Earth's orbit. Usually the moon lies above or below the Earth's orbit, and so cannot blot out the sun.

But twice a month the moon's orbit passes through the plane of the Earth's orbit. These points on the moon's orbit are called nodes, and shown as N and N′ on the picture below.

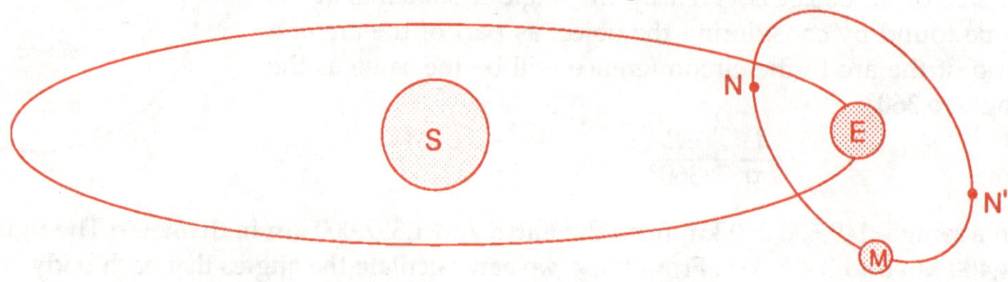

If the moon is at N or N′ at the time of a full moon, then there will be a lunar eclipse. If it is at N or N′ at the time of a new moon, there will be a solar eclipse.

Things are made more complicated by the fact that the positions of N and N′ are not fixed, relative to the sun or to the Earth or to the moon. These positions rotate around the moon's orbit, making a full circuit every 18.61 years. So to predict eclipses we have to keep track of N and N′ as well as of the sun and moon.

There are several different sorts of month. The time it takes to go from one new moon to the next is called a synodic month. It lasts 29.530589 days. The time it takes the moon to go from N to N′ and round to N again is a Draconian month. It is different from the synodic month because of the changing position of N and N′, and lasts 27.21222 days.

Suppose there is a solar eclipse. Then it must be a time of new moon. A whole number of synodic months later, there will be another new moon. If this time is also a whole number of Draconian months, then N and N′ will be at the same position as before. So there will be another solar eclipse.

The smallest interval of time for which this is approximately true is 6,585 $\frac{1}{3}$ days. Note that this represents 223.0004058 (near enough to 223) synodic months, and 241.9991214 (near enough to 242) Draconian months. So there is a cycle of this period, about 18 years long, after which eclipses repeat themselves. This period is called the Saros period. It has been known about for thousands of years.

Sunrise and moonrise

Nowadays we know that the Earth spins on its axis and goes around the sun. But this has been known only for a few centuries. For thousands of years before that, astronomy, in particular the prediction of eclipses, was done assuming that the Earth is fixed and that the sun moves round it.

For someone on the Earth, the path of the sun looks like an arc in the sky. The arc is not always the same, because the axis of the Earth is tilted. In winter, when the Earth is pointed away from the sun, the sun rises in the South East and the day is short. In summer, when the Earth is pointed towards the sun, the sun rises further North and the day is long.

Actual calculations of the directions of sunrise are very complicated. They depend on curved versions of the sine and cosine rules for the solution of triangles. But from experience primitive people were able to keep track of the seasons by seeing where the sun rises.

The motion of the moon is more complicated. It also appears to go round the Earth, which in this case is true. The point of moonrise varies throughout the month instead of throughout the year, but the degree of variation changes.

When the tilt of the moon's orbit is acting in the same direction as the tilt of the Earth's orbit, then the moon's orbit is most tilted relative to the Earth. Then there will be the greatest variation in the direction of moonrise, about 100°.

When the tilt of the moon's orbit is acting in the opposite direction to the tilt of the Earth's orbit, then the moon's orbit is least tilted relative to the Earth. Then there will be the least variation in the direction of moonrise, about 60°.

The time to go through this cycle of variation in the direction of moonrise is 18.61 years, which is the time for the points N and N′ to move round the moon's orbit.

If records of the direction of moonrise are kept over a long period of time, the pattern of the variation will be seen. It is then possible to find the position of the nodes N and N′ from the variation in moonrise. There is some evidence that primitive people were able to predict eclipses by measuring the direction of moonrise.

Errors

Even allowing from the inaccuracy of the measuring equipment available to prehistoric Man, there are several unavoidable causes of error in the sighting of the sun and moon. Three are as follows.

Parallax

The diagrams so far have had directions taken from the centre of the Earth. But when looking for sunrise or moonrise, we do so from the edge of the Earth.

The angle of the sun or moon is incorrect, by the small angle θ shown in the diagram. θ is given by $\sin\theta = \frac{r}{d}$, where r is the radius of the Earth and d is the distance.

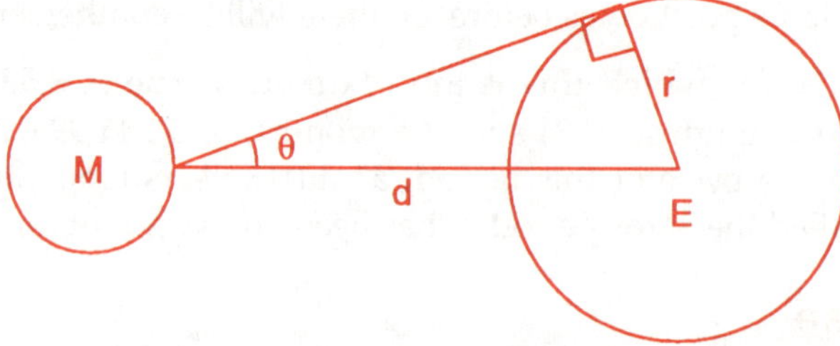

For the sun this angle is negligible. But for the moon it is 1°, so the angle of moonrise must be adjusted to take account of this.

Diffraction

When the sun or moon is coming over the horizon, its rays pass through the Earth's atmosphere. These gases form a sort of huge lens, which bend the light rays, and cause the sun or moon to seem higher in the horizon than it is. The correction necessary to take account of this is about 1°.

The development of Astronomy

Even when knowing all about the movements of the sun, moon and Earth, it is extraordinarily difficult to explain what the sky looks like from Earth, or to predict where the moon will be at a particular time. How much harder it is to go in the other direction! That is, from the motion of sun, moon and stars as seen from Earth, to find out what the real behaviour of the solar system is. The explanation of the solar system, from earliest times to Newton in the seventeenth century, is one of the greatest intellectual achievements of all.

The mathematics of eclipses

The explanation and prediction of eclipses requires a great deal of mathematics. Here material from Chapters 2, 4, 8, 13, 17 and 18 has been touched upon.

Extended task. Ringing the changes

Ringing the changes is a form of music unique to England. Church bells are rung in as many orders as possible, subject to various mathematical rules.

1) Suppose three bells are labelled 1, 2, 3. List the possible orders in which they can be rung. How many orders are possible with 4 bells, 5 bells, 6 bells?

   Note: the number of possible orders with n bells is $n!$ This function appears on a calculator. Use it to check your answers.

   A session begins with the bells in a descending sequence, 1 2 3 4 for four bells. Two rules are that a bell cannot move more than one place in the order, and a bell must not stay in the same place for more than two goes.

2) **Leads.** Two basic operations are:

   A. The bells in the first and second positions change places, and the bells in the third and fourth positions change places.

   B. The bells in the second and third positions change places.

   So the first few rounds are:

   1 2 3 4

   2 1 4 3 A

   2 4 1 3 B

   4 2 3 1 A

   Continue A and B until you are back to the beginning again. This sequence of changes is called a lead. How many changes were there?

   Describe the path of the number 1 bell.

   Apply A and B for a set of six bells. How many changes were there?

   How many changes would there be for 8 bells? Prove it, by considering the path of the number 1 bell.

3) **Dodge.** With 4 bells, the lead does not include all the changes. Just before 1 2 3 4 is returned to, i.e. at the end of the lead, the last two bells change places. This is a dodge.

   1 3 2 4

   1 3 4 2 dodge

   Show how all 24 changes are obtained with A, B and dodge.

4) **Bob.** With 6 bells, we need an extra way of changing. The bells in first and fourth position stay put, the second and third change, and the fifth and sixth. This is called a bob.

   1 2 3 4 5 6

   1 3 2 4 6 5 bob

   Write out the changes for 6 bells with A and B and bobs at the end of each lead.

5) By altering the dodges and bobs it is possible to get many different combinations on 6 bells. To avoid writing too much, do not write down every single order. It is only necessary to write out the beginning and ending of each lead. Try some combinations. Can you get all 720 orders?

6) What could be the patterns for 5 bells, or 7 bells?

7) If you are a computer programmer, you could write a program to produce a sequence of changes, either printed out or actually sounded.

Miscellaneous exercises

Group A

1) Expand: a) $(3x + 1)(2x - 5)$ b) $(m + 2n)(p - 3q)$

2) Factorize the following:

a) $x^2 + 8x + 7$ b) $x^2 + 3x - 40$ c) $x^2 - 12x + 27$

d) $x^2 - 9y^2$ e) $3a^2 - 3b^2$ f) $3x^2 + 2x - 1$

g) $10x^2 + 11x - 6$ h) $ab - 6 + 2b - 3a$ i) $pt + 6qs - 2qt - 3ps$

3) Solve: a) $x^2 + 12x - 13 = 0$ b) $6x^2 - 5x + 1 = 0$

4) Complete the square of the following:

a) $x^2 + 4x + 9$ b) $x^2 - 2x - 5$ c) $x^2 - x - 1$

5) Find the minimums of the expressions in Question 4.

6) In the following, change the subject to the letter in brackets.

a) $ax = bx + c$ (x) b) $2z + y = 3z - xy$ (y)

c) $P = \dfrac{M}{M-1}$ (M) d) $r = \dfrac{q-1}{q+1}$ (q)

7) Simplify the following fractions:

a) $\dfrac{3x}{9y}$ b) $\dfrac{7x^2y}{2y^2x}$ c) $\dfrac{x^2+6x+8}{x^2+4x+4}$

8) Express the following as single fractions, simplifying as far as possible:

a) $\dfrac{p}{q} \times \dfrac{q}{r}$ b) $\dfrac{8x^2}{y} \div \dfrac{2x}{y^2}$ c) $\dfrac{5p}{3} + \dfrac{p}{6} + \dfrac{p}{2}$

d) $\dfrac{7}{a} - \dfrac{3}{b}$ e) $\dfrac{1}{x-1} - \dfrac{1}{x+1}$

9) Solve the following equations, giving your answers to 3 significant figures where relevant:

a) $1 + 7x = 81 - 3x$ b) $3x + 2 = 5x - 18$ c) $x^2 + 8x - 9 = 0$ d) $x^2 - 2x - 7 = 0$

e) $x(x + 3) = 17$ f) $\dfrac{3}{x} = x + 1$ g) $7^{3x-2} = 49^x$ h) $9^{x+3} = 27^x$

10) The sides of a right-angled triangle are x, $x + 1$ and $2x$, where $2x$ is the longest side. Find x.

11) Draw the graph of $y = 2x^2 + x - 1$, taking values of x from –2 to 2. What is the least value of the function? What is its line of symmetry?

12) Draw the graph of $y = \dfrac{1}{2x+1}$.

For what value of x is it not defined?

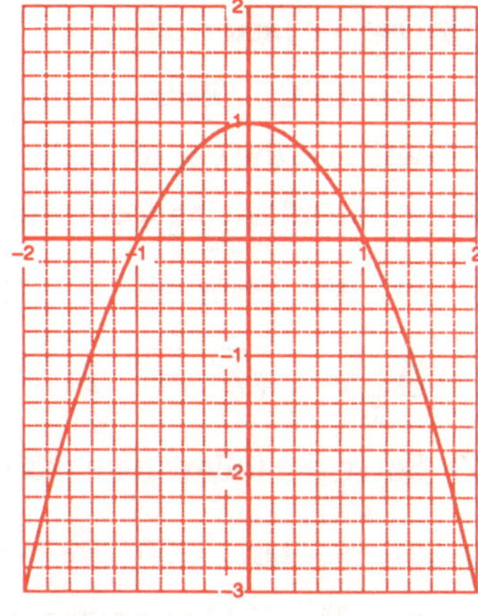

13) Draw the graph of $y = x^2 - \frac{2}{x}$, taking x to be $\frac{1}{4}, \frac{1}{2}, 1, 1\frac{1}{2}, 2, 3$.

On the same paper draw the graph of $y = x + 1$. Show that where they cross $x^3 - x^2 - x - 2 = 0$. Write down the solutions to this equation.

14) On the right is the graph of $y = 1 - x^2$. Use this graph to sketch the graphs of:

a) $y = 3 - x^2$ b) $y = 1 - (x - 1)^2$ c) $y = 1 - (2x)^2$

15) Find the equations of the straight lines through the following pairs of points:

a) (1,3) and (4,12) b) (4,5) and (7,6)

c) (-2,1) and (3,-2)

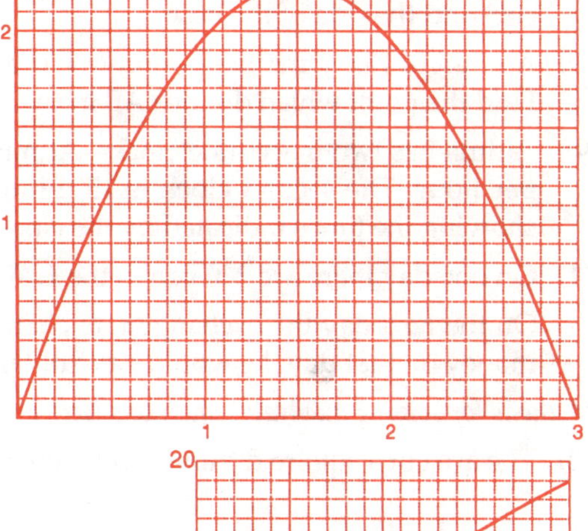

16) On the right is the graph of $y = x(3 - x)$, between $x = 0$ and $x = 3$. By drawing tangents find the gradient of the curve at $x = 1$ and $x = 2.5$.

17) By splitting the region under the graph of Question 16 into two triangles and four trapezia, estimate its area.

18) The graph on the lower right shows the speed of a car in the first 10 seconds after it has started. Estimate:

a) the acceleration 2 seconds after it has started

b) the distance travelled over the 10 seconds.

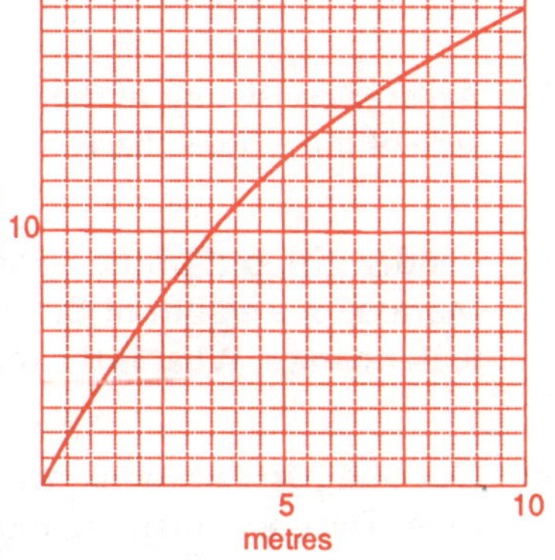

19) Fred walks away from home at 4 m.p.h. for 1 hour. He then talks to a friend for 20 minutes. He walks home at 3 m.p.h. Draw a distance-time graph of his journey.

Group B. Challenge questions

20) Find the greatest value of the expression $\dfrac{1}{x^2 + 4x + 5}$.

21) The area of a rectangle is 72 cm^2, and its perimeter is 34 cm. Find its sides.

22) The sides of the rectangle ABCD are said to be in the Golden Ratio if, when the square AXYD is removed, the remaining rectangle is similar to ABCD.

Let the ratio AB:AD be x. Show that $x^2 - x - 1 = 0$. Solve this equation.

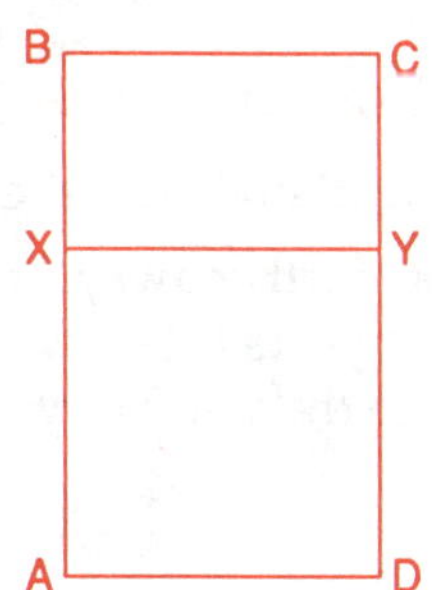

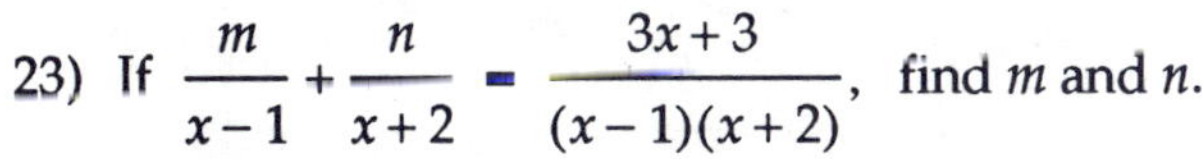

23) If $\dfrac{m}{x-1} + \dfrac{n}{x+2} = \dfrac{3x+3}{(x-1)(x+2)}$, find m and n.

24) If $\dfrac{kx+m}{x^2+1} + \dfrac{n}{x-1} = \dfrac{-2}{(x^2+1)(x-1)}$, find k, m and n.

25) Use the factorization $x^2 - y^2 = (x + y)(x - y)$ to evaluate:

a) $1000^2 - 999^2$ b) 9999^2,

without the use of a calculator.

26) In the following formulae change the subject to the letter in brackets:

a) $V = \frac{1}{3}\pi r^2 h$ (r) b) $\sqrt{x+y} = z$ $(x$

c) $c = \sqrt{a^2 + b^2}$ (a) d) $\frac{1}{a} = 1 - \frac{1}{b}$ (b)

27) Solve the following equations by trial and improvement, to the degree of accuracy shown:

a) $x + \tan x = 50$ (nearest whole number) b) $\frac{x}{20} + \sin(x) = 0.5$ (nearest whole number)

c) $3^x = 2$ (2 decimal places)

28) A cuboid has a square base, and its height is 1 cm less than the side of the base. If the volume is 6 cm^3 find the side of the base.

29) A straight line joins the points A(1,1) and B(2,6). Find the coordinates of the midpoint of the line. Find the point which divides AB in the ratio 2:3. Find the point which divides AB in the ratio m:n.

30) Fatima has two inaccurate clocks. At midday the first clock is 15 minutes fast, but it loses 5 minutes per hour. The second clock is 15 minutes slow, but it gains 15 minutes per hour. Draw a graph showing the times indicated by the clocks over the next 3 hours. When do they show the same time?

31) On one day there are 240 yen to the £. A man changes £x. How many yen does he get?

On the next day the exchange rate changes, so that there are 250 yen to the £. If he had changed his money on that day, he would have obtained 3,200 more yen. Form an equation in x and solve it.

Methods for solving quadratic equations have been known for years. Below are some old questions.

32) The area of a square diminished by the side of the square is 870. Find the side of the square.

(Babylon, 1800 BC)

33) An area consisting of the sum of two squares is 1,000. The side of one square is 10 less than $\frac{2}{3}$ of the side of the other square. What are the sides of the squares?

(Babylon, 1800 BC)

34) Tender girl, out of the swans on a certain lake, ten times the square root of their number went to Marasa, one eighth of the number went to the forest, three pairs remained on the lake, engaged in water games. What is the total number of swans?

(Bhaskara, India, 1150 AD)

35) Out of a party of monkeys, the square of one fifth of their number diminished by three went into a cave. The one remaining monkey was climbing a tree. What is the total number of monkeys?

(Bhaskara, India, 1150 AD)

Group C. Longer exercises

36) The planets and the sun

Planets further away from the sun have a longer year. A table of the distances of planets and the lengths of their years is below. The distances are in astronomical units (*au*), where 1 *au* is the distance from the Earth to the sun. The years are measured in Earth days.

Planet	*Distance*	*Year*
Mercury	0.387	88
Venus	0.723	225
Earth	1	365
Jupiter	5.203	4,329
Saturn	9.539	10,760
Neptune	30.058	60,193

The quantities are not proportional. In fact the cube of the distance is proportional to the square of the year.

Plot the distance cubed against the time squared, and show that the points lie roughly on a straight line.

a) Mars has a year of 687 days. How far is it from the sun?

b) Uranus is 19.182 au from the sun. How long is its year?

37) **Logic of inequalities**

a) On the number line on the right illustrate the inequality $x \leq 2$.

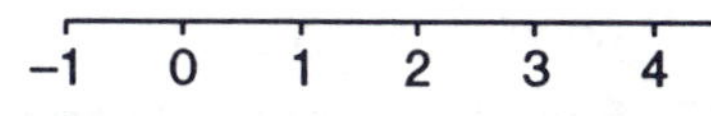

b) Describe the region not covered by the bar by an inequality. It could be called the negation of the original inequality.

c) Find the negations of $x \geq 1, x < 0, x > -1$.

d) On the number line of (a) illustrate the inequality $x \geq 0$. Describe the region covered by both the bars. it could be called the conjunction of the original inequalities.

e) Find the conjunctions of (i) $x > 0$ and$x < 5$ (ii) $x \leq 3$ and $x \leq 1$ (iii) $x < 1$ and $x > 4$.

f) On a number line illustrate the inequalities $x < 2$ and $x > 4$. Describe the region covered by either of the bars. (Or by both). It could be called the disjunction of the original inequalities.

g) Find the disjunctions of (i) $x \geq 1$ and $x \leq -3$ (ii) $x < 2$ and $x < 7$ (ii) $x \leq 3$ and $x \geq 1$.

h) Take the conjunction of (e) (i), and find its negation. How can you describe it in terms of disjunctions? Can you find a general rule?

Revision exercises

1) Simplify: a) $5PQ + 7QP + 5P - Q$ b) $5j^3 \times 8j^4$

2) Expand and simplify $4(t - 3) - 5(t + 8)$.

3) Factorize: a) $7pt + 21qt$ b) $6p^2q - 21q^2p$

4) The surface area of a cuboid is given by $A = 2(ab + bc + ca)$. Find the area when $a = 5$, $b = 6$ and $c = 1$.

5) The area of a triangle is given by $A = \sqrt{s(s-a)(s-b)(s-c)}$, where $s = \frac{1}{2}(a + b + c)$.

Find the area when $a = 5$, $b = 6$ and $c = 8$.

6) If $\frac{1}{r} = \frac{1}{u} - \frac{1}{v}$, find r when $u = 3$ and $v = 4$.

7) Find the value of $\dfrac{1+x}{1-x}$ when x is: a) 2 b) $\frac{1}{2}$ c) $-\frac{1}{2}$.

8) £100 is to be shared between g girls and b boys. How much does each get?

9) How many minutes are there between x minutes to 12 and y minutes past 3?

10) T boys play tennis, C boys play cricket, B boys play both. How many boys play:

a) tennis but not cricket b) tennis or cricket?

11) In the following change the subject to the letter indicated:

a) $5x + 2y = z$ (x) b) $x^2 + xy = z^2$ (y)

12) Solve the following equations:

a) $3x + 2 = 20$ b) $5 - x = 18$ c) $2x^2 + 1 = 99$

13) The length of a rectangle is three times its width. If 10 cm is added to both length and width, the length will be twice the width. What is the width?

14) An uncle is three times the age of his niece. Six years ago he was six times as old. How old is he now?

15) Solve the following by trial and improvement, to the degree of accuracy shown:

a) $x^3 + 5x = -8$ (1 Decimal Place)

b) $x^5 + 3x^3 = -20$ (1 DP) c) $x^3 + x = 4$ (2 DP)

16) Solve the following:

a) $3x + y = 3$
$5x + 3y = 7$

b) $4x + 3y = 5$
$2x + 4y = 0$

17) If I change £5 and \$10 to Spanish money I get 2100 pesetas, and if I change £12 and \$3 I get 2730 pesetas. How many pesetas are there to the £?

18) Illustrate the following inequalities on the number line:

a) $1 \le x \le 4$ b) $x^2 < 8$ c) $x^2 > 4$

19) Solve the inequalities:

a) $7x + 3 < 2x - 2$ b) $2x^2 + 1 < 5$

20) If I earn another £50, then I will earn more than half as much again as I have now. How much do I earn now?

21) On the same paper draw the graphs of $y = 2x + 3$ and $y = \frac{1}{2} - \frac{x}{2}$. Hence solve the simultaneous equations $y - 2x = 3$ and $2y + x = 1$.

22) A money changer will change money at a rate of 3 DM per £, and then charge a commission of 30 DM. How many DM do you get for:

a) £20 b) £50 c) £200?

Plot a graph with £ along the x-axis and DM up the y-axis.

Puzzles and paradoxes

1) If $x > y$ and $y > z$ then $x > z$, you will agree. So what is wrong with the following argument?

   Half a loaf is better than nothing

   Nothing is better than Heaven

   Therefore half a loaf is better than Heaven.

2) A Greek teacher trained his pupils as lawyers. But he only asked a pupil for payment if he won his first case. One pupil, after leaving the teacher, never took on a case. Eventually the lawyer sued the pupil, arguing as follows:

   If the court finds in my favour, then he must pay me my fees. If the court finds in my pupil's favour, then he has won his first case and must pay me my fees.

   The pupil argued:

   If the court finds in my favour, then I don't have to pay fees. If it doesn't find in my favour, then I have lost my first case and don't have to pay fees.

   Who is right?

3) On the first day of term, Teacher says to the class that there will be a surprise exam some day that term. The children go away and reason as follows:

   The exam cannot be on the very last day of term, because by then we would know it was coming and it wouldn't be a surprise. So we can cross the last day of term off the possible dates for the exam. The exam cannot be on the last but one day of term, because having eliminated the last day we would know it was coming and it wouldn't be a surprise. Working backwards, the exam cannot be on any day of the term – there will not be an exam at all!

   On the 17th day of term Teacher says: "There will be an exam today" and the children are surprised. What is wrong with their reasoning?

4) A dealer buys 72 identical books. Ink is spilled on the invoice, so that the total cost appears as £*67.9*. What are the hidden digits?

Chapter 13

Area and volume

The area of a semicircle is half the area of the full circle. But suppose we cut the circle a quarter of the way down. What is the area of the shaded portion? Is it a quarter of the full circle?

Fig 13.1

13.1 Sectors and arcs

The area and circumference of a circle with radius r are:

Area = πr^2, Circumference = $2\pi r$

If we have only part of the circle, then these expressions are reduced. Suppose we have a sector of a circle, in which the radii are θ apart.

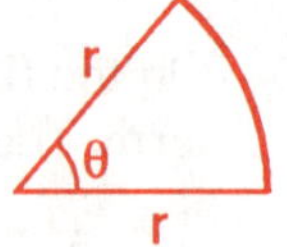

Fig 13.2

The area of the sector is found by decreasing the area of the circle in the ratio θ:360.

$$\text{Area of sector} = \pi r^2 \times \frac{\theta}{360}$$

The length of the arc is found by decreasing the circumference in the ratio θ:360.

$$\text{Length of arc} = 2\pi r \times \frac{\theta}{360}$$

13.1.1 Examples

1) A piece of wire is bent into the arc of a circle with radius 20 cm. If the arc subtends 17° at the centre what is the length of wire?

Solution Use the formula above, putting $r = 20$ and $\theta = 17$.

$$\textbf{Length of wire} = 2\pi \times 20 \times \frac{17}{360} = \textbf{5.93 cm.}$$

2) A sector of angle 30° occupies 25 cm². What is the radius of the circle?

Solution Putting $\theta = 30$ into the formula above, we obtain:

$$\pi r^2 \times \frac{30}{360} = 25$$

$$r^2 = 25 \times \frac{360}{30} \div \pi = 95.5$$

Square root to obtain r:

The radius is 9.77 cm

13.1.2 Exercises

1) Find the areas of the sectors below:

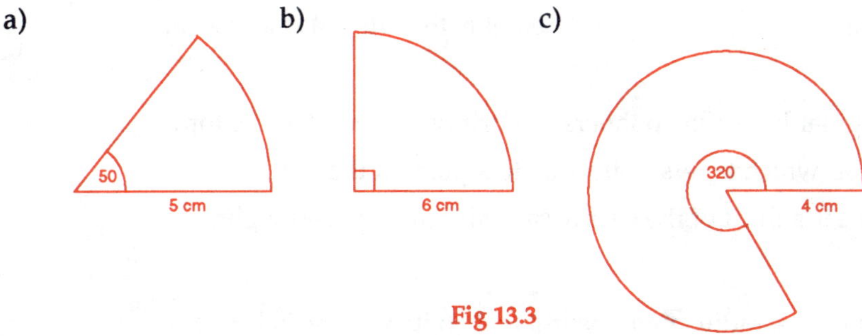

Fig 13.3

2) Find the lengths of the arcs below:

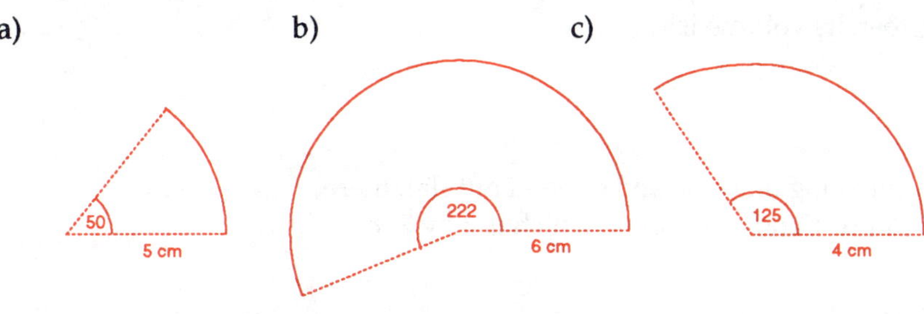

Fig 13.4

3) A sector of angle 20° is taken from a circle of radius 5 cm. What is its area?

4) A sector of area 10 cm^2 is taken from a circle of radius 15 cm. What is the angle of the sector?

5) A sector of angle 10° has area 20 cm^2. What is the radius of the circle from which it is taken?

6) An arc of length 30 cm is taken from a circle of radius 20 cm. What angle does the arc subtend?

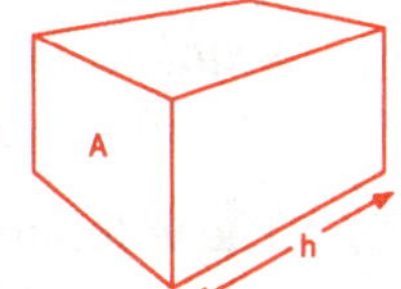

7) An arc of angle 45° has length 25 cm. What is the radius of the circle from which it is taken?

8) A circular racetrack has radius 60 m. An athlete runs part of the way round, turning through 88°. How far has she run?

9) If an athlete runs 200 m on the racetrack of Question 8, through what angle has he turned?

13.2 Volumes and surface areas of solids

Prisms

A prism is a solid with a constant cross-section.

If the cross-section is a rectangle, then it is a cuboid.

If the cross-section is a triangle, then it is a triangular prism.

If the cross-section is a circle, then it is a cylinder.

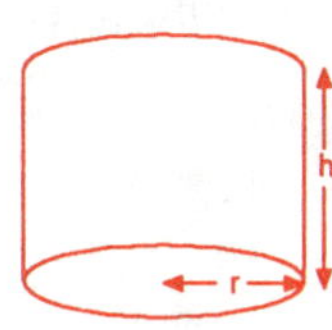

Fig 13.5

In all of these, the volume is found by multiplying the area of cross-section by the height.

$$\text{Volume} = Ah$$

In particular, if a cylinder has base radius r and height h, then its volume is $\pi r^2 h$.

Pyramids and cones

A pyramid has a rectangular base, which tapers uniformly to a point at the top.

A cone has a circular base, which tapers uniformly to a point at the top.

In both cases, the volume is a third of the base area multiplied by the height.

$$\text{Volume} = \frac{1}{3}Ah$$

In particular, if a cone has base radius r and height h, then its volume is $\frac{1}{3}\pi r^2 h$..

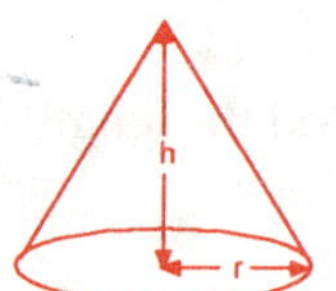

Fig 13.6

Spheres

If a sphere has radius r, then its volume is:

$$\text{Volume} = \frac{4}{3}\pi r^3$$

Surface area

Cylinder. If a cylinder is cut along one side and opened out flat, there will be two circles with radius r and a rectangle which is h by $2\pi r$. The surface area is:

$$\text{Area} = 2\pi r^2 + 2\pi rh = 2\pi r(r + h)$$

Sphere. The surface area of a sphere is:

$$\text{Area} = 4\pi r^2$$

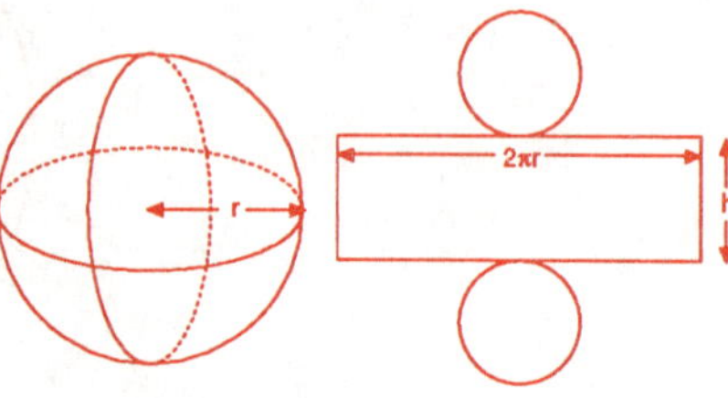

Fig 13.7 Fig 13.8

13.2.1 Examples

1) Find the volume of a pyramid with height 10 cm and square base of side 30 cm.

Solution Apply the formula, with $h = 10$ and $A = 30^2$.

The volume is $\frac{1}{3} \times 900 \times 10 = 3{,}000$ cm³

2) The volume of a cone is 23 cm³, and its height is 10 cm. Find the base radius.

Solution Letting the radius be r, use the formula for the volume of a cone:

$$23 = \frac{1}{3}\pi r^2 10$$

$$r = \sqrt{\frac{3 \times 23}{\pi \times 10}} = \mathbf{1.48\ cm}$$

3) The surface area of a sphere is 45 cm². Find its volume.

Solution First find the radius, using the formula for surface area.

$$45 = 4\pi r^2$$

$$r = 1.892 \text{ cm}$$

Now use the formula for volume:

The volume is $\frac{4}{3}\pi r^3 = 28.4$ cm³

13.2.2 Exercises

1) Find the volumes of the following:
   a) A cylinder with height 10 cm and base radius 0.5 cm.
   b) A pyramid with height 12 m and a rectangular base with sides 4 m and 5 m.
   c) A cone with height 4 cm and base radius 7 cm.
   d) A sphere with radius 4 cm.
2) A prism has height 12 cm and its base is a right-angled triangle with sides of 3 cm, 4 cm, 5 cm. Find its volume.
3) A cylinder has volume 60 cm^3 and base radius 4 cm. Find its height.
4) A cylinder has volume 8 m^3 and height 2 m. Find the base radius.
5) The base of a pyramid is a rectangle of sides 7 m and 8 m. If the volume is 112 m^3 find the height.
6) A pyramid with a square base has height 5 cm and volume 15 cm^3. Find the side of the base.
7) A cone has base radius 6 cm and height 7 cm. What is its volume?
8) A cone has volume 105 m^3 and base radius 7 m. Find its height.
9) A cone has volume 6 cm^3 and height 2 cm. Find the base radius.
10) Find the volumes of the spheres with radii:
    a) 5 cm   b) 12 m   c) 1.5 feet
11) Find the radii of the spheres with volumes:
    a) 46 cm^3 b) 12 cubic inches   c) 5.56 mm^3
12) Find the surface areas of the spheres of Question 10.
13) A sphere has volume 3.44 cm^3. What is its surface area?
14) A sphere has surface area 66 mm^2. What is its volume?
15) Find the surface areas of the cylinders:
    a) With base radius 4 cm and height 12 cm
    b) With base radius 2 m and height 0.1 m
    c) With base radius 6 mm and volume 16 mm^3
    d) With height 4 m and volume 44 m^3.
16) The base radius of a cylinder is 2 cm and its surface area is 40 cm^2. Find its height and its volume.

13.3 Combinations of figures

Suppose a compound shape is built up out of simple shapes. Then to find its area or volume we add the basic areas or volumes.

13.3.1 Examples

1) Find the area of the shape in Fig 13.9.

Solution Divide the shape into two rectangles, one 10 by 2 and the other 6 by 1.

The area is $10 \times 2 + 6 \times 1 = 26$

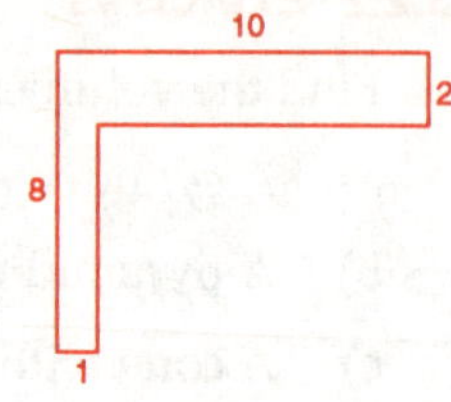

Fig 13.9

2) A barn is 12 m long, 3 m wide and 2.5 m high. The roof consists of half a cylinder. Find the volume.

Solution The shape is shown in Fig 13.10. The end walls are in the shape of a semicircle of diameter 3 m over a 3 by 2.5 rectangle.

Surface area of end wall $= \pi 1.5^2 \div 2 + 3 \times 2.5 = 11\ \text{m}^2$

Volume = length × area = $12 \times 11 = 132\ \text{m}^3$

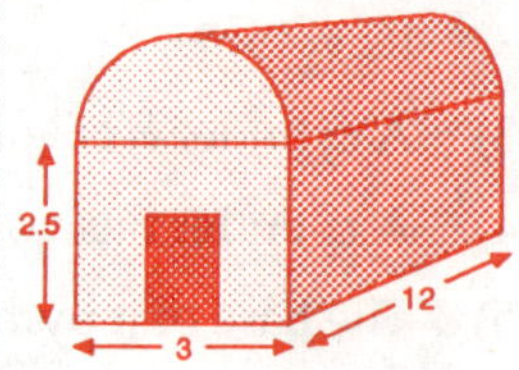

Fig 13.10

13.3.2 Exercises

1) Find the areas of the shapes below.

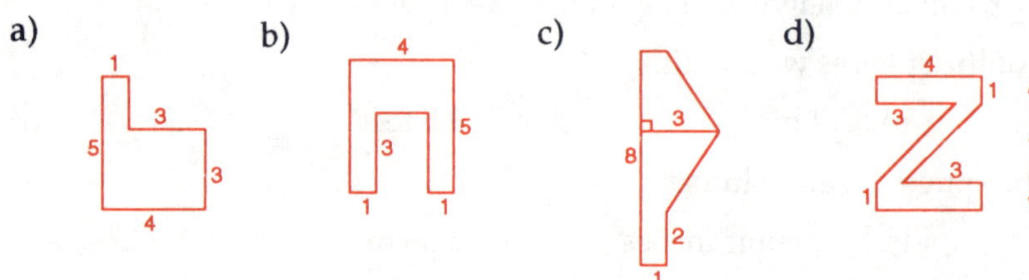

Fig 13.11

2) If the lines of the grid below are 1 unit apart find the areas of the dotted shapes shown.

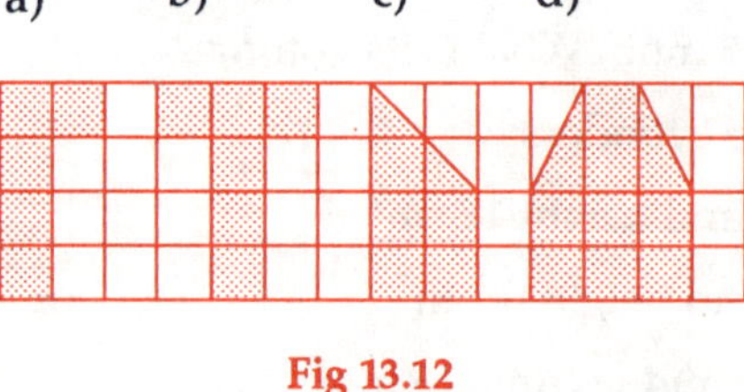

Fig 13.12

3) A running track consists of two parallel straight lines of length 50 m, separated by 20 m, and semi-circular ends. Find the length of the track and the area it encloses.

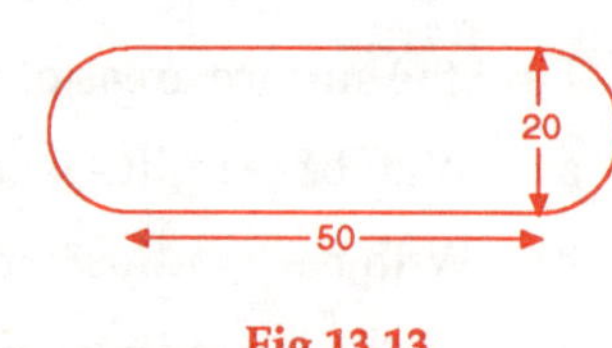

Fig 13.13

4) A window consists of a semi-circle on top of a rectangle. The rectangle is 60 cm high and 40 cm wide. Find the area of the window.

5) A test-tube consists of a cylinder with a hemisphere at one end. The length of the cylinder is 6 cm and its radius of cross-section is 1 cm. Find the volume and surface area of the tube.

6) A pencil is 12 cm long, and its cross-section is a circle of diameter 1 cm. The last 2 cm are sharpened to a conical point. Find the volume of the pencil.

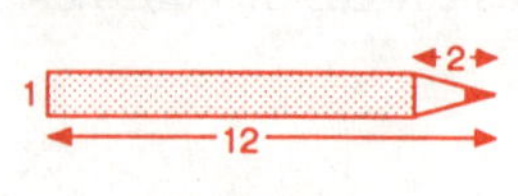

Fig 13.14

7) A cornet ice cream is a cone surmounted by a hemisphere. The total height is 5 inches and the radius of the hemisphere is 1 inch. Find the total volume.

8) A house is built on a rectangular base which is 6 m by 8 m. The walls are 10 m high, and the roof tapers to a point 12 m above the ground. Find the volume of the house.

13.4 Differences of shapes

To find the volume of a shape with a hole in it, find the original volume and subtract the volume of the hole.

Many problems involving the area or volume of a compound shape are best done by subtracting areas or volumes.

In particular, the area of a segment can be found by subtracting a triangle from a sector.

13.4.1 Examples

1) A chord subtends 50° at the centre of a circle of radius 5 cm. Find the area of the segment cut off by the chord.

Solution Use the method of 13.1 to find the area of the sector OAB.

Area of sector $= \pi 5^2 \times \frac{50}{360} = 10.91$ cm^2.

The base of triangle OAB is 5. Its height is $5 \times \sin 50°$.

Area of triangle $= \frac{1}{2} \times 5 \times 5 \times \sin 50° = 9.58$ cm^2

Subtract to find the area of the segment:

Area of segment = 1.33 cm^2

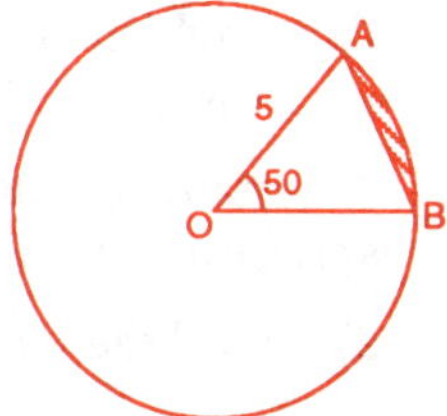

Fig 13.15

2) A hollow rubber ball has outside radius 6 cm and inside radius 5.5 cm. Find the volume of rubber.

Solution The volume is found by subtracting the volume of the hollow sphere inside from the volume of the whole ball.

Volume $= \frac{4}{3}\pi 6^3 - \frac{4}{3}\pi 5.5^3 = 208$ cm^3

13.4.2 Exercises

1) Find the areas of the shaded segments below:

a)

6
30

b)

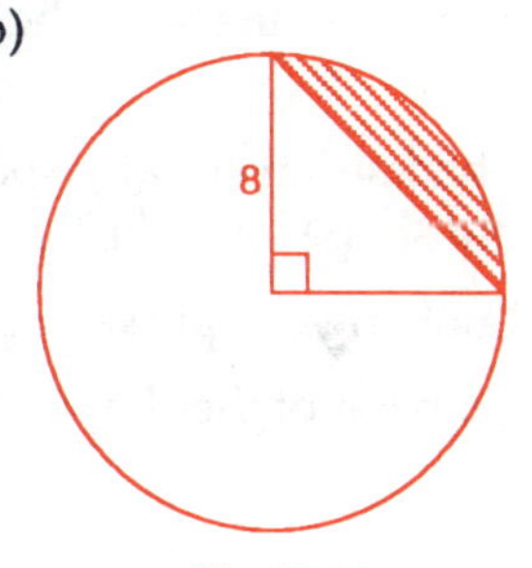

c)

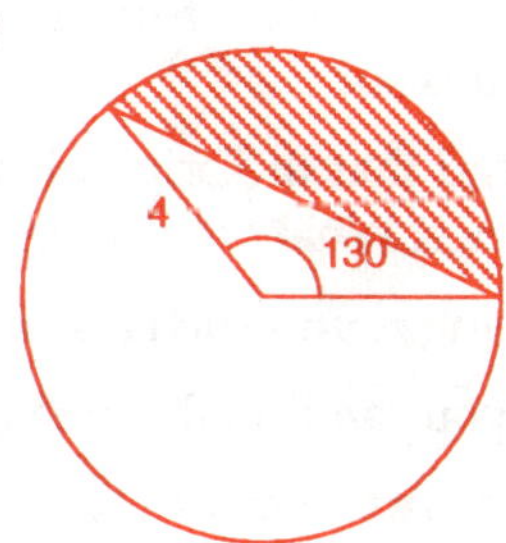

Fig 13.16

2) A chord subtends 60° at the centre of a circle, and the area of the segment cut off is 12 square inches. Find the radius of the circle.

3) A closed cuboid box is made out of wood which is 1 cm thick. The external sides are 22 cm, 17 cm and 14 cm. Find the volume of wood.

4) Fig 13.17 shows the cross- section of a copper pipe. The inside radius is 2 cm and the outside radius is 2.5 cm.

 a) Find the dotted area.

 b) Find the volume of copper in 40 m of the pipe.

Fig 13.17

5) An electrical cable consists of a copper cylinder surrounded by rubber. The diameter of the copper is 1.5 cm and the rubber is 0.25 cm thick. The cable is 100 m long.

 a) Find the volume of copper b) Find the volume of the cable

 c) Find the volume of rubber.

6) Paper which is 0.03 cm thick is rolled round a cylindrical core of radius 8 cm. The completed roll of paper is a cylinder with radius 20 cm. Find the length of the paper.

7) A certain sort of ball is a sphere with radius 2.5 cm. It is made by winding rubber string round a spherical core of radius 1 cm.

 a) Find the volume of rubber

 b) If the area of cross-section of the rubber string is 0.02 cm^2 find the length of the string.

8) The problem at the beginning of the chapter was about the area of a segment. The chord was a quarter of the way down from the top of the circle. Using trigonometry to find the angle subtended by the chord, find the proportion of the circle occupied by the segment.

13.5. Longer exercises

A. Shapes with constant diameter

A shape with constant diameter can roll along the ground, with its top always the same height above the ground. Circles and spheres and cylinders can do this. Are there any other shapes?

1) Draw a circle with radius 5 cm. Mark three points A, B, C equally spaced round the circumference.

2) Make an arc, with centre A, going through B and C. Repeat with the other two points.

3) Cut out the shape formed by the three arcs. Roll it along the table. You should find that the top of the shape is always the same height above the table. Why is this so?

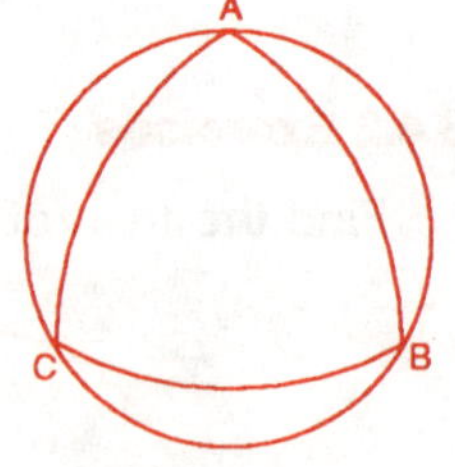

Fig 13.18

4) Suppose instead that the original circle had seven equally spaced points on its circumference. What would the cut-out shape look like?

5) Are you carrying round such a shape? Look in your purse or pocket!

6) (Hard) See if you can find the area or perimeter of the shape made in 1- 3.

B. Curved surface area of cone

The surface area of a cone can be found by "unwrapping" the side and laying it out flat.

1) Suppose the cone has height 24 cm and base radius 7 cm. Find the "slant height", i.e. the distance from the top to the rim of the base.
2) Suppose we now cut the curved surface along a slant height, and lay it flat. We obtain a sector as shown. What is the radius of this sector?
3) The arc of this sector is the circumference of the original base circle. Find the length of this arc.
4) Use the methods of 13.1 to find the angle of the sector and hence its area. This is the curved surface area of the cone.
5) A cone has height 4 cm and base radius 3 cm. What is its curved surface area?
6) Suppose we make a cone from a sector of angle 216° from a circle of radius 20 cm. Find the base radius and height of the cone.
7) See if you can find the general formula for the curved surface area of a cone with base radius r and height h.

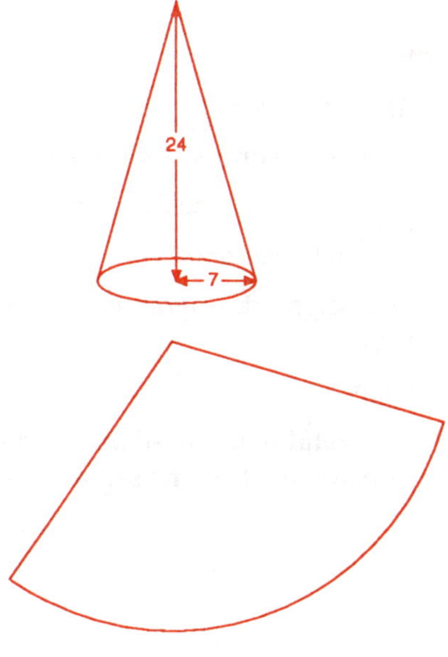

Fig 13.19

Multiple choice question *(Tick appropriate box)*

A and B are points on a circle with centre O, and $A\hat{O}B = 60°$. If the arc length AB is 6 cm, then the radius of the circle is:

a) 11.5 cm ☐

b) 6 cm ☐

c) 56.5 cm ☐

d) 0.955 cm ☐

e) 5.73 cm. ☐

Points to note

1) *Arcs and sectors*

   a) Don't confuse the arc AB with the straight line AB.

   b) Don't confuse the diameter of a circle with its radius.

2) *Pyramids and cones*

   The height of a pyramid or cone is the vertical height. It is not the height along the slanting face.

3) *Units*

   Be careful with questions in which the units are mixed. It is probably safest to express all the measurements in the same units.

Chapter 14
Circles

You are standing on the middle of a ladder which leans against a wall. It slides down slowly, until it lies flat on the ground. What path do you follow during the slide?

Fig 14.1

14.1 Angles within circles

Below are four theorems about angles made within circles. The proofs are in Longer exercise A at the end of the chapter.

I. **Angle at centre is twice angle at circumference**

In Fig 14.2, $A\hat{O}B = 2 \times A\hat{C}B$.

II. **Angle in a semicircle is 90°**

In Fig 14.3, $A\hat{C}B = 90°$

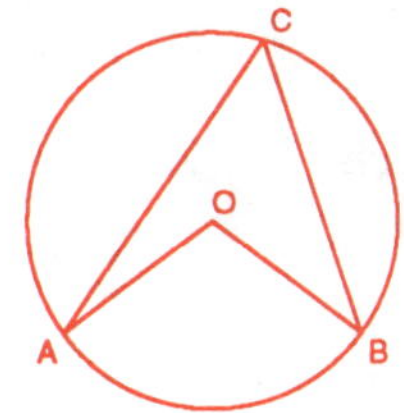

Fig 14.2

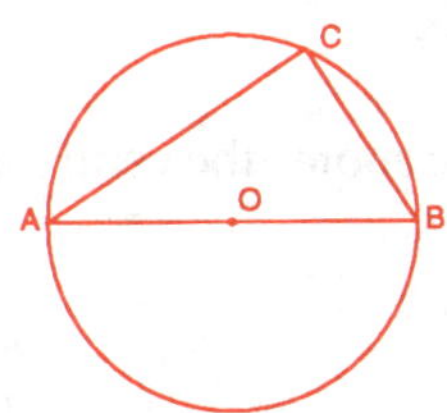

Fig 14.3

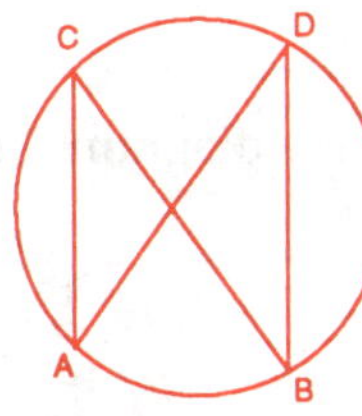

Fig 14.4

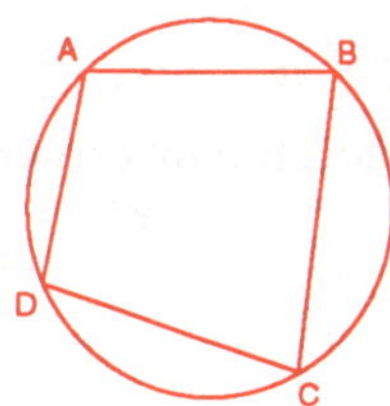

Fig 14.5

III. **Angles in same segment are equal**

In Fig 14.4, $A\hat{C}B = A\hat{D}B$.

IV. **Opposite angles of a cyclic quadrilateral add up to 180°**

In Fig 14.5, the points A, B, C, D lie on the circle. ABCD is a cyclic quadrilateral.

The theorem says that $A\hat{B}C + A\hat{D}C = 180°$.

14.1.1 Examples

1) AB is a diameter of the circle in the diagram. If $C\hat{A}B = 35°$ then find the other angles in the triangle.

Solution Because AB is a diameter it follows from II above that $A\hat{C}B$ is 90°. The other angle can be found by subtraction:

$A\hat{C}B = 90°$ and $C\hat{B}A = 55°$

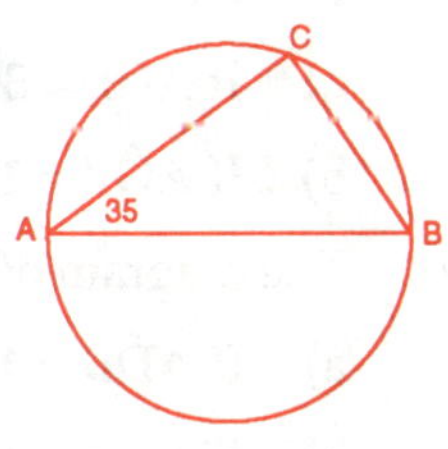

Fig 14.6

2) O is the centre of the circle in Fig 14.7, and $A\hat{O}B = 80°$. Find $\hat{C}$ and $\hat{D}$.

Solution Theorem I applies.

$\hat{C} = \frac{1}{2} A\hat{O}B = 40°$

ACBD is a cyclic quadrilateral. Hence Theorem IV applies.

$\hat{D} = 180° - \hat{C} = 140°$

3) The chords AB and CD of a circle cross at X. Show that Δ AXC is similar to Δ DXB.

Solution C and B are in the same segment of the circle defined by the chord AD. Theorem III applies.

$A\hat{C}D = A\hat{B}D$.

A and D are in the same segment of the circle defined by the chord BC. Theorem III applies.

$C\hat{D}B = C\hat{A}B$.

The angles $A\hat{X}C$ and $B\hat{X}D$ must also be equal.

Δ AXC is similar to Δ DXB

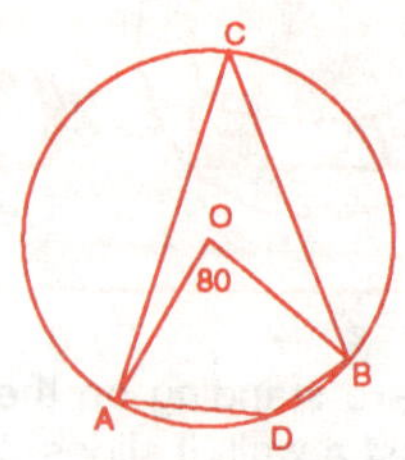

Fig 14.7

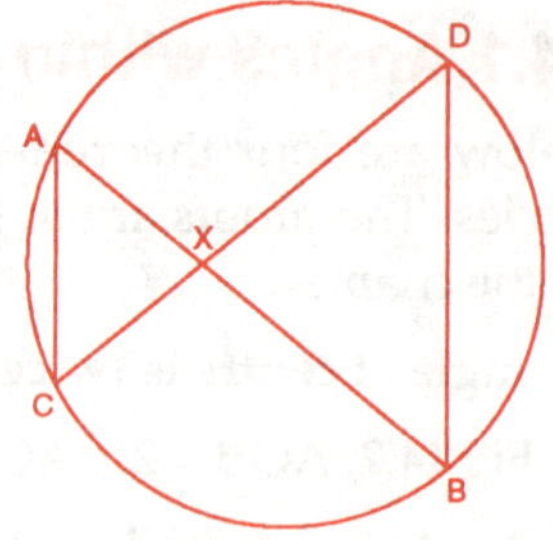

Fig 14.8

14.1.2 Exercises

1) Find the unknown angles in the diagrams below. O denotes the centre of the circle.

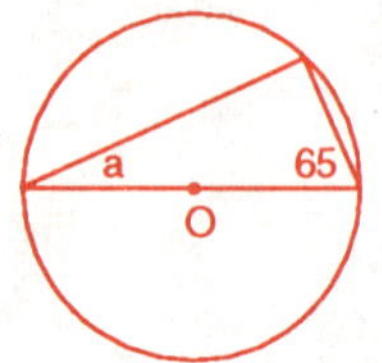

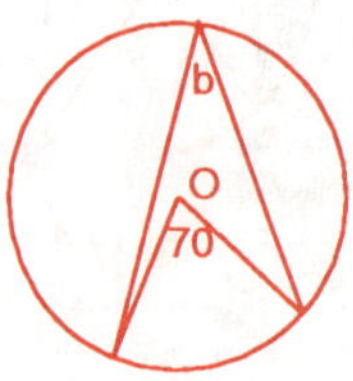

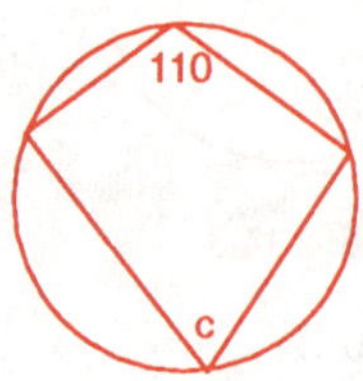

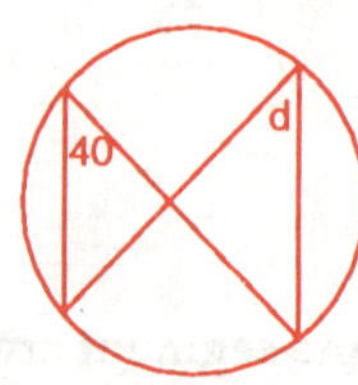

Fig 14.9

2) AB is the diameter of a circle, and C a point on the circumference. If $C\hat{B}A = 40°$ find $A\hat{C}B$ and $B\hat{A}C$.

3) O is the centre of the circle of Fig 14.10. The diagram is not to scale.

a) If $A\hat{C}B = 30°$ find $A\hat{O}B$.

b) If $A\hat{O}B = 126°$ find $A\hat{C}B$.

4) The diagram of Fig 14.11 is not to scale.

a) If $A\hat{D}B = 44°$ find $A\hat{C}B$.

b) Find an angle equal to $C\hat{A}B$.

c) Find two pairs of similar triangles.

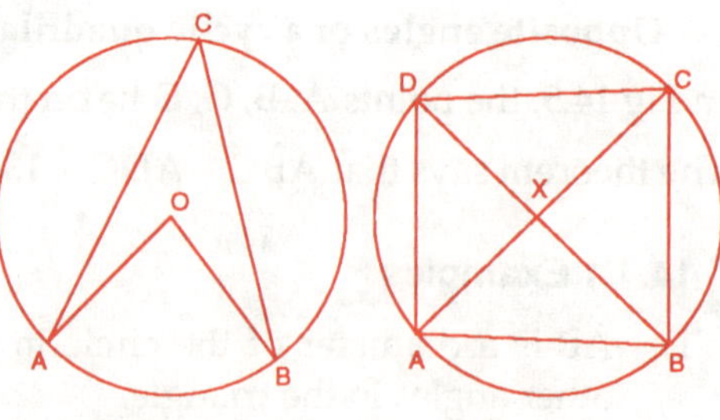

Fig 14.10 Fig 14.11

5) The diagram of Fig 14.12 is not to scale. ADE is a straight line.

a) If $\hat{A} = 56°$ find $\hat{C}$.

b) If $\hat{B} = 74°$ find $A\hat{D}C$ and $C\hat{D}E$.

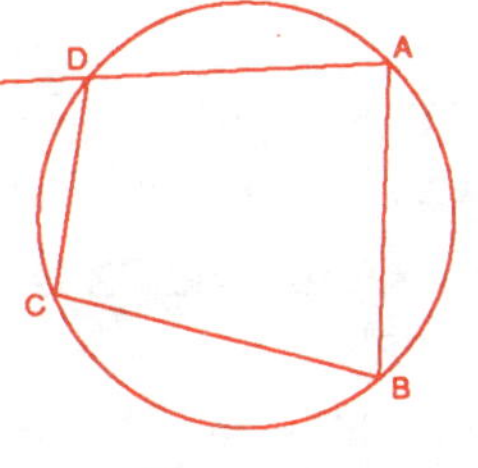

Fig 14.12

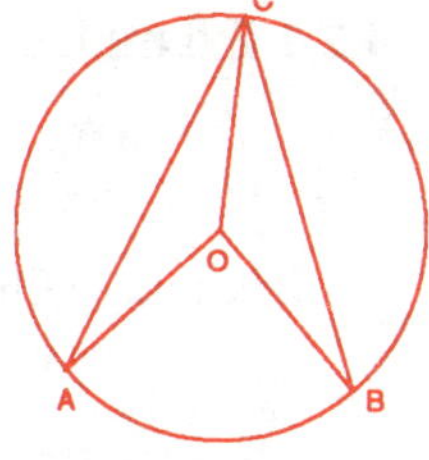

Fig 14.13

6) AB and CD are diameters of a circle. Show that ACBD is a rectangle.

7) In Fig 14.13 O is the centre of the circle. $A\hat{O}C = 108°$ and $C\hat{B}O = 56°$. Find $C\hat{O}B$ and $A\hat{O}B$.

8) In Fig 14.14 the chords AB and DC are parallel.

a) If $B\hat{A}X = 35°$, find $B\hat{D}C$, $D\hat{B}A$ and $B\hat{X}C$.

b) If $C\hat{X}B = 88°$ find $C\hat{A}B$ and $A\hat{C}D$.

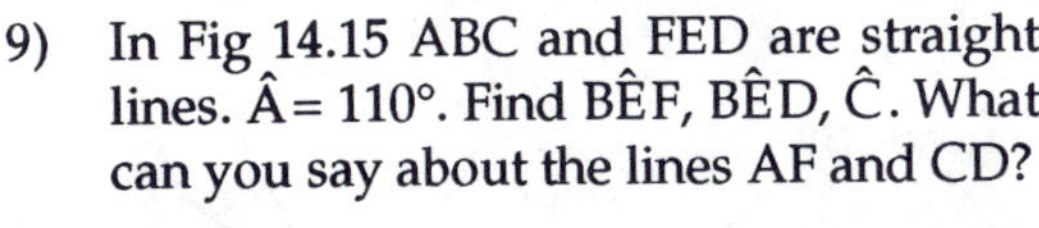

9) In Fig 14.15 ABC and FED are straight lines. $\hat{A} = 110°$. Find $B\hat{E}F$, $B\hat{E}D$, $\hat{C}$. What can you say about the lines AF and CD?

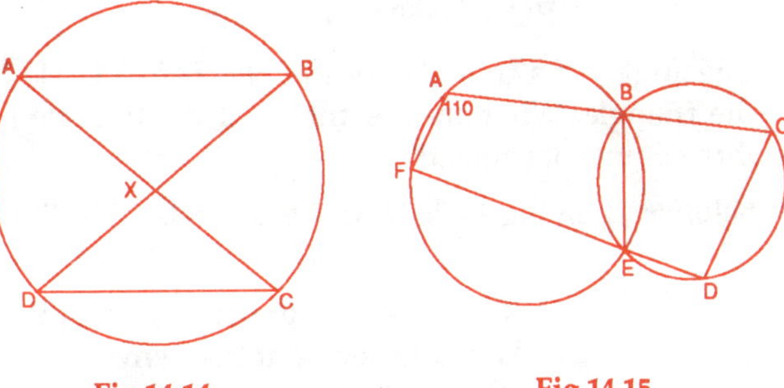

Fig 14.14

Fig 14.15

10) Look again at the problem at the beginning of the chapter. Let the ladder be the diameter of a circle, with you at its centre. Using Theorem II, what can you say about the point where the wall meets the ground? What is your distance from this point? What path do you follow?

14.2 Tangents to circles

Tangent and radius

A tangent to a circle touches it at exactly one point (Fig 14.16). The tangent is at right-angles to the radius at that point. $T\hat{P}O = 90°$.

Two tangents from a point

If two tangents are drawn from a point to a circle, then they are equal in length (Fig 14.17). TP = TQ.

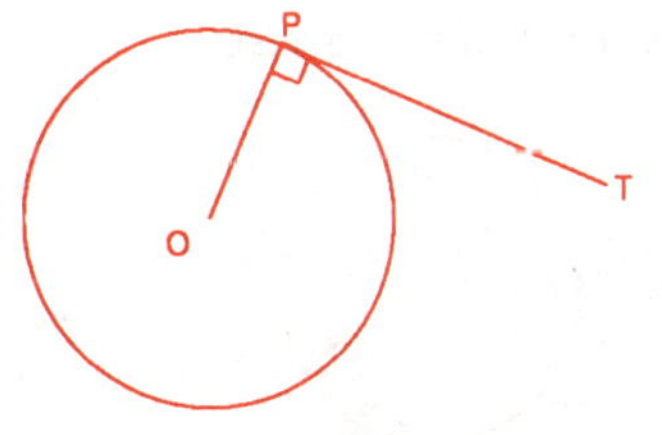

Fig 14.16

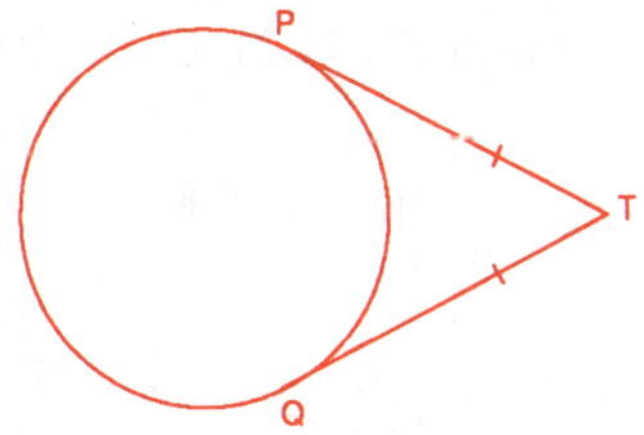

Fig 14.17

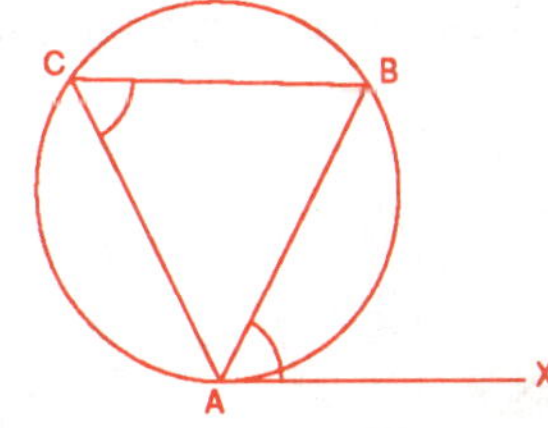

Fig 14.18

Alternate segment theorem

In the picture (Fig 14.18), the chord AB meets the tangent AX. Let C be in the opposite (alternate) segment. The Alternate Segment theorem states:

The angle between a chord and a tangent is equal to the angle in the alternate segment. $X\hat{A}B = A\hat{C}B$

14.2.1 Examples

1) In the diagram, XP is a tangent to the circle with centre O. OX cuts the circle at Q. If $P\hat{X}O = 28°$ find $P\hat{O}Q$ and $O\hat{P}Q$.

Solution OP is a radius and PX is a tangent. Hence they are at right-angles.

$P\hat{O}Q = 180° - 90° - 28° = 62°$

OP and OQ are equal radii of the circle. Hence $O\hat{Q}P = O\hat{P}Q$.

$O\hat{P}Q = \frac{1}{2}(180° - 62°) = 59°$

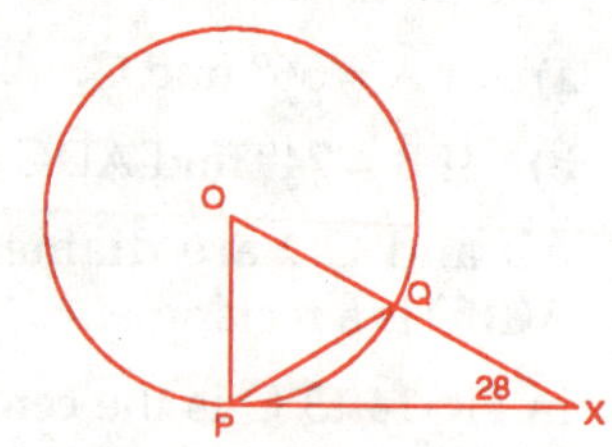

Fig 14.19

2) The angles of a triangle are 48°, 68°, 64°. A circle is inscribed in the triangle. What are the angles of the triangle formed by the three points of contact?

Solution In Fig 14.20, ΔAPR is isosceles. It follows that $A\hat{P}R = 66°$.

AP is a tangent to the circle, and PR is a chord. By the Alternate Segment theorem:

$P\hat{Q}R = A\hat{P}R = 66°$

By similar calculations:

$P\hat{R}Q = 56°$ and $R\hat{P}Q = 58°$

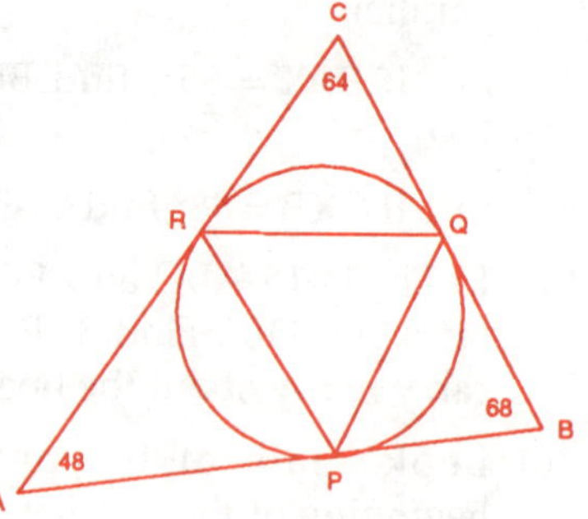

Fig 14.20

14.2.2 Exercises

1) Find the unknown angles in the diagrams of Fig 14.21. O denotes the centre of the circle.

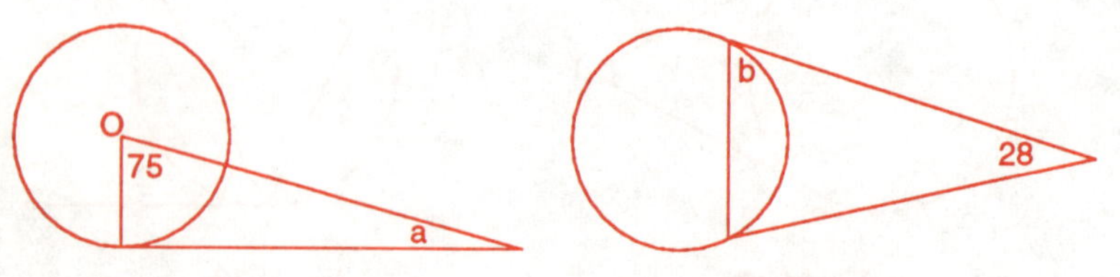

Fig 14.21

2) In Fig 14.22 AT is a diameter of a circle and TB is a tangent. If $\hat{A} = 55°$ find $\hat{B}$.
3) In Fig 14.23 TA and TB are tangents to the circle, centre O. If $\hat{T} = 72°$ find O.

4) In Fig 14.24 AB and CD are diameters, and the tangents at A, B, C, D meet at P, Q, R, S. Show that PQRS is a parallelogram.

5) In Fig 14.25 a quadrilateral ABCD is drawn round a circle. Show that AB + CD = BC + AD.

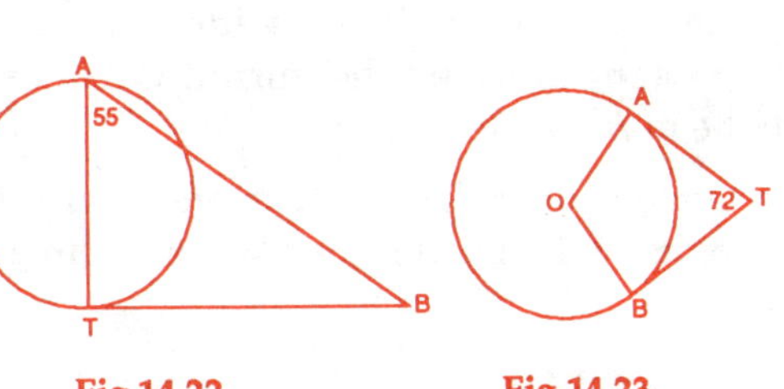

Fig 14.22 Fig 14.23

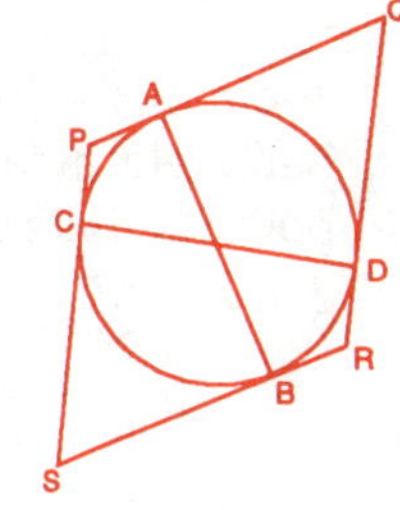

Fig 14.24

6) A triangle has angles 60°, 66°, 54°. A circle is drawn inside it. Find the angles of the triangle made by the points of contact.

7) A circle is drawn inside a triangle, and the triangle made by the points of contact has angles 55°, 63°, 62°. Find the angles of the original triangle.

8) The quadrilateral ABCD has angles 100°, 96°, 70°, 94° at A, B, C, D. A circle is drawn inside the quadrilateral, touching AB, BC, CD, DA at P, Q, R, S. Find the angles of PQRS.

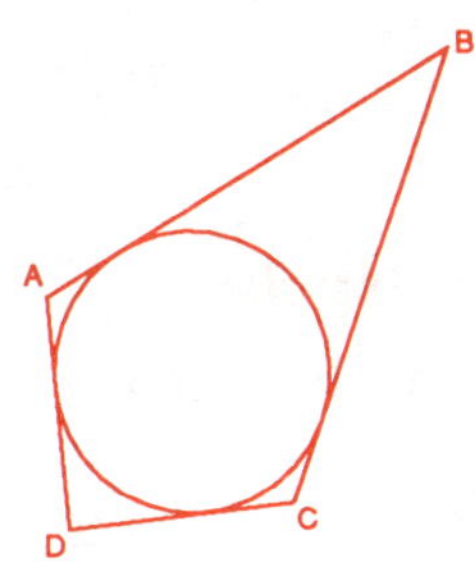

Fig 14.25

14.3 Intersecting chords

Intersecting chord theorem

AB and CD are chords of a circle meeting at X. (Either inside or outside the circle. See Fig 14.26). The Intersecting Chords Theorem states:

$$XA \times XB = XC \times XD$$

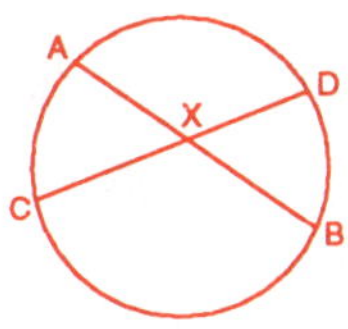

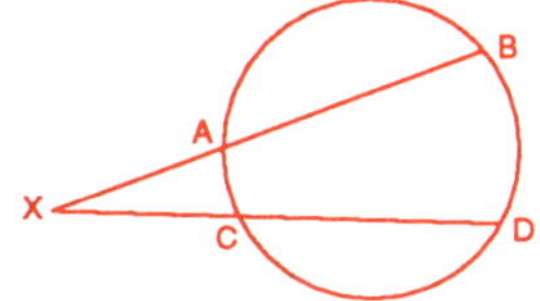

Fig 14.26

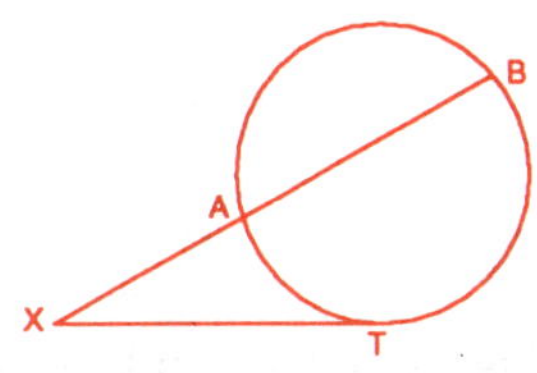

Fig 14.27

Tangents and chords

If AB meets a tangent XT at X, then:

$$XA \times XB = XT^2.$$

14.3.1 Examples

1) The chords AB and CD to a circle meet at X inside the circle. If XB = 3, XC = 2 and AB = 7 then find XD.

Solution Note that XA = 7 − 3 = 4. This gives the equation:

$$3 \times 4 = 2 \times XD$$

$$XD = 6$$

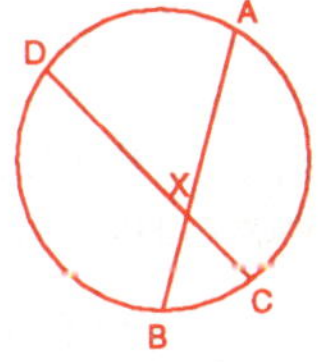

Fig 14.28

2) A circular mirror with radius 30 cm hangs with its centre 50 cm below a nail, held by a string wrapped round the mirror. What length of string is not in contact with the mirror?

Solution XT is a tangent to the circle. If A and B are the highest and lowest points of the mirror, then XA = 20 cm and XB = 80 cm. This gives:

$XT^2 = 20 \times 80 = 1600 \text{ cm}^2$.

XT = 40 cm.

The length of free string is $2 \times 40 = 80$ cm

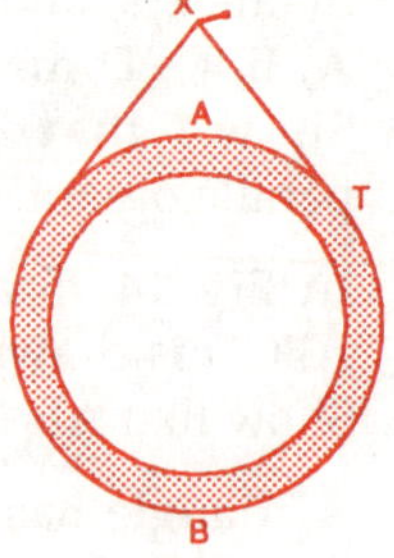

Fig 14.29

14.3.2 Exercises

1) Find the unknown lengths in the diagrams of Fig 14.30.

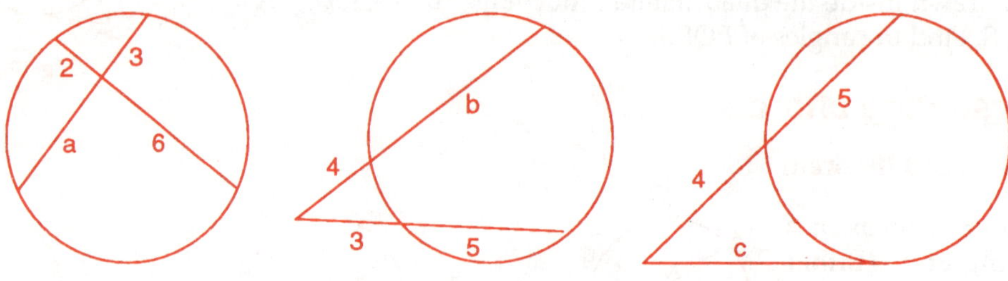

Fig 14.30

2) The chords AB and CD of a circle meet at X inside the circle. XA = 3, AB = 8, XC = 2. Find XD.

3) The chords AB and CD to a circle meet at X outside the circle. XA = 5, XB = 15, XC = 3. Find CD.

4) The chords AB and CD to a circle meet at X outside the circle, C being nearer to X than D. XC = 15, CD = 5, XB = 25. Find XA.

5) The chords PQ and RS to a circle meet at O outside the circle. OP = 3, PQ = 13, OS = 12. Find RS.

6) Fig 14.31 shows a bridge, which is in the shape of an arc of a circle. The width of the river is 12 m, and the highest point of the bridge is 4 m above the water. What is the radius of the circle?

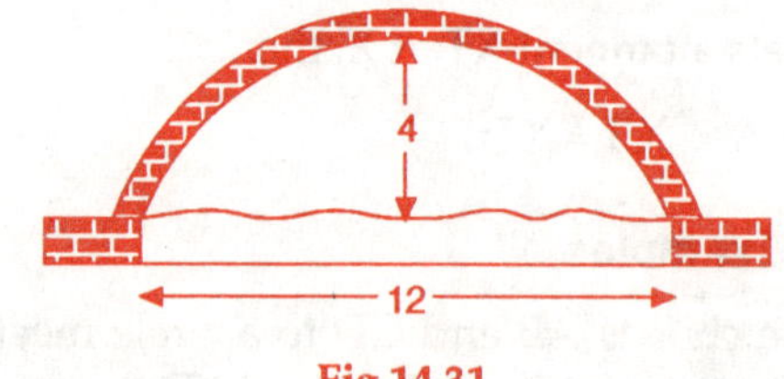

Fig 14.31

7) P, Q, R are points on a circle. The chord PQ meets the tangent at R at X. XR = 6, XP = 4. Find PQ.

8) The mast of a ship is 40 m above the level of the sea. How far can a lookout at the top of the mast see? (Take the radius of the Earth to be 6,400,000 m.)

14.4 Longer exercises

A. Proofs of theorems

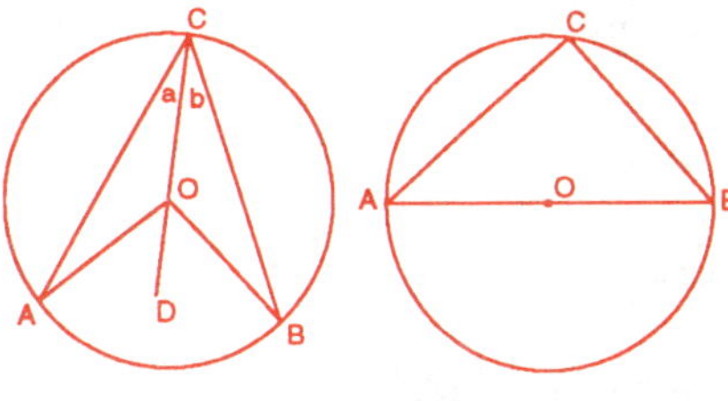

Fig 14.32 Fig 14.33

1) I. **Angle at centre is twice angle at circumference**

   Join C to O as shown (Fig 14.32). Let $A\hat{C}O = a$ and $B\hat{C}O = b$. Find $C\hat{A}O$ and $A\hat{O}D$ in terms of a. Similarly find $B\hat{O}D$ in terms of b. What is the relationship between $A\hat{O}B$ and $A\hat{C}B$?

2) II. **Angle in a semicircle is 90°**

   Apply the result I, in the case that AB is a diameter of the circle (Fig 14.33).

3) III. **Angles in the same segment are equal**

   Apply the result I, for $\hat{C}$ and for $\hat{D}$. (Fig 14.34).

4) IV. **Opposite angles of a cyclic quadrilateral add up to 180°**

   Apply the result I, for $A\hat{O}C$ and also for the reflex angle $A\hat{O}C$ (Fig 14.35).

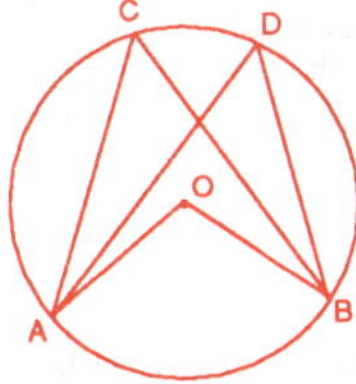

Fig 14.34

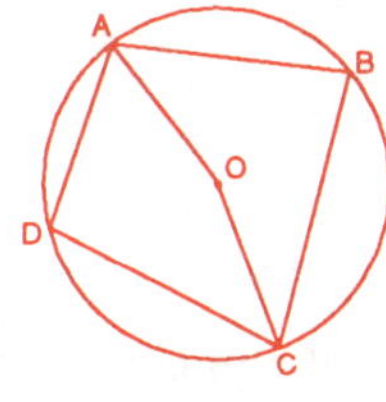

Fig 14.35

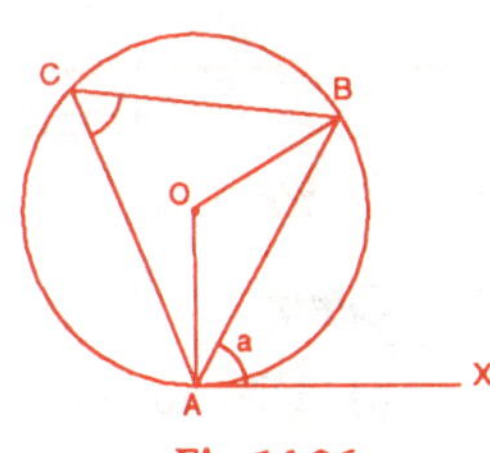

Fig 14.36

5) **Alternate segment theorem**

   Draw a perpendicular from the centre O. Let $B\hat{A}X = a$. (Fig 14.36). Find the other angles of the diagram in terms of a. You will need the result I.

6) **Intersecting chords theorem**

   Use III to find two pairs of equal angles. Find a pair of similar triangles. Write down the ratios between the sides of these triangles.

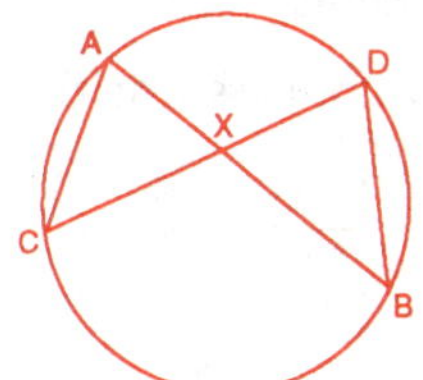

Fig 14.37

B. Ellipses

Take a disc, and hold it at an angle. The oval shape you can see is called an ellipse.

There are several ways of drawing ellipses. Here are some for you to try.

1) Put drawing-pins into two points A and B on a piece of paper. Tie a string loosely between them. Slide a pencil along the string, keeping it taut. The curve traced out is an ellipse. What curve do you get if A = B?

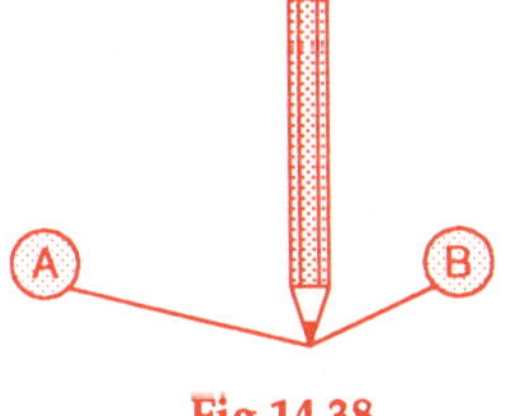
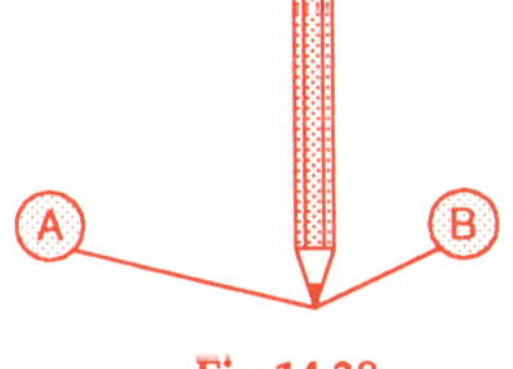

Fig 14.38

2) Take a circle, and a point F inside it. Cut out the circle, and fold it over so that the rim of the circle is on F. Repeat for several different folds. The set of creases should outline an ellipse. What happens if F is at the centre of the circle?

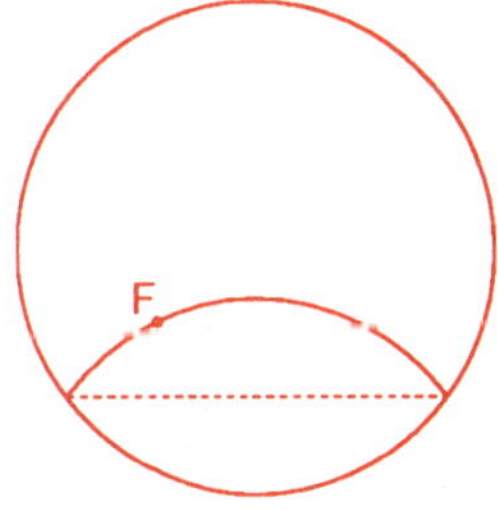

Fig 14.39

3) Can you think of natural examples of ellipses?

Multiple choice question *(Tick appropriate box)*

In the diagram, which of the following must be true?

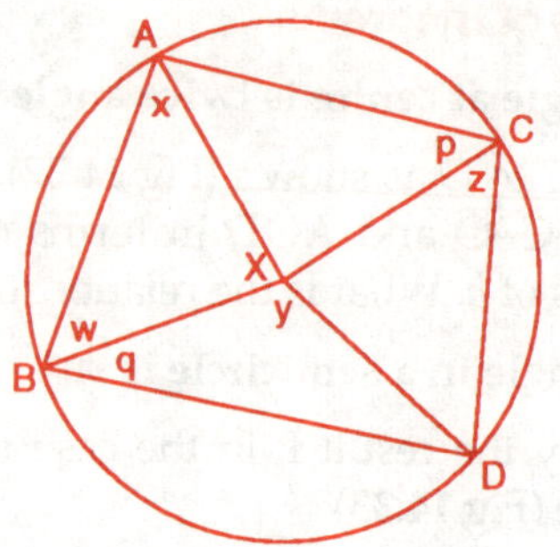

Fig 14.40

a) $y = 2z$ ☐

b) $w = z$ ☐

c) $x = z$ ☐

d) $p+z+w+q = 180°$ ☐

e) $p+z = w+q$ ☐

Points to note

1) *Centre*

   a) Do not assume that a point is the centre of a circle unless you are told so.

   b) Do not assume that a chord is a diameter unless you are told so.

2) *Chords*

   Do not assume that two chords cross in the centre of a circle unless you are told so.

Chapter 15

The general angle

When you first met sin, cos and tan they were defined only for acute angles. But even if the angle is bigger than 90° your calculator can still find these functions. Fill in the following table for sin:

x	20	40	60	80	100	120	140	160
$\sin x$								

Can you spot a pattern? Guess what the rule is, and check with other angles. Does the same rule work for cos or tan?

15.1 Trigonometry for obtuse angles

If P is an obtuse angle, then 180° – P is an acute angle. The trigonometric functions are defined as follows:

$$\sin P = \sin (180° - P)$$

$$\cos P = -\cos (180° - P)$$

$$\tan P = -\tan (180° - P)$$

This is justified by comparing the triangles shown.

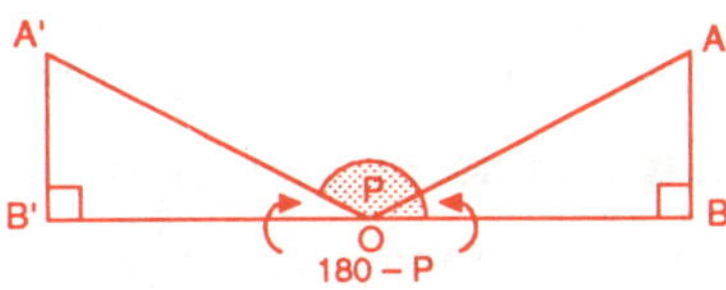

Fig 15.1

The HYP side OA has been swung round to OA′. The OPP sides AB and A′B′ of the two triangles are equal. But the ADJ side OB has been reversed to OB′, so OB′ = –OB. Hence the rules are:

$$\sin P = \frac{A'B'}{OA'} = \frac{AB}{OA} = \sin (180° - P)$$

$$\cos P = \frac{OB'}{OA'} = \frac{-OB}{OA} = -\cos (180° - P)$$

$$\tan P = \frac{A'B'}{OB'} = \frac{AB}{-OB} = -\tan (180° - P)$$

15.1.1 Examples

1) 1) Express in terms of the ratios of acute angles:

a) sin 124° b) cos 163°

Solution a) Put P = 124° into the first formula above:

sin 124° = sin (180° – 124°) = sin 56°

b) Putting P = 163° into the second formula:

cos 163° = –cos (180° – 163°) = –cos 17°

2) Find obtuse angles P and Q for which:

a) $\sin P = 0.75$ b) $\tan Q = -2$

Solution a) The acute angle whose sin is 0.75 is $\sin^{-1}0.75 = 48.6°$. Use the formula:

$\sin 48.6° = \sin(180° - 48.6°) = \sin 131.4°$

P = 131.4°

b) The acute angle whose tan is 2 is $\tan^{-1}2 = 63.4°$. Use the formula:

$\tan 63.4° = -\tan(180° - 63.4°) = -\tan 116.6°$

So $\tan 116.6° = -\tan 63.4° = -2$.

Q = 116.6°

15.1.2 Exercises

1) Express the following in terms of the ratios of acute angles:
   a) sin 138° b) cos 99° c) tan 176°
   d) sin 118° e) cos 103° f) tan 91°
2) Find obtuse angles which satisfy the following:
   a) $\sin x = 0.5$ b) $\cos x = -0.76$ c) $\tan x = -0.44$
   d) $\sin x = 0.2$ e) $\cos x = -0.68$ f) $\tan x = -2.7$
3) Find two values of x for which $\sin x = 0.6$.
4) x is an obtuse angle for which $\sin x = 0.8$. Find $\cos x$.
5) x is an obtuse angle for which $\cos x = -0.6$. Find $\tan x$.
6) Find two possible values of $\cos x$, given that $\sin x = 0.7$.
7) In the triangle of Fig 15.2, find sin P, cos P and tan P.
8) A ship sails 100 miles on a bearing of 110°. How far North and how far East has it gone?
9) The Big Wheel at a funfair has radius 6 metres. A customer starts at the bottom. If the wheel rotates through 150°, how far below the centre is he? How much has he moved to one side?
10) When you filled in the table at the beginning of the chapter, which of the rules did you verify?

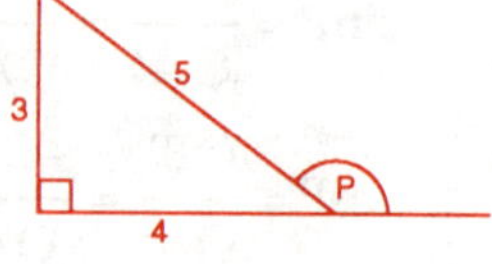

Fig 15.2

15.2 The general angle

The definitions of sin, cos and tan can be extended to all angles, as follows.

Consider a wheel of radius 1, placed so that its centre is at the origin (0,0). Let a point M start at (1,0) on the x-axis. Suppose that the wheel rotates anti-clockwise.

When it has rotated through an acute angle P, its y-coordinate will be sin P and its x-coordinate will be cos P.

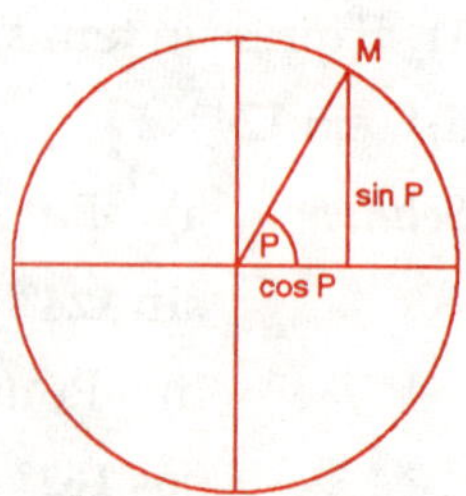

Fig 15.3

The definitions of sin, cos and tan for angles bigger than 90° follow this pattern. So whenever the wheel has rotated through P, the y-coordinate is always sin P and the x-coordinate is cos P.

When P is an obtuse angle, M lies in the second quadrant. So the y-coordinate is positive and the x-coordinate is negative. This confirms the rules given in the previous section (Fig 15.4).

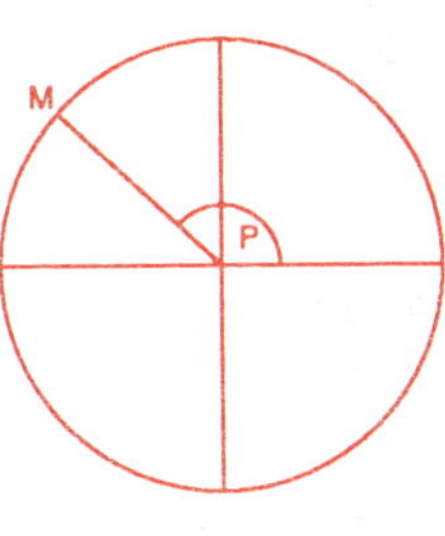

Fig 15.4

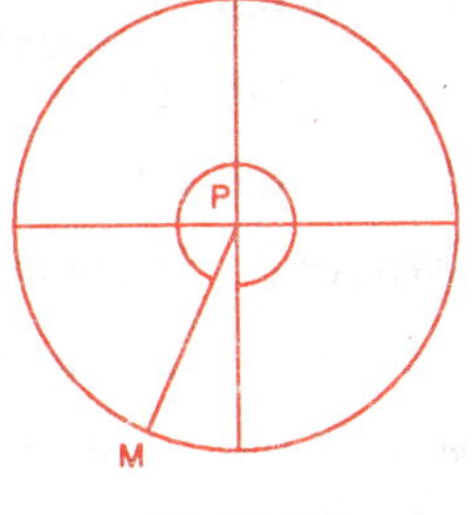

Fig 15.5

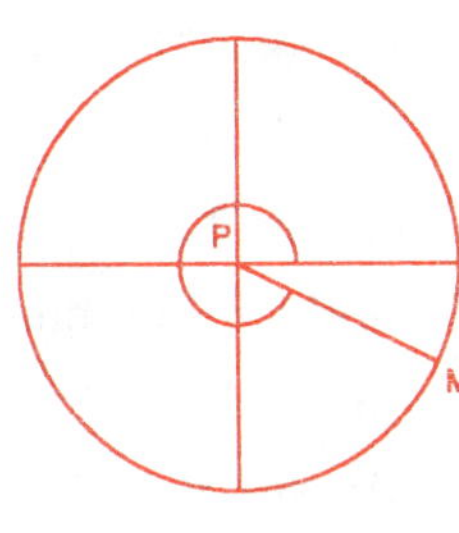

Fig 15.6

When P lies between 180° and 270°, M lies in the third quadrant (Fig 15.5). Note that P – 180° is an acute angle. Both the x and y coordinates are negative. The rules are:

sin P = –sin (P – 180°)

cos P = –cos (P – 180°)

tan P = tan (P – 180°)

In the fourth quadrant, P lies between 270° and 360° (Fig 15.6). Note that 360° – P is an acute angle.The x-coordinate is positive and the y-coordinate is negative. The rules are:

sin P = –sin (360° – P)

cos P = cos (360° – P)

tan P = –tan (360° – P)

15.2.1 Examples

1) Express in terms of the ratios of acute angles:

a) sin 200° b) cos 310°

Solution a) 200° is in the third quadrant. Apply the rule:

sin 200° = – sin (200° – 180°) = – sin 20

b) 310° is in the fourth quadrant. Apply the rule:

cos 310° = cos (360° – 310°) = cos 50°

2) Find two values of x for which:

a) $\sin x = 0.1$ b) $\tan x = -0.9$

Solution a) sin is positive in the first two quadrants. The solution in the first quadrant is found with the $\sin^{-1}$ button on a calculator. The solution in the second quadrant is found by subtracting the first answer from 180°.

x = 5.74° or 174.26°

b) tan is negative in the second and fourth quadrants. First use a calculator to find that $\tan^{-1}0.9 = 42°$, then subtract this angle from 180° and from 360°.

x = 138° or 318°

15.2.2 Exercises

1) Express the following in terms of the ratios of acute angles:

   a) sin 222° b) cos 245° c) tan 257°

   d) sin 325° e) cos 340° f) tan 289°

   g) sin 122° h) cos 322° i) tan 238°

2) Find two solutions for each of the following equations:

   a) $\sin x = 0.9$ b) $\cos x = 0.3$ c) $\tan x = 1$

   d) $\sin x = -0.3$ e) $\cos x = -0.6$ f) $\tan x = -4$

3) Find the value of x in the following:

   a) $\sin x = 0.6$ and $\cos x = -0.8$

   b) $\sin x = -\frac{5}{13}$ and $\cos x = \frac{12}{13}$.

   c) $\sin x = -0.6$ and $\tan x = 0.75$.

4) a) What angle has the same sin as 40°?

   b) What angle has the same cos as 130°?

   c) What angle has the same tan as 225°?

5) a) If $\sin x = -0.6$, find two values for $\tan x$.

   b) If $\cos x = 0$, find two values for $\sin x$.

   c) If $\tan x = 0.75$, find two values for $\cos x$.

6) A plane flies 200 miles on a bearing of 207°. How far North and how far East has it flown?

7) The Big Wheel at a funfair has radius 6 m. A customer starts at the bottom. After the wheel has turned clockwise through 325° how far below the centre is he? How far is he to the left of the centre?

15.3 Graphs of sin, cos and tan

If the wheel of Fig 15.3 rotates through 360°, then it is back where it started from. So when the wheel rotates from 360° to 720°, sin, cos and tan take the same values as between 0° and 360°.

The graphs of the three functions are as below.

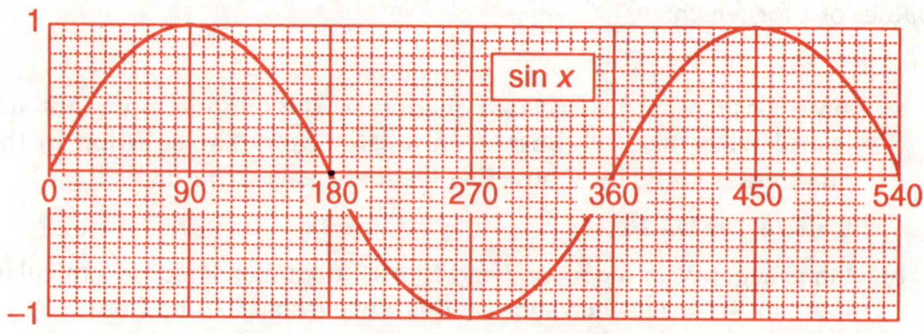

Fig 15.7

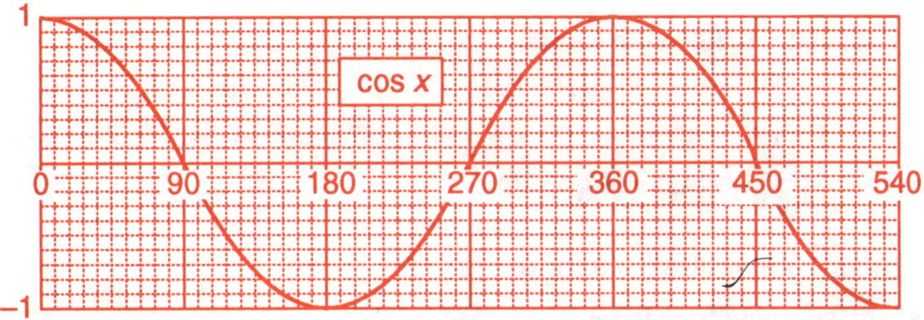

Fig 15.8

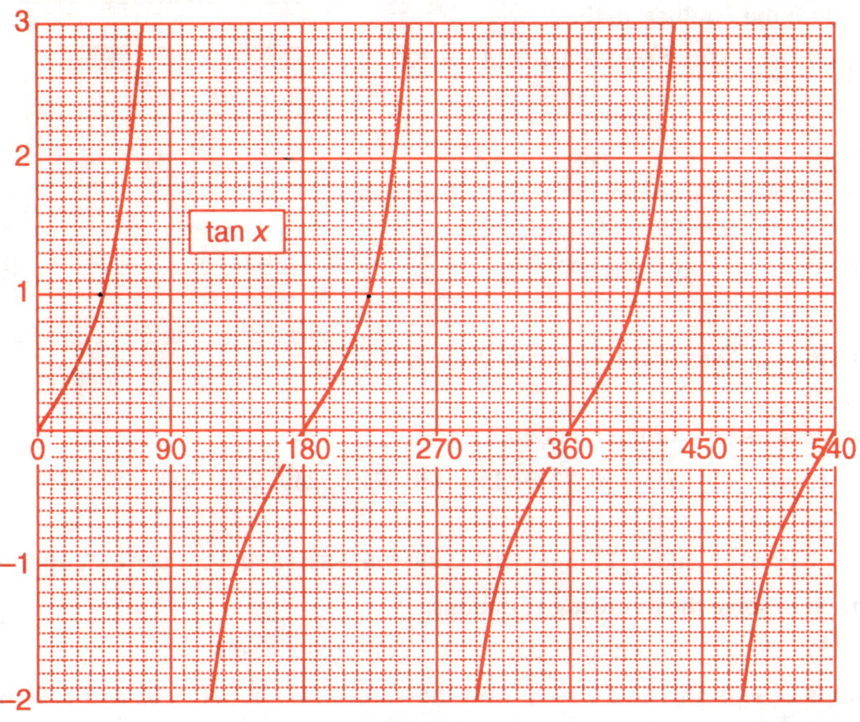

Fig 15.9

Notice that tan x is not defined for $x = 90°, 270°, 450°$ etc.

15.3.1 Example

Complete the table below for the function $y = \sin x + \cos x$.,and draw its graph.

x	0	30	60	90	120	150	180	210	240	270	300	330	360
y													

What is the greatest value of y?

Use the graph to solve the equation $\sin x + \cos x = -1.2$.

Solution Use a calculator to fill in the values:

x	0	30	60	90	120	150	180	210	240	270	300	330	360
y	1	1.37	1.37	1	.37	-.37	−1	−1.37	−1.37	−1	-.37	.37	1

The graph is shown below (Fig 15.10).

Read off the y-coordinate of the top value:

The greatest value for y is 1.4

There are two places for which $y = -1.2$. Read off the x values, to the nearest 10°:

$\sin x + \cos x = -1.2$ for $x = 260$ and $x = 190$

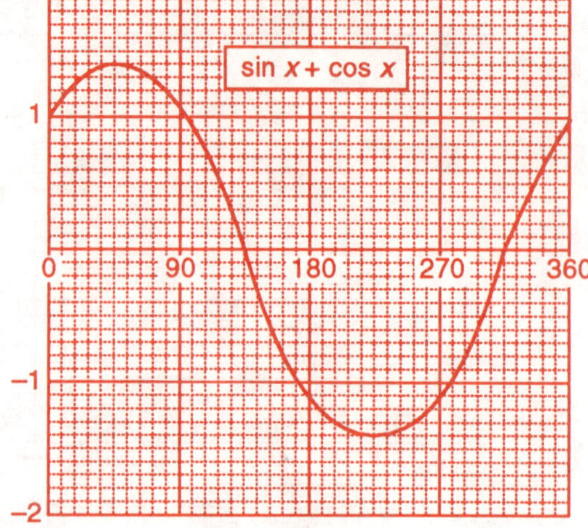

Fig 15.10

15.3.2 Exercises

1) Express the following in terms of ratios of angles under 360°:

 a) sin 500° b) cos 600°

 c) tan 700°

2) Express the ratios in Question 1 in terms of the ratios of acute angles.

3) Complete the table below for the function cos x:

x	0	30	60	90	120	150	180	210	240	270	300	330	360
cos x													

 Draw the graph of cos x, taking 1 cm per 60° along the x-axis and 2 cm per unit up the y-axis.

 Use your graph to solve the following equations:

 a) $\cos x = 0.5$ b) $\cos x = -0.5$ c) $\cos x = -0.6$

4) Use the graphs of Figs 15.7 and 15.8 to find the values of x between 0° and 360° which obey the following inequalities:

 a) $\cos x < 0$ b) $\sin x < 0$

 c) $\sin x > 0.5$ d) $\cos x < -0.5$.

5) Draw the graph of $y = 3 \sin x + 4 \cos x$, taking values from 0° to 360°.

 a) Find the maximum value of y.

 b) Solve the equation $3 \sin x + 4 \cos x = 2$.

6) Draw the graph of $y = \cos x - \sin x$, taking values from 0° to 360°.

 a) Find the maximum value of y.

 b) How is this graph related to the graph of Fig 15.10?

7) There is an upper limit to the size of angle that your calculator will work out. See if you can find this limit.

8) The Big Wheel at a funfair has radius 6 m. A customer starts from the bottom. The wheel rotates clockwise at 5° per second. After 7 minutes, how far below the centre of the wheel is the customer? How far is he to the left?

9) What is the line of symmetry for the graph of $y = \sin x$, for $0° < x < 180°$?

15.4. Longer exercise

The tides

Around the coasts of Britain the sea level rises and falls. This is caused by the attraction of the Moon. The level of the sea follows the pattern of a sin function.

The picture on the right shows a harbour wall. On a particular day, the depth of water is given by:

$$d = 6 + 4 \sin 30t$$

Here d is the depth in feet, and t is the time in hours after midnight.

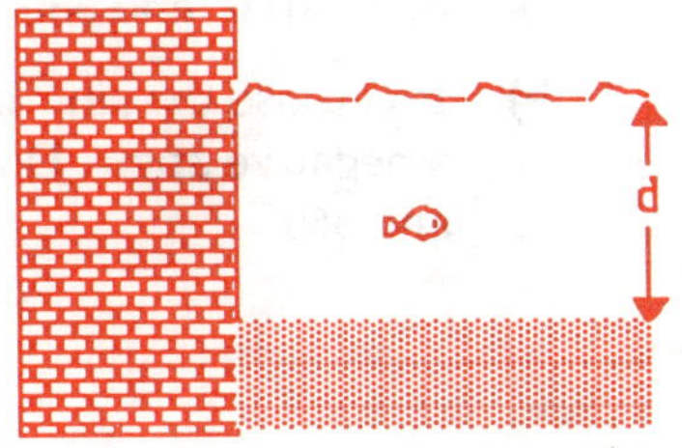

Fig 15.11

1) What is the depth at 2 a.m.? What is it at 7 a.m., at 4 p.m.?
2) When is high tide? (When water is deepest). What is the greatest depth?
3) When is low tide? What is the least depth?

The draught of a boat is the distance from the waterline to the bottom of the keel, i.e. it is the depth of water needed for it to float.

4) A boat has a draught of 5 feet. Can it come to the harbour wall at 8 a.m.? At 2 p.m.?
5) Another boat has a draught of 9 feet. Between which times can the boat dock at the harbour?

A more accurate formula for the depth might be:

$$d = 6 + 4 \sin 29t$$

6) Find the times of high tide for two successive days. Why are they different?

Multiple choice question *(Tick appropriate box)*

If $\sin x = -0.5$, with x between 0° and 360°, then x is:

a) 210° ☐

b) 30° or 150° ☐

c) 330° ☐

d) 210° or 330° ☐

e) 210° or -30° ☐

Points to note

1) *Negative values*

   Do not forget the minus signs, for example in the cos of an obtuse angle.

2) *Solving equations*

   a) When you are asked to solve a trig. equation, usually there will be two solutions between 0° and 360°.

   b) If you use the $\sin^{-1}$ or $\tan^{-1}$ buttons on your calculator for a negative value, you will get a negative angle. Don't give this as the answer if you are asked for solutions between 0° and 360°.

Chapter 16

Distances and angles

A pyramid has a base which is a rectangle of sides 7 m and 8 m. The height of the pyramid is 6 m.

If you want to run up to the top, what is the quickest route to take? What is the shallowest route?

Fig 16.1

16.1 Triangle problems

Finding the hypoteneuse

In the triangle shown, $\sin P° = \dfrac{a}{c}$ and $\cos P° = \dfrac{b}{c}$

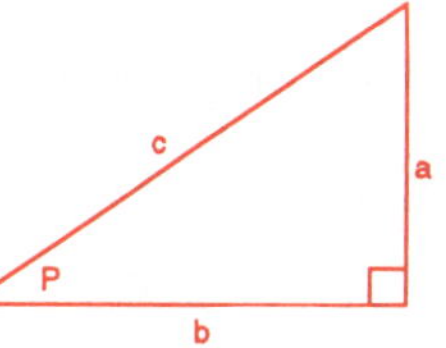

Fig 16.2

Suppose we know P and either a or b. Then c can be found from the equations:

$$c = \frac{a}{\sin P°} \text{ or } c = \frac{b}{\cos P°}$$

So to find the hypoteneuse we must divide by the ratio.

Isosceles triangles

Trigonometric ratios and Pythagoras' Theorem apply only to right-angled triangles. But if we are given an isosceles triangle, then we can convert it into two right-angled triangles by dropping a perpendicular as shown (Fig 16.3).

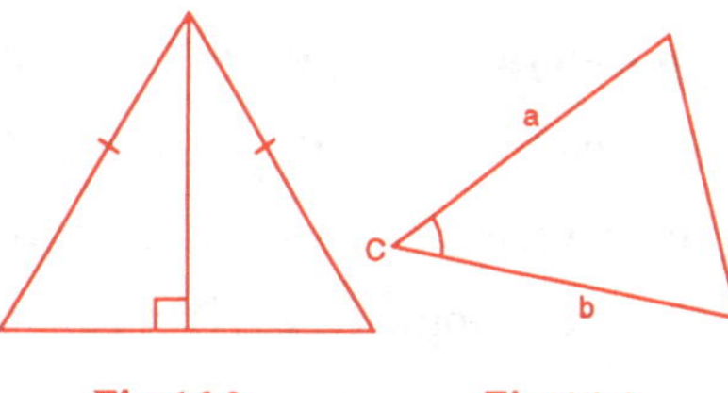

Fig 16.3 Fig 16.4

Area of triangles

Suppose a triangle has sides a and b, enclosing the angle $\hat{C}$ (Fig 16.4). Then its area is $\frac{1}{2}ab\sin\hat{C}$.

The base of the triangle is b, and its height is $a \times \sin\hat{C}$. Using the formula "half base times height" gives the result above.

16.1.1 Examples

1) In the triangle ABC of Fig 16.5, $\hat{B} = 90°$, $\hat{A} = 66°$, BC = 6 cm. Find BA.

Solution Applying the basic formula: $\tan 66° = \dfrac{6}{\text{BA}}$.

Multiply both sides by BA:

$\text{BA} \times \tan 66° = 6$

Now divide both sides by tan 66°:

$$\text{BA} = \frac{6}{\tan 66°} = \frac{6}{2.2460} = 2.67$$

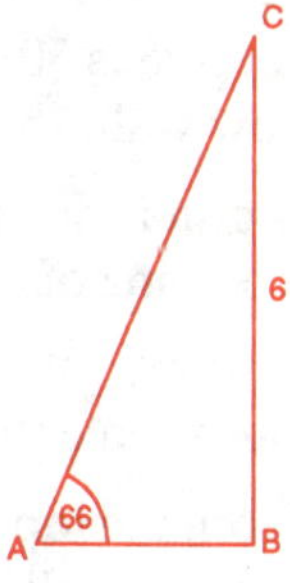

Fig 16.5

2) The legs of a pair of compasses are 3 inches long. The compasses are held vertically and used to draw a circle of radius 2 inches.

a) How high is the top of the compasses off the paper?

b) What is the angle between the legs of the compass?

Solution Drop a perpendicular from the top of the compasses. We now have two right-angled triangles.

a) The height can be found from Pythagoras:

Height $= \sqrt{3^2 - 1^2} = \sqrt{8} = 2.83$ **inches**

b) Use trigonometry in one of the triangles and then double the answer.

Angle $= 2 \times \sin^{-1}\frac{1}{3} = 38.9°$

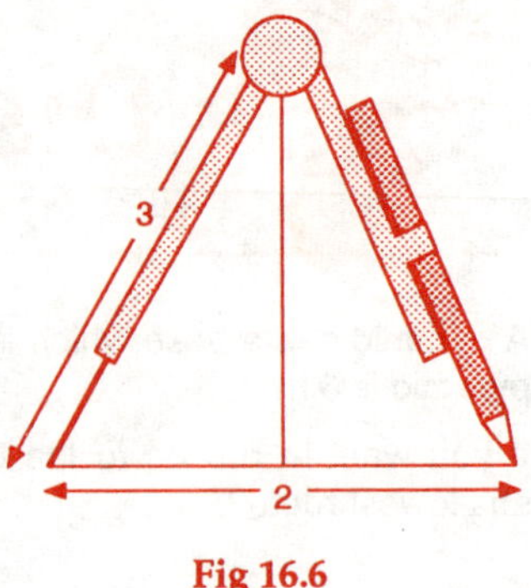

Fig 16.6

16.1.2 Exercises

1) Find the sides of the triangles shown in Fig 16.7.

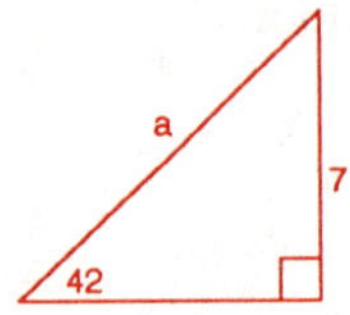

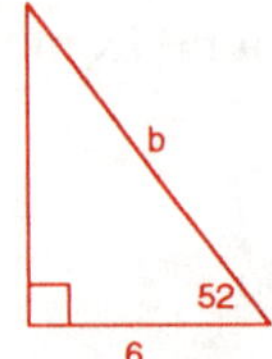

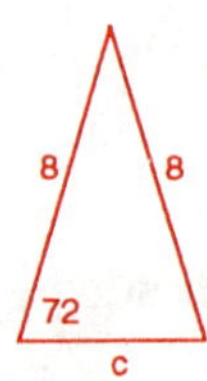

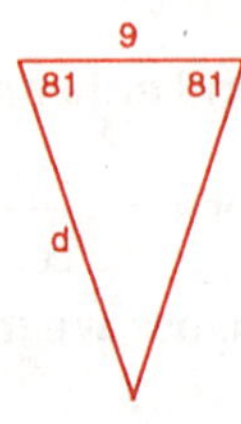

Fig 16.7

2) Find the angles of the triangles shown in Fig 16.8.

3) For the triangle ABC, BC = 3 and $\hat{B} = \hat{C} = 57°$. Find AB.

4) In triangle ABC, $\hat{A} = 90°$, AB = 8, $\hat{B} = 72°$. Find BC.

5) For the triangle XYZ, XY = XZ = 7, YZ = 4. Find $\hat{X}$.

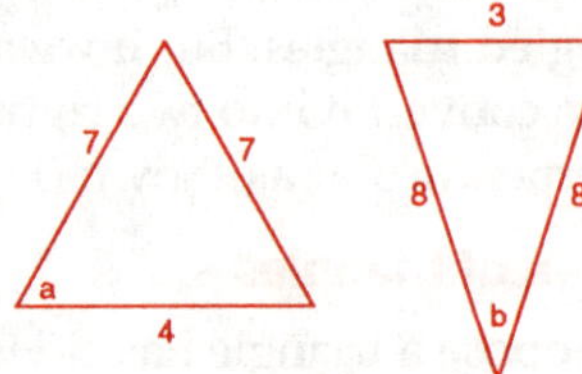

Fig 16.8

6) When the neck of a giraffe is at 20° to the vertical, it can reach leaves which are 4.5 m above the ground. Assuming that the shoulders of the giraffe are 2 metres high, how long is its neck?

7) In a circle of radius 12 cm a chord AB of length 7 cm is drawn. Find the distance of the chord from the centre of the circle. Find the angle which this chord subtends at the centre of the circle.

8) A spire is 50 metres high, and the angle of elevation is 15°. How far away am I from the base? If I now walk 150 m towards the spire, what is the new angle of elevation?

9) A gun is due South of its target. From an observation post 50 m due West of the gun, the target is on a bearing of 005°. Find the distance of the target from the gun.

10) Two men stand on opposite sides of a flagpole, which is 12 metres taller than they are. The angles of elevation of the top of the flagpole from the two men are 10° and 15°. How far apart are the men?

11) From the top of a 50 m cliff the angle of depression of a ship is 3°. How far away is the ship from the top of the cliff?

12) Find the areas of the triangles shown in Fig 16.9 on the next page.

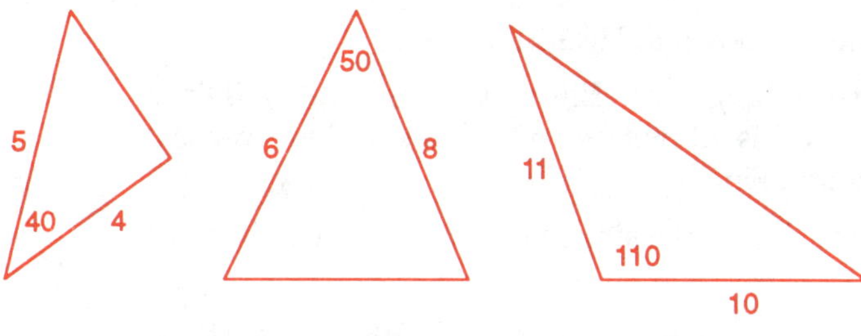

Fig 16.9

13) Inside a circle of radius 10 cm a regular octagon is drawn.
    a) Find the angle each side subtends at the centre.
    b) Find the area of the octagon.

16.2 Distances and angles within solids

So far all our problems have involved flat, two-dimensional triangles. But if we wish to find angles and distances in a three-dimensional figure, then we can still do so using two-dimensional trigonometry and Pythagoras.

It is essential to have a good picture for a solid object. Then we can see where the right-angles in the object are. It is often a good idea to make a separate drawing of the section of the solid which we want to deal with.

16.2.1 Examples

1) A room ABCDEFGH is a cuboid, 2.5 m high, 4 m long, 3 m wide. What is the length of the "space diagonal" AG? What angle does this line make with the horizontal?

Solution Make separate diagrams of the base rectangle ABCD and the triangle AGC.

The diagonal of the floor, AC, has length given by:

$AC^2 = 3^2 + 4^2$

$AC = \sqrt{9+16} = \sqrt{25} = 5.$

In the triangle AGC, $A\hat{C}G$ is a right angle. This gives:

$AG^2 = AC^2 + CG^2$

$AG = \sqrt{25+6.25} = \sqrt{31.25} = 5.59$ metre

For the angle, trigonometry gives:

$$G\hat{A}C = \tan^{-1}\frac{2.5}{5} = 26.6°$$

AG makes 26.6° with the horizontal

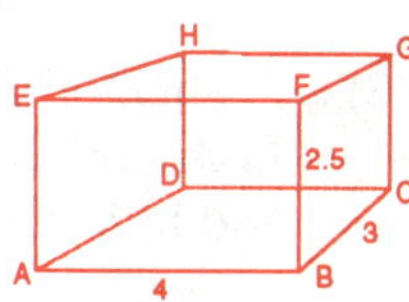

Fig 16.10

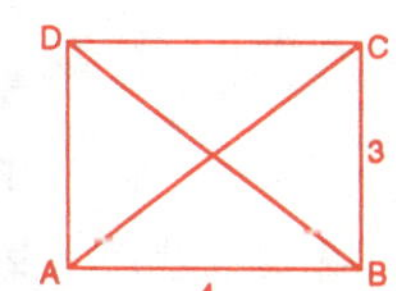

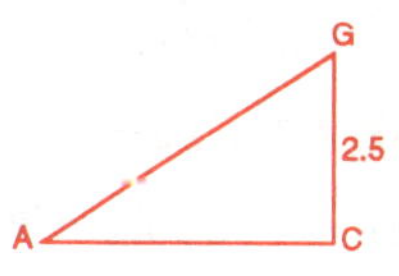

Fig 16.11

2) A section of a hillside is shown in Fig 16.12.

ABEF is a horizontal rectangle; AB, EF and CD are horizontal lines of length 50 metres. BE is 12 metres and FD and CE are vertical lines of length 5 metres. Find:

a) BC b) BD c) The slope of BC d) The slope of BD.

Solution Make separate diagrams of Δ BEC, ΔBCD and ΔBFD. BCE is a right-angled triangle. This gives:

$BC^2 = BE^2 + EC^2$

BC = √169 = 13

BCD is a right-angled triangle. This gives:

$BD^2 = CD^2 + BC^2$

BD = $\sqrt{2500 + 169}$ = $\sqrt{2669}$ = 52 metres

Using trigonometry in triangle BCE, tan $C\hat{B}E = \frac{5}{12}$

BC makes $\tan^{-1}\frac{5}{12}$ = 22.6° with the horizontal

Using trigonometry in triangle BDF:

$\sin D\hat{B}F = \frac{5}{BD}$

BD makes $\sin^{-1}\frac{5}{52}$ = 6^0 with the horizontal

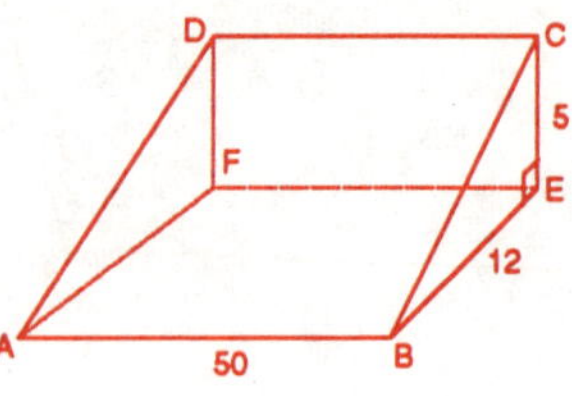

Fig 16.12

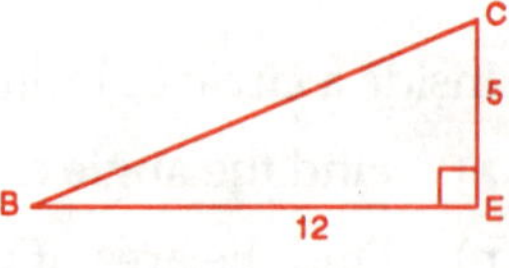

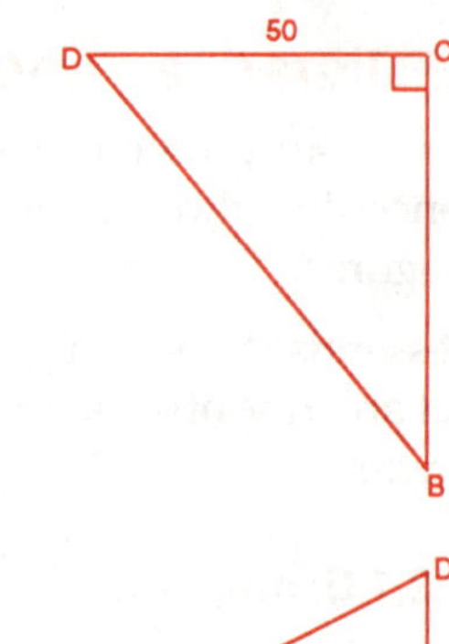

Fig 16.13

3) A stick of chocolate is shaped as a triangular prism 20 cm long. Each end is an equilateral triangle of side 2 cm. Find its volume and its surface area.

Solution Use the formula $\frac{1}{2}ab\sin\hat{C}$ for the area of a triangle.

Area of end triangle = $\frac{1}{2} \times 2 \times 2 \times \sin 60° = 1.732\ cm^2$.

Multiply this by the length of the stick.

Volume = 20 × 1.732 = 34.6 cm³

The surface area consists of the two ends and the three sides.

Area = 2 × 1.732 + 3 × 20 × 2 = 123.5 cm²

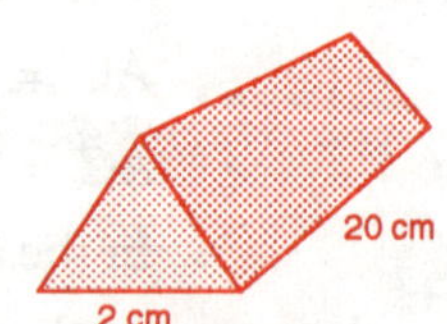

Fig 16.14

16.2.2 Exercises

1) A cuboid ABCDEFGH is shown in Fig 16.15.

Find the diagonal FD and the angles $F\hat{D}B$, $E\hat{H}B$, $F\hat{D}C$.

2) A wedge ABCDEF is shown in Fig 16.16. Find the lengths AF, AC, AE and the angles $A\hat{C}E$, $B\hat{C}A$.

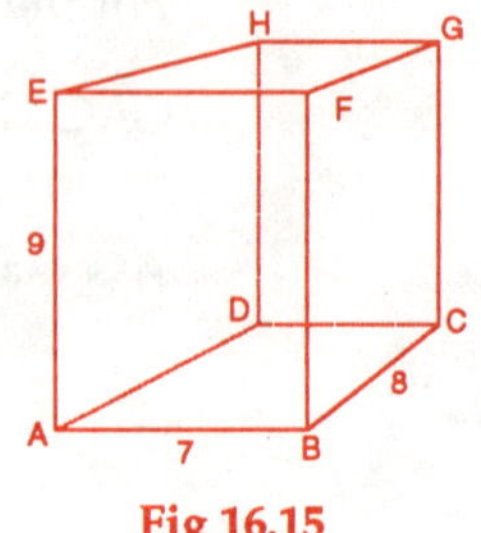

Fig 16.15

3) In Fig 16.17 the pyramid VABCD has a square base ABCD of side 4 cm. VA = VB = VC = VD = 6 cm. Find AC, and the height of V above the plane ABCD. Find the angles VÂC and VÂD.

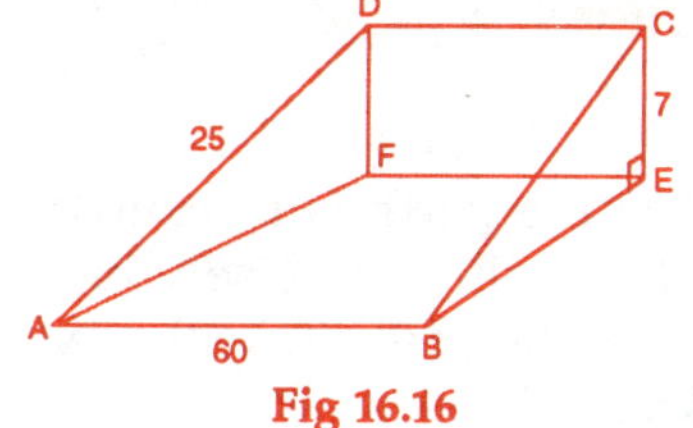

Fig 16.16

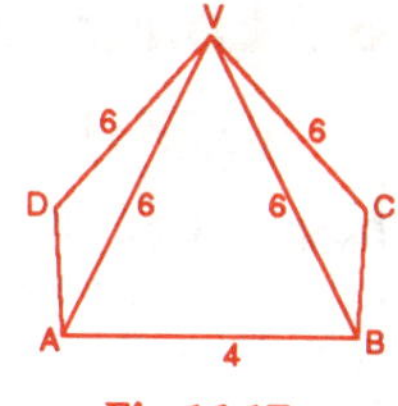

Fig 16.17

4) A prism is of height 10 cm and its cross-section is an equilateral triangle of side 3 cm. (Fig 16.18). Find the length AE. Find the angle BÂE.

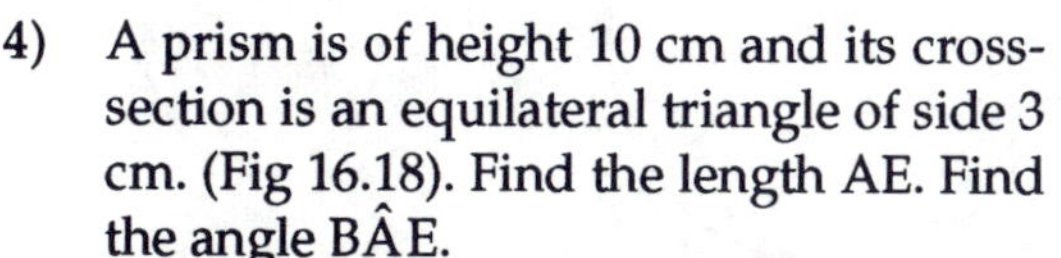

5) A cardboard carton is a cuboid with sides 2 ft, 1.5 ft, 2.5 ft. Find the length of the longest stick which can be put in the carton. Find the angles that the stick now makes with the faces of the carton.

6) In Fig 16.19 the pyramid VABCD is on a square base ABCD of side 100 metres, and V is 50 metres above the ground. Find:

a) The diagonal AC of the base.

b) The length of VA.

c) The distance from V to the midpoint X of AB.

d) The angle VÂC.

e) The inclination of VX to the horizontal.

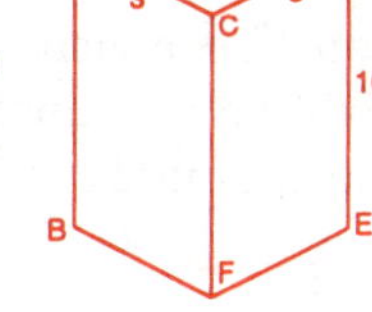

Fig 16.18

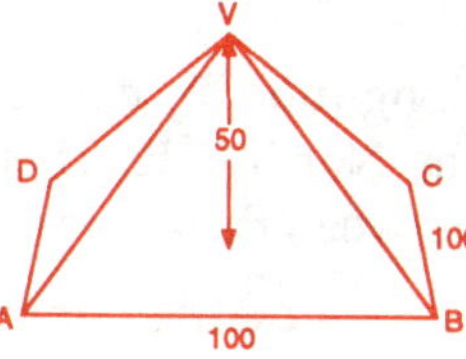

Fig 16.19

7) In Fig 16.20 ABCD is a regular tetrahedron, with all edges 8 cm. It is placed with BCD horizontal, so that A is vertically above the centre O of triangle BCD. X is the midpoint of BD. Find:

a) AX and XC.

b) The angle AX̂C.

c) XO and OC.

d) The angle AĈO.

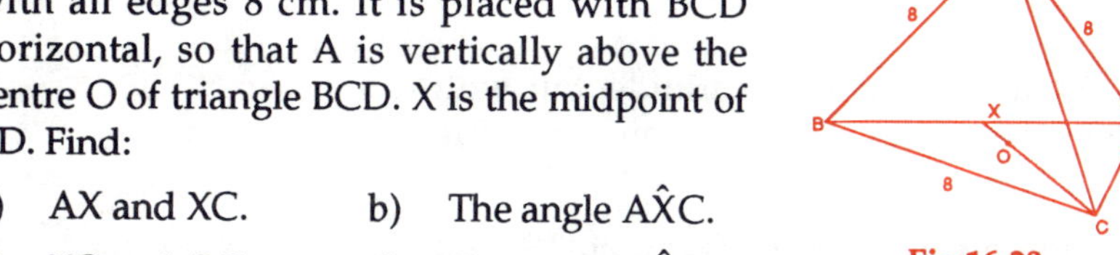

Fig 16.20

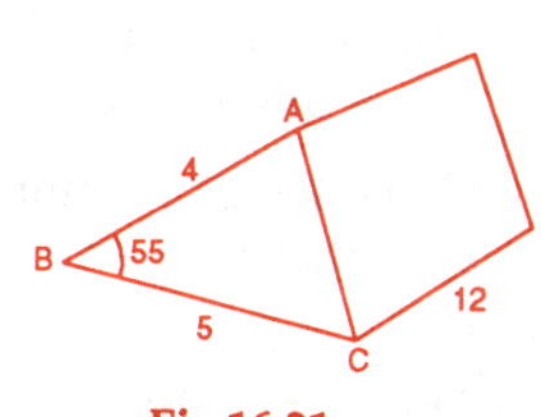

Fig 16.21

8) The prism of Fig 16.21 is 12 cm long, and its cross section is a triangle ABC with AB = 4 cm, BC = 5 cm, AB̂C = 55°. Find the area of∆ ABC and hence find the volume of the prism.

9) A prism is 10 cm long, and its cross section is an isosceles triangle with sides of length 7 cm, 7 cm, 8 cm. Find the area of the triangle, and hence find the volume of the prism.

10) The summit of a mountain is 3 km North and 1 km East of me, and is 600 m higher than me. Find the distance of the summit and its angle of elevation.

11) In the situation of Question 10, if I walk North until the angle of elevation is 20°, how far North will I have walked?

12) From the top of a 200 m cliff a boat is 1 km South and 300 m West. Find the distance of the boat and its angle of depression.

13) If the boat of Question 12 sails East until the angle of depression is 11°, how far will it have sailed?

14) The base ABCD of a pyramid is a rectangle of sides 6 and 8. The apex V is 5 m above the centre of ABCD. Show that AV̂C = 90°.

15) The problem at the beginning of the chapter was about a pyramid. Find the angles of slope of the edges and the faces.

16.3 Longer exercise

Latitude and longitude

The position of points on the Earth is measured by Latitude and Longitude. In this exercise you find distances between points on the Earth. Take the radius of the Earth to be 6,400 km.

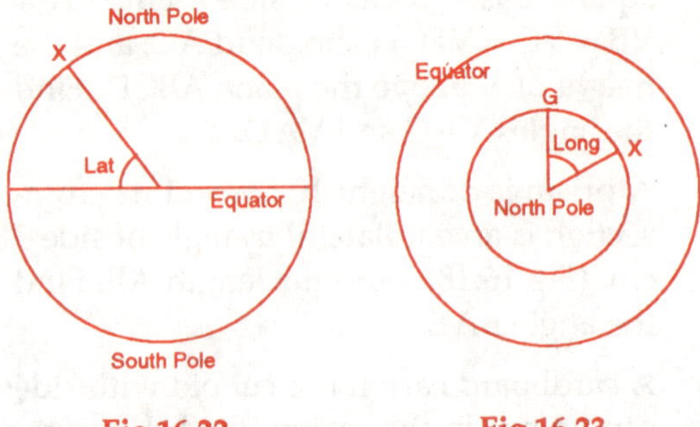

Fig 16.22 Fig 16.23

Latitude. Take a line from the centre of the Earth to a point X on its surface. This line makes an angle with the plane through the Equator. This angle is the Latitude of X. In particular, the Equator itself is at 0° Latitude.

Longitude. By convention, Greenwich is at 0° Longitude. Imagine looking down at the Earth from above the North Pole. There will be two lines from the North Pole, to Greenwich and to point X. The angle between these lines is the Longitude of X.

Points on the same longitude.

1) Suppose point A is at 10° Latitude, and point B at 70°. Both are on the same Longitude. To go from A to B one sails or flies due North. How many degrees of Latitude do you pass through? What fraction of the Earth's circumference is this? How far is it from A to B?

Points on the same latitude.

2) Consider the circle of Latitude 60° North. What is its radius? What is its circumference?

3) Consider two points C and D on this circle of Latitude, but with Longitudes 0° and 40°. How far is it from C to D if one sails due East?

   This is not the quickest way to go from C to D. (Why not? Think about a plane which flies from London to Tokyo, and almost goes over the North Pole). The quickest way is along a Great Circle, which is a circle whose centre is the centre of the Earth.

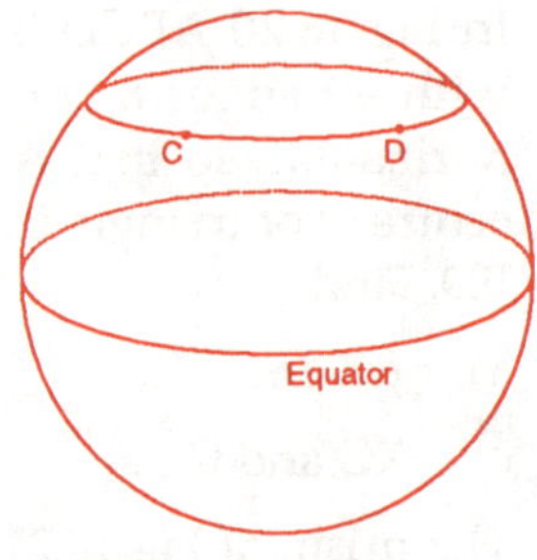

Fig 16.24

4) Find the straight line distance between C and D. (Tunnelling through the Earth.) Letting O be the centre of the Earth, find the angle $C\hat{O}D$. Hence find the Great Circle distance between C and D. Compare with your answer to (3).

5) To find the shortest distance between two general points on the Earth's surface is very hard. Try if you like to find the distance between E at Latitude 0° and Longitude 0°, and F at Latitude 30° and Longitude 80°.

Multiple choice question *(Tick appropriate box)*

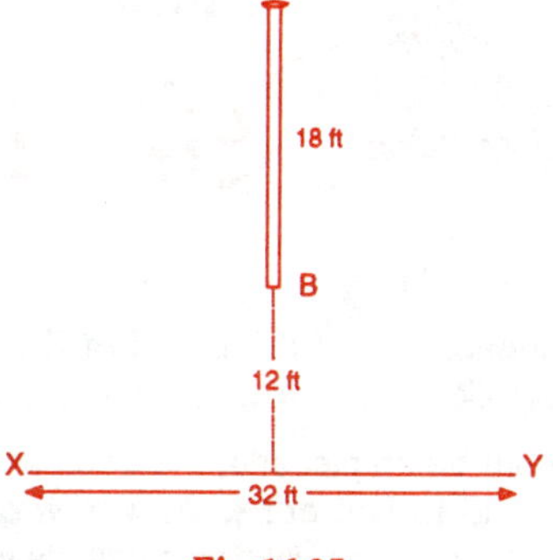

Fig 16.25

The base B of a 18 ft flagpole is 12 ft from the line XY. XY is 32 ft in length, and BX = BY. The angle of elevation of the top of the flagpole from X is:

a) 64° ☐

b) 42° ☐

c) 28° ☐

d) 60° ☐

e) 31° ☐

Points to note

1) *Finding the hypoteneuse*

   Suppose in a triangle $\hat{A} = 90°$, $\hat{B} = 30°$, AC = 4 To find the hypoteneuse BC you must divide AC by sin 30°.

   The hypoteneuse is the longest side of a triangle. In this case BC = 8. If you obtain BC = 2 then you have multiplied by sin 30°.

2) *Isosceles triangles*

   Pythagoras and trigonometry only work in right-angled triangles. If you have an isosceles triangle then cut it in half before doing any calculations.

3) *Diagrams*

   A picture of a three-dimensional object can be very confusing. Make sure that you do not think a triangle is right-angled when it is not, or miss a triangle which is right-angled. It is often a good idea to make a separate two-dimensional picture of the triangle you are using.

4) *Labelling*

   Once you have found a right-angled triangle in your diagram, make sure that you have labelled the sides correctly, as Hypoteneuse, Opposite, Adjacent. This is often necessary in three-dimensional diagrams.

Chapter 17
Similarity and congruence

The inhabitants of the island of Delos, in the Aegean Sea, built an altar to the god Apollo. The altar was in the shape of a cube.

Far from being pleased, the god sent plagues and famines. The Delians went to an oracle to find out what was wrong, and were told that the god was angry because the altar was too small. Its volume should be doubled.

They rebuilt the altar, doubling each side. But the plagues and famines continued.

What was the new volume of the altar, compared with the original volume? What should each side be multiplied by, in order to double the volume exactly?

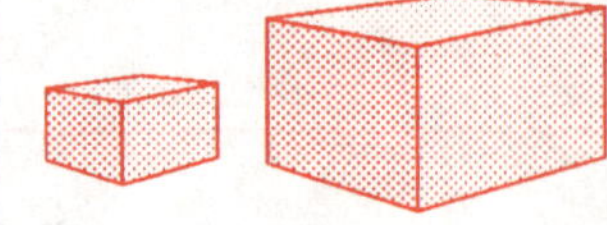

Fig 17.1

17.1 Ratios of sides, areas and volumes

Two figures are similar if they have the same shape. (But not necessarily the same size).

Similar figures have the same angles. There is a fixed ratio between the sides of the two figures. In particular, suppose the figures are two triangles ABC and DEF.

The ratio between the sides of Δ ABC and the sides of Δ DEF is constant, as below.

$$\frac{AB}{DE} = \frac{BC}{EF} = \frac{AC}{DF}$$

The ratio of sides is the same for both triangles.

$$\frac{AB}{BC} = \frac{DE}{EF}, \frac{AB}{AC} = \frac{DE}{DF}, \frac{AC}{BC} = \frac{DF}{EF}$$

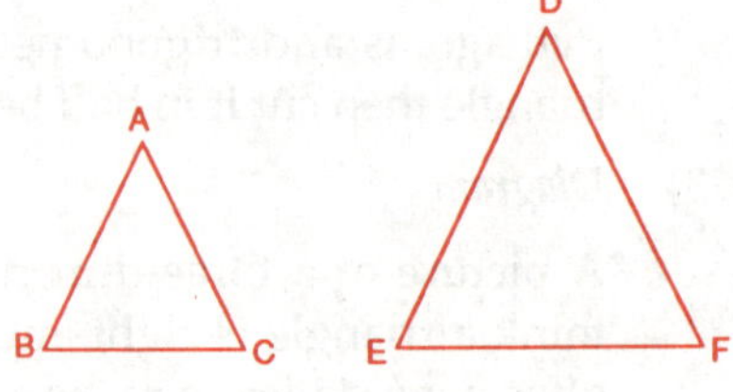

Fig 17.2

Ratio of areas

Suppose that two triangles T and T′ are similar, and the sides of T are twice the sides of T′. Then the base and the height of T are twice the base and the height of T′. Hence the area of T is $2 \times 2 = 4$ times the area of T′.

In general, suppose S and S′ are similar, with the sides of S being k times the sides of S′. Then the area of S is k^2 times the area of S′.

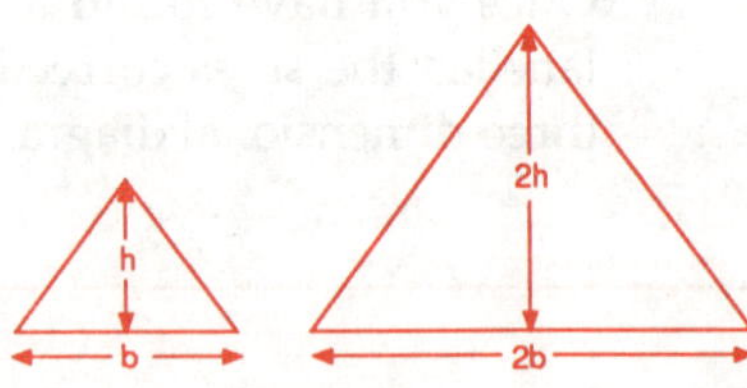

Fig 17.3

Ratio of volume

This principle applies to volumes. Suppose a cuboid is L by m by n. If its sides are now doubled, then it is $2L$ by $2m$ by $2n$. Its volume is $8Lmn$, which is 2^3 times the original volume.

In general, if lengths are in the ratio a: b, then the corresponding areas are in the ratio a^2: b^2, and the corresponding volumes are in the ratio a^3:b^3.

Area and volume units

Be careful with area and volume units. There are 100 centimetres in a metre. Hence there are 100^2 = 10,000 square centimetres in a square metre. Similarly there are 100^3 = 1,000,000 cubic centimetres in a cubic metre.

17.1.1 Examples

1) L and M are on the sides AB and AC of the triangle ABC. AL = 2, LB = 4, AM = 3, MC = 6. Find the ratio LM:BC. If ΔABC has area 27, what is the area of the quadrilateral BLMC?

Solution AB = 6 and AC = 9.

The triangles ABC and ALM have $\hat{A}$ in common.

The ratio AL:AM = 2:3 and the ratio AB:AC = 2:3.

Hence ΔABC is similar to Δ ALM. It follows that:

LM:BC = AM:AC = 1:3

The sides of ΔABC are 3 times the sides of ΔALM. Hence the area of Δ ABC is $3^2 = 9$ times the area of ΔALM.

It follows that the area of Δ ALM is 27 ÷ 9 = 3.

The area of BLMC is 27 – 3 = 24

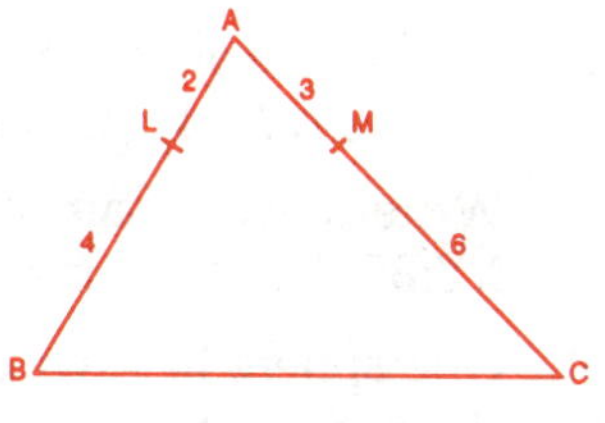

Fig 17.4

2) A model of a statue is in the scale 1:10. If the model is 200 cm^3 in volume, what is the volume of the real statue?

Solution The height, the length and the width of the real statue are each 10 times as big as in the model. Hence the volume of the original statue is 10 × 10 × 10 times as big as the model's volume.

Real volume = $10^3 \times 200 = 200{,}000$ cm^3

3) The scale of a map is 1:10,000. On a map the area of a lake is 50 cm^2. What is the area of the real lake, in m^2?

Solution The scale given is the ratio of lengths. Square this to get the ratio of areas. Multiply 50 by this area ratio.

Area of lake = $50 \times 10{,}000^2 = 5 \times 10^9$ cm^2.

There are 100 cm in a m, so there are 100^2 cm^2 in a m^2. Divide by 100^2.

The area of the lake is 500,000 m^2

17.1.2 Exercises

1) In Fig 17.5 overleaf, which triangles are similar?

2) X and Y are on the sides AB and AC of ΔABC, such that AX:XB and AY:YC are both equal to 1:3 (See Fig 17.6). Find the ratio XY:BC. If ΔABC has area 32, find the areas of ΔAXY and XYCB.

3) ABCD is a parallelogram, and E lies on AB so that AE:EB = 1:2. ED and AC meet at F (See Fig 17.7). Find a pair of similar triangles. What is the ratio of their areas?

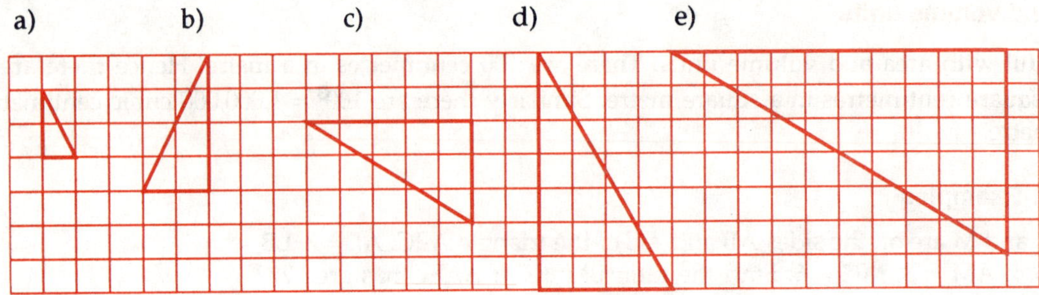

Fig 17.5

4) X and Y lie on the sides AB and AC of Δ ABC. AX = 2, XB = 3, AY = 4, YC = 6.

Write down a pair of similar triangles. Find the ratio XY:BC. If Δ AXY has area 8, find the area of XYCB.

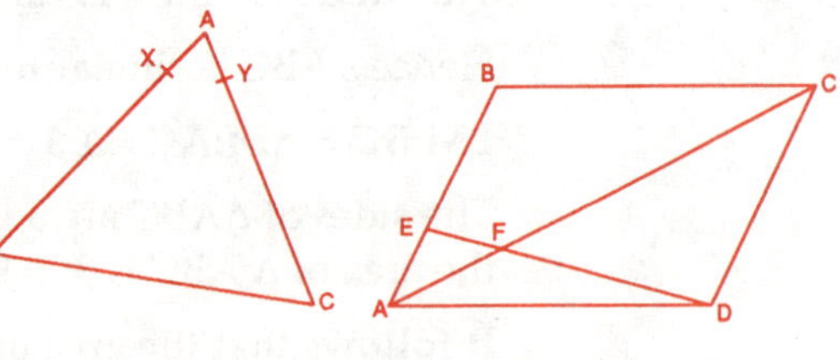

Fig 17.6 Fig 17.7

5) One sphere has twice the radius of another. What is the ratio of their surface areas? What is the ratio of their volumes?

6) An architect's model of a house is in the scale 1:10. If the living-room is 600 m^3, what is the volume of the model of the living-room?

7) A model of a boat is in the scale 1:20. If the model has volume 0.5 m^3, what is the volume of the boat?

8) A photograph is enlarged in the ratio 2:3. If sky occupies 10 cm^2 of the original photo, how much area does it occupy in the enlargement?

9) A model plane is in the scale 1:50.

a) The model is 8 cm long. How long is the plane in m?

b) The area of the wings is 10 m^2. What is the area of the wings of the model, in cm^2?

c) The volume of the fuselage of the model is 80 cm^3. What is the volume of the real fuselage, in m^3?

10) A model locomotive is in the scale 1:80.

a) The locomotive is 16 metres long. How long is the model?

b) The front of the model is 20 cm^2 in area. What is the area of the front of the real locomotive, in m^2?

c) The locomotive weighs 80 tonnes. Assuming that the model is made out of exactly the same materials as the real locomotive, what is the weight of the model, in kg?

11) A child has a model of Superman. The model is 10 cm high, while Superman is 2 metres high.

a) What is the scale of the model?

b) Superman's vest is 0.8 m^2 in area. What is the area of the vest on the model, in cm^2?

c) The model has ten fingers. How many fingers does Superman have?

12) In the problem at the beginning of the chapter there were two similar cubes. What is the ratio of their volumes? We want the volume ratio to be 1:2. If the length ratio is 1:x, write down an equation in x and solve it.

17.2 Congruent triangles

Two figures are congruent if they have the same size as well as the same shape. Congruence is a stronger condition than similarity. If figures are congruent, then they are similar.

If one plane figure is congruent to another, it could be cut out and placed exactly on top of the other.

If ΔABC is congruent to Δ DEF, then we write Δ ABC ≡ ΔDEF. The order of letters is important: from the congruency it follows that $\hat{A} = \hat{D}$ etc., BC = EF etc.

Conditions for congruence

It is not necessary to check that all the angles and all the sides are equal. Two triangles are congruent when they obey any of the following sets of conditions.

SSS The sides of one triangle are equal to the sides of the other triangle (See Fig 17.8). AB = DE, BC = EF, CA = FD.

ASA Two angles and the enclosed side of one triangle are equal to two angles and the enclosed side of the other triangle (See Fig 17.9). $\hat{A} = \hat{D}$, $\hat{B} = \hat{E}$, AB = DE.

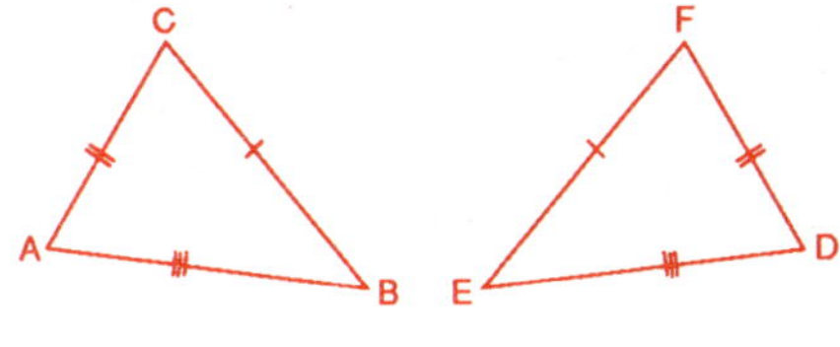

Fig 17.8

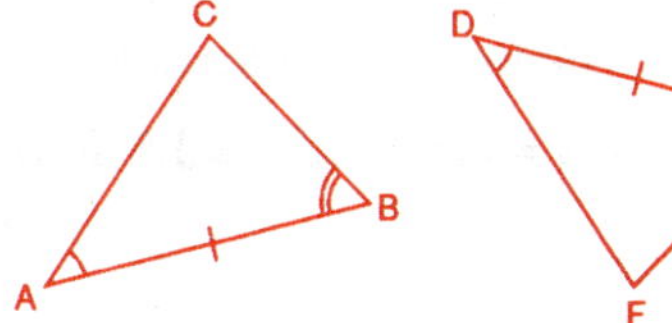

Fig 17.9

SAS Two sides and the enclosed angle of one triangle are equal to two sides and the enclosed angle of the other triangle (See Fig 17.10). $\hat{B} = \hat{E}$, AB = DE, BC = EF.

RHS Both triangles are right-angled, with the hypoteneuse and one other side of one triangle equal to the hypoteneuse and one other side of the other triangle (See Fig 17.11). $\hat{B} = \hat{E} = 90°$, CA = FD, BC = EF.

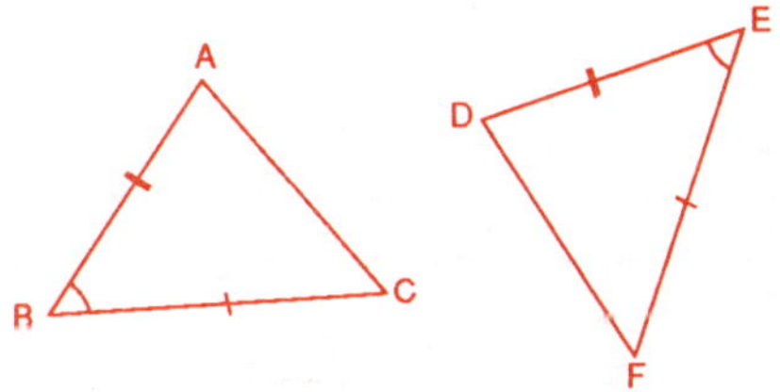

Fig 17.10

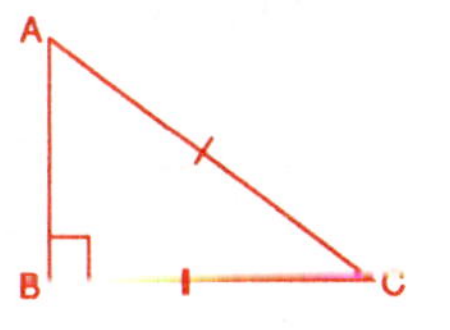

D
F
E

Fig 17.11

17.2.1 Examples

1) In the diagram ABCD is a kite, with AB = AD and CB = CD. The diagonals AC and BD cut at right-angles at E. Write down 3 pairs of congruent triangles, showing which conditions have been used.

Solution The sides of ACD are equal to those of ACB.

Δ ACD ≡ Δ ACB (SSS)

AED and AEB are both right-angled. They have their hypoteneuses equal and AE is common to both.

Δ AED ≡ Δ AEB (RHS)

The same argument applies to CED and CEB.

Δ CED ≡ Δ CEB (RHS)

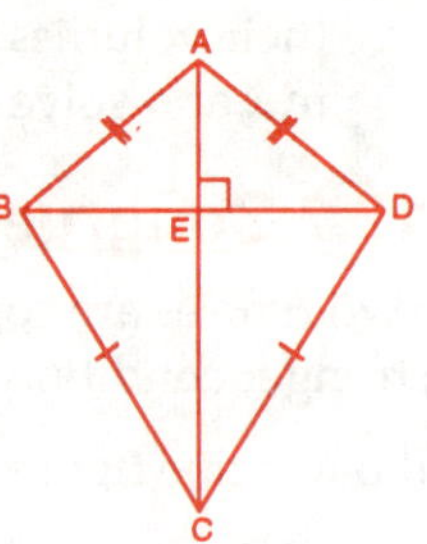

Fig 17.12

2) ABC is an equilateral triangle. L, M, and N are points on AB, BC, CA respectively such that AL = BM = CN. Show that Δ LMN is also equilateral.

Solution Consider the three triangles ALN, BML, CNM.

The angles $\hat{A}$, $\hat{B}$, $\hat{C}$ are equal to 60°.

AL, BM and CN are equal to each other, so AN, CM, and BL are also equal to each other.

The three triangles are congruent, by SAS. It follows that:

LN = NM = ML. Δ LMN is equilateral.

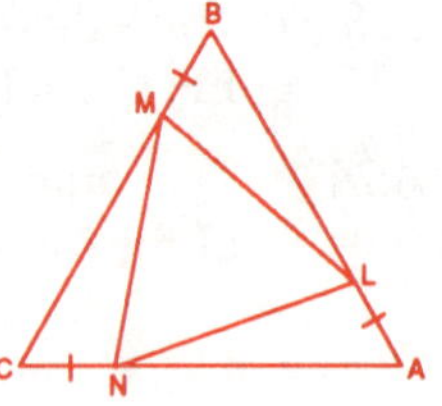

Fig 17.13

17.2.2 Exercises

1) Which of the following pairs of triangles are congruent?

a) 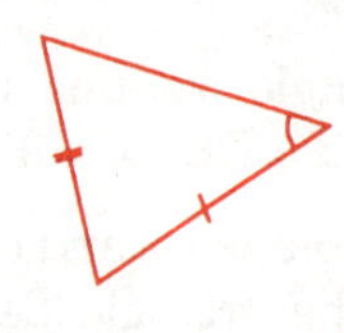

b) 

c) 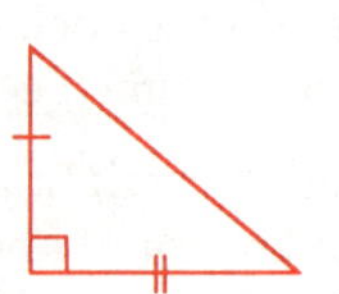 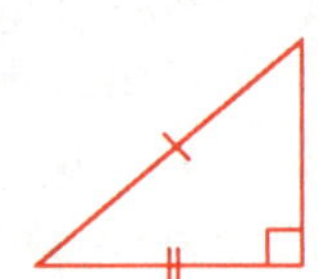

Fig 17.14

2) In the diagram below, which triangles are congruent?

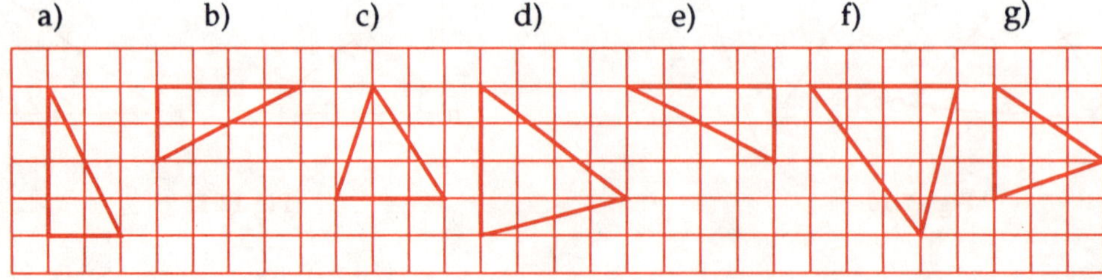

Fig 17.15

3) ABD and CBE are straight lines meeting at B (Fig 17.16). CB = BD and AB = BE. Find two congruent triangles. What condition have you used?

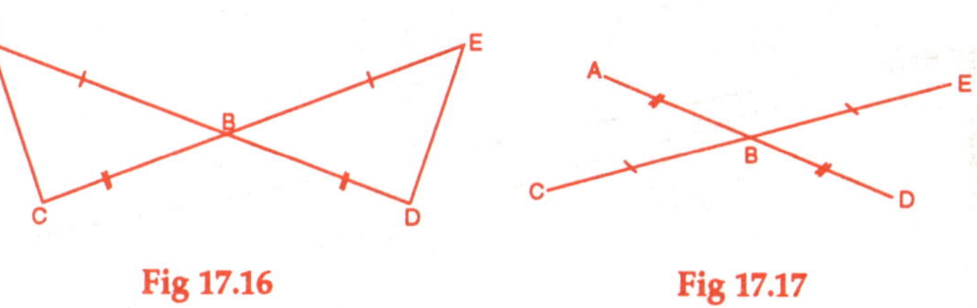

Fig 17.16

Fig 17.17

4) ABD and CBE are straight lines meeting at B (Fig 17.17). CB = BE and AB = BD. Find two pairs of congruent triangles. What condition have you used?

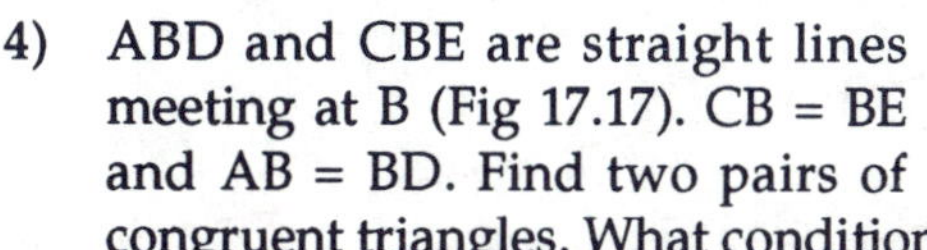

5) PQ and SR are equal and parallel lines. PR and SQ cross at X, as in Fig 17.18. Find two congruent triangles. What condition have you used?

6) ABCD is a parallelogram. The diagonals AC and BD meet at X. Write down as many pairs of congruent triangles as you can.

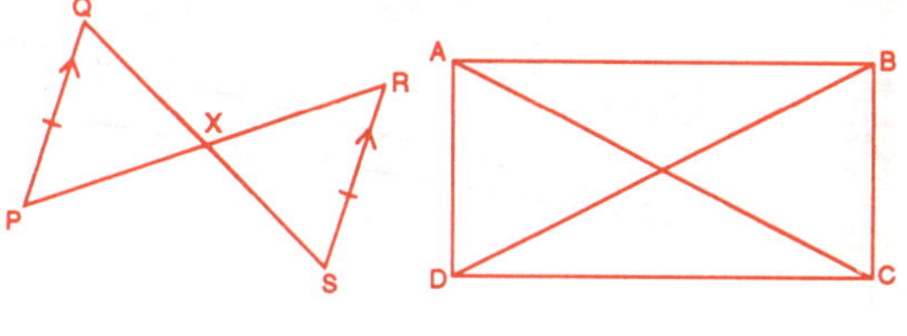

Fig 17.18

Fig 17.19

7) ABCD is a rectangle (see Fig 17.19). Show that the triangles ABC and BAD are congruent. Deduce that the diagonals AC and BD are equal.

8) ABCD is a rhombus. Let the diagonals AC and BD meet at X. Show that Δ ABX is congruent to ΔADX. Deduce that AC and BD are perpendicular.

9) ABCDE is a regular pentagon. X and Y are on BC and CD respectively, and CX = CY. Show that ΔABX ≡ ΔEDY. Deduce that AX = EY.

10) In Fig 17.20 ACDE and BCFG are squares on the equal sides of the isosceles triangle ABC. Show that AG = BE.

11) M is the midpoint of the side BC of Δ ABC (Fig 17.21). AM is extended to N, where AM = MN. Show that ABNC is a parallelogram.

12) ABCDE... are adjacent points of a regular 17 sided figure. Show that ΔABD ≡ Δ BCE.

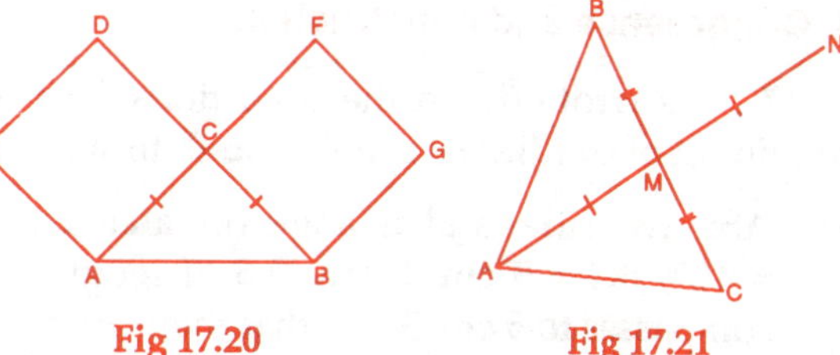

Fig 17.20

Fig 17.21

17.3 Longer exercises

A. Jacob's staff

Jacob's Staff is an old instrument for surveying. It consists of a rod of length about 3 or 4 feet. There is a cross-piece RS of width about 3 inches. The cross-piece can be moved up and down the rod, between marks which are a distance apart of RS.

R
P
S

Fig 17.22

It is used as follows. Suppose we want to find the width of an inaccessible object XY. Align the staff so that PRX and PSY are straight lines (See Fig 17.23). Now move the cross-piece one notch closer to P, and walk forwards until PRX and PSY are again straight lines. The distance you have walked will be the length of XY.

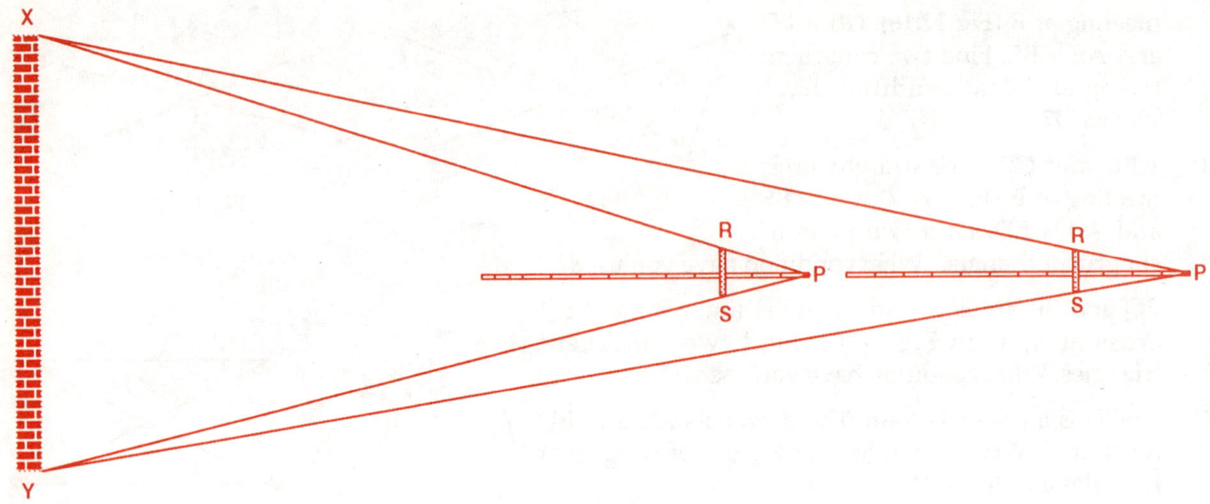

Fig 17.23

1) Make a Jacob's Staff out of stiff cardboard or wood. Use it to measure the width of various objects. Are your results accurate?

2) See if you can show why the method works. Say P is originally x from XY, and say you walk forwards y. Use similar triangles to find two equations in x and y. When you eliminate x you should find that y = XY.

B. Congruence and construction

In 17.2 we wrote down the conditions for congruence of two triangles. How could we show that a certain set of conditions is not enough to show congruence?

1) ASS (two sides and an angle not included) is not a condition for congruence. Suppose AB = 6 cm, $\hat{A}$ = 40°, BC = 5 cm. Draw AB of length 6 cm, construct an angle of 40° at A, and stretch your compasses to 5 cm. Show that there are two possible triangles satisfying the conditions given.

2) Suppose that AB = 7 cm, $\hat{A}$ = 40°, BC = 8 cm. Show that there is only one triangle satisfying the conditions given.

3) What is the difference between (1) and (2)? Can you say when conditions ASS will give us a unique triangle?

The situation with quadrilaterals is more complicated.

4) Is SSSS a condition for congruence for quadrilaterals? i.e., if we know the four sides of a quadrilateral, can we construct it uniquely?

5) What about AAAS?

6) Find some conditions for congruence for quadrilaterals.

Multiple choice question *(Tick appropriate box)*

X and Y lie on the sides AB and AC of ΔABC, dividing the sides AB and AC in the ratio 1:2. If Δ ABC has area 36, then BXYC has area:

a) 24 ☐

b) 32 ☐

c) 288 ☐

d) 27 ☐

e) 4 ☐

Points to note

1) *Similarity*

   a) If you are told that ΔABC is similar to Δ DEF, then the triangles are similar in that order. So $\hat{A} = \hat{D}$ etc..

   b) If you are told that L is on AB, with AL:LB = 1:3, then the ratio AL:AB is 1:4. Do not think that AL:AB is also 1:3.

   c) If two triangles are similar, in the ratio $1:k$, then the ratio of the areas is not $1:k$, it is $1:k^2$. In general, if the length ratio is $a:b$, then the area ratio is $a^2:b^2$ and the volume ratio is $a^3:b^3$.

   d) Be careful with area and volume units. There are 100 centimetres in a metre, but 100^2 = 10,000 cm^2 in a m^2. There are 100^3 = 1,000,000 cm^3 in a m^3.

2) *Congruence*

   a) If ΔABC is congruent to Δ DEF, then the triangles are congruent in that order. So $\hat{A} = \hat{D}$ etc., AB = DE etc.

   b) When you show that two triangles are congruent by ASA, then the equal sides must be inbetween the equal angles.

   c) When you show that two triangles are congruent by SAS, then the equal angle must be inbetween the sides. SSA, (two sides and an angle not enclosed), is not a condition for congruence.

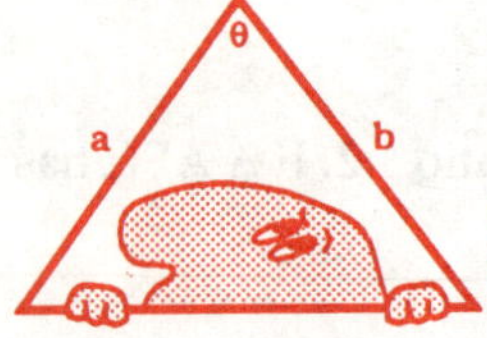

Chapter 18
Solution of triangles

The triangle shown is right-angled at C. By Pythagoras, $a^2 + b^2 = c^2$.

Suppose *a* and *b* are kept constant, and *c* is changed. For what sort of triangle is $a^2 + b^2 > c^2$? When is $a^2 + b^2 < c^2$?

What is the greatest possible value of c^2, and what is the least possible value? For what values of C are these achieved?

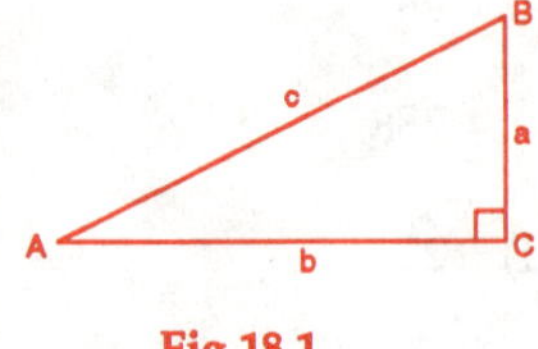

Fig 18.1

18.1 The sine rule

The sine rule and the cosine rule extend trigonometry to triangles which are not necessarily right-angled.

If we know one side and the three angles of a triangle, then the triangle can be constructed and the other sides measured. There is also a way to calculate the other sides of the triangle.

When labelling the sides and angles of the triangle ABC, the convention is that each side is labelled with the same letter as the opposite angle. So side c is opposite Ĉ etc.

Fig 18.2

Sine rule for angles

The sine rule is:

$$\frac{\sin\hat{A}}{a} = \frac{\sin\hat{B}}{b} = \frac{\sin\hat{C}}{c}$$

This form of the rule is used when we want to find the angles of a triangle.

Sine rule for sides

The rule can be written the other way up:

$$\frac{a}{\sin\hat{A}} = \frac{b}{\sin\hat{B}} = \frac{c}{\sin\hat{C}}$$

This form of the rule is used when we want to find the sides of a triangle.

18.1.1 Examples

1) In Fig 18.3, $\hat{Q} = 68°$, PQ = 4 and PR = 5. Find $\hat{R}$.

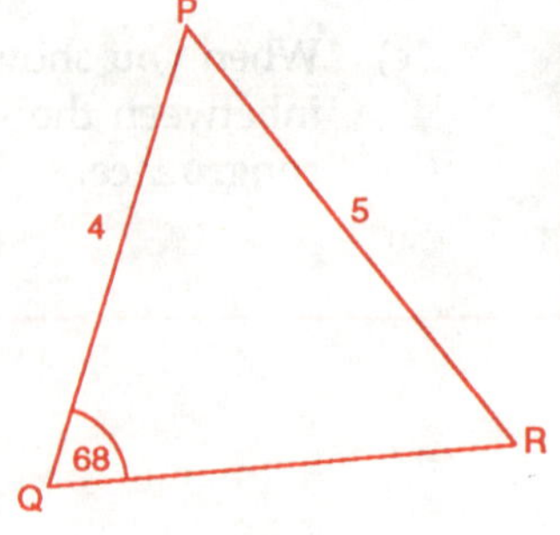

Fig 18.3

Solution The first version of the sine rule is used.

$$\frac{\sin\hat{R}}{4} = \frac{\sin 68°}{5}$$

Multiply across to obtain:

$\sin \hat{R} = \sin 68° \times \frac{4}{5}$

$\hat{R} = \sin^{-1}0.7417 = 48°$

2) Two men are 250 m apart. One is North of a tower, and one is South. They measure the angles of elevation of the top of the tower as 5° and 7°. Find the height of the tower.

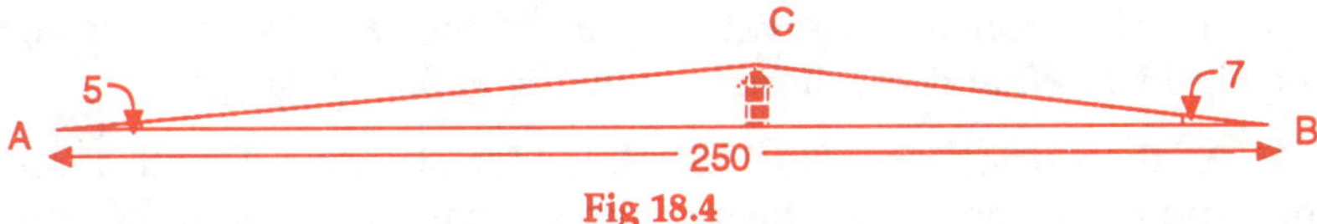

Fig 18.4

Solution Let C be the top of the tower, and A and B the two men. AB = 250, $\hat{C} = 180° - 5° - 7° = 168°$.

Use of the sine rule gives:

$$AC = \sin 7° \times \frac{250}{\sin 168°} = 146.5 \text{ metres}$$

Trigonometry now gives:

Height = AC × sin 5° = 13 metres

18.1.2 Exercises

1) Find the unknown sides in the following triangles:

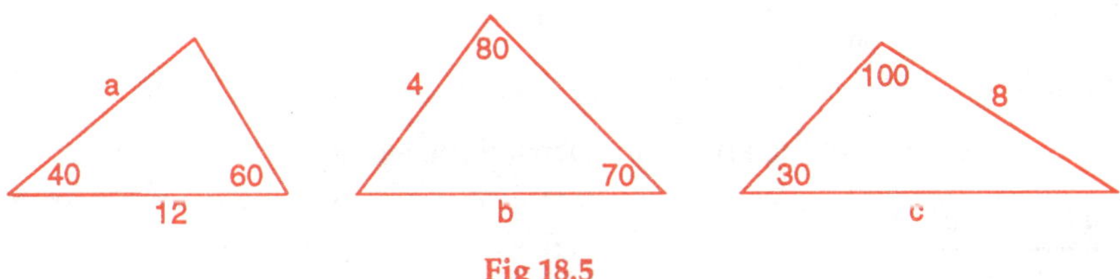

Fig 18.5

2) Find the unknown angles in the following triangles:

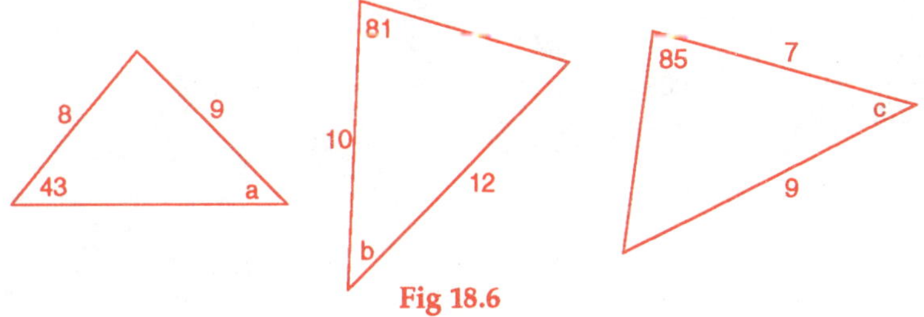

Fig 18.6

3) In the triangle ABC, $\hat{A} = 23°$, $\hat{B} = 68°$, AB = 5.6. Find the sides AC and CB.

4) In the triangle DEF, DE = 10, EF = 13, $\hat{D} = 62°$. Find the angles $\hat{F}$ and $\hat{E}$.

5) I measure the angle of elevation of a tree as 15°. I then walk 10 metres towards the tree, and the angle of elevation is now 23° (See Fig 18.7). Find my distance from the top of the tree, and hence find the height of the tree.

6) From a gun emplacement, the bearing of its target is 053°. From an observation point 30 metres west of the gun, the bearing of the target is 054° (See Fig 18.8). What is the distance from the gun to its target?

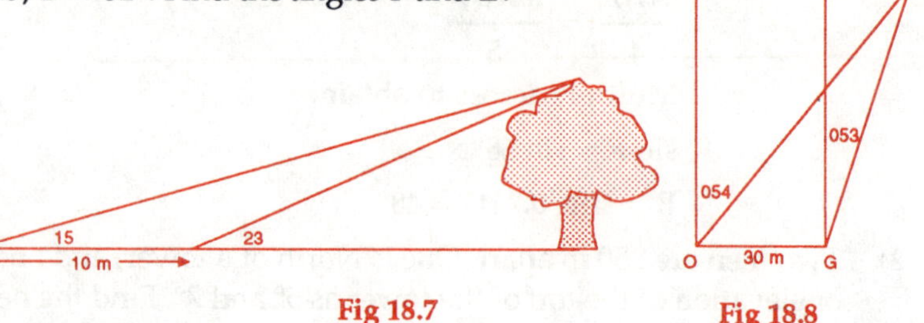

Fig 18.7

Fig 18.8

7) A wall leans at 15° to the vertical (See Fig 18.9). A ladder of length 2 metres is placed so that one end of the ladder is 1 metre from the base of the wall. What angle is the ladder leaning at? How far up the wall does the ladder reach?

8) Ship A leaves from port C at a bearing of 123°. Ship B leaves from port D, 200 miles south of C, on a bearing of 046°. How far from C do their paths cross?

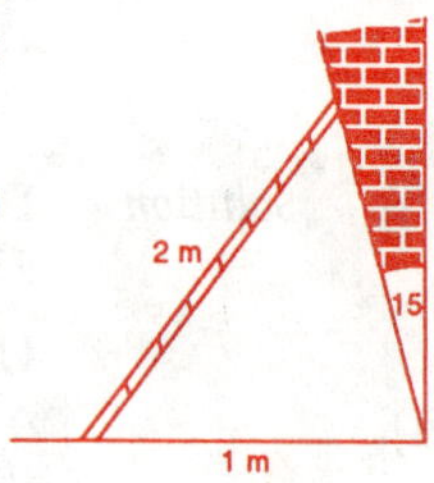

Fig 18.9

18.2 The cosine rule

Cosine rule to find sides

The cosine rule is:

$$c^2 = a^2 + b^2 - 2ab\cos\hat{C}\ .$$

This rule gives a side in terms of the other sides and the opposite angle.

The rule has been written so that c^2 is the subject. It could just as well be written in either of the two following forms:

$$a^2 = b^2 + c^2 - 2bc\cos\hat{A} \qquad b^2 = c^2 + a^2 - 2ca\cos\hat{B}$$

Cos rule to find angles

The rule can be re-arranged to give the angles in terms of the sides.

$$\cos\hat{C} = \frac{a^2 + b^2 - c^2}{2ab}$$

The rule has been written to make $\cos\hat{C}$ the subject. It could just as well be written in either of the two following forms:

$$\cos\hat{A} = \frac{b^2 + c^2 - a^2}{2bc} \qquad \cos\hat{B} = \frac{c^2 + a^2 - b^2}{2ca}$$

18.2.1 Examples

1) In the triangle PQR, PQ = 5, QR = 6.3, RP = 7.4. Find $\hat{P}$.

Solution The cosine rule gives, on putting $\hat{C} = \hat{P}$, $c = 6.3$, $a = 5$, $b = 7.4$:

$$\cos\hat{P} = \frac{5^2 + 7.4^2 - 6.3^2}{2 \times 5 \times 7.4}$$

$$\cos P = 0.5415$$

$$\hat{P} = 57.2°$$

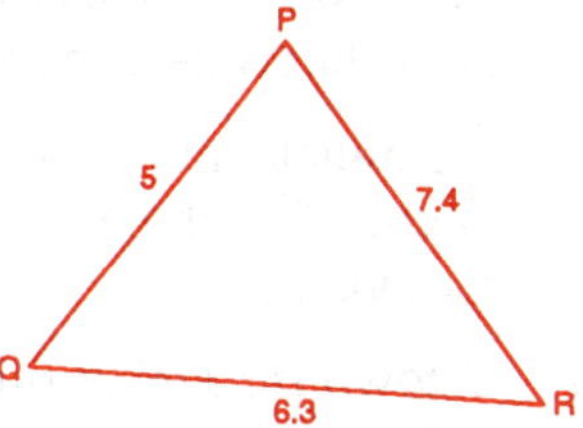

Fig 18.10

2) The hour hand of a clock is 15 cm long, and the minute hand is 20 cm long. How far apart are the tips of the hands at five o'clock?

Solution At five o'clock the angle between the hands is $360 \times \frac{5}{12} = 150°$.

Let d be the distance between the tips. Use the cosine rule:

$$d^2 = 15^2 + 20^2 - 2 \times 15 \times 20 \times \cos 150°$$

$$\mathbf{d = 33.8\ cm}$$

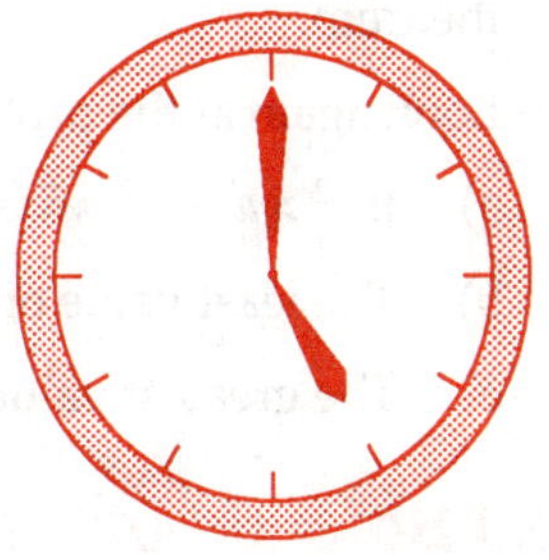

Fig 18.11

18.2.2 Exercises

1) Find the unknown sides in the following triangles.

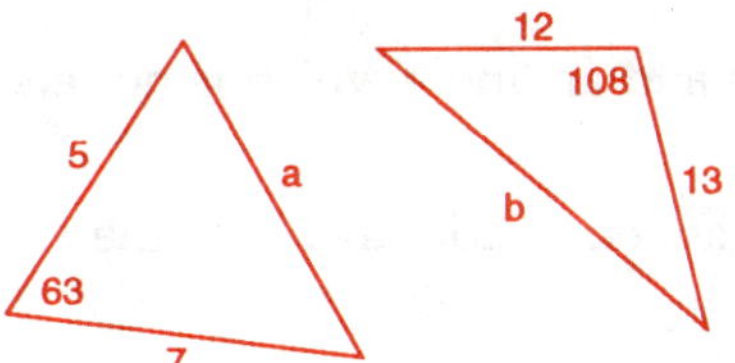

Fig 18.12

2) Find the unknown angles in the following triangles.

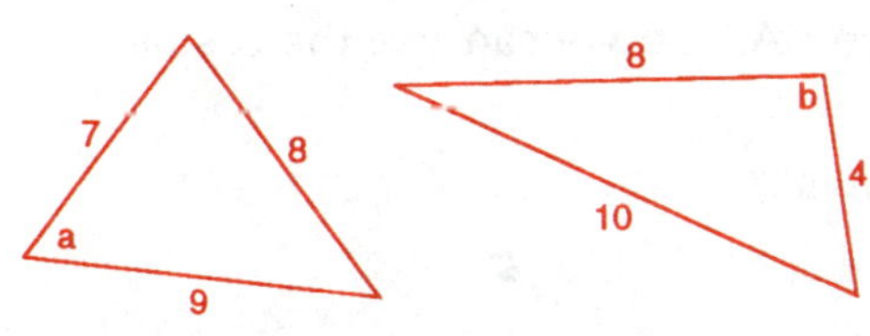

Fig 18.13

3) In triangle ABC, AB = 17, BC = 23, $A\hat{B}C = 43°$. Find AC.

4) In triangle DEF, DE = 45, EF = 52, DF = 27. Find $\hat{E}$.

5) A pilot flies his plane for 50 miles, then turns through 20° and flies a further 73 miles. How far is he from home?

Fig 18.14

6) The lower jaw of a crocodile is 58 cm, and the upper jaw is 52 cm. It can open its jaws to an angle of 43°. What is the greatest width of object it can grasp in its jaws?

7) A parallelogram has sides of length 12 and 7 cm, and the longer diagonal is 15 cm. Find the angles of the parallelogram. Find the length of the shorter diagonal.

8) Aytown is 50 miles due north of Beetown; Ceetown is 27 miles from Aytown and 33 miles from Beetown, and is west of them (See Fig 18.15). Find the bearings of Ceetown from Aytown and from Beetown.

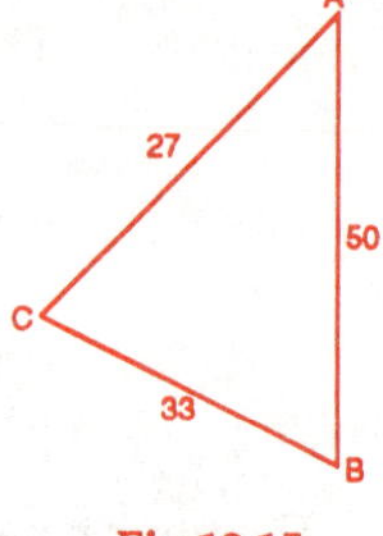

Fig 18.15

9) Show that if we put C = 90° in the cosine rule, we obtain Pythagoras' theorem.

10) Look again at the problem at the beginning of the chapter.

   a) If $c^2 > a^2 + b^2$, what does the cosine rule give for cos $\hat{C}$? What sort of angle is $\hat{C}$?

   b) The least value of $\hat{C}$ is 0°. Find cos 0°. What does the cosine rule give for c?

   c) The greatest value of $\hat{C}$ is 180°. Find cos 180°. What does the cosine rule give for c?

18.3 Solution of triangles

It is often hard to decide which rule to use when solving a triangle.

SSS. If you have the three sides of a triangle, then use the cosine rule to find the angles.

SAS. If you have two sides of a triangle and the enclosed angle, then use the cosine rule to find the third side.

SSA. If you have two sides of a triangle and an angle which is not enclosed, then use the sine rule to find the other angles.

ASA. If you have the angles of a triangle and a side, then use the sine rule to find the other sides.

Sometimes we have to use the rules more than once to solve a triangle.

18.3.1 Example

In the triangle ABC, AB = 8, BC = 7, $\hat{B}$ = 40°. Find $\hat{A}$

Solution Note that we have condition SAS. So we can use the cosine rule to obtain AC.

$$AC^2 = 8^2 + 7^2 - 2 \times 8 \times 7 \times \cos 40°$$

$$AC = 5.216$$

We now have three sides and one angle of the triangle. We have the conditions SSS and SSA. Using the sine rule:

$$\frac{\sin \hat{A}}{7} = \frac{\sin 40°}{5.216}$$

$$\hat{A} = 59.6°$$

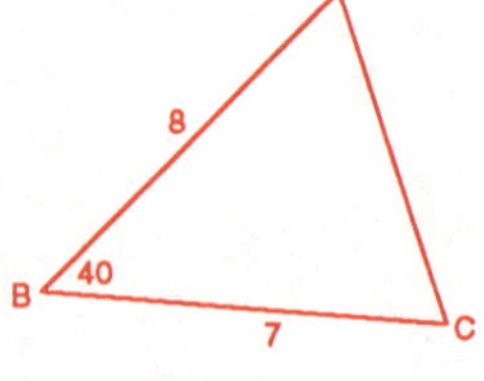

Fig 18.16

18.3.2 Exercises

1) Find the unknown sides of the following triangles.

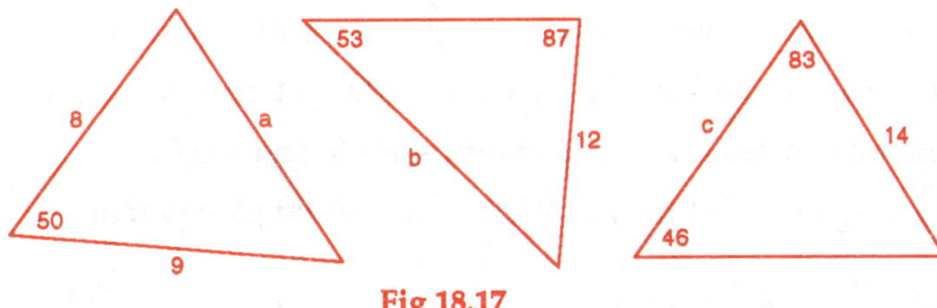

Fig 18.17

2) Find the unknown angles of the following triangles.

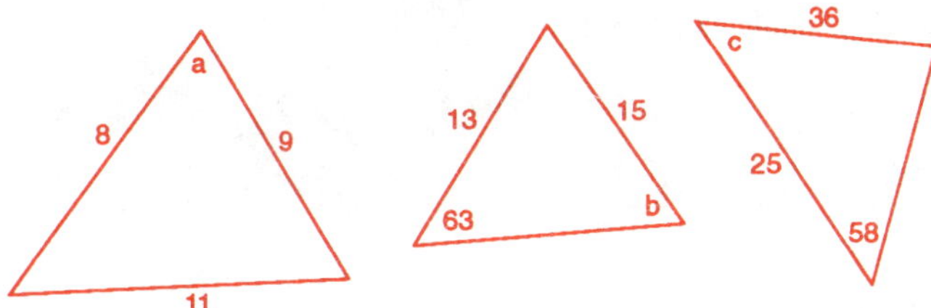

Fig 18.18

3) In triangle ABC, AB = 4.5, BC = 5.3, $\hat{B}$ = 39°. Find $\hat{A}$
4) In triangle XYZ,$\hat{Y}$= 59°, YZ = 11, XY = 12. Find $\hat{Z}$.
5) In triangle PQR, PQ = 17, PR = 23, $\hat{Q}$ = 48°. Find $\hat{R}$, $\hat{P}$ and QR.
6) In triangle LMN, LN = 4, $\hat{L}$ = 125°, MN = 4.5. Find $\hat{M}$, $\hat{N}$ and LM.
7) From a mountain top, A is 18 miles away due North. B is 27 miles away on a bearing of 063°. What is the bearing of B from A?
8) A 15 ft rod AB is held at 30° to the horizontal, with A on the ground (Fig 18.19). It breaks at $\frac{1}{3}$ of its length from A, so that the longer part rotates until B hits the ground. What is now the distance of A from B?

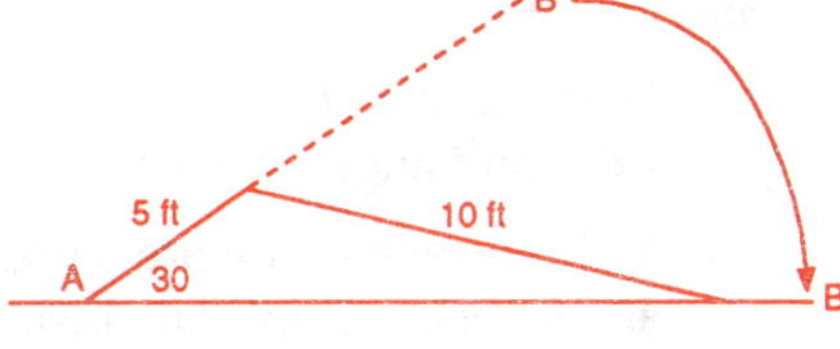

Fig 18.19

18.4 Longer exercise

Proof of the sin and cos rules

In Sections 1 and 2 of this Chapter the sin and cos rules were stated. In this exercise you prove them.

The sin rule

1) In the triangle ABC, drop a perpendicular from A to BC as shown. What is AD in terms of *c* and$\hat{B}$?
2) What is AD in terms of *b* and $\hat{C}$?
3) Equate your answers to (1) and (2), to eliminate AD.

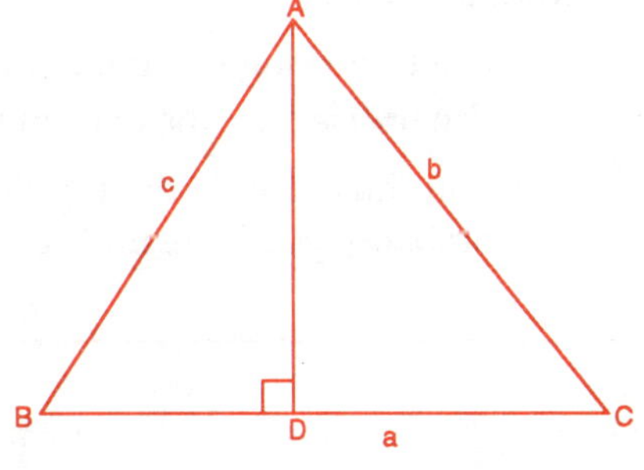

Fig 18.20

4) Re-arrange your answer to (3) to obtain part of the sin rule. Can you obtain the complete rule?

The cos rule

5) Using the same diagram as above, write an expression for BD in terms of c and cos $\hat{B}$.
6) Use Pythagoras in ΔABD, to find an expression for AD^2 in terms of c and cos B.
7) By subtraction, find an expression for CD in terms of a, c and cos B.
8) Now use Pythagoras again, this time in ΔADC. This should give you an expression for b^2 in terms of a, c and cos $\hat{B}$.
9) Re-arrange your answer to (8), until the cos rule is obtained

Multiple choice question *(Tick appropriate box)*

In ΔABC, A = 48°, AB = 0.3, AC = 0.4. Then $\hat{B}$ is:

a) 9.26° ☐

b) 48.2° ☐

c) 82.2° ☐

d) 135° ☐

e) 83.8° ☐

Points to note

1) *Sine and cosine rules*

a) When using either the sine rule or the cosine rule, be sure that you have labelled the sides and angles correctly. Side a is opposite angle $\hat{A}$, b is opposite $\hat{B}$, c is opposite $\hat{C}$.

b) Make sure that you are using the correct rule. Do not mistake the SAS condition for SSA, and so use the sine rule instead of the cosine rule.

2) *Use of calculator*

Calculator errors are easy to make, especially when using the cosine rule for finding an angle from the sides.

a) After working out the top line of the cosine formula, be sure to press the [=] button. Otherwise only the a^2 term will be divided by $2bc$.

b) You must divide the top line by the terms b and c. If your answer is bigger than 1 then probably you have multiplied.

Chapter 19
Vectors

> A river is flowing at 1 m/sec. You can swim at 2 m/sec. You wish to reach a point directly opposite, but if you swim straight across you will be swept downstream. Where should you aim for so that you do reach the point opposite?

Fig 19.1

19.1 Algebra of vectors

Translation

A vector can be thought of as a translation or displacement, of a certain distance in a certain direction.

To show that a quantity is a vector it is printed in bold type or underlined, as **a** or a̲.

If the displacement is of x units in the x-direction, and y units in the y-direction, then it is written as $\binom{x}{y}$.

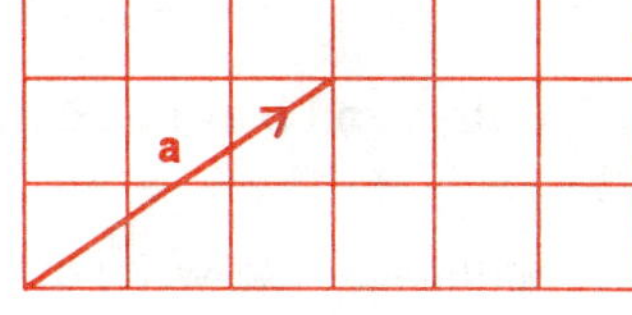

Fig 19.2

In Fig 19.2 the vector labelled **a** is $\binom{3}{2}$.

Modulus

The magnitude or modulus of a vector is its length. The magnitude of **v** is written $|\mathbf{v}|$. This can be found by Pythagoras:

$$\left|\begin{pmatrix} x \\ y \end{pmatrix}\right| = \sqrt{x^2 + y^2}. \text{ So } \left|\begin{pmatrix} 3 \\ 2 \end{pmatrix}\right| = \sqrt{13}$$

Vectors have size and direction. But they do not have position. A vector will be the same wherever it starts from. In the diagram **a** is the same as **b**.

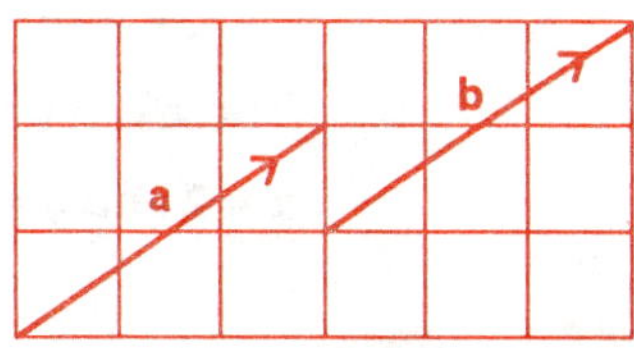

Fig 19.3

Adding and subtracting vectors

v + **u** is obtained by joining the tail of **u** to the head of **v**. Vectors can also be added by adding the coordinates. Vectors can be multiplied by ordinary numbers.

$$\begin{pmatrix} x \\ y \end{pmatrix} + \begin{pmatrix} p \\ q \end{pmatrix} = \begin{pmatrix} x+p \\ y+q \end{pmatrix}; \qquad n \times \begin{pmatrix} x \\ y \end{pmatrix} = \begin{pmatrix} nx \\ ny \end{pmatrix}$$

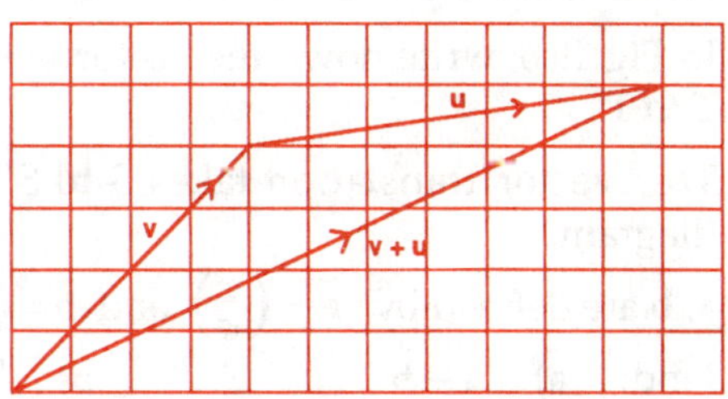

Fig 19.4

19.1.1 Examples

1) a) Let $\mathbf{a} = \begin{pmatrix} 3 \\ 2 \end{pmatrix}$ and $\mathbf{b} = \begin{pmatrix} -1 \\ 3 \end{pmatrix}$. Find a) $3\mathbf{a} + 2\mathbf{b}$ b) $|\mathbf{a} + \mathbf{b}|$.

Solution a) Multiply **a** by 3 and **b** by 2 and add.

$$3\mathbf{a} + 2\mathbf{b} = \begin{pmatrix} 3\times 3 \\ 3\times 2 \end{pmatrix} + \begin{pmatrix} 2\times -1 \\ 2\times 3 \end{pmatrix} = \begin{pmatrix} 7 \\ 12 \end{pmatrix}$$

b) Add **a** to **b**, to obtain $\begin{pmatrix} 2 \\ 5 \end{pmatrix}$. Use the formula for modulus:

$$|\mathbf{a} + \mathbf{b}| = \sqrt{2^2 + 5^2} = \sqrt{29} = 5.385$$

2) With **a** and **b** as in Example 1, illustrate on a graph **a**, **b** and **a** + **b**.

Solution For **a**, start from the origin, move 3 to the right and 2 up. **b** is drawn similarly.

For **a** + **b**, shift the tail of **b** to the head of **a**. Now join the origin to the head of **b**.

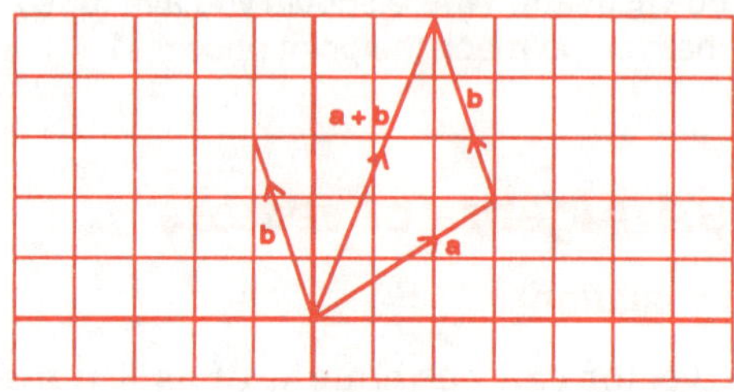

Fig 19.5

3) With **a** and **b** as in Example 1, solve the equation $x\mathbf{a} + y\mathbf{b} = \begin{pmatrix} 5 \\ 7 \end{pmatrix}$

Solution Re-write the equation as $x\begin{pmatrix} 3 \\ 2 \end{pmatrix} + y\begin{pmatrix} -1 \\ 3 \end{pmatrix} = \begin{pmatrix} 5 \\ 7 \end{pmatrix}$.

The top line is equivalent to $3x - y = 5$, and the bottom line gives $2x + 3y = 7$. So we have the simultaneous equations:

$$3x - y = 5$$

$$2x + 3y = 7$$

These can be solved to find:

$x = 2$ **and** $y = 1$

19.1.2 Exercises

1) Write down the vectors shown in Fig 19.6.
2) Find the moduli of the vectors of Question 1.
3) In Fig 19.6, write down the vector which has translated T to T′.

   This vector translation takes S to S′. Draw S′ on the diagram.

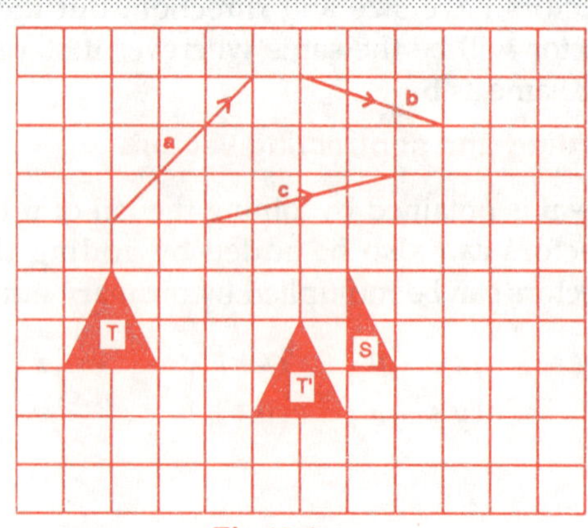

Fig 19.6

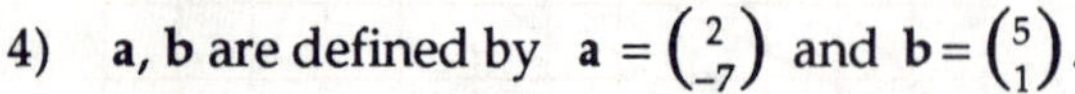

4) **a**, **b** are defined by $\mathbf{a} = \begin{pmatrix} 2 \\ -7 \end{pmatrix}$ and $\mathbf{b} = \begin{pmatrix} 5 \\ 1 \end{pmatrix}$.

   Find: a) $\mathbf{a} + \mathbf{b}$ b) $2\mathbf{a} + 5\mathbf{b}$

   c) $2\mathbf{a} - 3\mathbf{b}$ d) $\mathbf{b} - \mathbf{a}$

5) With the vectors **a** and **b** of Question 4, evaluate to 3 sig. figs.:

a) $|\mathbf{a}|$ b) $|\mathbf{b}|$ c) $|\mathbf{a}+\mathbf{b}|$

d) $|2\mathbf{a}+3\mathbf{b}|$ e) $|\mathbf{a}| + |\mathbf{b}|$

6) Find x and y from the following vector equation:

$$\binom{x}{2} + \binom{3}{y} = \binom{7}{9}$$

7) Find x and y from the following vector equation:

$$\binom{2}{1} + \binom{-1}{y} = \binom{x}{3}$$

8) With **a** and **b** as in Question 4, solve the following vector equations:

a) $\mathbf{v}+\mathbf{a}=\mathbf{b}$ b) $\mathbf{v}-\mathbf{b}=2\mathbf{a}$ c) $x\mathbf{a}+y\mathbf{b} = \binom{22}{-3}$ d) $x\mathbf{a}+y\mathbf{b} = \binom{9}{-13}$

9) On squared paper draw the vectors **a**, **b** of Question 4. Shift the tail of **b** to the head of **a**, and hence draw **a** + **b**.

10) Draw **c**, **d**, **c** + **d**, **c** – **d**, where $\mathbf{c} = \binom{2}{1}$ and $\mathbf{d} = \binom{3}{5}$.

19.2 Geometry of vectors

If A and B are two points in the plane the vector from A to B is written $\underline{AB}$ or as $\overrightarrow{AB}$.

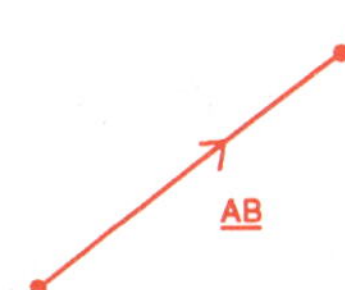

Fig 19.7

The vector from A(1,1) to B(3,2) is $\underline{AB} = \binom{2}{1}$.

The vector which goes from the origin to A is called the position vector of A. The position vector of A(1,1) is $\binom{1}{1}$.

Two vectors are parallel when one is a multiple of the other. So $\binom{4}{2}$ is parallel to $\binom{2}{1}$.

These ideas can be used to establish geometrical results.

19.2.1 Examples

1) A quadrilateral has vertices A(1,1), B(2,3), C(3,4), D(2,2). Show that ABCD is a parallelogram but is not a rhombus.

Solution The vectors of the sides of the quadrilateral are found by subtracting the co-ordinates.

$$\underline{AB} = \begin{pmatrix}2-1\\3-1\end{pmatrix} = \begin{pmatrix}1\\2\end{pmatrix},\ \underline{BC} = \begin{pmatrix}1\\1\end{pmatrix},\ \underline{DC} = \begin{pmatrix}1\\2\end{pmatrix},\ \underline{AD} = \begin{pmatrix}1\\1\end{pmatrix}$$

Since $\underline{AB} = \underline{DC}$ and $\underline{BC} = \underline{AD}$, opposite sides are equal and parallel. Hence ABCD is a parallelogram.

$$|\underline{AB}| = \sqrt{1^2+2^2} = \sqrt{5}. \quad |\underline{AD}| = \sqrt{1^2+1^2} = \sqrt{2}.$$

Since adjacent sides are not equal, ABCD is not a rhombus.

2) ABC is a triangle, and $\underline{AB} = \mathbf{b}$, $\underline{AC} = \mathbf{c}$. X and Y are the midpoints of AB and AC respectively. Express in terms of **b** and **c**:

a) $\underline{BC}$ b) $\underline{AX}$ c) $\underline{AY}$ d) $\underline{XY}$.

What can you conclude about BC and XY?

If Δ ABC has area 10, what is the area of Δ AXY?

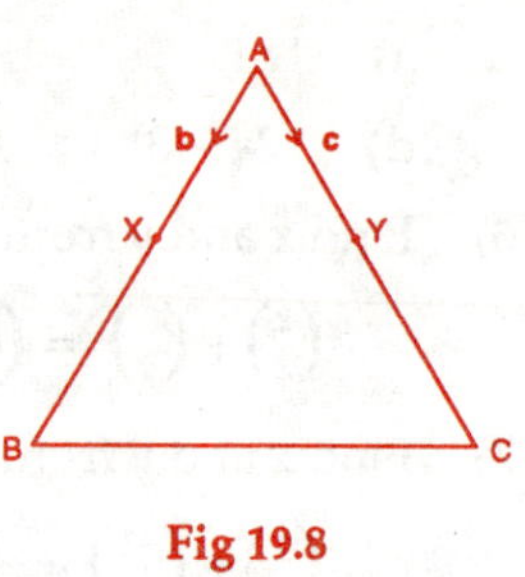

Fig 19.8

Solution Go from B to C by way of A. $\underline{BA}$ is minus $\underline{AB}$, which gives:

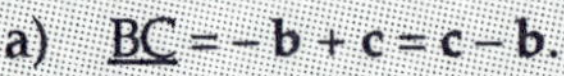

a) $\underline{BC} = -\mathbf{b} + \mathbf{c} = \mathbf{c} - \mathbf{b}$.

AX is halfway along AB. Hence:

b) $\underline{AX} = \frac{1}{2}\mathbf{b}$ and c) $\underline{AY} = \frac{1}{2}\mathbf{c}$

By similar reasoning to part (a):

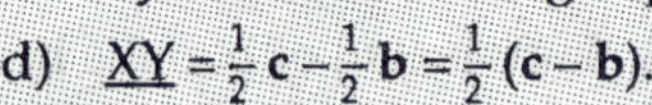

d) $\underline{XY} = \frac{1}{2}\mathbf{c} - \frac{1}{2}\mathbf{b} = \frac{1}{2}(\mathbf{c} - \mathbf{b})$.

Since $\underline{XY} = \frac{1}{2}$BC, conclude that XY is parallel to BC and half its length.

The two triangles are similar in the ratio 1:2. The base and height of AXY are half the base and height of ABC. So the area of AXY is $\frac{1}{2} \times \frac{1}{2} = \frac{1}{4}$ the area of ABC.

The area of ΔAXY is $\frac{10}{4} = 2.5$

19.2.2 Exercises

1) Four points in the plane are A(1,2), B(2,4), C(2,–4), D(4,0). Write down the vectors $\underline{AB}$, $\underline{AC}$, $\underline{CD}$, $\underline{BD}$, $\underline{DA}$. Which of these vectors are parallel to each other?

2) J(–3,1), K(–2,–2), L(–1,6), M(2,–3) are four points in the plane. Write down the vectors $\underline{JL}$, $\underline{JK}$, $\underline{ML}$, $\underline{MK}$, $\underline{MJ}$. Which of these vectors are parallel to each other?

3) Four points in the plane are A(2,3), B(5,9), C(2,2), D(3,4). Show that $\underline{AB}$ is parallel to $\underline{CD}$. What is the ratio of their lengths? Do the four points form a parallelogram?

4) A quadrilateral ABCD has vertices at A(–1,1), B(1,1), C(4,–1), D(3,–1). Show that ABCD is a trapezium. Is it a parallelogram?

5) Show that the four points P(1,0), Q(3,3), R(4,2), S(2,–1) form a parallelogram. Find the lengths of the sides. Is PQRS a rhombus?

6) A quadrilateral has its vertices at W(1,6), X(1,1), Y(4,5), Z(4,10). Show that WXYZ is a rhombus.

7) J(1,2), K(5,4), L(6,2), M(2,0) are the four vertices of a quadrilateral. Show that they form a parallelogram. By considering the lengths of the diagonals show that they form a rectangle.

8) A(–4,4), B(–1,3), C(1,2), D(5,1) are four points in the plane. By considering the vectors between them, find out which three of them lie on a straight line.

9) Given the three points A(1,1), B(2,3), C(1,2) find the point D such that ABCD is a parallelogram.

10) Given L(0,–2), M(–1,3), N(4,4) find the point P so that LMNP is a parallelogram.

11) Find x to ensure that A(1,1), B(2,5), C(x,9) lie on a straight line.

12) In the diagram shown $\underline{OA} = \mathbf{i}$ and $\underline{OB} = \mathbf{j}$. Find in terms of **i** and **j**:

a) $\underline{OC}$ b) $\underline{CD}$ c) $\underline{DC}$.

Suppose $\underline{OE} = -2\mathbf{i} + 2\mathbf{j}$. Place E on the diagram.

Suppose $\underline{CF} = \underline{OE}$. Place F on the diagram.

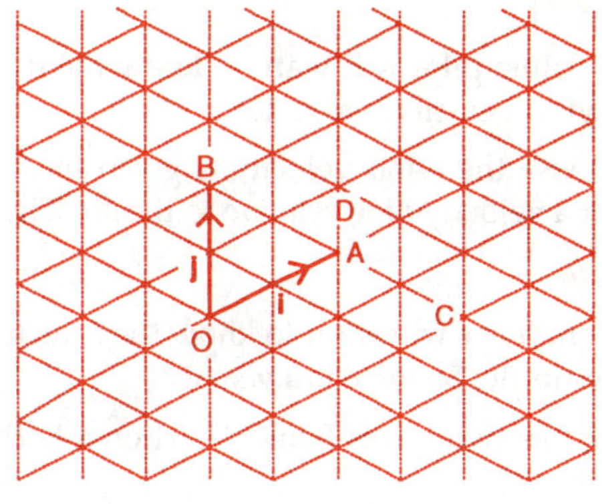

Fig 19.9

13) ABC is a triangle, and $\underline{AB} = \mathbf{b}$, $\underline{AC} = \mathbf{c}$. D and E lie on AB and AC respectively so that AD = $\frac{1}{4}$ AB and AE = $\frac{1}{4}$ AC (See Fig 19.10). Express in terms of **b** and **c**:

$\underline{BC}$, $\underline{AD}$, $\underline{AE}$, $\underline{DE}$, $\underline{DC}$.

Which of these vectors are parallel to each other?

If ΔABC has area 32, what is the area of DBCE?

14) Fig 19.11 shows three triangles arranged in a row. $\underline{AB} = \mathbf{b}$, $\underline{AC} = \mathbf{c}$. Express in terms of **b** and **c**:

$\underline{BD}$, $\underline{CD}$, $\underline{AE}$, $\underline{BC}$.

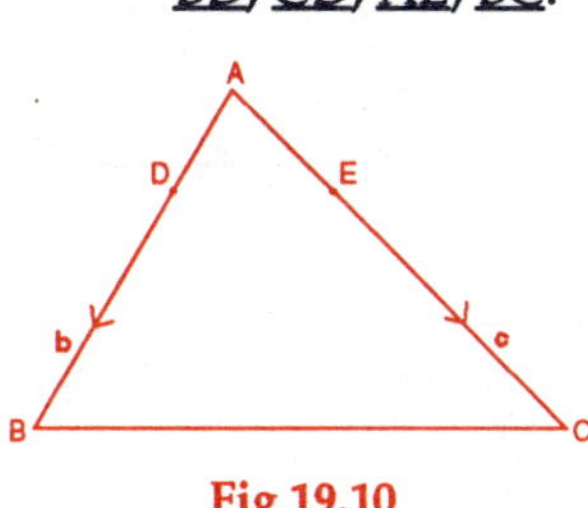

Fig 19.10

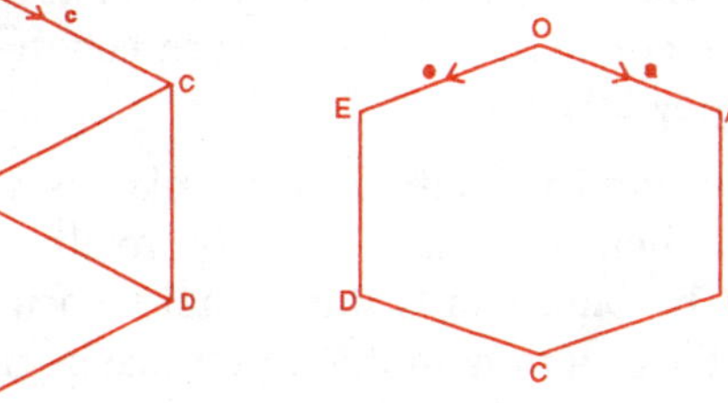

Fig 19.11

Fig 19.12

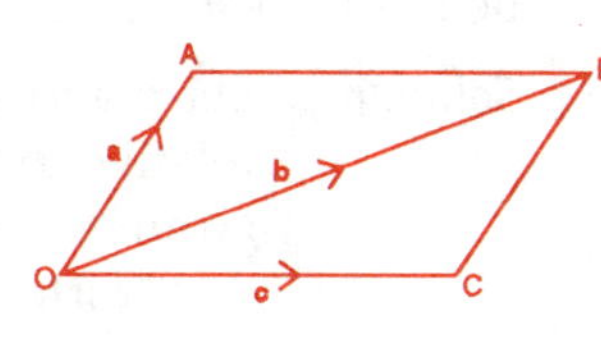

Fig 19.13

15) OABCDE is a hexagon, with the position vectors of A and E relative to O being **a** and **e** respectively (See Fig 19.12). Express in terms of **a** and **e**:

$\underline{BC}$, $\underline{CD}$, $\underline{EB}$, $\underline{OB}$.

16) Which three of the points with position vectors **a**, **b**, **a** + **b**, **a** – **b** lie on the same straight line?

17) OABC is a parallelogram, in which the position vectors of A, B, C relative to O are **a**, **b**, **c** respectively (See Fig 19.13). Let X and Y be the midpoints of the diagonals OB and AC respectively.

Express **b** in terms of **a** and **c**.

Find expressions for $\underline{AC}$, $\underline{AY}$, $\underline{OX}$, $\underline{OY}$.

What can you say about the points X and Y?

18) In the triangle ABC, $\underline{AB} = \mathbf{b}$ and $\underline{AC} = \mathbf{c}$. X lies on AB so that AX = $\frac{3}{4}$AB. Y is the midpoint of AC, and Z is the midpoint of CX.

Find in terms of **b** and **c** the vectors $\underline{AY}$, $\underline{AX}$, $\underline{CX}$, $\underline{CZ}$, $\underline{AZ}$, $\underline{ZY}$. What can you say about ZY?

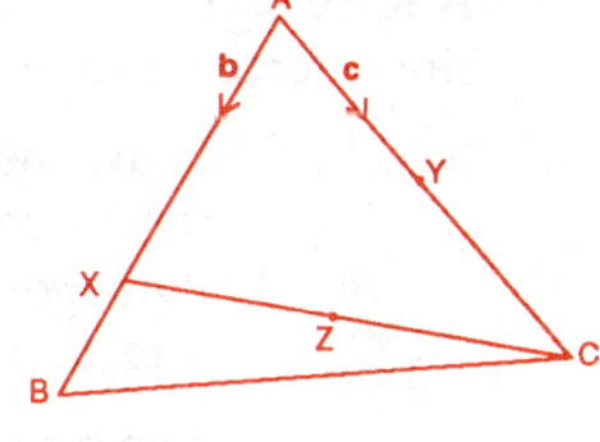

Fig 19.14

19.3 Applications of vectors

Vectors have direction as well as size. There are many physical quantities which are best described by vectors.

Velocity

An airline pilot will want to know the direction of the wind as well as its speed. So wind velocity is a vector.

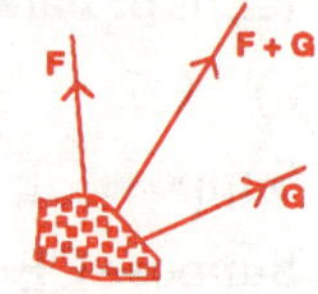

Suppose the wind velocity is given by the vector **v**. Suppose that the pilot flies with a velocity of **u**, relative to the air. The actual velocity of the plane is **v** + **u**.

Force

An engineer will want to know the direction of a force in a structure as well as its magnitude. So force is a vector.

Suppose two forces **F** and **G** act on a body. They are equivalent to a single force **H** = **F** + **G**.

If three forces **a**, **b**, **c** cancel each other out then they must form a closed triangle as shown.

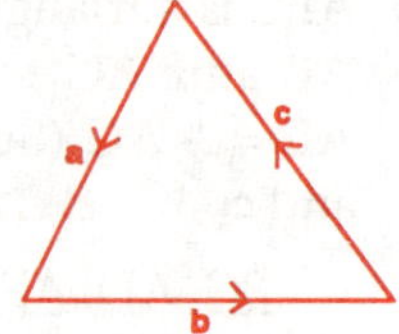

Fig 19.15

19.3.1 Examples

1) A plane can fly at 200 m.p.h. The pilot wishes to fly 400 miles North, but there is a wind from the East of 40 m.p.h. In which direction should he fly? How long will the journey take him?

Solution Let **v** and **u** be the wind velocity and the plane's velocity relative to the air. Then the actual velocity, relative to the ground, is **v** + **u**. The pilot wants this actual velocity to be due North. Hence the diagram on the right must be fitted.

The direction in which the pilot should steer is given by trigonometry. Take $\sin^{-1}$ of $\frac{40}{200}$:

He should steer at a bearing of 011.5°

His actual speed, relative to the ground, is given by Pythagoras:

Actual speed $= \sqrt{200^2 - 40^2} = 196$ m.p.h.

Time taken $= \frac{400}{196} = 2.04$ hours

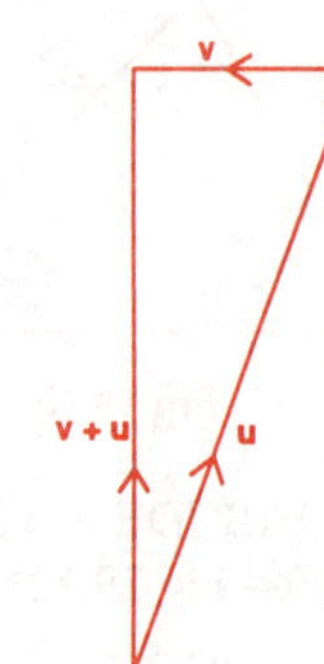

Fig 19.16

2) A force of 5 N acts due North, and a force of 6 N acts due East. Find a single force which will counterbalance them.

Solution Draw the forces as shown. The third side of the triangle is the force which will cancel out the original forces. Use Pythagoras to find its length, and trigonometry to find its direction.

The counterbalancing force is 7.81 N at 230°

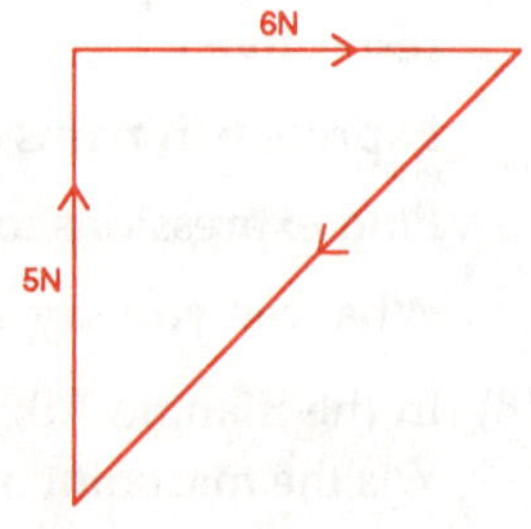

Fig 19.17

3) Two forces are $F = \begin{pmatrix} 3 \\ 4 \end{pmatrix}$ and $G = \begin{pmatrix} 1 \\ 4 \end{pmatrix}$.

Find: a) the magnitude of F b) the force which will counterbalance both of them.

Solution a) Use Pythagoras to find the magnitude of **F**.

$|F| = \sqrt{3^2 + 4^2} = 5$

b) Add F and G to obtain $\begin{pmatrix} 4 \\ 8 \end{pmatrix}$.

The counterbalancing force will be minus this.

The counterbalancing force is $\begin{pmatrix} -4 \\ -8 \end{pmatrix}$.

19.3.2 Exercises

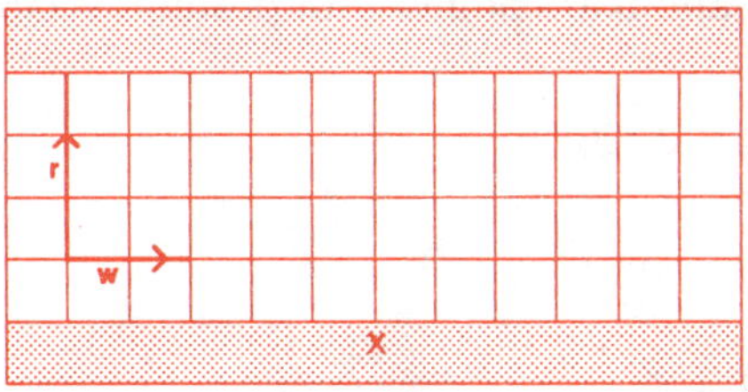

1) The grid shown represents a river. **w** is the water velocity and **r** is the velocity of a rower relative to the water. Draw the vector representing the velocity of the boat relative to the bank. If the boat starts at X where does it reach the other side?

Fig 19.18

2) A river flows at 3 km.p.h. A man can row at 5 km.p.h. If he points the boat directly across the river, find his actual speed and direction.

3) If the rower of Question 1 wishes to go directly across the river, in what direction should he steer? If the river is 0.2 km wide, how long will it take him to cross?

4) A plane can fly at 400 m.p.h. There is a 50 m.p.h wind from North to South. If the plane is pointed East, what bearing and speed will it fly at?

5) If the pilot of Question 4 wishes to fly East, what bearing should be set? What will be the speed of the plane?

6) Two forces are of 5 N due North and 7 N due East. Find the size and direction of the single equivalent force.

7) Two forces are of 6 N North West and of 7 N North East. Find the size and direction of the single force which will counterbalance them.

8) Two forces are given by $\mathbf{A} = \begin{pmatrix} 2 \\ 8 \end{pmatrix}$ and $\mathbf{B} = \begin{pmatrix} 3 \\ 4 \end{pmatrix}$.
Find the single equivalent force **C**. Find $|\mathbf{A}|$, $|\mathbf{B}|$, $|\mathbf{C}|$.

9) Find in vector form the force needed to counteract 3**A** + 2**B**, where **A** and **B** are as in Question 8.

10 Look again at the problem at the beginning of the chapter. Advise the swimmer on the direction to swim to reach the opposite bank.

19.4 Longer exercise

Hanging weights

Suppose we have three weights, of 4 kg, 5 kg, 3 kg, joined on a rope in that order. They are slung over two pegs as shown. The middle one will sink, and after bobbing up and down for a while will come to rest. What angles P° and Q° will the ropes make?

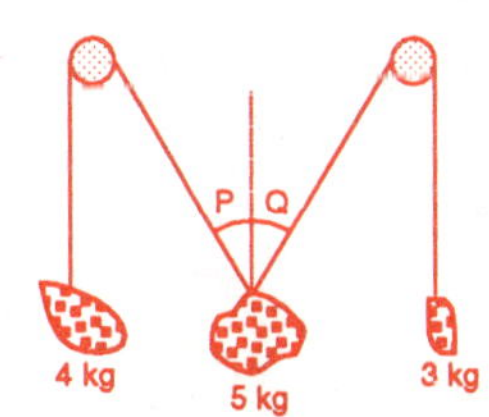

Fig 19.19

There are three forces acting on the middle weight – its own weight, and the tensions in the two ropes on either side of it. Once it has stopped moving, these three forces will cancel each other out. Hence the three forces must form a closed triangle.

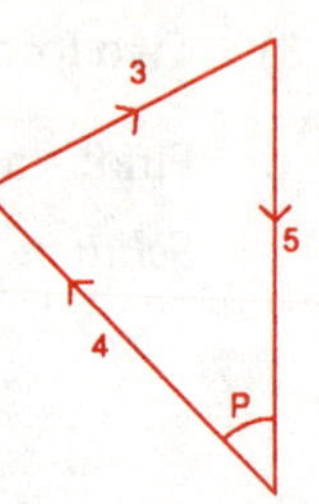

Fig 19.20

The 5 kg acts vertically down. The 4 kg acts up and to the left, making P° with the vertical. Draw the third side of the triangle. What sort of triangle is it? By trigonometry find P° and Q°.

Suppose the weights are 7 kg, 9 kg, 8 kg. Find the angles made by the ropes with the vertical. You could find them by a scale drawing or by the cosine rule of Chapter 18.

Suppose the weights are 9 kg, 21 kg, 10 kg. What happens when you try to draw the triangle of forces? What happens to the weights?

Multiple choice question *(Tick appropriate box)*

A and B are points with position vectors $\binom{12}{5}$ and $\binom{4}{3}$ respectively. The modulus of $\underline{AB}$ is:

a) $\sqrt{320}$ ☐

b) 5 ☐

c) 8 ☐

d) $\sqrt{68}$ ☐

e) 10 ☐

Points to note

1) *Co-ordinates*

Be careful not to confuse vectors with points. (3,4) is a point, and $\binom{3}{4}$ is a vector which goes from the origin to that point.

The vector will also go from (1,1) to (4,5), or from (–1,–3) to (2,1) and so on. The vector does not have any position: it can start from anywhere in the plane.

2) *Modulus*

Be careful when working out the modulus of a vector. If **v** is the vector $\binom{3}{4}$, then its modulus is given by $|\mathbf{v}| = \sqrt{3^2 + 4^2} = 5$.

The modulus of **v** is not equal to 3 + 4 = 7.

Similarly, when adding vectors do not add the moduli.

$|\mathbf{a} + \mathbf{b}| \neq |\mathbf{a}| + |\mathbf{b}|$.

Be careful with negative signs. The modulus of $\binom{-3}{4}$ is 5, not $\sqrt{7}$.

3) *Vector geometry*

a) A vector is only a position vector if it starts from the origin. Otherwise take account of where it starts.

b) The vector from (3,2) to (5,7) is $\binom{2}{5}$, not $\binom{-2}{-5}$.

c) If A has position vector **a**, and B has position vector **b**, then $\underline{AB}$ is **b** – **a**. It is not equal to **b**, or **a** + **b**, or **a** – **b**.

4) *Relative velocity*

Make sure you do not confuse relative velocity (relative to the water or the air) and absolute velocity.

Chapter 20

Transformations and matrices

A wardrobe has to be moved along a wall. It is too heavy to be lifted, and the floor is too rough for it to slide.

You find that you can just tilt the wardrobe and turn it about one corner of its base. How can you move it along the wall?

Fig 20.1

20.1 Finding the centre and angle of rotation

Centre

If a shape is rotated, then one point must remain fixed. This point is the centre of rotation.

Suppose in the rotation A has gone to A′. The centre C must be an equal distance from A and A′. So the centre must lie on the perpendicular bisector of AA′.

Similarly, if B is taken to B′, the centre lies on the perpendicular bisector of BB′.

Construct both these lines. The centre C will lie on their intersection point.

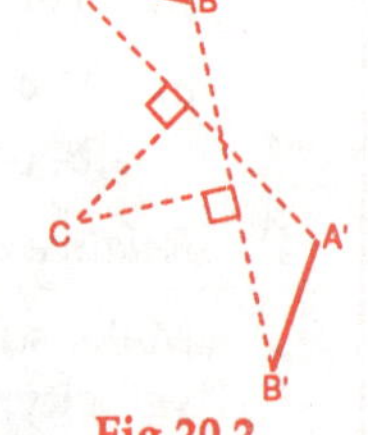

Fig 20.2

Angle

During the rotation, AB has been moved to A′B′. The angle of rotation is the angle between AB and A′B′.

20.1.1 Example

A triangle has vertices at A(1,1), B(1,3), C(2,3). It is rotated, so that its new vertices are at A′(3,1), B′(5,1), C′(5,0). Find the centre and angle of rotation.

Solution The triangles before and after rotation are shown. The perpendicular bisector of AA′ is the vertical line $x = 2$. The perpendicular bisector of CC′ is dotted. They cross at (2,0).

The centre of rotation is (2,0)

AB is vertical, and A′B′ is horizontal.

The angle of rotation is 90° clockwise

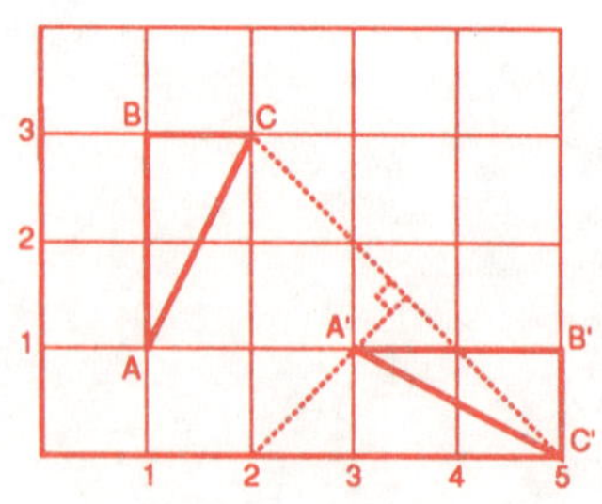

Fig 20.3

20.1.2 Exercises

1) Find the angles of rotation on the diagrams of Fig 20.4. Find the coordinates of the centres, relative to the bottom left corner of the grid.
2) A triangle has vertices at A(1,1), B(3,1), C(3,2). It is rotated, so that its new vertices are at A′(1,3), B′(–1,3), C′(–1,2). Find the centre and angle of rotation.
3) The triangle ABC of Question 2 is rotated to A″(1,–1), B″(1,1), C″(0,1). Find the centre and angle of rotation.

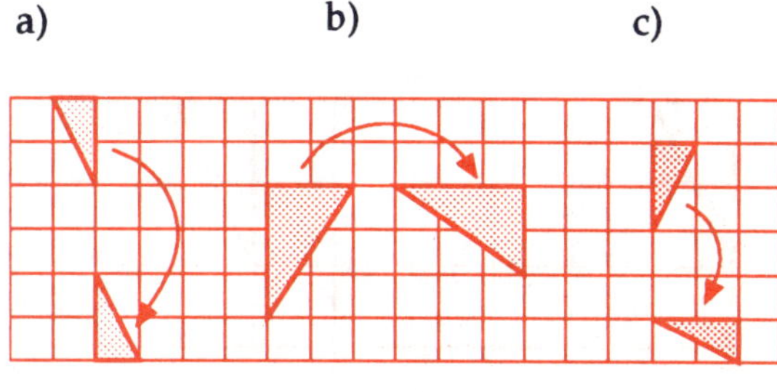

Fig 20.4

4) A rectangle has vertices at P(1,1), Q(2,1), R(2,–1), S(1,–1). It is rotated so that its vertices become P′(0,0), Q′(0,–1), R′(–2,–1), S′(–2,0). Find the centre and angle of rotation.
5) The rectangle PQRS of Question 4 is rotated to P″(4,1), Q″(3,1), R″(3,3), S″(4,3). Find the centre and angle of rotation.

20.2 Combination of transformations

If one transformation is followed by another, the final result is a combined transformation.

If transformation P is followed by transformation Q, the combined transformation is written QP. In particular, if P is done twice then the transformation is written P^2.

Often the combined transformation can be simplified to a single transformation. Below are some examples:

Translations. The composition of two translations is another translation. Suppose the first translation moves x to the right and y up, and the second moves z to the right and w up. The composition moves $x + z$ to the right and $y + w$ up.

Rotations. The composition of two rotations about a point is also a translation about the same point. If the first rotation is of P° and the second of Q°, then the combination is of P° + Q°.

Enlargements. The composition of two enlargements is another enlargement. If their scale factors are a and b, then the scale factor of the composition is $a \times b$.

Reflections. The composition of two reflections is either a translation or a rotation. If the mirror lines are parallel then it is a translation. If the mirror lines meet it is a rotation about the meeting point.

20.2.1 Examples

1) The triangle T with vertices at A(1,1), B(1,3), C(2,3) is reflected in the line $x = 2$, giving the triangle T′. T′ is reflected in the line $x = -1$, to give the triangle T″.

   Draw the three triangles on graph paper. Describe the transformations which take T to T″ and which take T″ to T.

   Solution The triangles are shown in Fig 20.5 on the following page. T is taken to T″ by a translation, of 6 units to the left. T″ is taken to T by a translation of 6 units to the right.

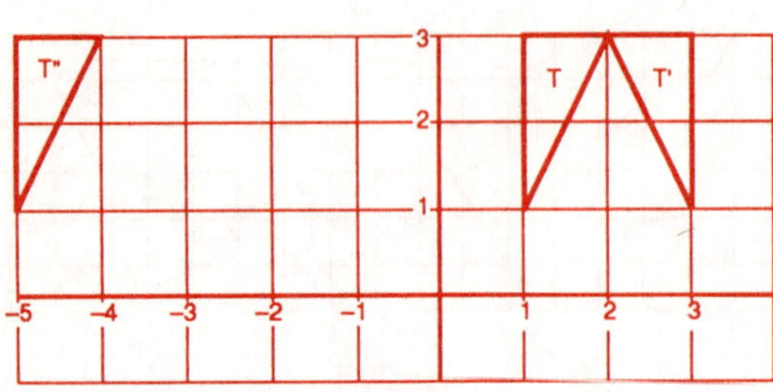

Fig 20.5

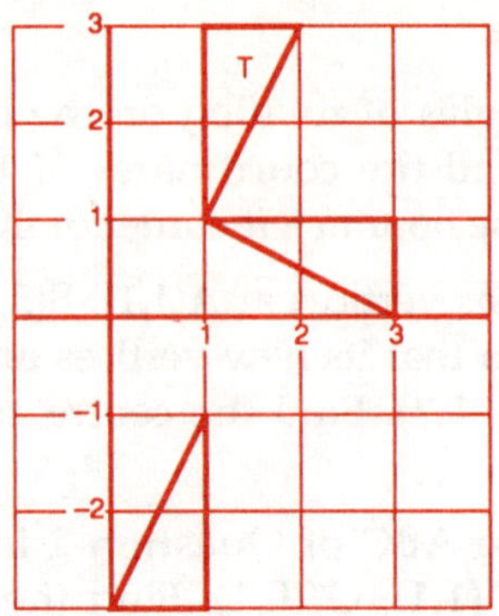

Fig 20.6

2) The triangle T of Example 1 is rotated through a quarter turn clockwise about (1,1), then through a further quarter turn clockwise about (0,0). To what single transformation is this equivalent?

Solution The three triangles are shown in Fig 20.6. The two rotations of 90° give a rotation of 180°. The point (1,0) remains fixed.

A rotation of 180° about (1,0)

20.2.2 Exercises

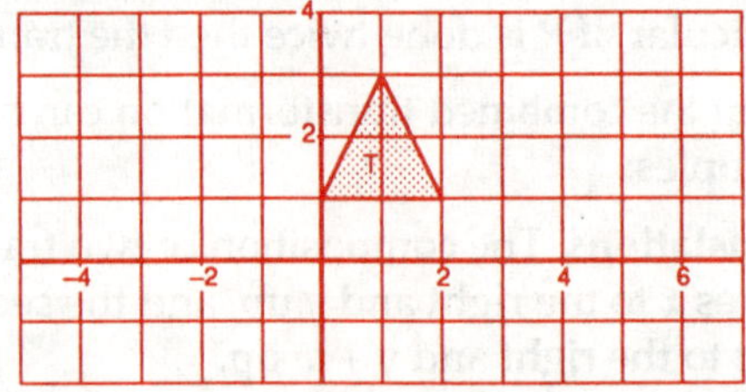

Fig 20.7

1) The triangle T of Fig 20.7 is reflected in $x = 2$ to T'. T' is reflected in $x = 0$ to T". Draw T' and T" on the grid. Describe the single transformation which will take T to T".

2) Triangle T of Question 1 is reflected in $y = 1$ to T*. T* is reflected in $x = 3$ to T**. Draw T* and T** on the grid, and describe the single transformation which will take T to T**.

3) The triangle S with vertices A(1,1), B(2,2), C(4,1) is reflected in the line $x = 1$ and then in the line $x = 2$. Find the single transformation equivalent to the two reflections.

4) The triangle S of Question 3 is reflected in $y = 1$ and then in $y = -1$. Find the single transformation equivalent to the two reflections.

5) The triangle S of Question 3 is reflected in $x = 1$ and then in $y = 1$. Describe the single equivalent transformation.

6) The triangle S of Question 3 is reflected in $y = -1$ and then in $x = 2$. Describe the single equivalent transformation.

7) LMN is the triangle with vertices L(0,2), M(3,2), N(0,1). Describe the single transformation equivalent to the following successive transformations:

   a) Rotation of 90° clockwise about L.

   b) Rotation of 90° anti-clockwise about (0,0).

8) With Δ LMN as in Question 7, describe the single transformation equivalent to the following successive transformations:

a) Rotation of 180° about (2,3).

b) Rotation of 180° about (1,0).

9) The problem at the beginning of the chapter involved moving a heavy wardrobe. The positions of the wardrobe are shown on the right.

Describe successive rotations which will move it from T to T′.

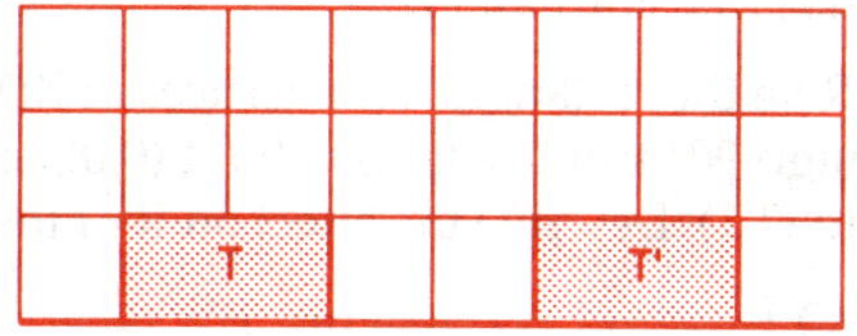

Fig 20.8

20.3 Inverses of transformations

If a transformation P takes A to A′, the inverse transformation which takes A′ back to A is written P^{-1}.

The inverses of some simple transformations are as follows:

Translations. The inverse of a translation is a translation in the opposite direction. If the translation moves x to the right and y up, then its inverse moves x to the left and y down.

Rotations. The inverse of a rotation of P° is a rotation of P° in the opposite direction.

Enlargements. The inverse of an enlargement, with scale factor k, is an enlargement of scale factor $\frac{1}{k}$.

Reflections. A reflection is its own inverse. That is, the inverse of a reflection is the same reflection.

20.3.1 Example

A transformation takes T to T′, as shown in Fig 20.9. Describe the inverse transformation.

Solution The original transformation is a translation, of 2 units to the right and 3 up. The inverse will be 2 to the left and 3 down.

The inverse is the translation $\begin{pmatrix} -2 \\ -3 \end{pmatrix}$

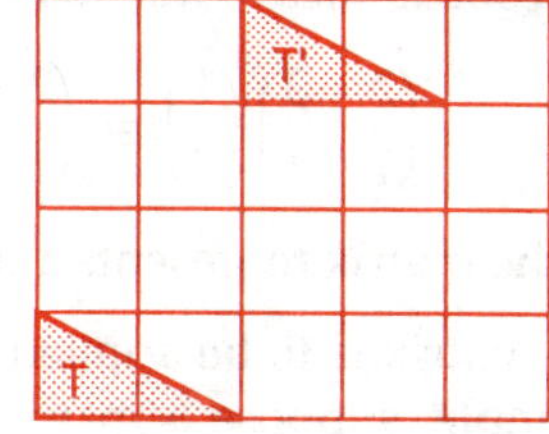

Fig 20.9

20.3.2 Exercises

1) Write down the inverses of the following transformations:

a) A translation of $\begin{pmatrix} 2 \\ 3 \end{pmatrix}$

b) A translation of $\begin{pmatrix} -3 \\ 1 \end{pmatrix}$

c) A rotation of 90° clockwise about (1,0)

d) A rotation of 120° anti-clockwise about (3,2)

e) A rotation of 180° about (0,0)

f) An enlargement of scale factor 2 about (2,3)

g) An enlargement of scale factor $\frac{1}{2}$ about (1,2)

h) An enlargement of scale factor –1 about (0,0)

i) A reflection in the line $x = 3$

j) A reflection in the line $y = 2x$.

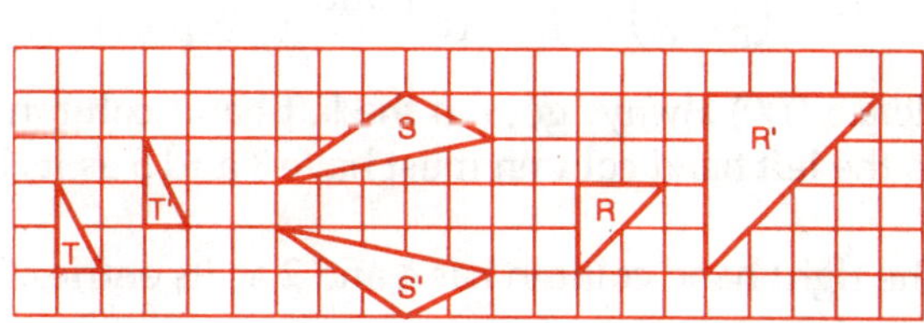

Fig 20.10

2) In the grid of Fig 20.10, T has been transformed to T′, S to S′, R to R′. In each case describe the inverse transformation.

3) Let R be the rectangle with vertices at X(1,1), Y(1,3), Z(2,3), W(2,1). Let P be the operation of rotation through 90° anti-clockwise about (0,0), and let Q be the operation of rotation through 90° clockwise about (1,1). Describe the effect on R of the following combined transformations:

a) Q^{-1} b) P^{-1} c) PQ d) QP
e) $(PQ)^{-1}$ f) $(QP)^{-1}$ g) $P^{-1}Q^{-1}$.

What can you conclude about inverses of combined transformations?

4) Let T be the triangle with vertices at J(–1,1), K(0,3), L(2,1). Let F be the operation of reflection in the line $x = y$, and G the operation of reflection in $y = 0$. Describe the effect on T of the following transformations:

a) F^{-1} b) G^{-1} c) FG
d) GF e) $(FG)^{-1}$ f) $(GF)^{-1}$.

20.4 Matrices

A matrix is a block of numbers. They can be used to represent transformations. When a matrix is applied to a point, the coordinates of the point must be written vertically. Each row of the matrix then multiplies the coordinates of the point, as shown below.

$$\begin{pmatrix}2 & 3\\1 & 4\end{pmatrix}.\begin{pmatrix}1\\2\end{pmatrix} = \begin{pmatrix}2\times1+3\times2\\1\times1+4\times2\end{pmatrix} = \begin{pmatrix}8\\9\end{pmatrix}$$

So the matrix represents a transformation which takes (1,2) to (8,9).

If a matrix is to be applied to several points, it saves time to write all the coordinates in one block. For example, suppose a matrix is to be applied to the triangle with vertices at (1,2), (3,4), (8,1). Write the coordinates vertically and put them in a 2 by 3 block. Apply the matrix:

$$\begin{pmatrix}2 & 3\\1 & 4\end{pmatrix}.\begin{pmatrix}1 & 3 & 8\\2 & 4 & 1\end{pmatrix} = \begin{pmatrix}8 & 18 & 19\\9 & 19 & 12\end{pmatrix}$$

The transformed triangle has vertices at (8,9), (18,19), (19,12).

Finding the matrix

Suppose that we wish to find the matrix which takes (1,0) to (3,5) and (0,1) to (4,2). Note that for a general matrix:

$$\begin{pmatrix}a & b\\c & d\end{pmatrix}.\begin{pmatrix}1\\0\end{pmatrix} = \begin{pmatrix}a\\c\end{pmatrix} \text{ and } \begin{pmatrix}a & b\\c & d\end{pmatrix}.\begin{pmatrix}0\\1\end{pmatrix} = \begin{pmatrix}b\\d\end{pmatrix}$$

Hence (1,0) always goes to the left hand column of the matrix, and (0,1) goes to the right hand column. So the left hand column must have 3 and 5 as its entries.

The right hand column has 4 and 2 as its entries. The matrix can be written down as $\begin{pmatrix}3 & 4\\5 & 2\end{pmatrix}$.

Standard transformations

Some matrices which perform standard transformations are below.

Rotations

The matrices $\begin{pmatrix} 0 & 1 \\ -1 & 0 \end{pmatrix}$ and $\begin{pmatrix} 0 & -1 \\ 1 & 0 \end{pmatrix}$ represent rotations of 90°, clockwise and anti-clockwise respectively.

Reflections

The matrices $\begin{pmatrix} -1 & 0 \\ 0 & 1 \end{pmatrix}$, $\begin{pmatrix} 1 & 0 \\ 0 & -1 \end{pmatrix}$ and $\begin{pmatrix} 0 & 1 \\ 1 & 0 \end{pmatrix}$ represent reflections, in the y-axis, the x-axis and the line $y = x$ respectively.

Enlargements

The matrix $\begin{pmatrix} k & 0 \\ 0 & k \end{pmatrix}$ represents an enlargement of scale factor k.

20.4.1 Example

The points of the triangle T are A(1,1), B(3,1), C(1,2). Draw the triangle T on graph paper.

The points ABC are transformed to A′B′C′, forming the triangle T′, by the matrix M where M = $\begin{pmatrix} 0 & -1 \\ 1 & 0 \end{pmatrix}$.

Draw the triangle T′ on the same graph paper. What transformation does A perform?

T is reflected in the x-axis, to obtain T″. Draw T″ on the graph paper. What single matrix would send T to T″?

Solution Plot A, B, C on the graph. Apply the matrix M to the points.

$$\begin{pmatrix} 0 & -1 \\ 1 & 0 \end{pmatrix} \cdot \overset{\quad A \quad B \quad C}{\begin{pmatrix} 1 & 3 & 1 \\ 1 & 1 & 2 \end{pmatrix}} = \overset{\quad A' \quad B' \quad C'}{\begin{pmatrix} -1 & -1 & -2 \\ 1 & 3 & 1 \end{pmatrix}}$$

Plot the points A′, B′, C′. Note that the triangle has been turned through 90° anticlockwise.

M represents an anticlockwise rotation of 90°

Reflect the triangle T in the x axis. Notice that the y coordinates have all been multiplied by –1. Hence the matrix of this transformation is:

$$\mathbf{N} = \begin{pmatrix} 1 & 0 \\ 0 & -1 \end{pmatrix}$$

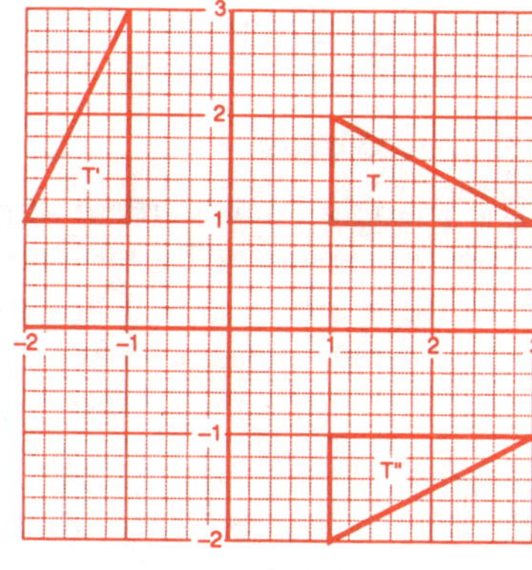

Fig 20.11

20.4.2 Exercises

1) Let T be the triangle with vertices L(1,2), M(3,2), N(2,1). Find the image of T after action by the following matrices:

$$A = \begin{pmatrix} 1 & 0 \\ 0 & -1 \end{pmatrix},\ B = \begin{pmatrix} -1 & 0 \\ 0 & 1 \end{pmatrix},\ C = \begin{pmatrix} 0 & 1 \\ -1 & 0 \end{pmatrix},\ D = \begin{pmatrix} 0 & -1 \\ 1 & 0 \end{pmatrix},\ E = \begin{pmatrix} 0 & -1 \\ -1 & 0 \end{pmatrix}$$

2) Repeat Question 1, for the rectangle with vertices at P(1,1), Q(1,3), R(2,3), S(2,1).

3) Describe the action of the matrices A, B, C, D, E defined in Question 1.

4) Let S be the unit square with vertices at (0,0), (1,0). (1,1), (0,1). Find the image of S after action by the following matrices:

$$F=\begin{pmatrix}3 & 0\\ 0 & 3\end{pmatrix},\ G=\begin{pmatrix}\frac{1}{2} & 0\\ 0 & \frac{1}{2}\end{pmatrix},\ H=\begin{pmatrix}\frac{1}{2} & 0\\ 0 & 1\end{pmatrix},\ J=\begin{pmatrix}1 & 0\\ 0 & 2\end{pmatrix},\ K=\begin{pmatrix}-2 & 0\\ 0 & -2\end{pmatrix}$$

5) Describe the action of the matrices F, G, H, J, K defined in Question 4.

6) Find the matrix which takes (1,0) to (4,–2) and (0,1) to (2,–1).

7) Find the matrix which takes (2,0) to (4,6) and (0,3) to (9,6).

8) A certain matrix takes the square with vertices (0,0), (3,0), (3,3), (0,3) to the parallelogram with vertices (0,0), (2,5), (6,7), (4,2). Find the matrix.

20.5 Multiplying matrices

Suppose that P and Q are two transformations, which can be performed by matrices A and B respectively. Then we can multiply the matrices A and B, so that the product AB represents the transformation of Q followed by P.

Matrices are multiplied together as shown below.

$$\begin{pmatrix}2 & 1\\ 3 & 4\end{pmatrix}\cdot\begin{pmatrix}3 & 4\\ 2 & 5\end{pmatrix}=\begin{pmatrix}2\times3+1\times2 & 2\times4+1\times5\\ 3\times3+4\times2 & 3\times4+4\times5\end{pmatrix}=\begin{pmatrix}8 & 13\\ 17 & 32\end{pmatrix}$$

20.5.1 Example

The triangle T has vertices at (1,1), (2,4), (3,1). Draw T on graph paper. Draw the image of T after it has been operated on first by A and then by B, where are A and B are the matrices given below. What single transformation has been applied to T?

$$A=\begin{pmatrix}0 & 1\\ 1 & 0\end{pmatrix},\ B=\begin{pmatrix}0 & 1\\ -1 & 0\end{pmatrix}$$

Solution There is no need to perform the transformations individually. The combined transformation is performed by the product matrix BA.

$$BA=\begin{pmatrix}0 & 1\\ -1 & 0\end{pmatrix}\cdot\begin{pmatrix}0 & 1\\ 1 & 0\end{pmatrix}=\begin{pmatrix}1 & 0\\ 0 & -1\end{pmatrix}$$

Apply this to T:

$$BA=\begin{pmatrix}1 & 0\\ 0 & -1\end{pmatrix}\cdot\begin{pmatrix}1 & 2 & 3\\ 1 & 4 & 1\end{pmatrix}=\begin{pmatrix}1 & 2 & 3\\ -1 & -4 & -1\end{pmatrix}$$

Plot T and its image under the transformation. Notice that all the y coordinates have been multiplied by –1.

BA performs a reflection in the x axis

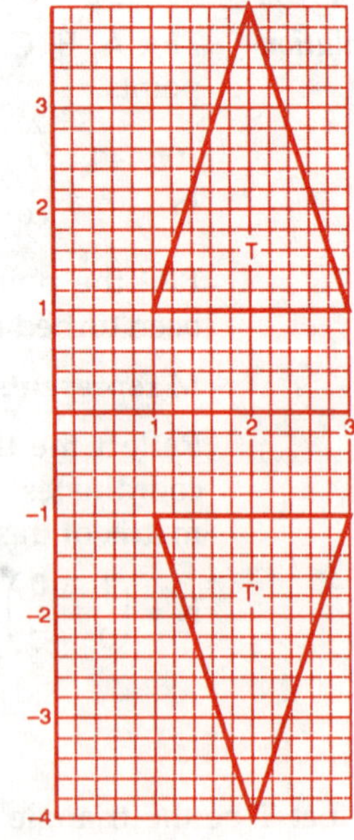

Fig 20.12

20.5.2 Exercises

1) Evaluate the following matrix multiplications:

a) $\begin{pmatrix}1 & 2\\0 & 1\end{pmatrix}\cdot\begin{pmatrix}3 & 4\\1 & 1\end{pmatrix}$ b) $\begin{pmatrix}-1 & 2\\1 & -3\end{pmatrix}\cdot\begin{pmatrix}2 & 0\\1 & 3\end{pmatrix}$ c) $\begin{pmatrix}-1 & 2\\-2 & 1\end{pmatrix}\cdot\begin{pmatrix}2 & -3\\-3 & 2\end{pmatrix}$

2) On squared paper plot the triangle T with vertices (1,2), (1,–1), (2,2).

T is taken to U by the matrix $A = \begin{pmatrix}0 & 1\\-1 & 0\end{pmatrix}$

Plot U on the same squared paper.

U is now taken to V by the matrix $B = \begin{pmatrix}-1 & 0\\0 & 1\end{pmatrix}$

Plot V on the same paper. What single matrix will take T to V?

3) Let S be the square with corners at (1,1), (1,2), (2,2), (2,1).

Plot S on squared paper. S is sent to S′ by the matrix $C = \begin{pmatrix}1 & 2\\0 & 1\end{pmatrix}$

Plot S′ on the paper. S′ is taken to S″ by the matrix $D = \begin{pmatrix}1 & 0\\0 & -1\end{pmatrix}$

Plot S″ on the same paper. What single matrix will take S to S″?

4) On squared paper plot the triangle with vertices at (1,4), (5,4), (1,3). Draw the image of the triangle after action by A, A^2, A^3, A^4, where:

$$A = \begin{pmatrix}0 & 1\\-1 & 0\end{pmatrix}$$

5) Let M be the rectangle with corners at (1,1), (1,5), (2,5), (2,1). Plot this rectangle on squared paper, and its image after action by B, C and BC where:

$$B = \begin{pmatrix}1 & 0\\0 & -1\end{pmatrix},\ C = \begin{pmatrix}-1 & 0\\0 & 1\end{pmatrix}$$

20.6 Longer exercise

Wallpaper

Of course, there is no limit to the number of wallpaper patterns. But they can be classified into a small number of types.

1) The square on the right is the basic motif. For the pattern shown it is copied horizontally and vertically, after a reflection for each copying.

Different patterns are obtained by different ways of copying. Some you could try are:

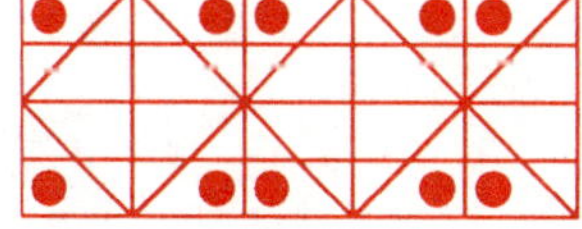

Fig 20.13

Translate the motif horizontally and vertically.

Translate the motif horizontally, but reflect it vertically.

Translate the motif vertically, but rotate it horizontally.

See how many different patterns you can obtain.

2) Start with a triangular motif on a triangular grid, as shown. See how many different patterns you can obtain by rotating or reflecting or translating the motif.

It can be shown that there are only 17 types of wallpaper patterns. How many did you get?

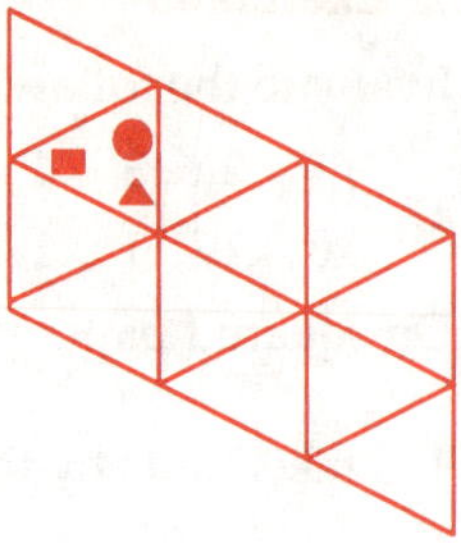

Fig 20.14

Multiple choice question *(Tick appropriate box)*

A square has points at A(2,1), B(3,1), C(3,0), D(2,0). It is reflected first in $x = 1$ then in $y = x$. The combined transformation is:

a) 90° clockwise rotation about (1,1) ☐

b) Translation of 2 to left, 1 down ☐

c) Reflection in $y = 3 - 2x$ ☐

d) 90° anti-clockwise rotation about (1,1) ☐

e) Enlargement of scale factor –1 about ($1\frac{1}{2}$,0). ☐

Points to note

1) *Combined transformations*

The order in which transformations are done is important. PQ is not the same as QP. Be sure to remember that PQ means that Q is done first and then P.

2) *Transformation matrices*

a) Usually, the co-ordinates of a point may be written either horizontally or vertically. But when a matrix is applied to a point, its co-ordinates must be vertical.

b) Be careful when multiplying matrices to give a combined transformation. The product AB is a transformation which does B first and then A. It is easy to get this the wrong way round.

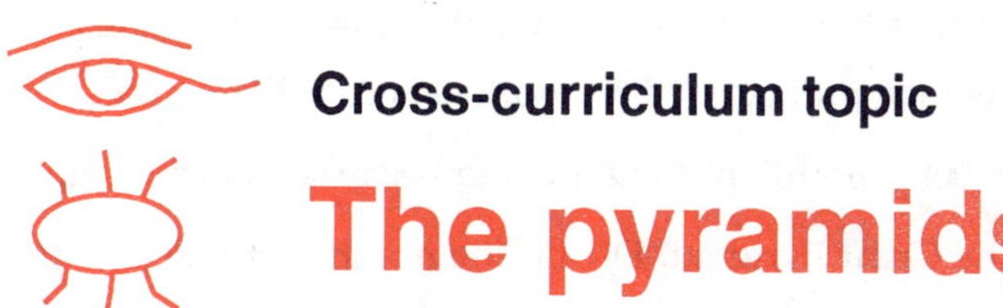

Cross-curriculum topic

The pyramids

Outside Cairo, the capital of Egypt, is a place called Giza. Three of the ancient kings of Egypt, the Pharaohs, were buried here almost 5,000 years ago. Their tombs are known as the pyramids, and are still standing. They are so huge that they have survived the centuries and the attempts made to destroy them. They are in a simple Mathematical shape, built out of solid stone. The photograph below shows the three pyramids.

The biggest pyramid is the oldest of the three. It is known as the Great Pyramid. It was built as a tomb for the Pharaoh Khufu, also known as Cheops. He lived in about 2,650 BC.

The Second Pyramid was built by Khufu's son Khafre. It is 10 m lower than the Great Pyramid.

Khafre's son was Menkaure. He built the Third Pyramid. His pyramid is about a tenth as big as the Great Pyramid.

When these pyramids were built Man's knowledge of engineering and Mathematics was very limited. Yet somehow these huge constructions were made, to an astonishing degree of accuracy. In the following pages we look at some facts about the size and shape of the Pyramids.

How were they built?

The Pyramids are bigger than anything built nowadays. But at the time of their construction there were no machines to cut the stone. There was not even any iron – all the stone had to be cut with copper tools. There were no lorries or trains to transport the blocks. They all had to be dragged, by sheer muscle power, up from the river and onto their positions on the Pyramid.

Some people have thought that the Pyramids could not have been built by human means, and that supernatural forces, or creatures from outer space, were responsible for their construction. But it is possible to explain how they were built, if a very large number of men were involved over long periods of time.

Herodotus was a Greek historian who visited Egypt in 450 BC. (Note that at this time the Pyramids were already over 2,000 years old). It is from him that we get our first details of the construction of the Pyramids. He was told that the Great Pyramid had taken 20 years to build, and that 100,000 men had been employed. Let us see what this means in terms of the work each man would have to do.

Say that the labour force was organized into gangs of 10 men each. That would mean 10,000 gangs.

Say that they worked for 300 days each year. The total number of days worked is $20 \times 300 = 6{,}000$.

So the total number of "gang-days" is $10{,}000 \times 6{,}000 = 6 \times 10^7$, putting the number in standard form.

There are estimated to be 2.3×10^6 blocks in the Great Pyramid. Divide the number of blocks into the number of days available:

$$6 \times 10^7 \div 2.3 \times 10^6 = 26 \text{ approximately.}$$

This means that each gang would be required to cut and shift one block per month. This is possible, even though the average weight of the blocks was 2,500 kg, and they had to be moved a mile or so from the quarry to the pyramid.

Volume

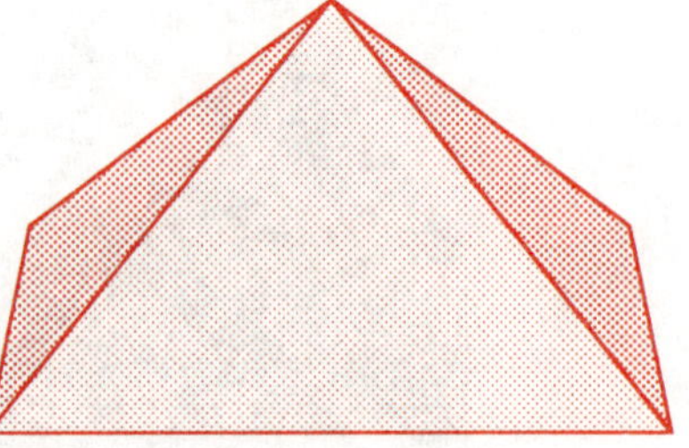

The immediately impressive thing about the Pyramids is their sheer size. Here we find the volume of some of the Pyramids.

As a geometrical figure, a pyramid is defined as having a rectangular base, from which flat sides rise to a point. The height of the pyramid refers to the height of the point above the base. The volume of the pyramid is given by:

$$\text{Volume} = \tfrac{1}{3} \text{ base area} \times \text{height}$$

The Egyptian Pyramids all have square bases. If the side of the square base is a, and the height is h, then the volume V is given by:

$$V = \tfrac{1}{3}a^2h$$

Here are the dimensions of the Pyramids of Giza, and the names of the Pharaohs who were buried in them.

Name	Pharaoh	Height	Base Side	Volume
Great	Khufu	147 m	230 m	2.6×10^6 m^3
Second	Khafre	144 m	216 m	2.24×10^6 m^3
Third	Menkaure	66 m	108 m	2.6×10^5 m^3

Numbers by themselves do not give much of an idea of the size of these buildings. Here are some facts about the Great Pyramid to show how huge it is.

Weight. The weight of the Great Pyramid is 30 times that of the Empire State Building in New York.

Area of base. In the square base one could fit several European cathedrals. The illustration shows how Salisbury Cathedral, itself the tallest cathedral in Britain, would fit comfortably inside the Great Pyramid.

Area of faces

From a distance, the Pyramids seem to have perfectly straight edges. Close to, the sides and edges are jagged. On one face of the Great Pyramid there is a large hole. This was caused by Arab excavators who used battering rams to open the pyramid, and by an English traveller called Colonel Howard Vyse, whose method of archaeology was to use large quantities of gunpowder to blast open the building.

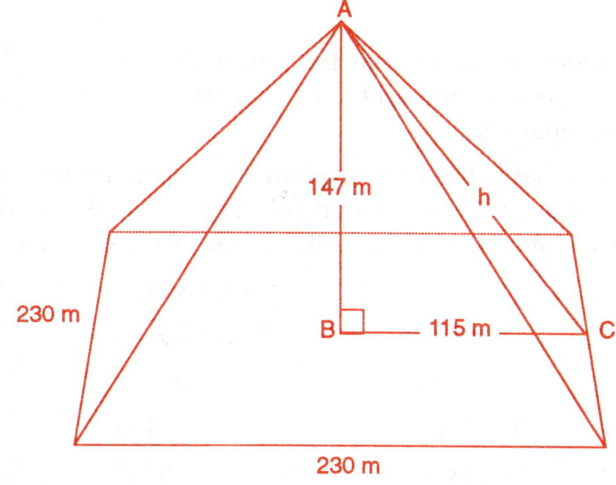

But originally the pyramid had a smooth surface. The whole surface was covered with polished limestone. The covering was removed about a thousand years ago, and used for the construction of buildings in Cairo.

Each face is a triangle. The base side of the triangle is 230 m. What is its height?

Look at the Pyramid from the side, as shown on the right. A right-angled triangle is formed by the top of the pyramid A, the middle of the base B and the centre of one side C.

Using Pythagoras's theorem we can find the height h of the triangular face.

$$h = \sqrt{115^2 + 147^2} = 187 \text{ m.}$$

The area of the faces is now easy to obtain. Use the formula for the area of a triangle, half base times height:

Area of face = 21,500 m^2. Total area = 86,000 m^2

This area is about 21 acres. It is equivalent to 12 football pitches, or to 330 tennis courts.

Slope

It is now illegal to walk on the pyramids. Earlier it was common for tourists to climb to the top. The steepest and quickest route to the top is by starting at the middle of one of the base sides, marked C in the diagram on the right. The shallowest and longest route is by starting at one of the corners, D.

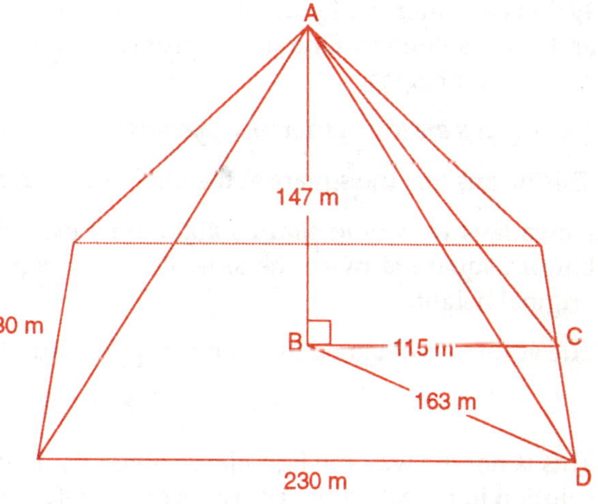

The steepest angle is found from triangle ABC. The opposite side is the height of the pyramid, 147 m, and the adjacent side is half the base side, 115 m.

Steepest angle = $\tan^{-1}\frac{147}{115} = 52°$.

For the shallowest angle we use triangle ABD. The side BD can be found first, by Pythagoras in triangle BCD, to be 163 m.

Shallowest angle = $\tan^{-1}\frac{147}{163} = 42°$.

Accuracy

Earlier we found that the pyramids could have been built by the methods of the time, using huge numbers of men over very long periods. There is no need to appeal to supernatural or extraterrestrial explanations.

But what is harder to explain is the accuracy with which the Pyramids were built. They were designed to be square, aligned along North-South and East-West directions. With no compass to guide them, how accurately were the sides laid? Here are the directions and lengths of the sides of the Great Pyramid:

	Length	Difference from NS or EW
North side	230.251 m	0.04°
East side	230.391 m	0.09°
South side	230.454 m	0.03°
West side	230.357 m	0.04°

So the maximum error in the directions is 0.09 of a degree.

The greatest difference between the sides is 230.454 – 230.251, which is about 0.2 m or 20 cm. This is tiny considering the size of the building. The relative error is the ratio of the error to the quantity we are measuring or constructing. In this case the relative error is:

$$0.2 \div 230 = 0.00087$$

Another way of expressing the relative error is by the percentage error. This can be done by multiplying by 100.

$$\text{Percentage error} = 0.087\%$$

Egyptian mathematics

Nothing is known of Egyptian Mathematics at the time of the construction of the Pyramids. There is no evidence that they knew of Pythagoras's theorem, even though the angles at the base of the Great Pyramid are almost exactly 90°. The earliest surviving text of Egyptian Mathematics dates from 1850 BC, 1,000 years after the Pyramids were built. It is called the Moscow Papyrus, and consists of 25 problems and their solutions. One of the problems deals with a truncated pyramid, i.e. a pyramid with its top removed. It begins:

If you are told: a truncated pyramid, 6 for the vertical height by 4 on the base by 2 on the top.

This means that the square at the top has side 2, and the base side is 4. The height is 6.

Nowadays we would find its volume by extending the pyramid to its peak as shown. The side of the bottom square is twice the side of the top square. Hence the completed pyramid must be twice the original height.

The volume is obtained by subtracting the extra bit A from the completed pyramid C.

$$\text{Volume} = \tfrac{1}{3} \times 12 \times 4^2 - \tfrac{1}{3} \times 6 \times 2^2 = 56$$

This is not the way the Egyptians solved it. Their method is shown at the top of the following page. The solution in the Moscow Papyrus is on the left, with modern notation on the right.

You are to square 4, result 16	$4^2 = 16$

You are to double 4, result 8 $2 \times 4 = 8$

You are to square 2, result 4 $2^2 = 4$

You are to add the 16, 8 and 4, result 28 $16 + 8 + 4 = 28$

You are to take one third of 6, result 2 $\frac{1}{3} \times 6 = 2$

You are to take 28 twice, result 56 $2 \times 28 = 56$

See, it is 56. You will find it right.

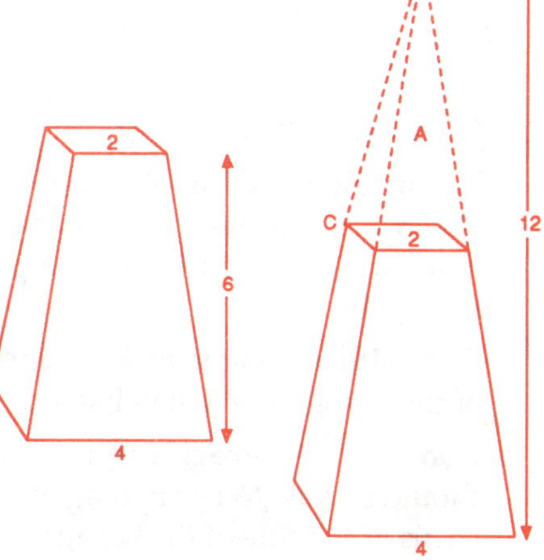

What rule or formula was being followed here? There is a modern formula for the volume of a truncated pyramid: if the height is h and the squares at top and bottom have sides a and b:

$$\text{Volume} = \tfrac{1}{3} h(a^2 + ab + b^2)$$

The solution in the Moscow Papyrus seems to use this formula, or something very like it. Perhaps Mathematics 4,000 years ago was more advanced than we thought. This problem and its solution has been referred to as the "Greatest Egyptian Pyramid".

Mathematics and the pyramids

The study of the pyramids involves the mathematics of measurement. Here material from Chapters 2, 4, 13 and 16 has been touched upon.

Extended task. Squaring the circle

One of the oldest problems in Mathematics is that of "Squaring the Circle". The problem is to find a square with the same area as a given circle. It can be shown that it is equivalent to "Circling the Square", which is to find a circle with the same area as a given square.

Both problems are equivalent to finding the value for π, which is the ratio of the circumference of a circle to its diameter.

1) **Historical values**

Various values of π have been given, as follows. In each case find the percentage error in the value.

$\frac{22}{7}$ *(Archimedes, Greece, 225 BC)*

$\frac{355}{113}$ *(Tsu Ch'ung-Chih, China, 470 AD)*

$\frac{3927}{1250}$ *(Bhaskara, India, 1150 AD)*

$\sqrt{10}$ *(Ch'ang Hong, China, 125 AD)*

$$\frac{88}{\sqrt{785}}$$ *(Tycho Brahe, Denmark, 1580 AD).*

2) **Inscribed polygons**

The method used by Archimedes and by a Chinese Mathematician called Liu Hui was to draw polygons inside a circle. As we take more and more sides then the perimeter of the polygon approaches that of the circle.

Start with a hexagon inside a circle of radius 1. What is the perimeter of the hexagon? What value does this give for π?

Convert the hexagon to a 12 sided figure. (A dodecagon). You should be able to use Pythagoras to find the side of the dodecagon in terms of the side of the hexagon. What value does this give for π?

Repeat, finding the perimeter of a 24 sided figure, a 48 sided figure, and so on. Archimedes went up to a 96 sided figure, Liu Hui up to 192 sides. If you can program a computer to do the calculations, you will be able to go much further than this.

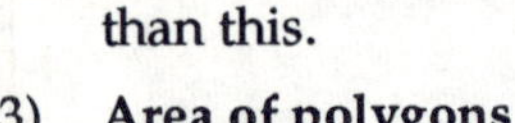

3) **Area of polygons**

The area of a triangle is given by the formula $\frac{1}{2}ab \sin \hat{C}$. Use this formula to find the area of an inscribed polygon. By taking more and more sides you will get closer to the area of the circle. Probably you used a calculator to find the values of sin – why does this assume the answer?

4) **Series and products**

The number π occurs throughout Mathematics, often in situations which seem far removed from circles. There are many ways of calculating π from series and products. Try some of the following: see how many terms you must take to get reasonably close to π.

a) $$\frac{1}{4}\pi = 1 - \frac{1}{3} + \frac{1}{5} - \frac{1}{7} + \frac{1}{9} - \ldots$$ *(Leibnitz, 1673)*

b) $$\frac{1}{3}\pi = 1 + \frac{1^2}{4\times6} + \frac{1^2\times3^2}{4\times6\times8\times10} + \frac{1^2\times3^2\times5^2}{4\times6\times8\times10\times12\times14} + \ldots$$ *(Matsunaga,1739)*

c) $$\frac{\sqrt{3}}{6}\pi = 1 - \frac{1}{3\times3} + \frac{1}{3^2\times5} - \frac{1}{3^3\times7} + \frac{1}{3^4\times9} - \ldots$$ *(Sharp, 1717)*

d) $$\frac{1}{4}\pi = \frac{2\times4\times4\times6\times6\times8\times8\times10\times10\times12\times12\times\ldots}{3\times3\times5\times5\times7\times7\times9\times9\times11\times11\times13\times13\times\ldots}$$ *(Wallis, 1655)*

The answer to the problem of squaring the circle is that it is impossible to do exactly: π is not a number which can be expressed exactly in terms of fractions or square roots or cube roots and so on. This was proved in 1888 by Lindemann.

Miscellaneous exercises

Group A

1) A square is drawn inside a circle of radius 5 cm. What is the length of the circle between adjacent corners of the square?

2) The diameter of a cartwheel is 120 cm, and the boss in the centre of the wheel has diameter 15 cm. How long are the spokes of the wheel? If the cart travels 100 m, how many times has the wheel turned?

3) A long-playing record has diameter 12 inches, and the playing surface ends 2 inches from the centre. What is the area of the playing surface?

4) What is the volume of 1,000 cm of wire, if the cross-section is a circle of diameter 0.05 cm?

5) A cylinder which holds 1 litre has height 20 cm. What is the radius of the base circle?

6) A hemispherical bowl of radius 7 cm is full of water. It is emptied into a cylindrical jar of base radius 5 cm. How deep is the water in the cylinder?

7) A cylindrical pipe delivers 3 litres per second. If the radius of cross section is $1\frac{1}{2}$cm find the speed of water in the pipe.

8) In the diagrams on the right the dot represents the centre of the circle. Find the unknown angles.

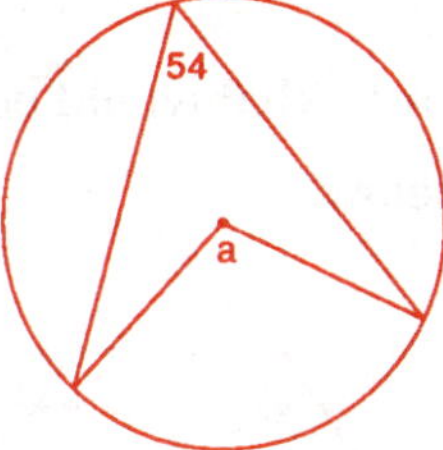

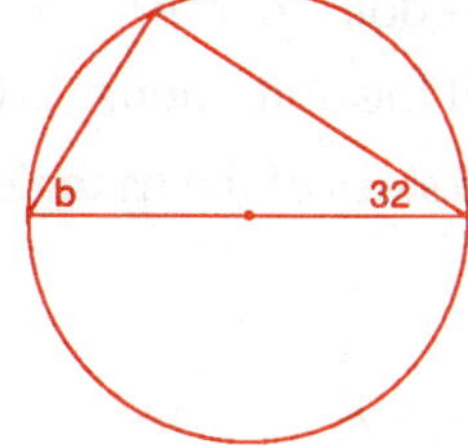

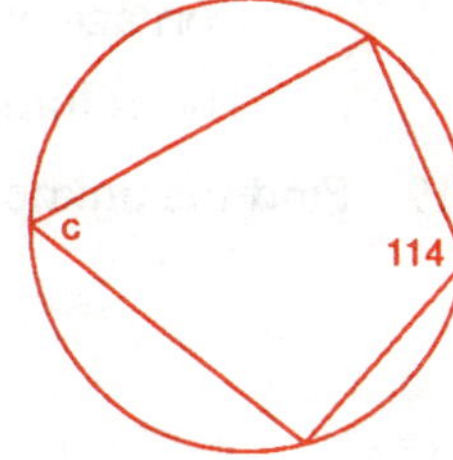

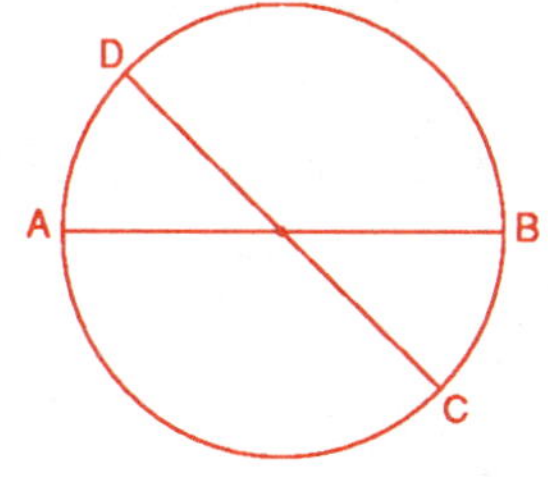

9) AB and CD on the diagram on the left are diameters of the circle shown. Prove that ACBD is a rectangle.

10) Find the unknown angles in the diagrams below.

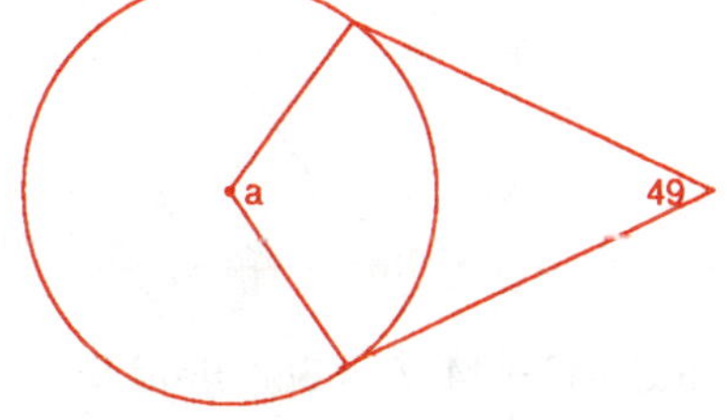

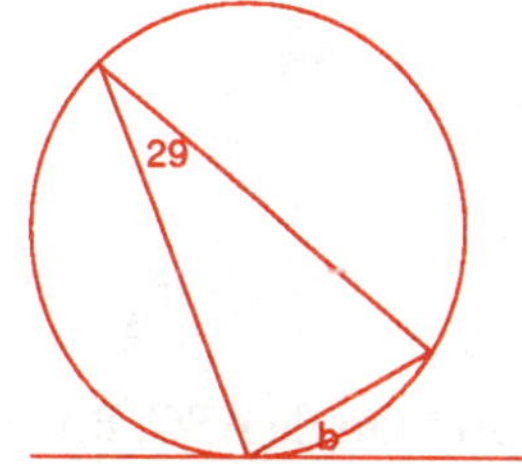

11) Chords AB, CD of a circle meet at X inside the circle. BX = 4, CX = 2, CD = 18. Find AX.

12) AB is a chord of a circle, with AB = 15. XAB is a straight line, with X outside the circle and XA = 5. Find the length of the tangent from X to the circle.

13) Find obtuse angles for which

a) $\sin x = 0.7$ b) $\cos x = -0.3$

c) $\tan x = -2.6$.

14) A ship sails 50 miles on a bearing of 325°. How far North and how far East has it gone?

15) Draw the graph of $y = 3 \cos x - \sin x$, taking values of x from 0° to 360°. Find the maximum value of $3 \cos x - \sin x$. Solve the equation $3 \cos x - \sin x = 2$.

16) In the diagram, the base of the figure is a triangle right-angled at A, with AB = AC = 8 cm. V is 5 cm vertically above A. X is the midpoint of BC.

Find a) VB b) AX c) $V\hat{B}A$ d) $V\hat{X}A$.

17) In Δ ABC, M is on AB and N is on AC, with MN parallel to BC and AM = $\frac{1}{4}$MB.

a) Write down a pair of similar triangles.

b) Find the ratio MN:BC.

c) If the area of Δ ABC is 100, what is the area of BCNM?

18) A dolls' house is in the scale 1:20.

a) If the doll's house is 1.1 m high, how high would the real house be?

b) If the frontage of the real house is 500 m^2 in area, what is the frontage of the dolls' house?

c) The volume of the dolls' house is 0.8 m^3. What would be the volume of the real house?

19) Find the unknown sides of the triangles below.

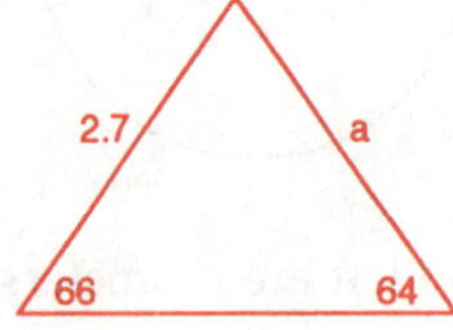

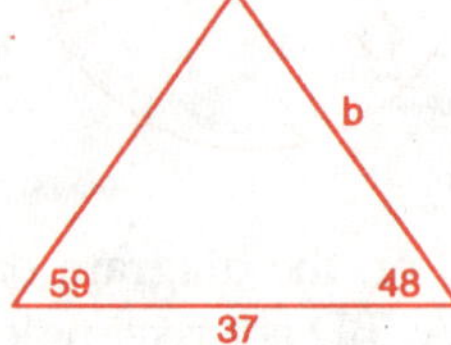

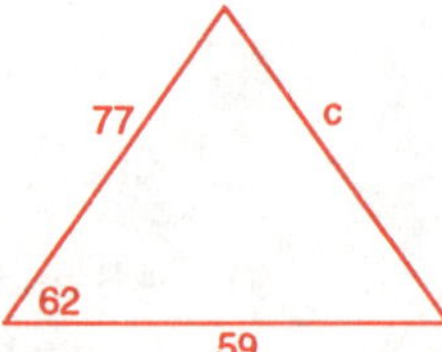

20) Find the unknown angles of the triangles below.

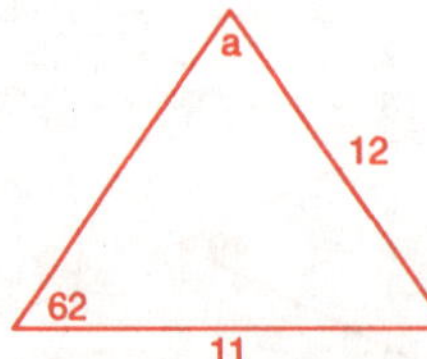

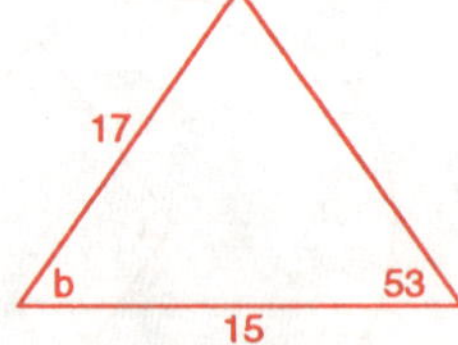

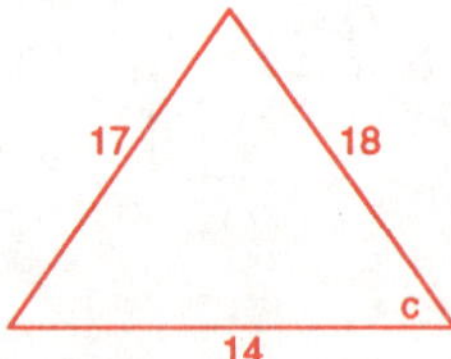

21) In triangle ABC, BA = 12 and AC = 14. $\hat{A} = 38°$. Find $\hat{B}$.

22) In triangle PQR, PQ = 12 and QR = 17. $\hat{P} = 47°$. Find PR.

23) Let $\mathbf{a} = \begin{pmatrix} 4 \\ 7 \end{pmatrix}$ and $\mathbf{b} = \begin{pmatrix} 8 \\ -2 \end{pmatrix}$. Find the following:

a) $3\mathbf{a} + 2\mathbf{b}$

b) $|\mathbf{a}|$, $|\mathbf{b}|$ and $|\mathbf{a} + \mathbf{b}|$

c) x and y such that $x\mathbf{a} + y\mathbf{b} = \begin{pmatrix} 28 \\ 17 \end{pmatrix}$.

24) W(1,2), X(2,4), Y(5,3) and Z(4,1) are the vertices of a quadrilateral. Show that WXYZ is a parallelogram. Is it a rectangle? Is it a rhombus?

25) Which three of J(2,1), K(4,1), L(–2,–2) and M(0,–1) lie on a straight line?

26) ABCD is a parallelogram, with $\underline{AB}$ = **b** and $\underline{AD}$ = **d**. X and Y are the midpoints of AB and CD respectively. Express in terms of **b** and **d**:

$\underline{AC}$, $\underline{AX}$, $\underline{AY}$, $\underline{XY}$

What can you say about XY?

27) The current in the sea is 1 km/hr due East. A boat can be rowed at 3 km/hr.

a) If the boat is pointed due North, what is its actual speed and direction?

b) In what direction should the boat be pointed, if it is to travel due North? What will be its speed?

28) A triangle has vertices at A(–1,1), B(1,3), C(4,1). It is rotated to A′(0,2), B′(2,0), C′(0,–3). Find the centre and angle of rotation.

29) The triangle ABC of Question 28 is reflected first in $y = x$ then in $x = 0$. Find the combined transformation.

30) Find the matrices equivalent to the transformations of Question 29. Multiply these matrices to find the matrix equivalent to the combined transformation.

Group B. Challenge questions

31) ABCD is a cyclic parallelogram. Draw a diagram of ABCD. What else can be said about it?

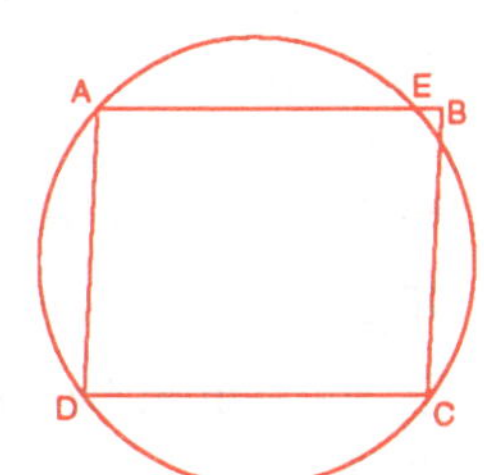

32) In the figure ABCD is a parallelogram. The circle through ADC cuts BA at E. Show that Δ CBE is isosceles.

33) The chords AB and CD of a circle meet at X outside the circle. XA = 12, XB = 10, CD = 7. Find XC and XD.

34) The pyramid shown has a square base of side 50 m, and has height 30 m. Find the angle of slope if one climbs:

a) From the midpoint of a side to the top.

b) From one of the corners of the base to the top.

If one wants to climb to the top at an angle of 45°, where along a base side should one start?

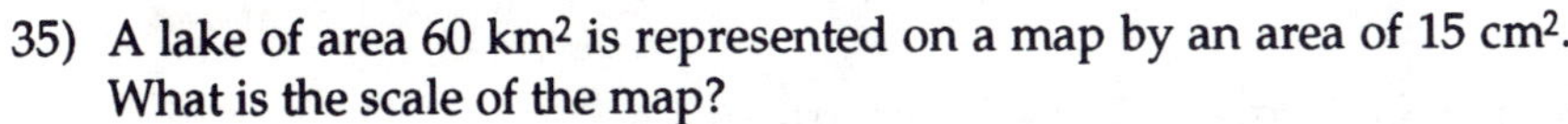

35) A lake of area 60 km^2 is represented on a map by an area of 15 cm^2. What is the scale of the map?

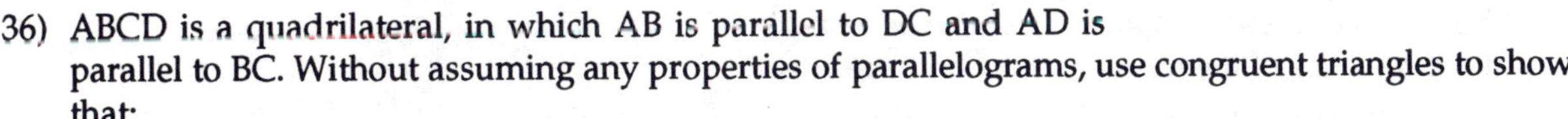

36) ABCD is a quadrilateral, in which AB is parallel to DC and AD is parallel to BC. Without assuming any properties of parallelograms, use congruent triangles to show that:

a) AB = DC and AD = BC b) $\hat{A} = \hat{C}$ and $\hat{B} = \hat{D}$.

37) In Δ ABC, AB = 8, BC = 9, CA = 18. Find $\hat{B}$

What has gone wrong? Find conditions on the sides of ΔABC for it to exist.

38) In Δ PQR, PQ = 12, $\hat{Q}$ = 63°, PR = 8. Find $\hat{R}$.

What has gone wrong? How could the value of PR be changed so that Δ PQR exists?

39) A regular octagon is drawn outside a circle of radius 10 cm. Find the area of the octagon.

40) Let $\mathbf{a} = \begin{pmatrix}4\\5\end{pmatrix}$ and $\mathbf{b} = \begin{pmatrix}2\\1\end{pmatrix}$. Find values of x so that $|\mathbf{a} + x\mathbf{b}| = 12$.

41) A pyramid has a square base of side 12 cm. Its height is 10 cm. A hoop of radius 4 cm is placed on top of the pyramid. Find the depth of the hoop below the apex of the pyramid.

42) The matrix which performs a rotation of P° is $\begin{pmatrix}\cos P & -\sin P\\ \sin P & \cos P\end{pmatrix}$.

Use this matrix to perform a rotation of 60° on the triangle of Question 28.

43) If a circle is rotated about a diameter, what is the solid region it passes through?

If an isosceles triangle is rotated about its axis of symmetry, what solid region does it pass through?

What area would you rotate in order to pass through a cylindrical region of space?

Group C. Longer exercise

44) Quadratic equations by construction

This is a geometric way of solving a quadratic equation.

Suppose the equation is $x^2 - gx + h = 0$. Plot B at (0,1) and H at (g,h). Draw the circle whose diameter is BH. Where this cuts the x-axis are the solutions of the equation.

a) Try this method for the equations $x^2 - 4x + 2 = 0$ and $x^2 + 6x - 5 = 0$. Check that your answers agree with those obtained by the formula.

b) Can you show algebraically why the method works?

Revision exercises

1) The base radius of a cylinder is 2 cm. If the volume is 25 cm³ find the height.

2) A trapezium has area 60 cm² and height 10 cm. If the parallel sides are in the ratio 1:2 what are they?

3) Parquet tiles are rectangles which are 4 cm by 12 cm. How many are needed to cover a floor of 12 m by 8 m?

4) AB is a chord of a circle with centre X. If $A\hat{X}B = 47°$ find $B\hat{A}X$.

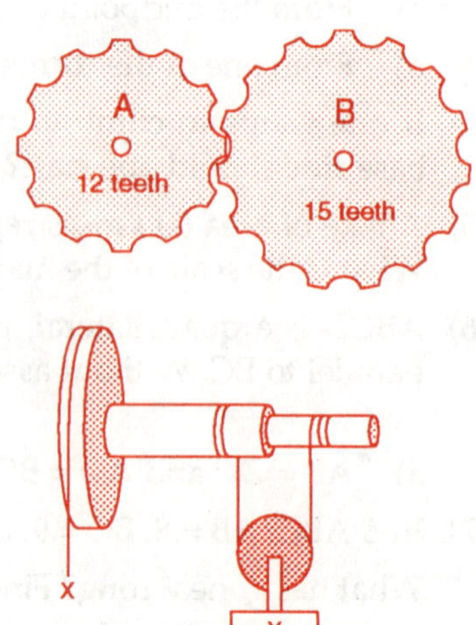

5) Construct the triangle ABC with AB = 8 cm, BC = 9 cm, CA = 8.5 cm. Measure $\hat{A}$. Construct the circle which goes through A, B and C. Find the radius of this circle.

6) In the triangle PQR, PQ = 8 cm, PR = 7 cm and $\hat{P} = 48°$. Construct the triangle. Measure QR. Construct the triangle which touches the three sides of the triangle, and find its radius.

7) In the diagram above right, the wheel A rotates clockwise at 3 revolutions per minute. Predict the motion of wheel B.

8) In the diagram on the right the wheel has radius 40 cm, and the two axles have radii 6 cm and 5 cm. The rope passes round a

pulley, from which hangs a weight Y. The rope at X is pulled down at 1 m per second. Predict the motion of Y.

9) Find the interior angle of a regular polygon with 18 sides.

10) The interior angle of a regular polygon is 100° greater than the exterior angle. Find the number of sides of the polygon.

11) Try to construct a triangle ABC with AB = 10 cm, BC = 5 cm, CA = 4 cm. What has gone wrong? What conditions on the sides are necessary for you to be able to construct a triangle?

12) Try to construct a triangle XYZ with XY = 8 cm, YZ = 4 cm, $\hat{X} = 35°$. What has gone wrong? How could you change the angle $\hat{X}$ to enable you to construct the triangle?

13) ABCDE is a regular pentagon. Find $A\hat{B}C$, $A\hat{D}E$, $A\hat{C}D$.

14) ABCDEF is a regular hexagon. Find $A\hat{B}C$, $A\hat{C}D$, $A\hat{D}E$, $A\hat{D}F$. What can you say about ACDF?

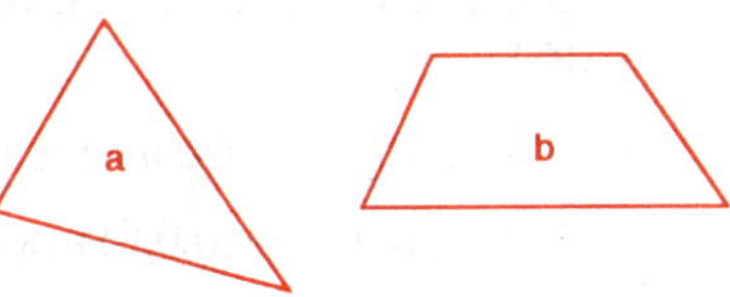

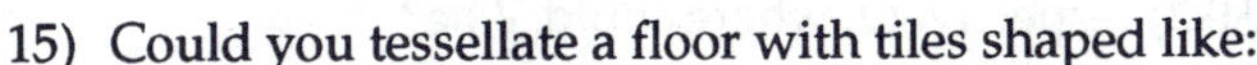

15) Could you tessellate a floor with tiles shaped like:

a) irregular triangles b) trapezia?

16) A cuboid is 8 high, 4 wide, 7 long. The origin is at the centre of the cuboid. What are the coordinates of the vertices?

17) Use isometric paper to make a drawing of the cuboid of Question 16.

18) Draw the plan and elevations of the cuboid of Question 16.

19) An octahedron has 8 faces which are equilateral triangles. How many edges and vertices does it have? Draw the net for an octahedron.

20) The figure shows a square based pyramid. X and Y are the midpoints of AD and BC.

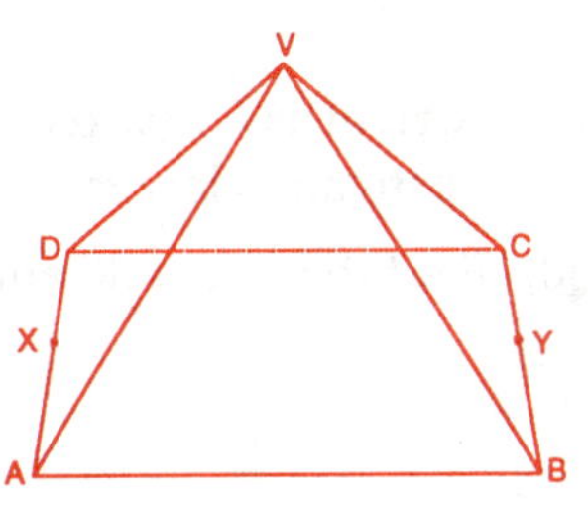

a) The pyramid is cut in half by the plane through VXY. What is the name of the solid formed by one of the halves? How many faces, edges and vertices does it have?

b) The pyramid is cut in half by the plane through VAC. What is the solid formed by one of the halves? How many faces, edges and vertices does it have?

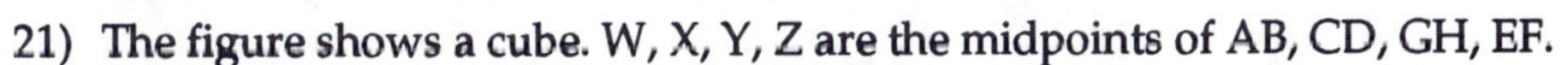

21) The figure shows a cube. W, X, Y, Z are the midpoints of AB, CD, GH, EF.

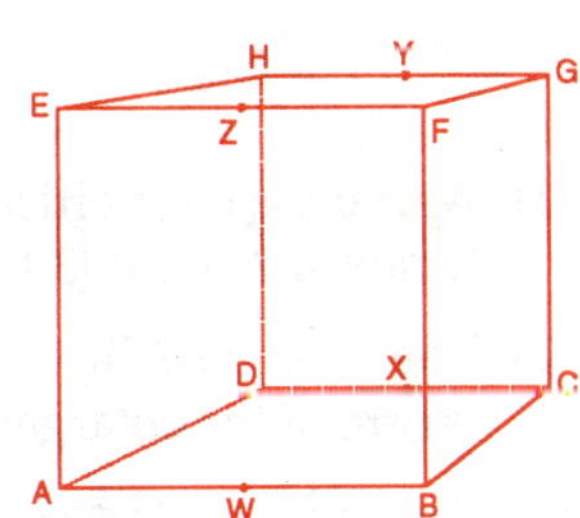

a) The cube is cut in half by the plane through WXYZ. What is the name of the solid formed?

b) The cube is cut in half by the plane through ACGE. What is the name of the solid formed?

c) The cube is cut in two by the plane through BED. What is the name of the smaller solid formed?

22) The greatest distance within the cube of Question 21 could be AG. Name three other lines in the cube which have the same length.

23) Draw the plan and elevation of a regular tetrahedron.

24) How many planes of symmetry are there for the following:

a) A pyramid with a square base.

b) A pyramid with a rectangular base.

c) A cuboid which is 3 by 4 by 5.

d) A cuboid which is 3 by 3 by 4.

e) A cube.

25) Let $\mathbf{a} = \begin{pmatrix} 2 \\ -5 \end{pmatrix}$ and $\mathbf{b} = \begin{pmatrix} 3 \\ 2 \end{pmatrix}$. Find $\mathbf{a} + 2\mathbf{b}$ and $2\mathbf{a} - 4\mathbf{b}$.

Where would the translation corresponding to $\mathbf{a} + 2\mathbf{b}$ take (4,7)?

26) What is the vector between (8,3) and (5,4)? Where would this vector take the point with coordinates (1,-2)?

27) A pyramid has a square base ABCD of side 2, and its vertex V is 3 from the centre of the base ABCD.

a) If A, B, C, D are at (0,0,0), (0,2,0), (0,2,2), (0,0,2) respectively, where could V be?

b) If A, B are at (0,0,0) and (0,2,0) respectively, where could C, D, V be?

c) If A is at (0,0,0), where could B, C, D, V be?

28) Find the unknown sides in the triangles below:

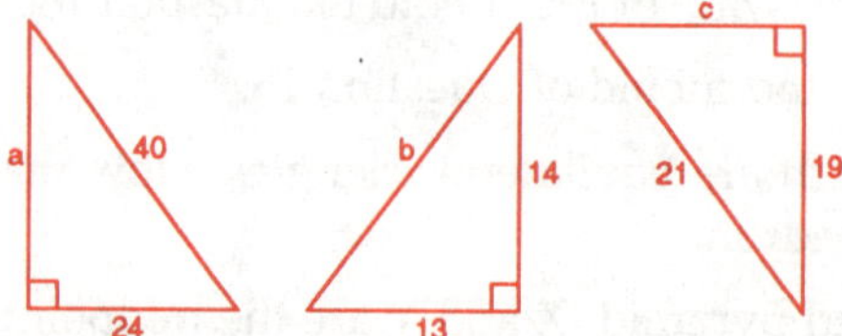

29) A river is 80 yards wide. I am standing opposite a tree on the other bank. I now walk 20 yards upstream. How far am I now from the tree?

30) Find the sides and angles of the triangles below:

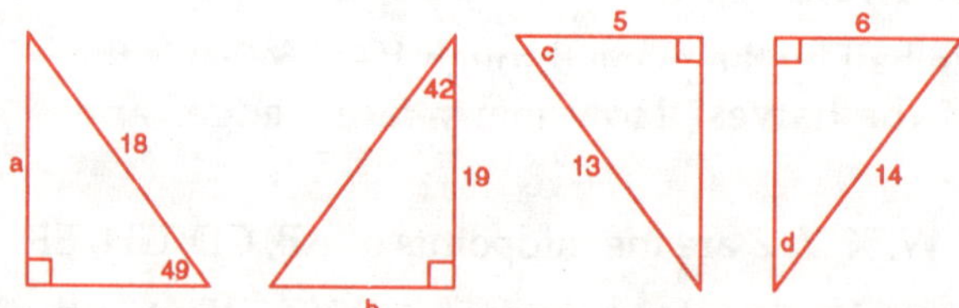

31) A triangle has vertices at A(2,3), B(3,4), C(4,1). Draw ΔABC on graph paper, and enlarge it by a scale factor of 2 about (3,1). Write down the coordinates of the new vertices.

32) The triangle ABC of Question 31 is enlarged to A′(0,3), B′(3,6), C′(6,-3). Find the scale factor and centre of the enlargement.

33) A quadrilateral has vertices at W(0,2), X(2,3), Y(1,5), Z(-1,4). Plot WXYZ. Enlarge it by a scale factor of $\frac{1}{2}$ from (0,3). Write down the new coordinates.

34) The quadrilateral WXYZ of Question 33 is enlarged by a scale factor of –3 about (1,4). Plot the enlarged quadrilateral, and write down the new vertices.

35) Δ ABC is similar to ΔXYZ. A is at (1,1), B at (3,1), C at (3,2): X is at (0,4), Y at (4,4). Find two places where Z could be.

36) The figure shows two overlapping circles, with centres at X and Y. Draw the two common tangents, touching the left circle at A and B and the right circle at C and D.

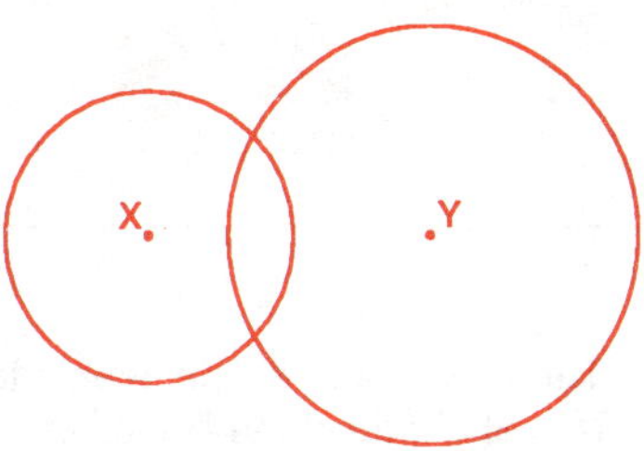

What figure is ABDC? What is the line of symmetry of the diagram?

37) The radius of the Earth is 6,400,000 m. A tower is 100 m high. How far is the horizon from the top of the tower?

Puzzles and paradoxes

1) This paradox shows that all lengths are equal. In the similar triangles shown

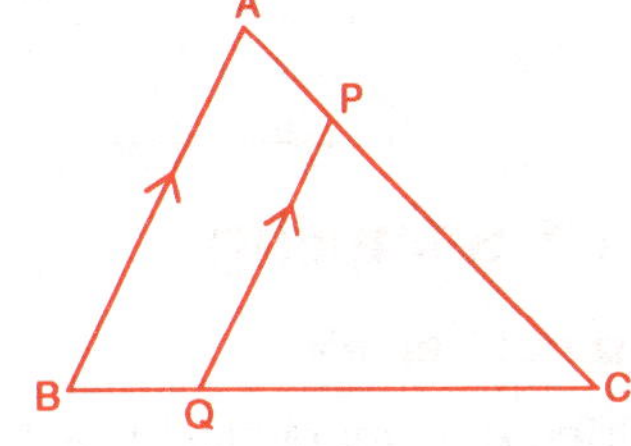

$$\frac{AB}{PQ} = \frac{AC}{PC}$$

Multiply across to obtain AB.PC = AC.PQ. Multiplying both sides of this equation by AB – PQ, we obtain:

$$AB^2.PC - AB.PC.PQ = AC.PQ.AB - AC.PQ^2$$

Rearrange to get $AB^2.PC - AC.PQ.AB = AB.PC.PQ - AC.PQ^2$.

Both sides can be factorized, to obtain:

$$AB.(AB.PC - AC.PQ) = PQ.(AB.PC - AC.PQ)$$

Notice that the term in brackets is the same. Divide by it to obtain AB = PQ. What has gone wrong?

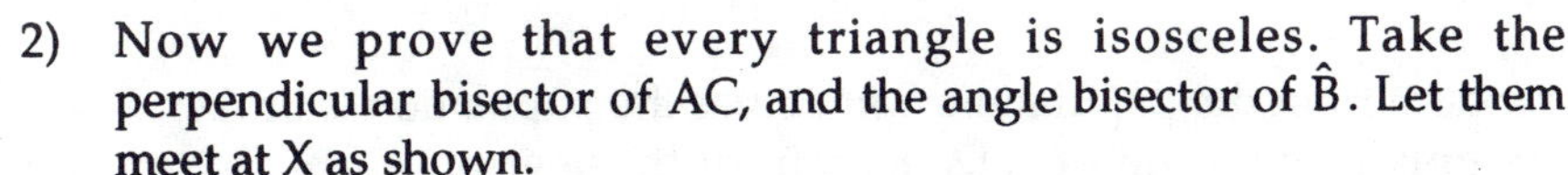

2) Now we prove that every triangle is isosceles. Take the perpendicular bisector of AC, and the angle bisector of $\hat{B}$. Let them meet at X as shown.

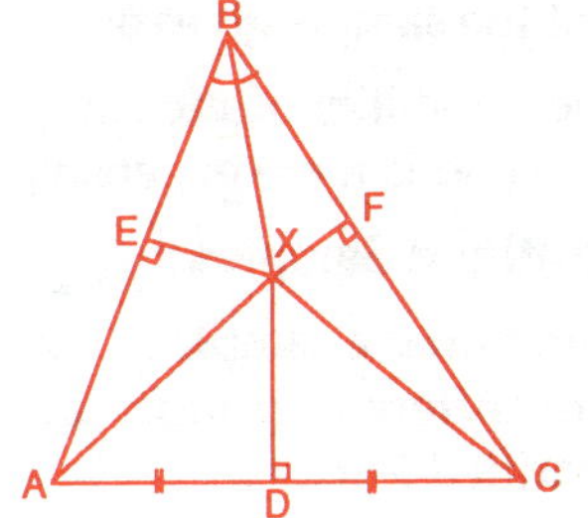

BXE and BXF are congruent. (ASA). DXA and DXC are congruent. (SAS). Now EXA and FXC are congruent. (RHS). It is easy to show now that BA = BC. What has gone wrong?

Chapter 21

Samples

The newspaper article seems to show that the Progress Party is well ahead of the Reaction Party. But the item does not say how many people were questioned in the poll. What could you conclude if you knew that the size of the sample was:

a) 100 b) 1,000 c) 10,000?

Progress Party storms ahead in poll shock

The Progress Party has opened up a 20% lead over the Reaction Party according to a poll published today.

The results give 60% for the Progressives, against 40% for the Reactionaries. If repeated at a General Election that would give a massive majority of 200 seats in Parliament.

Fig 21.1

21.1 Sampling

Size of Sample

Often it is impractical to ask everybody concerned about a certain issue. In this case we ask only a small number of people, called a sample, and hope that the sample is representative.

For example, only in a General Election is everyone asked for their political views. In between General Elections there are opinion polls, which ask a sample of people whom they would vote for. It is hoped that the sample gives a reliable guide for the voting intentions of the population.

The reliability of the sample can be improved by increasing its size. But then the sampling takes more time and is more expensive.

Stratified Samples

Sometimes a sample is taken at random from the population. Sometimes the population is broken down into different groups, and the sample is made up of selections from those groups. This is called a stratified sample.

When an opinion poll is taken, the population is classified by occupation, sex, age, region and so on. The composition of the sample should reflect the composition of the population, otherwise allowance should be made for the bias.

21.1.1 Examples

1) A die was rolled 100 times. The results are below. Find the average score after:

a) 10 rolls b) 50 rolls c) 100 rolls.

What is the best estimate for the average score of the die?

45332 53666 46241 43426
32646 16663 22146 42433
62433 21553 52463 41544
62233 34132 21453 36522
35225 16354 41331 63161

Solution Adding up the first 10 and dividing by 10 we obtain 4.3. Similarly the average after 50 rolls is 3.74, and after 100 rolls it is 3.52. The most reliable average is the one from the largest sample.

The averages are 4.3, 3.74 and 3.52.

The best estimate of the average score is 3.52

2) A washing powder company finds that 20% of its products are bought by men and 80% by women. A sample of 100 men and 200 women are asked whether they would prefer the packets to come in smaller sizes: 50 men and 80 women said they would. Estimate the support for this change for all the people who buy the washing powder.

Solution The sample does not quite represent the customers, so allowance should be made for this. Multiply the support in each group by its proportion among the people who buy the washing powder.

$$\frac{50}{100}\times 0.2+\frac{80}{200}\times 0.8=0.42$$

42% of the customers support the change

21.1.2 Exercises

1) Ann, Bee, Chas, Dave and Edgar take turns to spin a coin 20 times. Ann and Bee each got 7 Heads, Chas got 10, Dave 9 and Edgar 15. What is the proportion of Heads

a) for each person b) for the group as a whole?

2) A computer was programmed to pick 200 random numbers, and to add them up in groups of 20. The results are below.

Group	1	2	3	4	5	6	7	8	9	10
Total	8.3	7.3	10.4	6.8	12.7	9.8	11.5	10.3	10.5	11.2

Find the average random number:

a) of the first 40 b) of the first 100 c) of all 200.

In Questions 3, 4 and 5 the use of a computer will make the experiment quicker and quieter.

3) Roll a die many times, to see the average number of 6's you get in

a) 10 rolls b) 50 rolls c) 100 rolls.

4) Spin a coin many times, to see the average number of Heads you get in

a) 10 spins b) 50 spins c) 100 spins.

5) Look again at the problem at the beginning of the chapter. Suppose the parties have 50% of the vote each. How likely is it that an opinion poll of 100 people would give the result reported? You could spin a coin 100 times to simulate the opinion poll.

6) In an opinion poll 40% of the men questioned supported the Government and 35% of the women. Assuming that there are equal numbers of men and women in the electorate, what is the overall support for the Government?

7) A soft drinks company does research into the popularity of its product. The results are below.

Age range	0 – 18	19 – 39	40 +
Number asked	120	80	80
Total number of cans per week	480	160	8

If the age groups form 30%, 40%, 30% of the population respectively, estimate the average consumption of the drink for the whole population.

8) A survey is done into the weekly spending of the pupils at a school. The girls spent an average of £8.50 each, and the boys an average of £10. If 45% of the school are girls, estimate the average spending for the school as a whole.

9) Cars are classified by their engine capacity, into under 1,100 c.c., between 1,100 and 2,000 c.c., over 2,000 c.c. These groups form 20%, 55% and 25% of the cars in the U.K. The average weekly petrol consumption for these groups is 4 gallons, 5 gallons, 6.5 gallons respectively. Find the average petrol consumption for the cars in the U.K. as a whole.

21.2 Dispersion

When we collect a mass of data, we often want to know how widely spread the numbers are. This is the dispersion of the numbers. There are several ways of measuring dispersion, as follows:

Interquartile range

The lower quartile of a set is the number which separates the bottom quarter from the top three quarters. Similarly the upper quartile separates the top quarter from the bottom three quarters. The interquartile range is the difference between the two quartiles. It contains the central half of the numbers.

Mean deviation

First find the mean of the numbers. Then find all the differences from the mean and average them. This is the mean deviation.

Take the four numbers a, b, c, d with mean m. Suppose m is bigger than a and b but less than c and d.

$$\text{The mean deviation is: } \frac{(m-a)+(m-b)+(c-m)+(d-m)}{4}$$

Standard deviation

First find the mean, then find the squares of the differences from the mean. Average these squares, then take the square root. The result is the standard deviation.

Suppose we have four numbers a, b, c, d, whose mean is m.

$$\text{The standard deviation is: } \sqrt{\frac{(a-m)^2+(b-m)^2+(c-m)^2+(d-m)^2}{4}}$$

This definition sounds complicated and unnatural, but it is the most widely used measure of dispersion.

21.2.1 Examples

1) The army is considering which make of field gun to order. Both were set for 1,000 m and were each fired 8 times. The results, in m, are below. Find the interquartile range for each gun. Which is the better gun?

A: 1008, 990, 989, 999, 1002, 1010, 1005, 1013

B: 1000, 1001, 999, 1004, 996, 999, 1003, 1002

Solution Arrange each of these sets of figures in increasing order.

A: 989, 990, 999, 1002, 1005, 1008, 1010, 1013

B: 996, 999, 999, 1000, 1001, 1002, 1003, 1004

The lower quartile for A is halfway between the second and third number, 994.5. Similarly the upper quartile is 1009.

The interquartile range for A is 14.5

The quartiles for B are 999 and 1002.5.

The interquartile range for B is 3.5

B has a smaller interquartile range. Half of its shells will be landing in a smaller area, and so it is more accurate.

Gun B is better

2) Find the mean deviation and standard deviation for the numbers in Example 1.

Solution Find the means for A and B by adding and dividing by 8.

Mean for A = 1002. Mean for B = 1000.5

Go through all the A figures, and find their differences from 1002. We obtain $1002 - 989 = 13$, $1002 - 990 = 12$ and so on. Add all these differences and divide by 8.

The mean deviation for A is 7

Repeat this procedure for B, taking the differences from 1000.5.

The mean deviation for B is 2

The squared differences for A are 13^2, 12^2 and so on. The sum of these squares is 552. The average of the squares is 69. Square root to obtain:

The standard deviation for A is $\sqrt{69} = 8.31$

Apply the same procedure for B, squaring the differences from 1000.5.

The standard deviation for B is $\sqrt{5.75} = 2.40$

Note that in all three cases the dispersion for A was greater than for B.

21.2.2 Exercises

In Questions 1 to 4 find the interquartile range, the mean deviation and the standard deviation.

1) 50, 70, 57, 63, 45, 48, 51, 64.

2) 90, 97, 97, 92, 94, 95, 92, 95.

3) 30, 26, 25, 36, 38, 32, 33, 27, 23.

4) 36.4, 35.2, 35.9, 36.1, 31.3, 34.2, 35.0, 35.6, 35.3.

5) Eight cats and eight dogs were weighed. The results, in kilograms, are given below. Find the interquartile range for each set of figures, and comment on the result.

Cats: 3.3, 3.8, 2.9, 3.0, 3.4, 3.4, 3.1, 2.9.

Dogs: 5.6, 50, 20.1, 33, 2.0, 43, 10.2, 41.

6) 10 boys and 10 girls each took a test. The results are below. Find and compare the means and the mean deviations.

Boys:	12	13	9	14	17	20	5	14	8	18
Girls:	11	12	13	13	15	14	14	16	17	15

7) Two makes of batteries were tested by seeing how many hours they lasted. The results are below. Find the means and the standard deviations. Comment on your results.

Type A: 21 26 24 23 19 27 24 25 20 24 19 24

Type B: 21 33 15 25 32 39 13 20 12 14 31 27

21.3 Longer exercise

Use of calculator

If you have a scientific calculator then it will be able to find out automatically the mean and standard deviation of data.

1) Get into the SD mode. (SD stands for standard deviation). Make sure that all the memories are clear. Suppose we want to find the mean and standard deviation of 5, 6, 6, 7, 10.

For Casio calculators, the key to enter numbers is M+. (For Texas it is STO.) The sequence for the first number is [5] [M +]. Repeat for the other numbers.

To find the mean, press $\bar{x}$. (This usually requires the shift button). You should get 6.8.

To find the standard deviation, press the button labelled σ_n. You should get 1.72.

Try this procedure with some of the examples of this chapter, and make sure that the answers agree.

2) Your calculator will also be able to find means and standard deviations from frequency tables. For each entry, press the number, then ×, then its frequency, then M+. Repeat for all the other values. Try this for the following frequency table:

Value	2	3	4	5	6
Frequency	5	10	11	14	10

The buttons for the first entry are [2] [×] [5] [M +].

Repeat with the other values, and find the mean and standard deviation. (You should get 4.28 and 1.2655.)

3) How does your calculator do it? Suppose we have 4 values *a*, *b*, *c*, *d*, with mean *m*. The formula we have for standard deviation is:

$$\text{SD} = \sqrt{\frac{(a-m)^2 + (b-m)^2 + (c-m)^2 + (d-m)^2}{4}} \qquad (*)$$

In fact, your calculator uses the following formula for standard deviation:

$$SD = \sqrt{\frac{a^2 + b^2 + c^2 + d^2}{4} - m^2} \qquad (**)$$

By expanding out the brackets in (*) show that it is equivalent to (**). You will need the fact that $m = \frac{1}{4}(a + b + c + d)$.

4) How much memory is needed for each formula? Can you show why a calculator must use the formula (**) rather than (*)?

5) Would it be possible to have a calculator which worked out the mean deviation or the interquartile range?

Multiple choice question *(Tick appropriate box)*

The standard deviation for 6, 7, 8, 7, 6, 5, 7, 7, 8, 9 is:

a) 0.8 ☐

b) 1.2 ☐

c) 0 ☐

d) 7 ☐

e) √1.2 ☐

Points to note

1) *Samples*

If a sample comes from two different groups, then take account of the sizes of these groups. If the sample gives an average of 40% for one group and 60% for the other, then the overall average is not 50% unless the two groups are equal in size.

2) *Dispersion*

a) Read the question carefully to make sure you give the measure of dispersion that you are being asked for.

b) When working out the mean deviation, make sure you take all the differences to be positive. Otherwise you will get a mean deviation of 0.

c) When working out the standard deviation, make sure you do the operations in the correct order. Square the differences, then average, then square root.

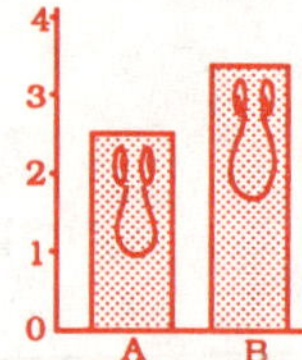

Chapter 22
Histograms

"Britain's trains are getting later and later! We logged the arrival time of 100 trains, and found that all but 20 of them arrived more than a quarter minute after the scheduled time. 40 of the trains were more than 4 minutes late. The diagram shows the disgraceful record of BR."

The diagram does seem to show that a huge proportion of trains are arriving late. But is the diagram fair? How should the diagram be redrawn so that it does give a fairer picture?

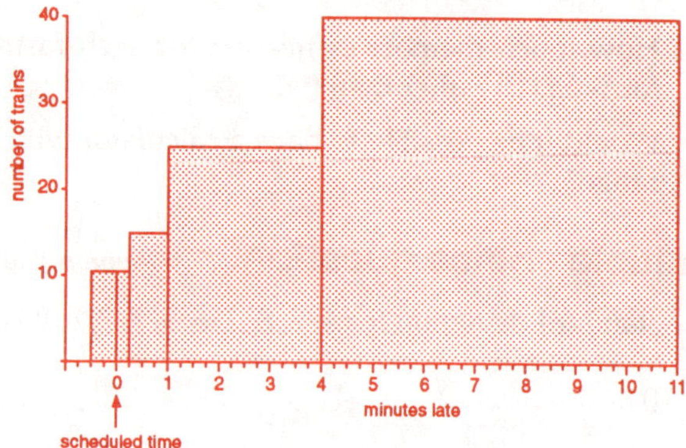

Fig 22.1

22.1 Display of data

There are many ways in which statistical figures can be illustrated. There are pie-charts, bar-charts, frequency polygons and histograms.

If the intervals of a histogram are not of equal width, an adjustment has to be made to take account of this.

We judge the number of elements in an interval by the area of its bar. If the interval is smaller than the rest, then the bar will be thinner than the rest, and there will seem to be too few elements in the interval. If the interval is larger than the rest, then the bar will be fatter than the rest, and there will seem to be too many elements in the interval. The heights of the bars should be adjusted to compensate for this.

The height of a bar on a histogram represents the frequency per unit interval. Hence if an interval is twice the normal width, then its height must be halved. If an interval is one third the normal width, then its height must be tripled.

22.1.1 Example

The marks of 120 candidates in an exam were given by the following table:

% Marks	0–29	30–39	40–49	50–59	60–64	65–69	70–79	80–100
Frequency	12	10	16	24	17	14	19	8

a) Construct a histogram to show this information.

b) What is the modal class?

c) Estimate the proportion of candidates who got at least 55%.

Solution Notice that the intervals are not even. There must be a corresponding adjustment to the height of the bars.

The most common interval is of 10 marks.

The intervals at the beginning and the end are of 30 and 20 marks respectively. Divide each of their frequencies by 3 and 2 respectively.

The intervals in the 60's are of 5 marks each. Double the frequencies in those intervals.

a) The histogram is in Fig 22.2.

b) The modal class is the one in which the population is densest. This is equivalent to the highest bar on the histogram.

The modal group is 60–64

c) Assume that half the candidates in the 50–59 range got at least 55%. This gives 12+17+14+19+8 = 70 candidates in all.

The proportion is $\frac{70}{120} = \frac{7}{12}$

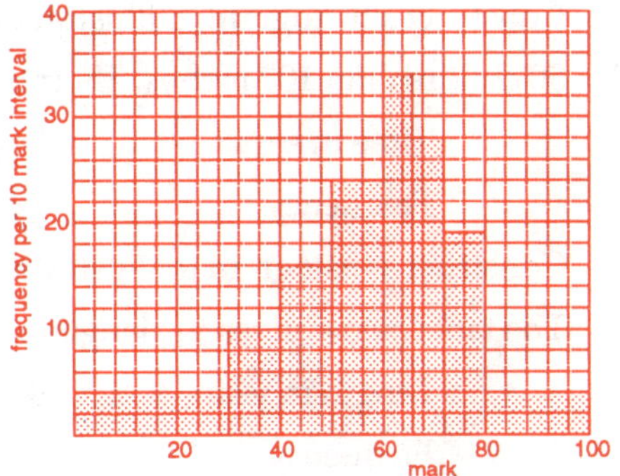

Fig 22.2

22.1.2 Exercises

1) The ages of a group of 500 people at a cinema were as follows:

Age range	10–20	20–25	25–30	30–35	35–40	40–70
Frequency	74	73	104	116	67	66

a) Construct a histogram, using a span of 5 years as the basic interval.

b) What is the modal class?

c) Estimate the proportion of the audience who were over $32\frac{1}{2}$.

2) The averages of 80 cricketers were compared. The figures are shown in the following table:

Average	0–20	20–30	30–40	40–50	50–80
Frequency	22	18	16	12	12

a) Draw a histogram to illustrate this data.

b) Find the modal class.

c) Estimate the percentage of cricketers whose average was less than 35.

3) The salaries of 100 employees of a firm were analysed, and the following table shows the distribution:

Salary in £1,000's	7–9	9–10	10–11	11–12	12–13	13–16
Frequency	24	15	17	19	10	15

Draw a histogram to show the distribution.

4) 60 cats were weighed. The results were as follows:

Weight in kg.	1–3	3–3.5	3.5–4	4–4.5	4.5–6
Frequency	20	9	15	10	6

Construct a histogram to illustrate these figures.

5) 50 children ran 100 metres. Their times are given in the following table.

Time in secs.	12–14	14–15	15–15.5	15.5–16	16–17	17–20
Frequency	4	13	9	11	4	9

Construct a histogram to illustrate these times.

6) The table below gives the length of service of 100 employees at a company:

Length in years	0–1	1–2	2–4	4–6	6–8	8–20
Frequency	16	12	15	13	8	36

Construct a histogram to illustrate these figures.

7) Out of 160 families, 33 had 0 children, 26 had one child, 45 had 2 children, 26 had 3 children, and 30 had 4, 5 or 6 children. Construct a histogram to show these figures.

8) A bridge player always counts the number of hearts in his hand. After 130 games, he finds that he has the following figures:

Number of hearts	0 or 1	2	3	4	5	6	7–13
Frequency	23	19	25	27	13	9	14

Show this information on a histogram.

9) Look at the histogram of Fig 22.1 at the beginning of the chapter. Redraw it so that it is fair.

22.2 Shape of histogram

Symmetry and skewness

The shape of a histogram or frequency polygon can tell a lot about the data it illustrates. If it is symmetrical, then the numbers are balanced on both sides of the mean. If the histogram is skewed to the left then the data contains a lot of small numbers and a few very large numbers.

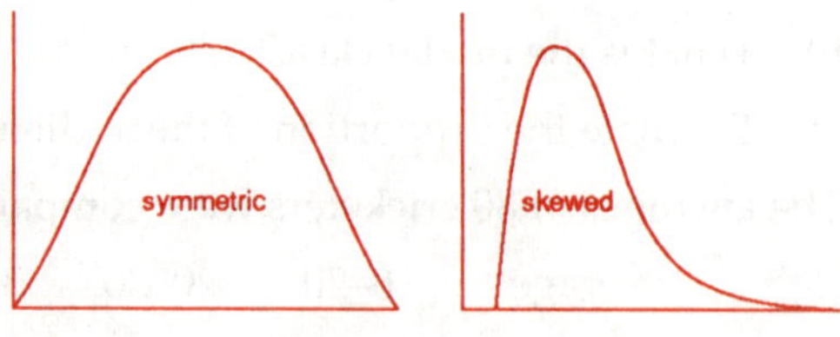

Fig 22.3

Width of histogram

If the histogram is thin, then the data is concentrated near the mean, and if it is fat then the data is widely spread (Fig 22.4).

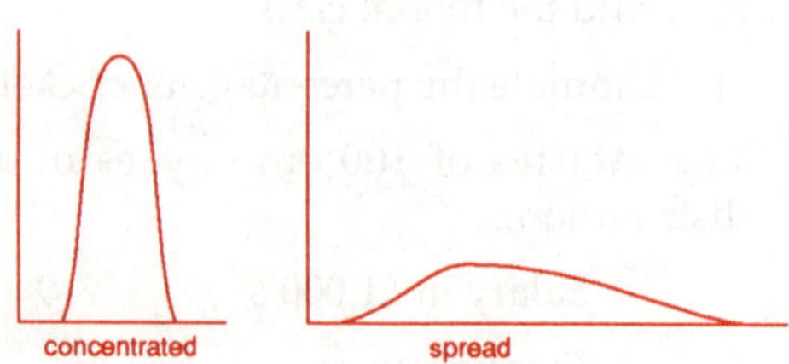

Fig 22.4

The normal curve

When we take a large amount of data, the histogram or frequency polygon often approaches the curve shown in Fig 22.5 (on the following page).

This is known as the normal curve. The mean, mode and median are all together at the top point.

Standard deviation

There are two points on the normal curve, marked with an x, where the curve changes from convex to concave. The distance from either of these points to the mean is a measure of the dispersion of the data. It is called the standard deviation of the data. The numerical formula for finding standard deviation was given in Chapter 21.

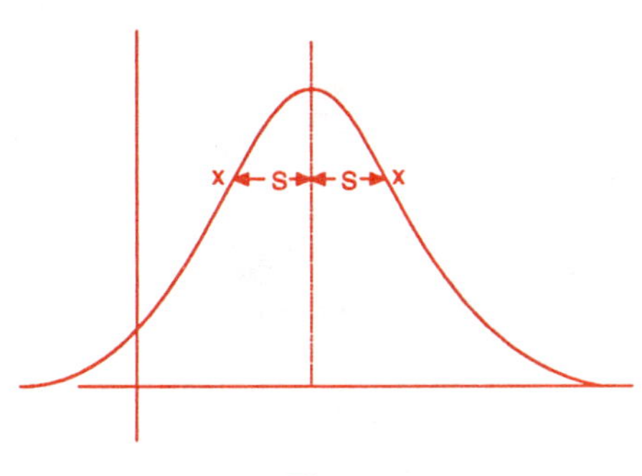

Fig 22.5

Fig 22.6

22.2.1 Example

The diagram above (Fig 22.6) shows the marks obtained by two classes for the same exam. Comment on the difference.

Solution The mean mark for class B is higher than for A. The frequency curve for class B is wider.

Class B did better on average.

The ability in class B is more widely spread

22.2.2 Exercises

1) The numbers of runs scored over a season by two cricket teams are illustrated in the diagram below. Comment on the difference.

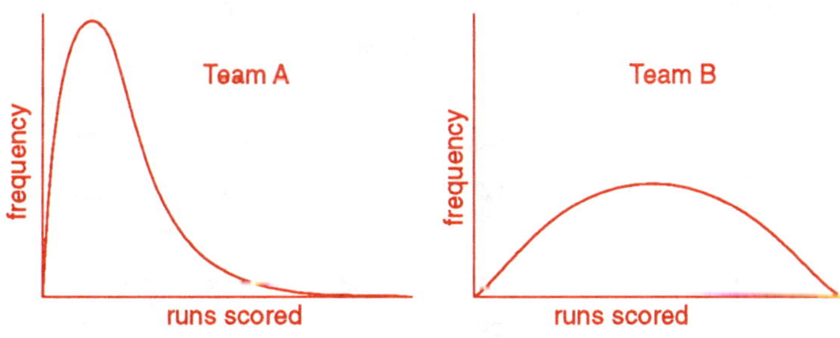

Fig 22.7

2) The histograms of Fig 22.8 show the weights of 2 groups of people. Describe the difference between the groups.

3) The histograms of Fig 22.9 show the salaries for the employees of two firms. Describe the difference.

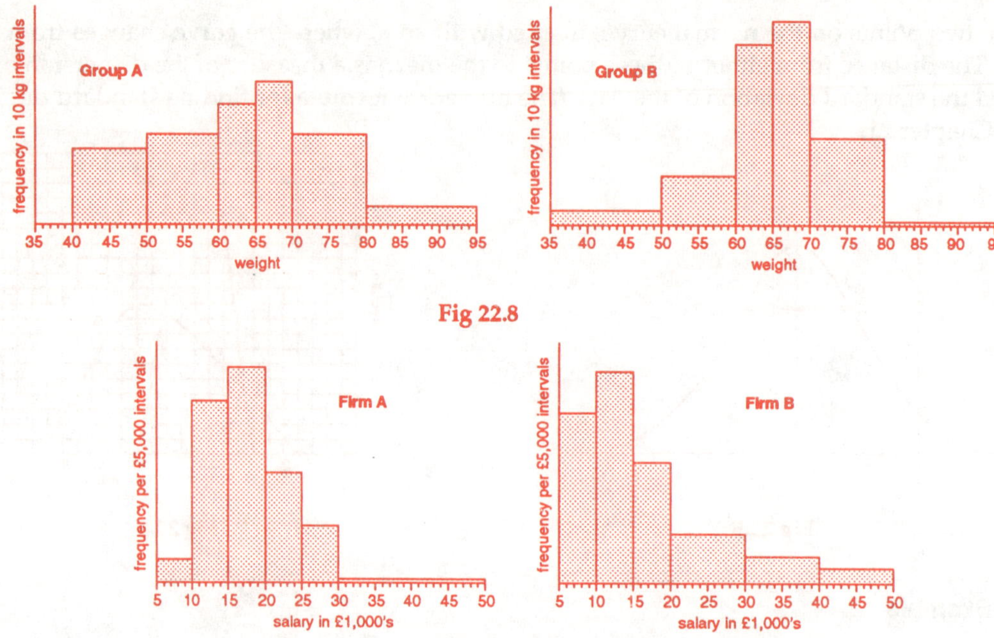

Fig 22.8

Fig 22.9

4) Two different makes of battery were tested by taking 100 of each and seeing how many hours they lasted. Plot histograms and comment on the difference.

Make A

Time	5–10	10–15	15–20	20–25
Frequ.	10	35	42	13

Make B

Time	5–10	10–15	15–20	20–25
Frequ.	19	27	30	24

5) Two different groups of motorists were asked how many years they had owned their cars. Results are below. Plot histograms and comment on the difference.

Group I

Years	0–1	1–2	2–3	3–4	4–5	5–10
Frequ.	45	32	12	6	5	20

Group II

Years	0–1	1–2	2–3	3–4	4–5	5–10
Frequ.	25	33	28	15	2	5

6) Jane and Joe both play 30 rounds of golf over the same course. They have the same average of 90, but Jane is much more consistent than Joe. Sketch frequency curves which show their scores.

7) In a certain country most people earn round about £15,000 per year, but there are a few people who earn a great deal more than that. Draw an approximate histogram which shows the income distribution in that country.

8) The frequency curves below are of normal distributions. In each case estimate the mean and standard deviation.

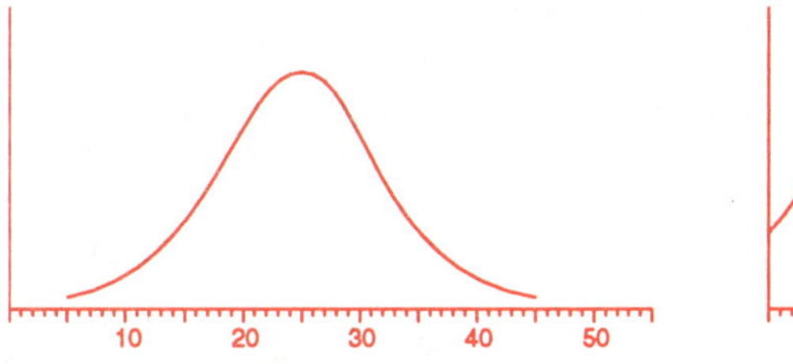

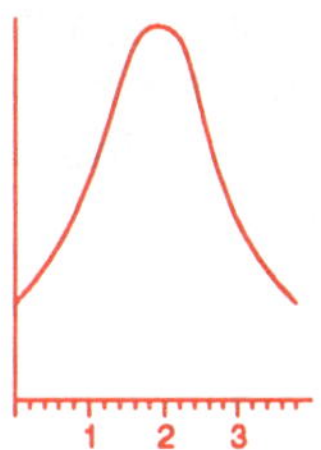

Fig 22.10

9) Sketch the normal distributions:

a) with mean 3 and standard deviation 0.5

b) with mean 5 and standard deviation 2.

22.3 Longer exercise

"Central Limit Theorem"

If we take large samples, the distribution of the average will almost always be approximately normal. This result is known as the Central Limit Theorem. Its proof requires advanced Mathematics, but it can be verified in numerical cases.

A computer was used to pick 10 random numbers, and their average of 0.549 was found. This was repeated 100 times. The full results are below.

.549	.530	.333	.561	.503	.561	.504	.575	.316	.424
.424	.553	.444	.325	.489	.371	.393	.488	.587	.580
.514	.561	.507	.699	.506	.614	.333	.422	.513	.437
.445	.414	.627	.545	.523	.311	.489	.373	.441	.521
.682	.575	.470	.525	.341	.533	.480	.576	.545	.547
.636	.497	.620	.438	.500	.385	.439	.553	.332	.506
.524	.356	.487	.502	.540	.436	.619	.583	.502	.303
.478	.434	.471	.590	.410	.409	.454	.549	.459	.735
.406	.457	.566	.513	.528	.711	.468	.512	.670	.630
.699	.576	.625	.457	.491	.520	.337	.253	.371	.429

1) Group these figures into appropriate class intervals. Plot the histogram. Does your result look like the normal curve?

2) Find the standard deviation of these figures,

a) from the graph

b) using the formula given in Chapter 21. How close are your results?

3) If a larger sample size is taken, the shape of the curve becomes closer to the normal curve. If you can program a computer, use it to find the average of 50 random numbers, 100 times over. You may be able to extend the program so that the numbers are sorted into a frequency table. Repeat (1) and (2).

Multiple choice question

(Tick appropriate box)

Classes A and B compete in a race. Class A were faster on average, but the members of Class B all had about the same time. Frequency curves of their times could be:

a) ☐

b) ☐

c) ☐

d) ☐

a)

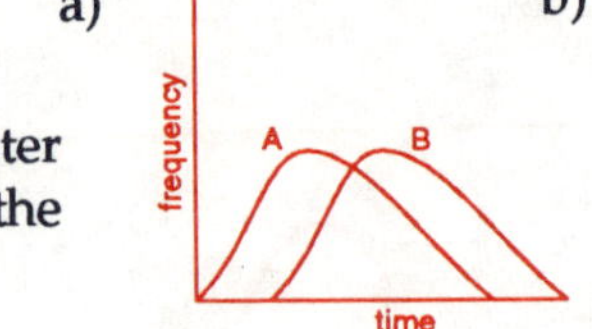

b)

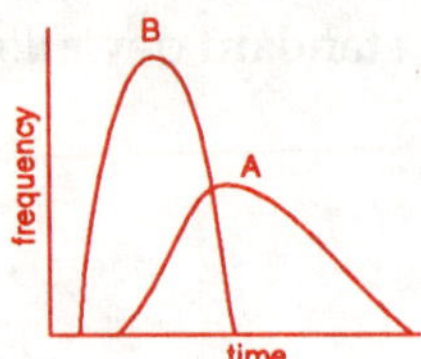

c)

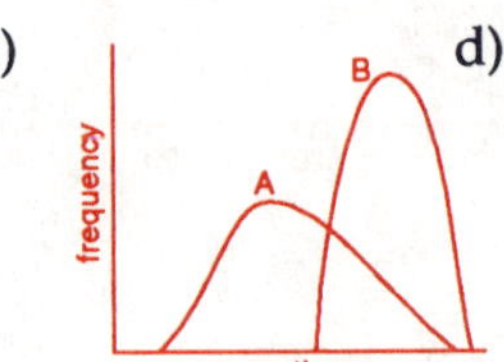

d)

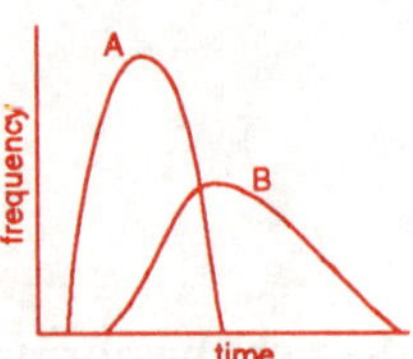

Fig 22.11

Points to note

1) *Width of interval*

Be sure that you adjust the height of the bars to compensate for the different widths of the intervals. If you do not do so, the histogram will be misleading. The example of 22.1.1., without such compensation, would be as shown.

We can see that too much importance is given to the end intervals, and too little importance to the middle intervals.

2) *Labelling*

Be sure that you label the vertical axis clearly. It is not enough to label it "Frequency", you must also explain what the basic interval is. Label it "Frequency per 5 marks", or "Frequency per 10 cm" etc.

3) *Modal group*

The modal group is not necessarily the group with the greatest number in it. It is the group with the greatest density, i.e. it is the group with the tallest bar.

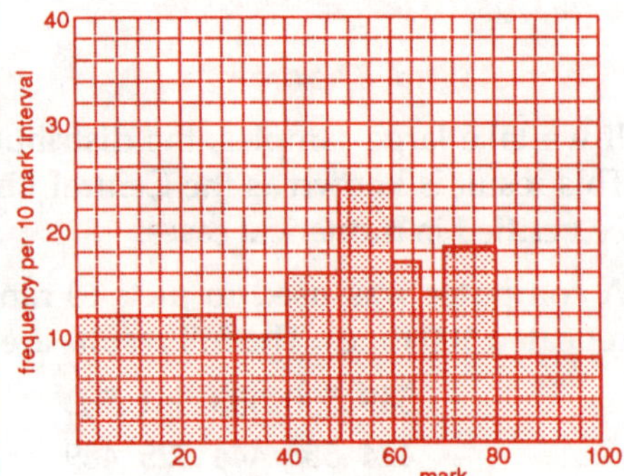

Fig 22.12

Chapter 23

Matrices and networks

You invited the members of two hockey teams for tea after a match, but have forgotten completely about it. The match is Saturday afternoon, and it is already Saturday morning. You haven't made any preparations for the tea.

Your friend tells you not to panic, but to write down all the necessary tasks in an orderly way. How could this be done?

Fig 23.1

23.1 Information matrices

Matrices are rectangular blocks of numbers. In Chapter 20 they were used to represent transformations. They can also be used to represent information, when items are classified under two headings.

The matrix

$$\begin{array}{c} \\ A \\ B \end{array} \begin{array}{c} \text{Bread} \quad \text{Milk} \\ \begin{pmatrix} 80 & 34 \\ 75 & 32 \end{pmatrix} \end{array}$$

might represent the prices of bread and milk in two shops A and B.

If we have a shopping list for 2 loaves of bread and 3 pints of milk, then we can form a matrix product which will show how much we would spend in each shop.

$$\begin{pmatrix} 80 & 34 \\ 75 & 32 \end{pmatrix} \cdot \begin{pmatrix} 2 \\ 3 \end{pmatrix} = \begin{pmatrix} 80 \times 2 + 34 \times 3 \\ 75 \times 2 + 32 \times 3 \end{pmatrix} = \begin{pmatrix} 262 \\ 246 \end{pmatrix}$$

So we would spend £2.62 in shop A or £2.46 in shop B.

23.1.1 Example

Four schools P, Q, R, S play each other in a football league. The results are given in the table on the right. The side is read first, so for example school R lost to school Q.

a) Represent this information as a matrix A, showing the numbers of games won, drawn and lost by each team.

b) Form the matrix product AV, where V is given by $V = \begin{pmatrix} 3 \\ 1 \\ 0 \end{pmatrix}$.

What does this product represent?

	P	Q	R	S
P	X	L	D	L
Q	W	X	W	L
R	D	L	X	D
S	W	W	D	X

Solution a) With one row per team, the following matrix is obtained.

$$\begin{array}{c} \\ P \\ Q \\ R \\ S \end{array}\begin{array}{c} \begin{array}{ccc} W & D & L \end{array} \\ \begin{pmatrix} 0 & 1 & 2 \\ 2 & 0 & 1 \\ 0 & 2 & 1 \\ 2 & 1 & 0 \end{pmatrix} \end{array} = A$$

b) $$\begin{pmatrix} 0 & 1 & 2 \\ 2 & 0 & 1 \\ 0 & 2 & 1 \\ 2 & 1 & 0 \end{pmatrix} \times \begin{pmatrix} 3 \\ 1 \\ 0 \end{pmatrix} = \begin{pmatrix} 1 \\ 6 \\ 2 \\ 7 \end{pmatrix}$$

The product represents the total points for each team, on the system of 3 points for a win and 1 for a draw.

23.1.2 Exercises

1) Four children Albert, Beatrice, Cynthia and David took exams in Maths, English and French. Their percentage marks were:

	Maths	English	French
Albert	57	63	83
Beatrice	85	54	66
Cynthia	43	75	43
David	73	96	56

Consider this as a matrix. Let $U = (\frac{1}{4}\ \frac{1}{4}\ \frac{1}{4}\ \frac{1}{4})$ and $V = \begin{pmatrix} 1 \\ 1 \\ 1 \end{pmatrix}$.

a) Form the products UM and MV. What do they represent?

b) The marks are scaled to that Maths and English account for 40% each of the total mark, and French accounts for the remaining 20%. Find a matrix W so that MW gives the total percentage marks for each child.

2) Emilia has a job delivering newspapers. She delivers the Post, the Bugle and the News to Acacia Avenue and Beech Close. The numbers of papers are given by:

	Post	News	Bugle
Acacia Avenue	24	32	18
Beech Close	42	21	13

Consider this as a matrix N.

a) Find a matrix T so that NT represents the numbers of papers she delivers to the two streets, and evaluate this product.

b) Find a matrix R so that RN represents the numbers of copies of each of the three papers. Evaluate this product.

c) The Post costs 25 p, the News 30 p, the Bugle 40 p. Find a matrix P such that RNP represents the total price of the newspapers, and evaluate this product.

3) A survey was carried out to see how the pupils in the three forms of a year came to school. The results were:

	Car	Bus	Train	Foot	Bike
Form 1	2	6	8	10	2
Form 2	3	3	7	12	1
Form 3	5	4	2	9	4

Consider this as a matrix T.

a) Find a matrix P so that TP gives the numbers of pupils in each form.

b) Find a matrix Q so that QT gives the numbers of pupils who use each form of transport.

c) Find matrices S and R so that STP and QTR both give the total number of pupils in the year. Verify that the two products give the same result.

4) A baker makes two sorts of pastry: type A is half butter and half flour, type B is two fifths butter to three fifths flour. Express this as a matrix showing the amounts of butter and flour for 1 kilogram of each type of pastry. If he is going to make 15 kg of type A and 30 kg of type B, form a matrix product which will give the total amounts of butter and flour he will use.

23.2 Route matrices

Suppose there are several towns connected by road or rail or airplane routes. A route matrix tells us how many direct routes there are connecting each pair of towns. When this matrix is squared, it gives the number of two stage routes between pairs of towns.

23.2.1 Example

Fig 23.2 shows the roads which connect three villages X, Y, Z. The arrow denotes a one-way road. Find the route matrix A for this map.

Find A^2. How many two stage journeys are there from Y back to Y?

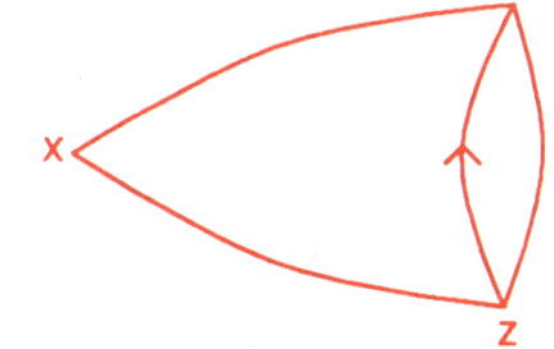

Fig 23.2

Solution There are 3 villages, so the matrix will have 3 rows and 3 columns. The side is read before the top, so for example there is 1 road from Y to Z. The matrix is below.

$$A = \begin{pmatrix} 0 & 1 & 1 \\ 1 & 0 & 1 \\ 1 & 2 & 0 \end{pmatrix} \quad \begin{matrix} X \\ Y \\ Z \end{matrix} \qquad (\text{columns } X \ Y \ Z)$$

Square A to obtain $A^2 = \begin{pmatrix} 0 & 1 & 1 \\ 1 & 0 & 1 \\ 1 & 2 & 0 \end{pmatrix} \times \begin{pmatrix} 0 & 1 & 1 \\ 1 & 0 & 1 \\ 1 & 2 & 0 \end{pmatrix} = \begin{pmatrix} 2 & 2 & 1 \\ 1 & 3 & 1 \\ 2 & 1 & 3 \end{pmatrix}$

There are 3 two stage journeys from Y to itself.

23.2.2 Exercises

1) Write down the route matrices for the maps below. In each case find the square of the matrix.

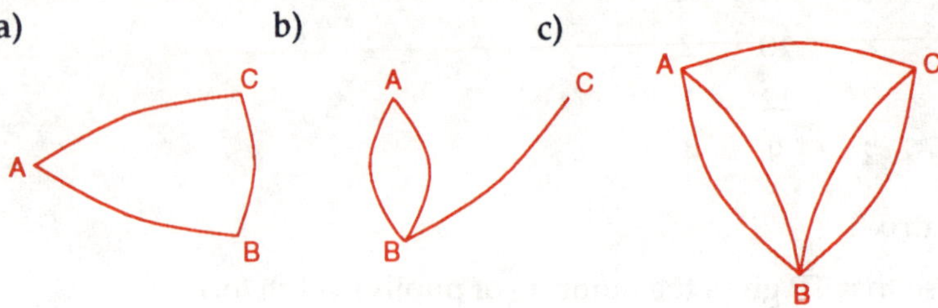

Fig 23.3

2) In the following maps the arrows indicate one-way streets. Write down the route matrices for these maps.

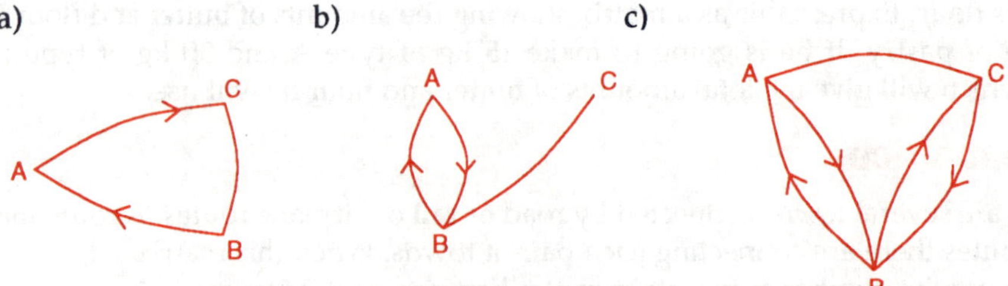

Fig 23.4

3) Three towns A, B, C are connected by the map of Fig 23.5. The council introduces a system of one-way roads, so that the route matrix is as below. Insert arrows on the map to show which roads are now one-way.

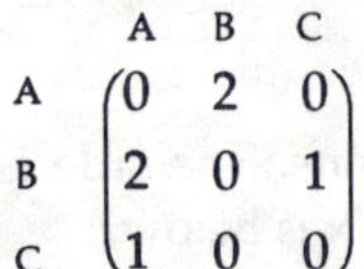

$$\begin{array}{c} \\ A \\ B \\ C \end{array} \begin{array}{c} \begin{array}{ccc} A & B & C \end{array} \\ \begin{pmatrix} 0 & 2 & 0 \\ 2 & 0 & 1 \\ 1 & 0 & 0 \end{pmatrix} \end{array}$$

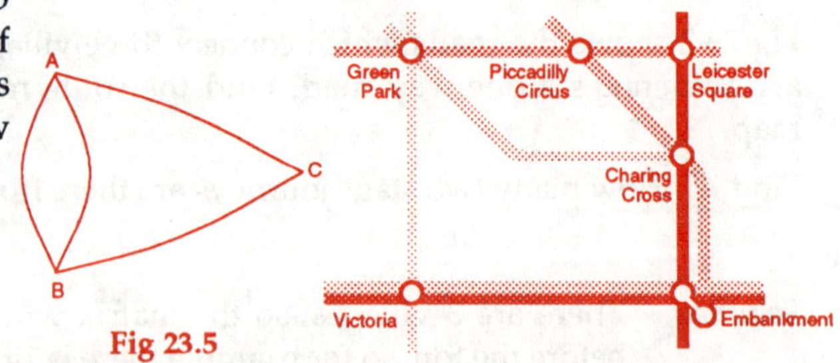

Fig 23.5

Fig 23.6

4) Fig 23.6 shows a map of part of the London Underground system. Write down a route matrix for the six stations shown.

23.3 Networks for jobs

Networks can be used to show the structure of complicated jobs.

Suppose we have a large complicated job. It can usually be broken up into smaller tasks. These tasks are then arranged to make it clear which task must be done first.

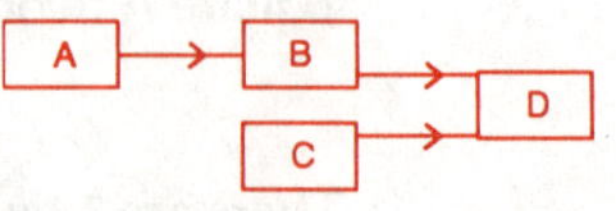

Fig 23.7

In the diagram to the right, Task A must be done before B. It does not matter whether C or A is done first. Both B and C must be finished before D is started.

Fig 23.8 shows a listing of the various tasks. To the right of each task are written the tasks which must be completed first.

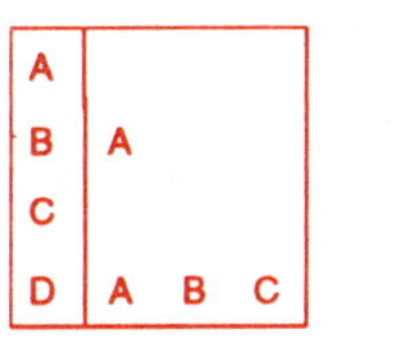

Fig 23.8

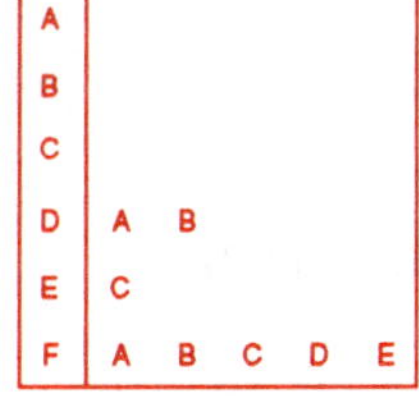

Fig 23.9

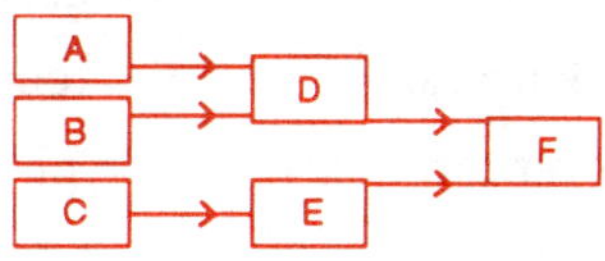

Fig 23.10

23.3.1 Example

A job is broken down into tasks A, B, C, D, E and F as listed in Fig 23.9. Draw the network diagram for the job.

Solution Notice that Tasks A, B and C do not depend on any other. So they can be put at the beginning of the network. D depends on A and B, so it must follow from them. E follows from C. Finally F depends on all the tasks, and so is shown at the end of the network. The diagram is Fig 23.10.

23.3.2 Exercises

1) The listings for the tasks of three jobs are shown below. Draw the network diagrams.

a)

A	
B	A
C	A B
D	
E	A B C D

b)

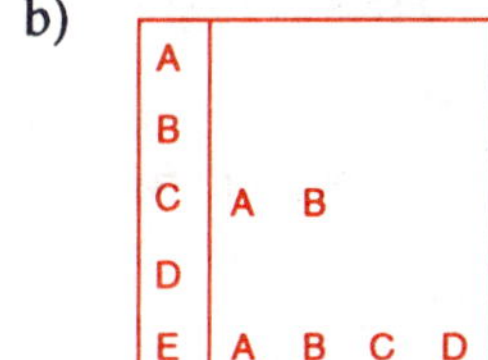

c)

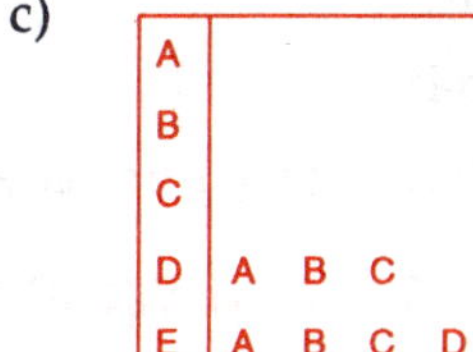

Fig 23.11

2) Construct the listings of the tasks in the networks below, showing which tasks must be done first.

a)

A → B → C → D

b)

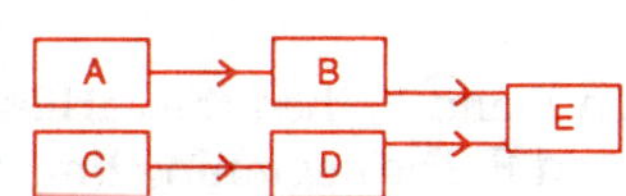

Fig 23.12

3) The job of preparing breakfast is broken down into tasks as below. Show which tasks depend on others, and draw the network diagram.

A = boil water in Kettle B = Boil water in saucepan

C = Cut bread D = toast bread

E = butter toast F = put food on table

G = warm and put tea in pot H = infuse tea

I = boil egg

4) The job of changing a car wheel is broken up into tasks as below. List the tasks showing their precedence, and draw the network.

A = loosen nuts　B = get spanner and jack　C = get spare wheel
D = jack up car　E = remove old wheel　F = put on new wheel
G = lower car　H = put away tools and old wheel
I = tighten nuts

5) A room has to be cleared up after being used for a sports exhibition. The tasks are:

A: re-lay carpets　B: return furniture
C: clear away cups and plates　D: wash up cups and plates
E: remove rows of chairs　F: sweep up
G: put cups and plates in cupboard　H: lock up
I: switch off lights.

List the tasks showing their precedence, and draw a network.

6) Before going on holiday the following must be done.

A: apply for passport　B: collect passport
C: apply for foreign money　D: collect foreign money
E: book flight　F: find dates of flights
G: book hotel　H: go to airport.

List the tasks showing their precedence, and draw a network.

23.4 Shortest time and critical path

Each individual task of a job takes a certain time to complete. This can be shown on the diagram. Fig 23.13 shows that A takes 5 minutes and B takes 10.

Suppose that Task B depends on Task A. Then the earliest beginning time for B is the finishing time for A. So the beginning time for B is 5 minutes, and the ending time 15 minutes.

If Task G depends on E and F, then the earliest time to begin G is the later of the finishing times of E and F. The beginning time for G is 6 minutes.

The whole diagram can then be filled in, and the total time for completion can be found.

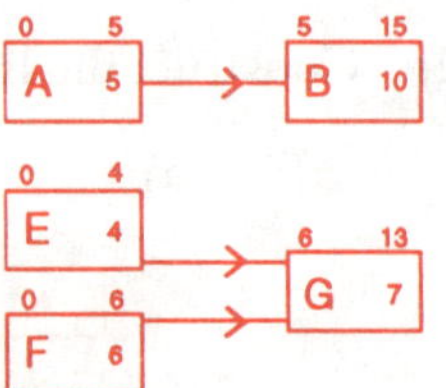

Fig 23.13

The tasks which must be completed on time are critical tasks. Above F is critical, but E is not. There is a path through the whole network consisting of critical tasks, which is called a critical path.

If a task is not critical, then it can be delayed, without extending the time for the whole job. The time by which it can be delayed is the slack time. The slack time for E above is 2 minutes.

23.4.1 Example

The diagram below shows the network for a job. The time in minutes for each task is indicated. Find the completion time for the whole job, and find the critical path. Find the slack time for the first non-critical task.

Solution A, B and C can all begin after 0 minutes. A takes 5 minutes, so the finishing time for A is 5. Similarly the finishing times for B and C are 7 and 8 minutes.

D can begin when A is finished, after 5 minutes. E has to wait until both B and C are done, after 8 minutes. The ending times for D and E are found by adding on the times for the tasks.

Finally, the starting time for F is the larger of the finishing times for D and E. The whole diagram is Fig 23.15.

The total time for the job is 27 minutes

Notice that F began immediately after E was finished. But there could be a delay of up to 2 minutes in the completion of D. So E is critical and D is not. Similarly C is critical, while B is not.

The critical path is C - E - F

A is the first non-critical task. It could be delayed for an extra 2 minutes, without altering the start time of F.

The slack time of A is 2 minutes

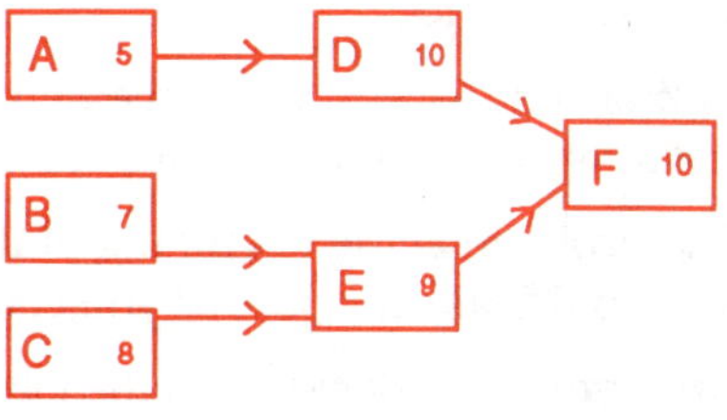

Fig 23.14

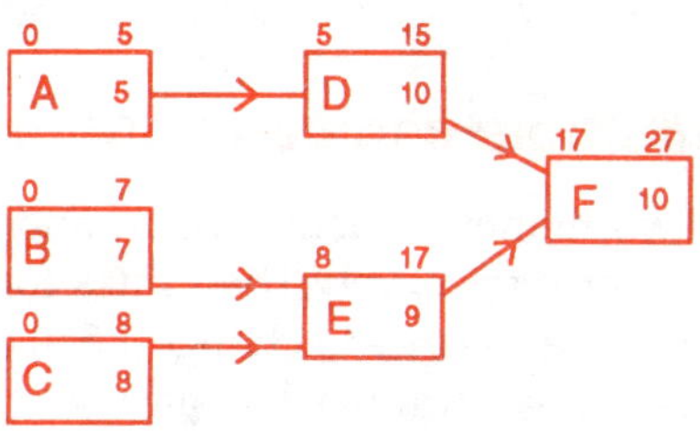

Fig 23.15

23.4.2 Exercises

1) In each of the following diagrams, find the completion times and the critical path.

a) b) c)

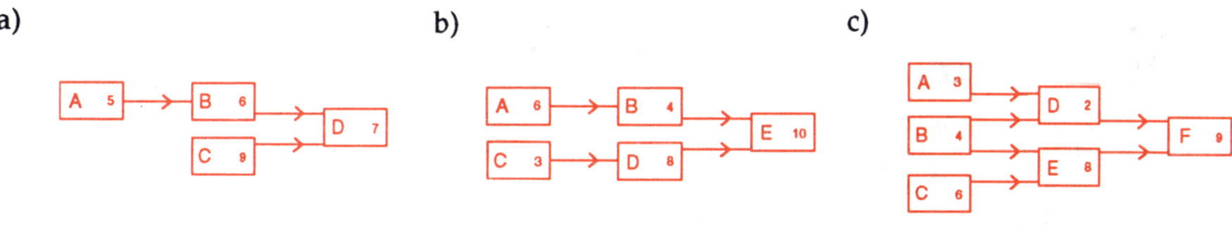

Fig 23.16

2) List the non-critical tasks of the jobs of Question 1. Find the slack times of these tasks.

3) Suppose the tasks of Question 4 of 23.3.2 took the following times (in minutes). Find the completion time and the critical path.

A: 2 B: 5 C: 2 D: 15 E: 1 F: 3 G: 4 H: 6 I:3

4) Suppose the tasks of Question 5 of 23.3.2 took the following times (in minutes). Find the completion time and the critical path.

A: 10 B: 6 C: 8 D: 15 E: 12 F: 10 G: 5 H: 2 I: 1

5) Estimate the times for the tasks of Question 3 of 23.3.2. Hence find the completion time and the critical path.

23.5 Longer exercise

Analysing a job

In this chapter you have been given the tasks into which the jobs have been split, and you were given the times which the tasks would take. Now you are ready to do the whole operation yourself.

The problem at the beginning of the chapter involved getting tea ready for two teams of hockey players. You could take this job, or you could think up one of your own.

Once you have decided on the job, you must do the following:

- Split the job up into simple tasks.
- Estimate the time for each task.
- List the tasks, showing their precedence.
- Draw the network, find the completion time and the critical tasks.

Multiple choice question *(Tick appropriate box)*

Two money dealers, Adams and Brown, will change dollars into pounds at rates of £0.58 and £0.59 per dollar respectively.Their rates for changing Deutschmarks are £0.35 and £0.34 per DM respectively. An exporter wishes to change 1,500 dollars and 4,000 DM. The matrix product which represents how much he will get from each dealer is:

a) $\begin{pmatrix} 0.58 & 0.35 \\ 0.59 & 0.34 \end{pmatrix} \times \begin{pmatrix} 1500 \\ 4000 \end{pmatrix}$ ☐

b) $\begin{pmatrix} 1500 \\ 4000 \end{pmatrix} \times \begin{pmatrix} 0.58 & 0.35 \\ 0.59 & 0.34 \end{pmatrix}$ ☐

c) $\begin{pmatrix} 0.58 & 0.59 \\ 0.35 & 0.34 \end{pmatrix} \times \begin{pmatrix} 1500 \\ 4000 \end{pmatrix}$ ☐

d) $(1500 \quad 4000) \times \begin{pmatrix} 0.58 & 0.59 \\ 0.34 & 0.35 \end{pmatrix}$ ☐

e) $\begin{pmatrix} 0.58 & 0.35 \\ 0.59 & 0.34 \end{pmatrix} \times (1500 \quad 4000)$ ☐

Points to note

1) *Information matrices*

   a) Make sure that you know which information goes into rows and which into columns.

   b) The order of a matrix product is important. The meaning as well as the result depends on it.

2) *Listings*

   The listings show what must be completed before each task, not what comes after.

3) *Completion time*

   If one task depends on two or more previous tasks, then make sure you take their latest completion time, not their earliest.

4) *Critical paths*

   Make sure you give all the critical tasks. There must be a continuous path of them from start to finish of the job. There may be more than one critical path.

Chapter 24

Straight line inequalities

There are 64 pupils of your school who are to go on a day trip. You are to organize the transport.

There is a choice between hiring minibuses, which will take 9 pupils and cost £42 to hire, or asking teachers to use their own cars, which will take 3 pupils and cost £6 in mileage expenses. 16 teachers have offered either to drive their cars or to drive a minibus.

How many minibuses and cars should be used, so that all the pupils are transported, using at most 16 drivers? Can you do it within a budget of £210?

Fig 24.1

24.1 Representation of inequalities

An inequality in one variable is something like $3x + 1 < 5$. It can be represented as a range along the number line.

An inequality in two variables is something like $2x + 3y < 12$ or $y \geq 4x - 1$. It can be represented by a region on a plane.

Suppose, for example, we wish to illustrate the region of the points which satisfy $2x + 3y \leq 12$. The procedure is as follows:

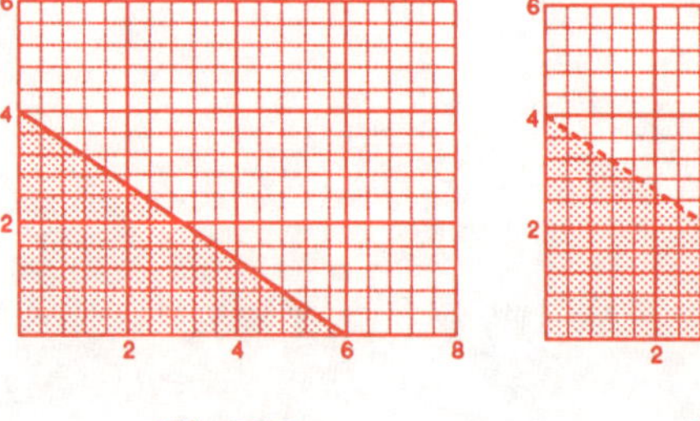

Fig 24.2

Fig 24.3

First draw the line $2x + 3y = 12$. This can be done by joining up the points (6,0) and (0,4).

We want $2x + 3y$ to be less than 12. So we want the region below the line. Shade this region. The result is shown in Fig 24.2.

Notice that the line is filled in. That is because we want to include the line itself. To illustrate the inequality $2x + 3y < 12$, draw a broken line as shown in Fig 24.3.

Simultaneous inequalities

Suppose there are two or more simultaneous inequalities. The region of points satisfying all of them consists of the intersection or overlap of the individual regions.

The diagram can get very muddled. To prevent this it is usual to shade out the regions which we don't want, rather than to shade in the regions which we do want.

24.1.1 Examples

1) Illustrate on graph paper the solution set of the simultaneous inequalities
$x > \frac{1}{2}, y > \frac{1}{2}, 4x + 3y \le 12, 3x + 4y \le 12.$
Find the pairs of whole numbers which satisfy these inequalities.

Solution First draw the lines corresponding to the 4 equalities. Note that the lines $x = \frac{1}{2}$ and $y = \frac{1}{2}$ are dotted.

The region required is above the line $y = \frac{1}{2}$, to the right of the line $x = \frac{1}{2}$, and below the two slanting lines. Shade out the regions which are not required.

The pairs of points within the required region are:

(1,1), (1,2), (2,1)

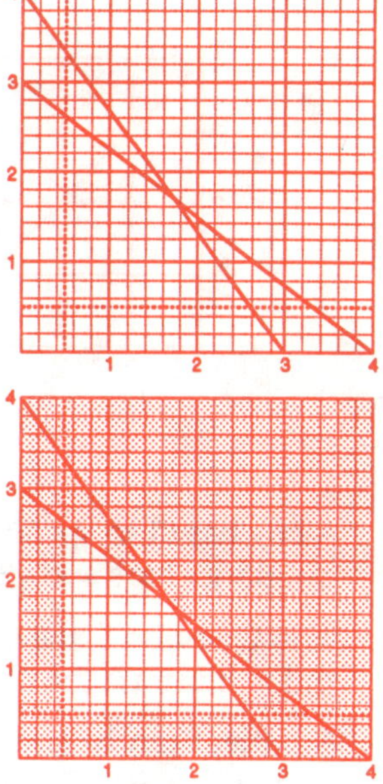

Fig 24.4

2) A man has £10 to spend on cigars. Superbas cost 50 p each, and Grandiosos cost 75 p. If he buys x Superbas and y Grandiosos, obtain an inequality in x and y. Illustrate this inequality on a graph.

Solution The total amount he spends on cigars is given by:

$50x + 75y$ p.

This must be less than or equal to 1,000 p.

$50x + 75y \le 1000$

$\mathbf{2x + 3y \le 40}$

This is illustrated by the shaded region of Fig 24.5.

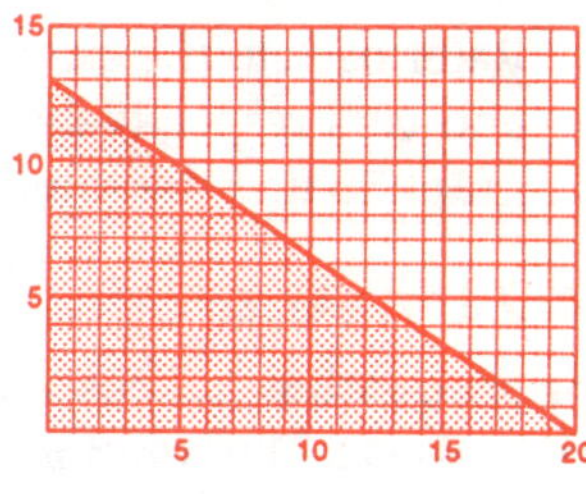

Fig 24.5

24.1.2 Exercises

1) Illustrate on graph paper the regions corresponding to the following inequalities:

a) $x + y \le 1$ b) $2x + 4y \le 8$ c) $3x + 5y < 15$ d) $4x + 3y \le 12$

e) $x + 2y \ge 4$ f) $3x + 2y > 12$ g) $x - y \ge 0$ h) $2x - 3y \le 6$

i) $y - 3x < 6$ j) $5y - 4x \ge 20$

2) Illustrate the following inequalities on graph paper. Each group should be illustrated simultaneously by shading out.

a) $x \ge 0, y \ge 0, x + y \le 6$ b) $x \ge 0, y \ge 0, x + y \ge 3, x \le 7, y \le 8$

c) $x \ge 0, y \ge 0, 2x + 3y \le 1$ d) $x > 0, y > 0, x + 3y \le 9, 2x + y \le 10$

e) $y \ge 0, y \le x, 3x + 4y \ge 12, 3x + 4y \le 18$

f) $x - y > 1, x - y < 3, x + y < 8, x + y > 4$

3) Describe the unshaded regions of Fig 24.6 by inequalities in x and y.

4) For each of the regions of Question 2, find the top bounds of x and y.

5) For the regions (c), (d), (e) and (f) of Question 2, list the integer value points which satisfy all the inequalities.

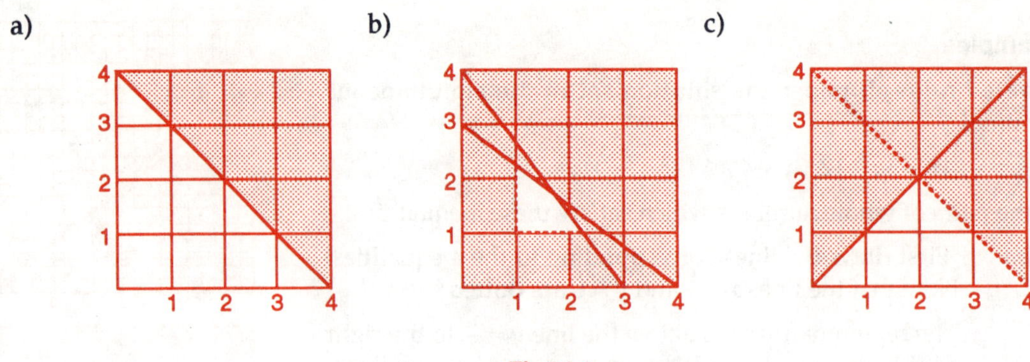

Fig 24.6

6) A boy has £1 to spend on sweets. Liquorice bars cost 10p each, and toffee bars cost 15p. Say he buys x liquorice bars and y toffee bars. Find an inequality in x and y, and illustrate it on a graph.

7) If, in Question 6, the boy's mother tells him not to buy more than 8 bars, find another inequality in x and y. Illustrate the new inequality on the same graph.

8) A patient can be prescribed either tablets or pills. Tablets contain 3 units of vitamin A, and pills contain 4 units. The daily intake must be at least 15 units. If the patient takes x tablets and y pills, obtain an inequality in x and y and illustrate it on a graph.

9) Refer back to the example at the beginning of this chapter. Let x and y be the numbers of minibuses and cars respectively. Write down inequalities which express the conditions. Illustrate them on a graph to find the solution to the example.

24.2 Linear programming

The inequalities discussed in 24.1 can be used to represent restrictions, of money, of space, of raw materials etc. The solution region then gives the values which comply with all the restrictions.

Often we wish to find the point which represents the maximum or minimum value of a quantity. For example, a businessman wants to maximize his profit. The method of finding the maximum point is Linear Programming.

Suppose the region of points which obey all the restrictions is as shown in Fig 24.7. Suppose that we wish to make $x + y$ as large as possible.

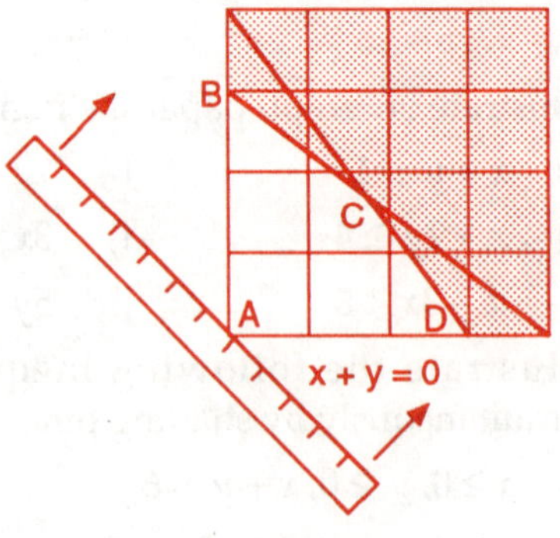

Fig 24.7

The greatest value of $x + y$ must occur at one of the corners of the region. There are two methods of finding the greatest value:

I. Find the coordinates of all the corner points, A, B, C, D. Evaluate $x + y$ at each of them, and take the greatest value.

II. Draw the line $x + y = 0$ as shown. Keep your ruler parallel to this line, and slide it up the diagram until it is only just in the region. The edge of the ruler will then be at the point which gives the greatest value of $x + y$.

24.2.1 Example

Fire regulations require that a cinema should admit at most 400 people. Each cheap seat occupies 1 m^2 of space, and each expensive seat occupies 2 m^2. There is 600 m^2 of space available. Cheap seats are to cost £3, and expensive seats £5. Letting x and y be the numbers of cheap and expensive seats respectively, form inequalities in x and y and illustrate them on a graph. What allocation of seats will bring in the most money?

Solution The total number of seats must be at most 400. This gives the inequality $x + y \le 400$.

The total space used by the seats must be at most 600 m^2. This gives the inequality $x + 2y \le 600$.

x and y cannot be negative. Hence $x \ge 0$ and $y \ge 0$.

Illustrate the four inequalities on a graph as shown.

The money received by the cinema is £$(3x + 5y)$.

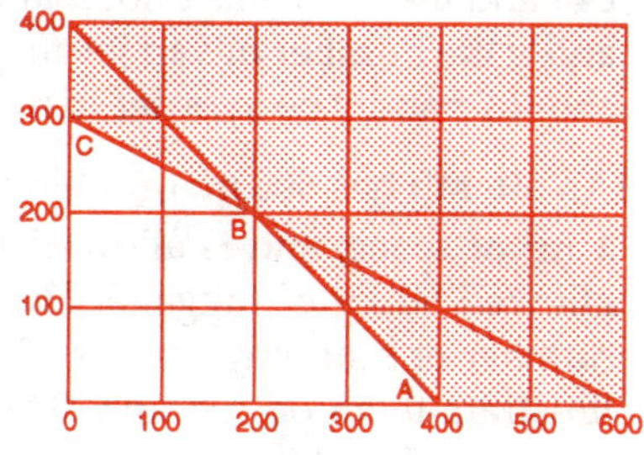

Fig 24.8

Using the first method to find the maximum of this function:

The corners of the region are O(0,0), A(400,0), B(200,200), C(0,300). Evaluate $3x + 4y$ at these points, to obtain 0, 1200, 1600, 1500 respectively. The maximum value is 1600.

The best allocation is 200 cheap and 200 expensive seats

24.2.2 Exercises

1) A factory manager is to buy two sorts of machines. Type 1 occupies 3 m^2 and costs £200, type 2 occupies 2 m^2 and costs £400. There is 40 m^2 of space available, and £4000 to spend. Let x be the number of type 1 machines, and y the number of type 2 machines.

   Show that the restrictions can be expressed by the inequalities:

   $3x + 2y \le 40$ and $x + 2y \le 20$.

   Illustrate these inequalities on a graph. If type 1 produces 100 items per hour, and type 2 150 items, find how many of each should be bought to maximize production.

2) In a car park there is 6000 m^2 of land available. A car space occupies 15 m^2, and a lorry space 30 m^2. There must be space for at least 50 lorries, and there must be at least twice as many car spaces as lorry spaces. Let c be the number of car spaces, and L the number of lorry spaces.

   Show that the restrictions can be expressed by the inequalities:

   $c + 2L \le 400$, $L \ge 50$ and $c \ge 2L$.

   Illustrate these inequalities on a graph. The parking fees are £2 for a car and £3 for a lorry. How should the spaces be arranged to bring in the most profit?

3) A shop has space for 5 refrigerators. The shop buys them from the manufacturers, at a price of £200 for type A, and £300 for type B, and there is £1200 available. The profits on types A and B are £45 and £70 respectively. If x of type A and y of type B are bought, express the restrictions in the form of inequalities. Illustrate the inequalities on a graph, and find the maximum profit.

4) Food A contains 4 units of protein and 5 units of starch per kg, and food B contains 6 units of protein and 3 units of starch per kg. The minimum daily intake of protein is 16 units, and the minimum daily intake of starch is 11 units. Let X be the number of kg of A to be eaten, and Y the number of kg of B. Obtain inequalities in X and Y, and illustrate them on a graph. What are the values of X and Y which ensure that the least weight of food is eaten?

5) A mail order firm must deliver 900 parcels using a lorry which takes 150 at a time or a van which takes 80 at a time. Each journey costs £5 for the lorry and £4 for the van. The total cost cannot exceed £44 and the lorry must not make more journeys than the van. Let x be the number of lorry journeys, and y the number of van journeys. Find inequalities in x and y and illustrate them on a graph. What should x and y be in order to make the total number of journeys as small as possible?

6) An aircraft has 600 m^2 of cabin space, and can carry 5000 kg of luggage. An economy passenger gets 3 m^2 of space, and is allowed 20 kg of luggage. A first class passenger gets 4 m^2 of space, and is allowed 50 kg of luggage. There must be space for at least 50 economy passengers. Let x be the number of economy seats, and y the number of first class seats. Obtain inequalities in x and y, and illustrate them on a graph. The profit from a first class seat is £100, and is £40 from an economy class seat. What is the greatest profit?

24.3 Longer exercise

Constructing a problem

In this chapter the situation of each problem was given to you. Here you try to set up the situation yourself.

Suppose we want to find a problem for which the only answer is (5,7).

1) Mark out axes on graph paper, taking x from 0 to 10 and y from 0 to 15. Mark the point P at (5,7)
2) Draw three straight lines on the paper, enclosing a triangle in which the only integer-valued point is P. It will help if your straight lines go through integer points on the x and y axes.
3) Find the equations of your straight lines.
4) Define the triangle enclosed by the lines by means of three inequalities.
5) See if you can find a situation to match your diagram. You need a situation in which you have a choice between two items, measured by x and y. There must be three constraints on the amounts of x and y you can use, giving rise to the three inequalities.

Multiple choice question *(Tick appropriate box)*

The unshaded region on the right is defined by the following inequalities:

a) $y \le x, x + y \le 2, y \ge \frac{1}{2}$ 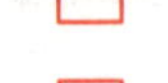

b) $y \ge x, x + y < 2, y \ge \frac{1}{2}$ 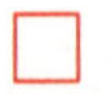

c) $y \le x, x + y < 2, y \ge \frac{1}{2}$ 

d) $y \ge x, x + y > 2, y \le \frac{1}{2}$  

e) $y \le x, x + y > 2, y \ge \frac{1}{2}$ 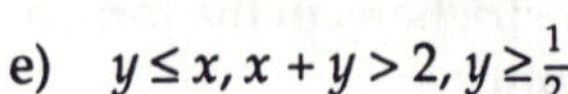

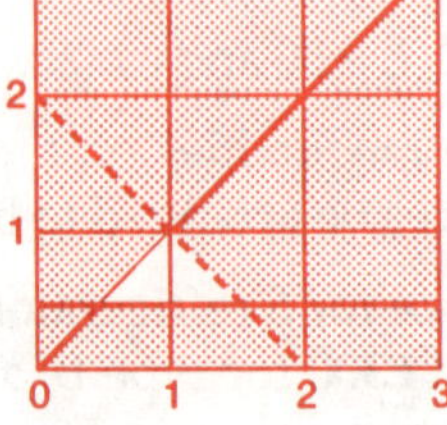

Fig 24.9

Points to note

1) *Two-dimensional inequalities*

   a) Be sure to draw the correct line. The line $2x + 3y = 6$ goes through (3,0) and (0,2).

      But do not draw the vertical and horizontal lines through these points. Fig 24.10 shows the correct and incorrect diagrams.

   b) Be sure that you take the correct side of the line. If in doubt, take a test point. If your inequality is $2x + 3y \leq 6$, then test by putting $x = 1$ and $y = 1$.

      $2 \times 1 + 3 \times 1 < 6$, so the point (1,1) must lie in the region.

   c) If an inequality involves < or >, then its boundary is dotted.

2) *Linear programming*

   a) Make sure that your variables stand for the unknown quantities, not for the known restrictions. In the example of 24.2.1, do not let x stand for the number of people and y the amount of floor space. These are known to be 400 and 600 respectively.

   b) If you have two inequalities, then the maximum point is often at the intersection of the two. But not assume this until you have tested – the maximum point may be at where one of the inequality lines crosses the axes.

   c) When dealing with a problem, make sure that you obtain the full inequalities.

      If a boy buys x items at 20p, and y items at 30p, out of a budget of 60p, then the inequality is $20x + 30y \leq 60$.

      Do not put $x \leq 3$ and $y \leq 2$. These do not express the full situation.

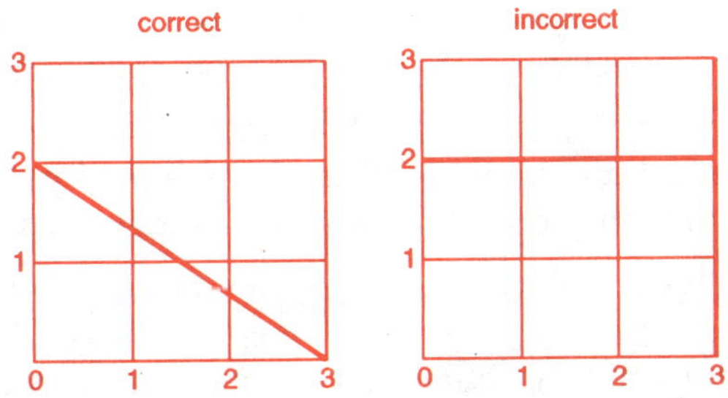

Fig 24.10

Chapter 25

Combined probability

In a lucky-dip at a fete a third of the tickets will win prizes. Your friend says:

"I shall buy three, then I'm sure of a prize."

You say that he might be unlucky. But he says:

"If there were only three tickets and one prize, then I'd be certain of getting the prize if I bought all three tickets."

How do you explain the difference? What is the probability he wins a prize?

Fig 25.1

25.1 Dependent and independent events

The probability of an event measures our belief that it will happen. This probability may change when we get more information. If the information makes the event more likely, then its probability increases. If the information makes it less likely, then the probability decreases.

Dependent events

Suppose that two events are connected, so that information about one of them alters the probability of the other. The events are said to be dependent.

Suppose two cards are drawn from a pack. If the first card is an Ace, then the second card is less likely to be an Ace. (Because there is one fewer Ace in the pack). So the two events, of picking an Ace on the first and second cards, are dependent on each other.

Independent events

Suppose that two events are not connected, so that information about one of them does not alter the probability of the other. The events are said to be independent.

Suppose two dice are rolled. If the first die shows a 6, then the probability of a 6 on the second die is still $\frac{1}{6}$. So the two events, of a 6 for the first and second die, are independent of each other.

25.1.1 Examples

1) A bag contains 5 red and 7 blue marbles. Jake and Bet each pick one out. What is the probability that Bet's marble is red,

a) without any information about Jake's marble

b) if we are told that Jake's marble is blue?

Solution a) Bet is equally likely to chose any of the 12 marbles, and there are 5 red ones.

The probability of a red marble is $\frac{5}{12}$

b) If we know that Jake has picked a blue marble, then Bet has a choice of 11 marbles, of which 5 are red.

The probability of a red marble is $\frac{5}{11}$

2) A roulette wheel has the numbers 1 to 36. It is spun twice. The first spin gives 25: what is the probability that the second spin will give 17?

Solution Information about the first spin does not alter the probabilities of the results of the second spin. There are still 36 equally likely numbers.

The probability of a 17 is $\frac{1}{36}$

25.1.2 Exercises

1) Two cards are drawn from a pack.
   a) If the first is a King, what is the probability that the second is a King?
   b) If the first is a King, what is the probability that the second is a Queen?
   c) If the first is a Spade, what is the probability that the second is a Heart?
   d) If the first is a Spade, what is the probability that the second is a black card?
2) Two dice are rolled.
   a) If the first die shows a 5, what is the probability that the second shows a 4?
   b) If the first die shows a 6 what is the probability that the total score is 8?
   c) If the first die shows a 1, what is the probability that the total score is 9?
3) A bag contains 4 toffees and 6 chocolates. Two children each pick one out.
   a) If the first is a toffee, what is the probability that the second will be a chocolate?
   b) If the first is a chocolate, what is the probability that the second will also be a chocolate?
4) Two cards are drawn from a pack.
   a) If the first is a King, what is the probability that the second is a Spade?
   b) If the first is a Club, what is the probability that the second is a Jack?
   c) If the first is a King, what is the probability that it is a Diamond?
   d) If the first is a Heart, what is the probability that it is an Ace?
   e) If the first is a red card, what is the probability that it is a Diamond?

25.2 Multiplying probabilities

Problems concerning two or more events are often best solved by a tree diagram.

Dependent events

Suppose we want to find the probability of drawing two Aces from a pack of cards. The tree diagram is set up as below.

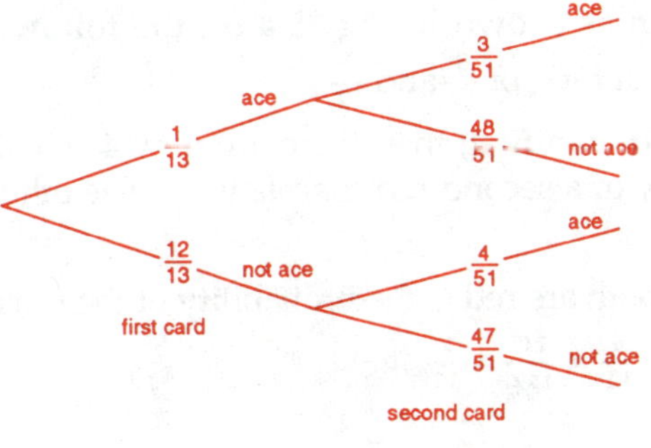

Fig 25.2

The first fork tells us whether or not we got an Ace for the first card. The probabilities are $\frac{1}{13}$ and $\frac{12}{13}$. The second forks tell us whether or not we got an Ace for the second card. Note that the probabilities depend on the result of the first drawing. The probability of $\frac{3}{51}$, for example, is the probability that the second card is an Ace, given that the first card is an Ace.

The probability of two Aces is the probability of the top branch. This is found by multiplying the probabilities along it.

$$\text{Probability of two Aces} = \frac{1}{13} \times \frac{3}{51} = \frac{1}{221}$$

Independent events

The tree diagram below is for the rolling of two dice.

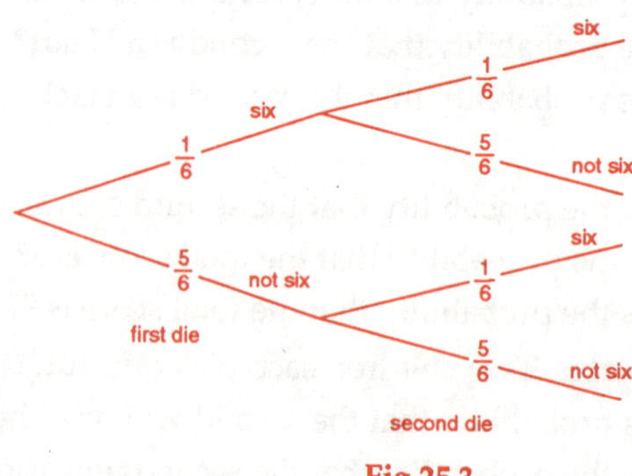

Fig 25.3

Note that the probabilities for the second die are not altered by the result of the first die. Multiplying the top branch:

$$P(\text{double } 6) = \frac{1}{6} \times \frac{1}{6} = \frac{1}{36}$$

So the probability that both dice give a 6 is found by multiplying the probabilities for each die. In general:

If A and B are independent, then P(A & B) = P(A) × P(B)

25.2.1 Examples

1) A bag contains 5 red and 7 blue marbles. Two are drawn in succession. Find the probability that they are both red.

Solution Draw a tree-diagram as shown in Fig 25.4 on the following page. Mark in the probabilities at the first fork, of $\frac{5}{12}$ and $\frac{7}{12}$.

Note that if a red is drawn first, then there are now 4 red and 7 blue marbles left. Hence the probability of a second red marble is $\frac{4}{11}$. The other branches are filled in similarly.

The probability that both are red is the probability of the top branch.

$$\text{P(Both are red)} = \frac{5}{12} \times \frac{4}{11} = \frac{20}{132} = \frac{5}{33}$$

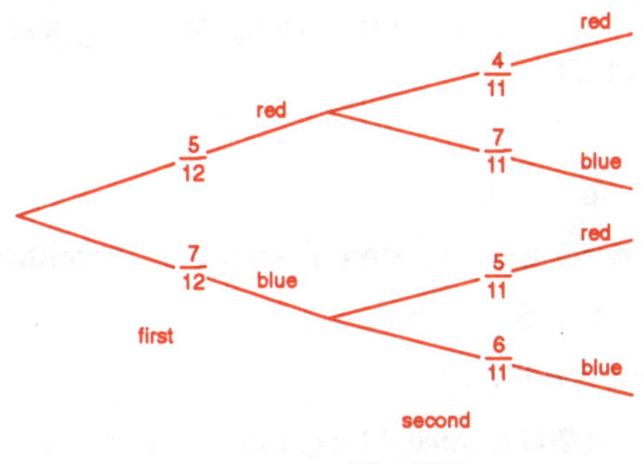

Fig 25.4

2) Three fair six-sided dice are thrown. What is the probability that the result is a treble six?

Solution For each single die, the probability of a six is $\frac{1}{6}$. The three dice cannot affect each other. The probability that all the dice give sixes is therefore:

$$\frac{1}{6} \times \frac{1}{6} \times \frac{1}{6} = \frac{1}{216}$$

25.2.2 Exercises

1) One in ten flash cubes is faulty. I buy 2. Complete the tree diagram.

   Find the probability that both flash cubes work.

2) 3 white and 4 black balls are in a bag. 2 are drawn at random. Complete the tree diagram.

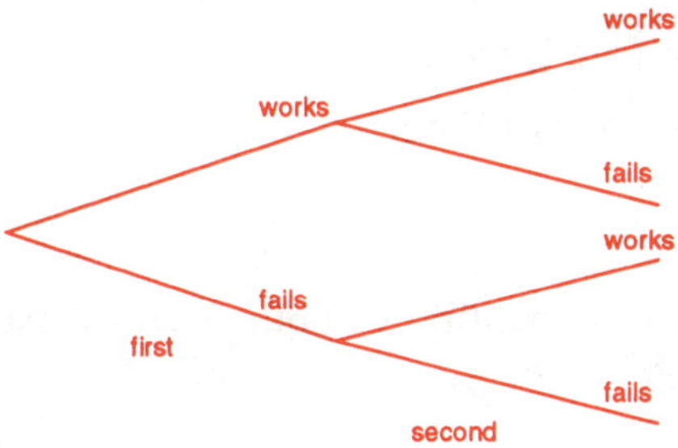

   Find the probability that both are black.

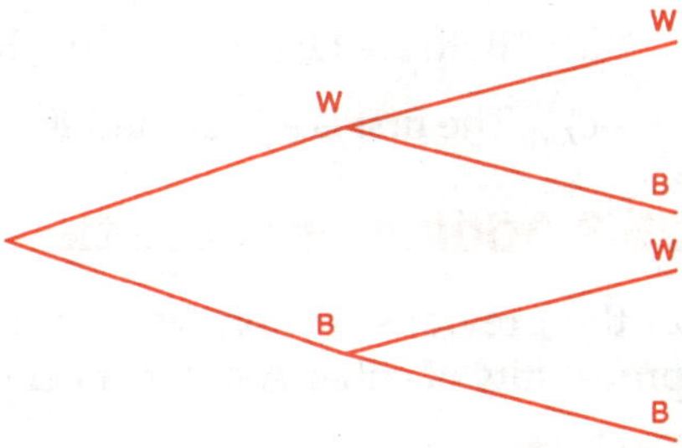

Fig 25.5

Fig 25.6

3) Two letters are chosen from the word SCROOGE. What is the probability that both O's are chosen?

4) Two people are chosen from 5 women and 4 men. What is the probability that they are both men?

5) A box contains 7 red and 12 yellow counters. Two are chosen. What is the probability that the first is red and the second yellow?

6) A box of chocolates contains 12 soft-centred and 14 hard-centred chocolates. Two are selected; find the probabilities that:

   a) Both are soft-centred.

   b) The first is soft-centred and the second hard-centred.

7) In a multiple choice exam, each question has 5 possible answers. A candidate answers three questions at random: find the probability that all three answers are right.

8) A roulette wheel has the numbers 1 to 36. For the first spin I bet that an even number will come up, and for the second spin that a number divisible by 3 will come up. What is the probability that I win both my bets?

9) A football team has probabilities $\frac{1}{2}, \frac{1}{3}, \frac{1}{6}$ of winning, losing, drawing respectively. It the team plays two matches, find the probabilities that:

a) Both matches are drawn.

b) The first match is won and the second lost.

10) Two fair dice are thrown and the scores are recorded. Find the probabilities that:

a) Both are fives b) the first is 5 and the second 3

c) The first is even and the second is odd.

11) Jane will enter either the 100 m or the 200 m race. She cannot enter both. Her chances of winning are $\frac{1}{10}$ and $\frac{1}{8}$ respectively. If she is equally likely to choose either race, find the probabilities that:

a) She enters the 100 m and wins b) She enters the 200 m and loses.

12) If it is fine today, the probability that it will rain tomorrow is $\frac{1}{5}$. If it is rainy today, the probability that it will rain tomorrow is $\frac{2}{3}$. The probability that today is fine is $\frac{1}{2}$.

Find the probabilities that:

a) It will be fine on both days. b) It will be wet on both days.

13) Two cards are drawn from a well-shuffled pack. Find the probabilities that:

a) Both are hearts. b) Both are Queens.

c) The first is a heart and the second is a King.

25.3 Adding probabilities

In the previous section we found the probability of both A and B happening. Here we discuss the probability of either A or B happening.

Exclusive events

In a dice game you want either an odd number or a 6. The probability that you get this is $\frac{4}{6}$. Note that this is the sum of the probabilities.

P(Odd or 6) = P(Odd) + P(6).

If A and B cannot happen simultaneously, then we say that A and B are exclusive. In this case we can just add the probabilities.

If A and B are exclusive:

P(A or B) = P(A) + P(B)

Non-exclusive events

If A and B are not exclusive, then more work has to be done. Three ways are as follows:

Tree diagram. Draw a tree diagram as shown on the right. In three of the branches, shown ticked, either A or B is true. Add up the probabilities of the branches.

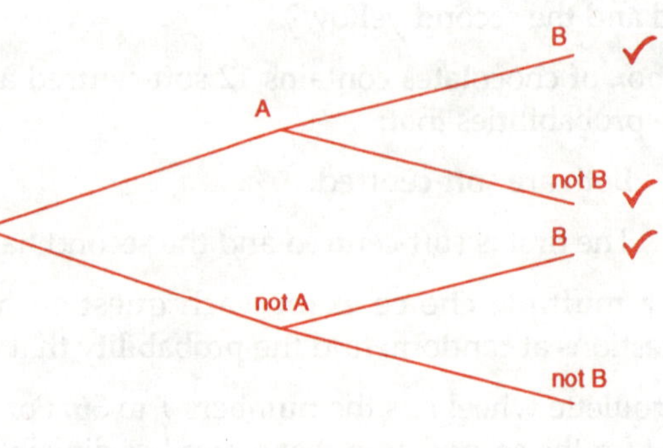

Fig 25.7

Reverse the question. If neither A nor B is true, then both are false. Hence:

P(A or B) = 1 – P(not A & not B)

Formula. If we add P(A) and P(B), then P(A and B) will have been counted twice. So subtract it away:

P(A or B) = P(A) + P(B) – P(A and B)

25.3.1 Examples

1) In his drawer a man has 4 left shoes and 5 right shoes. In the dark he draws out two. What is the probability that he has a left and a right?

Solution Draw a tree diagram as shown.

The middle branches will give a left shoe and a right shoe.

The probability is $\frac{4}{9}\times\frac{5}{8}+\frac{5}{9}\times\frac{4}{8}=\frac{5}{9}$

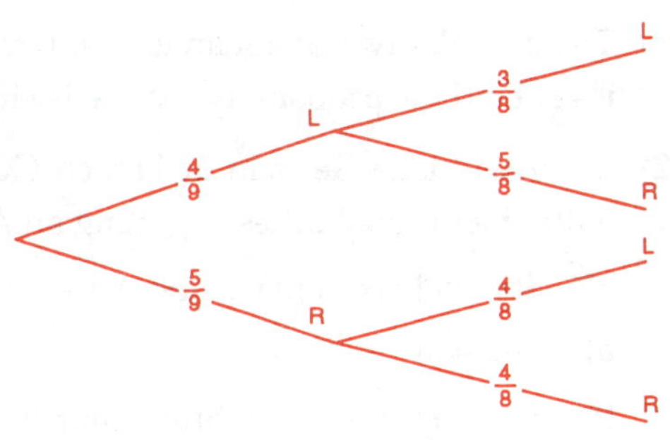

Fig 25.8

2) In a dice game I need to throw a 6 to start. What is the probability that I will get a 6 in one of the first three throws?

Solution The probability that I won't throw a 6 is $\frac{5}{6}$.

The probability that I won't get a 6 in three goes is $\left(\frac{5}{6}\right)^3=\frac{125}{216}$. Subtract this from 1.

The probability that I will get a 6 in three throws is $\frac{91}{216}$

3) For hot-air ballooning, the weather must not be windy or rainy. The probability of wind is $\frac{1}{4}$, the probability of rain is $\frac{1}{3}$, and the probability of both is $\frac{1}{6}$. Find the probability that the weather will prevent ballooning.

Solution Use the formula above.

P(wind or rain) = P(wind) + P(rain) – P(wind and rain)

The probability is $\frac{1}{3}+\frac{1}{4}-\frac{1}{6}=\frac{5}{12}$

25.3.2 Exercises

1) A bag contains 5 red and 6 blue marbles. I draw out two: what is the probability that either of them is red?
2) I draw two cards from a well-shuffled pack. What is the probability that either of them is an Ace?
3) Two dice are rolled. What is the probability that either is a 6?
4) One in ten flash cubes is faulty. If I buy two, what is the probability that at least one of them will work?
5) Two different letters are chosen from the word COMPUTER. Find the probability that at least one is a vowel.
6) My chances of passing the driving-test are $\frac{1}{4}$. What is the chance that I will pass in the fourth attempt or sooner?
7) A fair dice is rolled four times. What is the probability of at least one 6?

8) In a lottery, one in ten of the tickets will give a prize. If I buy 10 tickets, what is the probability that I have won a prize?

9) A gun has a probability $\frac{1}{10}$ of hitting a target. What is the probability that it will hit the target in 8 shots?

10) The probabilities that Monday and Tuesday will be wet are $\frac{1}{6}$ and $\frac{1}{5}$ respectively. The probability that both days will be wet is $\frac{1}{8}$. Find the probability that either Monday or Tuesday will be wet.

11) The probability that a man is over 6 ft is $\frac{1}{4}$, and that he is over 16 stone is $\frac{1}{10}$. The probability of both is $\frac{1}{15}$. Find the probability that he is either over 6 ft or over 16 stone.

12) Mary will take German or French GCSE with probabilities $\frac{1}{3}$ and $\frac{2}{3}$ respectively. (She cannot take both). Her probabilities of getting an A grade are $\frac{1}{6}$ and $\frac{1}{8}$ respectively. Find the probabilities that:

    a) She will take French and get an A,

    b) She will get an A.

13) If it is rainy, the probability that Barchester City will win their match is $\frac{1}{3}$, and if it is fine the probability is $\frac{1}{2}$. The probability of rain is $\frac{1}{4}$. Find the probabilities that:

    a) It will be fine and Barchester will win.

    b) Barchester will win.

14) A woman goes to work by bus, by car or on foot with probabilities $\frac{1}{2}, \frac{1}{3}, \frac{1}{6}$ respectively. For each type of transport, the probabilities that she will be late are $\frac{1}{10}, \frac{1}{5}, \frac{1}{50}$ respectively. Find the probabilities that:

    a) She will go by car and be late.

    b) She will be late.

15) Look again at the problem at the beginning of the chapter. If your friend buys 3 tickets, what is the probability that they will all lose? What is the probability that one will win?

25.4 Longer exercises

A. Pontoon

Pontoon, also known as 21 or as Blackjack, is a card game for two players. The object is to get 2 or more cards whose total is as high as possible, without going over 21.

The standard pack of cards with no jokers is used. The suits do not matter. Aces can be either 1 or 11, picture cards (Jack, Queen, King) count as 10, and other cards count as their face value.

You play against the dealer. You each get 2 cards. You can ask for extra cards, provided your total does not go over 21. If your score is higher than the dealer's, then you win. Otherwise the dealer wins. Obviously the best score to get is 21, which can be obtained with an Ace and a picture card or a 10.

1) Your first card is an Ace. What is the probability that your second card will give you 21?

2) What is the probability that your first 2 cards will give you 21?

3) Your first two cards are a King and a 6. If you ask for another card, what is the probability that your total score will be over 21?

4) What should be the total of your first two cards, if it is to be worth your while to ask for another card?

   Normally you are allowed to see the first of the dealer's two cards. How does this affect your decision in (4)?

B. Deduction

In this chapter we used probability to predict the likelihood of something happening. Probability can also be used the other way round, to deduce things after something has happened. The following examples will show how this is done.

2% of the population has a certain disease. There is a test for the disease, but the test is not perfect. The test is positive for 90% of the people with the disease, but it is also positive for 5% of people without the disease.

1) If a person is picked at random, what is the probability that he/she has the disease and the test is positive?
2) If a person is picked at random, what is the probability that he/she does not have the disease and the test is positive?
3) What proportion of the population would give a positive result for the test?
4) Of the people in (3), what proportion actually have the disease?
5) If a person is picked at random, and the test is positive, what is the probability that he/she has the disease?
6) If a person is picked at random, and the test is negative, what is the probability that he/she does not have the disease?

Here is another example. A certain wine-bar contains lawyers and journalists in the ratio 1:2. Lawyers speak the truth with probability $\frac{2}{3}$, and journalists speak the truth with probability $\frac{3}{4}$.

7) In the wine-bar you meet someone who says: "I am a lawyer". What is the probability that he is telling the truth?

Multiple choice question *(Tick appropriate box)*

A bag contains 3 red and 2 blue marbles. Two are drawn. The probability that either is red is:

a) $\frac{9}{10}$ ☐

b) $\frac{3}{10}$ ☐

c) $\frac{3}{5}$ ☐

d) $\frac{6}{5}$ ☐

e) $\frac{1}{10}$ ☐

Points to note

1) *Multiplication of probabilities*

   Probabilities are only multiplied together if the events do not affect each other.

   If event A makes event B either more likely or less likely,
   then it is *not* true that P(A & B) = P(A) × P(B).

2) *Exclusive and independent events*

   These words refer to pairs of events, not to single events. It does not make sense to say: "A is an independent event."

3) *Use of "or"*

   In Mathematics, when we say "A or B" we include A and B. Do not confuse this with the common English usage in which "A or B" means A or B but not both.

4) *Adding probabilities*

   If A and B are not exclusive, then P(A or B) is not the sum of P(A) and P(B).

Cross-curriculum topic

Ciphers and cipher breakers

In war or diplomacy or business, it is often very important to keep information secret. So when a message is transmitted, it is often sent in a cipher.

The original message is called the plaintext. The sender rewrites this according to some system, and the receiver is able to recreate the plaintext by knowledge of the system. If the message is intercepted, by an enemy or a business rival, it will seem to be a string of meaningless letters. The cipher can only be broken with a great deal of difficulty.

There are two requirements for a successful cipher, which conflict with each other to some extent. It must be fairly easy to cipher and decipher, for those who know the system or the key. If anyone else intercepts the message, it must be very hard for them to decipher it. Here we look at various cipher systems.

There are basically two ways of ciphering messages. In a Transposition cipher, the letters remain the same but their order changes. In a Substitution cipher, the letters change but their order remains the same.

Transposition ciphers

An early transposition cipher was used by the Spartans in ancient Greece. A long strip of leather was wound round a post, and a message written on it. When the strip was unwound the letters seemed to be meaningless. The receiver of the message could easily recover the original, by winding the strip round a post of the same diameter. Of course, anyone who intercepted the message could do the same, so the cipher was not particularly safe.

Another fairly simple transposition cipher is called the Rail-fence cipher. The plaintext is written as two rows. It is ciphered by writing it down the columns, in groups of five letters.

Plain text MYHEARTACHESANDADROWS

YNUMBNESSPAINSMYSENSE

Ciphered Text MYYNH UEMAB RNTEA SCSHP EASIA NNSDM AYDSR EONWS SE

Deciphering is the transposition which is inverse to the original. Just write the ciphered message in columns, and the plaintext appears along the rows.

But anyone else who knows that the rail-fence system is being used can decipher it just as easily.

A more sophisticated system is the Keyed column method. Write the message as a rectangle, then write the key word along the top. Suppose the key word is BRAVELY. Give numbers to the letters according to their alphabetic order.

```
B R A V E L Y
2 5 1 6 3 4 7
M Y H E A R T
A C H E S A N
D A D R O W S
Y N U M B N E
S S P A I N S
M Y S E N S E
```

The ciphered message is obtained by writing the columns in order of the keyword letters. We write the column under the A first, then the column under the B and so on.

```
HHDUP  SMADY  SMASO  BINRA  WNNSY  CANSY  EERMA  ETNSE  SE
```

With knowledge of the keyword, deciphering is easy. Just write the ciphered message in columns and order them in the way determined by the keyword. The plaintext appears.

Suppose that an enemy intercepts the message, and knows that the keyed column method is being used. Without knowledge of the keyword, the enemy will not know how many columns there are, or the order in which the columns should be arranged. With 7 columns, the number of possible arrangements is:

$$7 \times 6 \times 5 \times 4 \times 3 \times 2 \times 1 = 5{,}040.$$

It would take a very long time to try them all!

In practice, this sort of cipher can be broken fairly easily, by recognizing combinations of letters which are likely to come next to each other. So often a second transposition takes place, perhaps with a different keyword. To decipher one has to perform the inverses of both the transpositions, in the opposite order.

Substitution ciphers

In a substitution cipher, the letters of the plaintext are changed to other letters or to symbols. An example of a substitution cipher is given in the Conan Doyle story, "The Dancing Men".

The detective Sherlock Holmes is sent pictures of little dancing men, as below.

He recognizes that they form a cipher. Once he has enough examples, he is able to count the number of times each symbol occurs. The symbol on the right of the message above occurs most frequently, so it almost certainly represents "e", as this is the most common letter in English. Soon he was able to decipher the whole message.

Nothing can be deduced from a short message. But if we have several hundred letters, the commonest letter is almost certainly e. The next commonest will probably be t, n, r, o, a or i. With a bit of trial and error basic words like "the" or "and" will be found, and then the whole plaintext can be recovered.

So ciphers in which each letter is always changed to the same symbol are fairly easily to decipher, by this method. Below is a histogram showing the frequencies of letters in English, in percentages. Notice how "e" stands out by itself, as twice as frequent as the other vowels. The five commonest consonants are 25 times as frequent as the five rarest consonants.

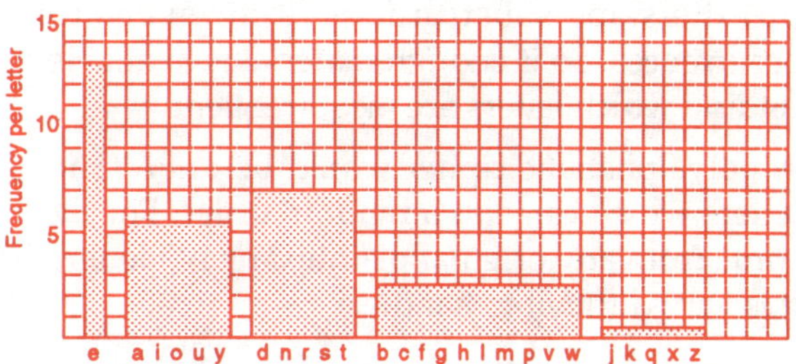

One way to make a substitution cipher more secure is by changing letters by pairs instead of singly. Several methods are available: the following uses matrices.

Give each letter a number according to its position in the alphabet. So A is 1, B is 2 and so on. Suppose the word we want to cipher is BABE. In numbers this will be 2 1 2 5.

Let the cipher matrix be $\begin{pmatrix} 5 & 7 \\ 2 & 3 \end{pmatrix}$. Apply it to the pairs of numbers:

$$\begin{pmatrix} 5 & 7 \\ 2 & 3 \end{pmatrix} \times \begin{pmatrix} 2 \\ 1 \end{pmatrix} = \begin{pmatrix} 17 \\ 7 \end{pmatrix} \text{ and } \begin{pmatrix} 5 & 7 \\ 2 & 3 \end{pmatrix} \times \begin{pmatrix} 2 \\ 5 \end{pmatrix} = \begin{pmatrix} 45 \\ 19 \end{pmatrix}$$

So the ciphered message is 17 7 45 19. Notice that the letter B is represented first by 17 and then by 45. So the cipher cannot be broken as easily as if a letter was always changed in the same way.

To decipher, we apply the inverse matrix, $\begin{pmatrix} 3 & -7 \\ -2 & 5 \end{pmatrix}$.

$$\begin{pmatrix} 3 & -7 \\ -2 & 5 \end{pmatrix} \times \begin{pmatrix} 17 \\ 7 \end{pmatrix} = \begin{pmatrix} 2 \\ 1 \end{pmatrix} \text{ and } \begin{pmatrix} 3 & -7 \\ -2 & 5 \end{pmatrix} \times \begin{pmatrix} 45 \\ 19 \end{pmatrix} = \begin{pmatrix} 2 \\ 5 \end{pmatrix}$$

So the plaintext reappears.

This sort of cipher can be broken, by recognizing common pairs of letters, such as "TH", or "HE", or "AN". But obviously this is much more difficult.

Polyalphabetic ciphers

A polyalphabetic cipher is a substitution cipher in which one letter is changed to another, but by varying rules. Several different arrangements of the alphabet are written out, and the one that is used depends on a keyword.

		A B C D E F G H I J K L M N O P Q R S T U V W X Y Z
Key letter	a	B C D E F G H I J K L M N O P Q R S T U V W X Y Z A
	b	C D E F G H I J K L M N O P Q R S T U V W X Y Z A B
	c	D E F G H I J K L M N O P Q R S T U V W X Y Z A B C
	d	E F G H I J K L M N O P Q R S T U V W X Y Z A B C D
	e	F G H I J K L M N O P Q R S T U V W X Y Z A B C D E
	..	.. ..

Suppose the key word is *bad*, and the plaintext is ATTACK. The first letter of the plaintext is ciphered by the row of the first letter of the keyword. So the first letter A is ciphered by the b row, obtaining C. The second letter is ciphered by the a row, obtaining U. The third letter is ciphered by the d row, obtaining X. Now we use the b row again. The final ciphered word is CUXCDO.

Notice that the letter T was represented by a different letter each time, so this cipher is much harder to break.

But the same substitutions occur every three letters. Notice that A was ciphered as C in both occurrences. So if enough material is available the cipher can be broken by taking every third letter and finding which letters are most frequent.

A polyalphabetic cipher would be unbreakable if the key word was arbitrarily long, and consisted of letters which came in a random order. For then any ciphered message, 100 letters long say, could have come from any original plaintext of 100 letters. The reason why this cipher is not used in practice is that it is very difficult to handle.

The Enigma Machine

Ciphering and deciphering are made much quicker and more reliable if they are done by machine rather than by hand. Probably the most famous cipher machine is the Enigma Machine, which was used by the German armed forces throughout the Second World War. A photograph is below.

As each letter was keyed in, an electrical current would pass through wires connected to the three dials, successively changing the letter. The ciphered letter would be shown by a bulb being switched on. After each letter the dials would rotate, so that the substitution would be different for the next letter.

So the Enigma Machine produced a polyalphabetic cipher. The same alphabet would not be repeated until the dials returned to their original setting. As there are 26 letters in the alphabet, this would happen only after $26^3 = 17{,}576$ letters. So the length of the keyword was over 17,500 letters! It was impossible to break this cipher by the methods described above, and it was thought that this cipher was unbreakable by any means.

But by advanced mathematical techniques, and with the help of early computers, methods were found to break the cipher. By the end of the war most of the Enigma messages were being broken. This was of enormous advantage to Britain in winning the War.

Public key ciphers

In all cipher systems, the procedure of deciphering is the inverse of the procedure of ciphering. For the systems described so far, they have been of equal difficulty. But there are some operations for which the inverse is much harder than the original operation. For example, factorizing an algebraic expression is much harder than expanding out brackets!

Consider something as simple as multiplication. To multiply together two 4 digit numbers takes a few seconds on a calculator, or a few minutes with paper and pencil. Suppose the result is the 8 digit number 32596357.

The inverse of this operation is factorizing. Can you find the two original numbers? Unless you are very lucky it will take you several hours with a calculator to find the factors of 32596357.

A public key cipher exploits this. Two 100 digit numbers are multiplied together, giving a 200 digit number. To cipher a message, only the 200 digit number is needed. To decipher the message, the original 100 digit numbers are required. So the 200 digit number is made public, and anyone can use it to send messages. Only the people who know the original 100 digit numbers can recover the plaintext.

To break this cipher, it is necessary to factorize a 200 digit number. With present mathematical techniques, this would take thousands of years, even on the fastest of computers. But if mathematicians can find a quick way to factorize large numbers, the cipher will be broken and all the secret messages will become exposed.

The mathematics of ciphers

Constructing and breaking ciphers requires a lot of mathematics. Here material from Chapters 6, 20, 21, 22 and 23 has been touched upon.

Extended task. The sine function

The sine function is defined in terms of lengths of a right-angled triangle. But a calculator or computer can work out values of sine, without having to draw a triangle and measure its sides. In this investigation you use a spreadsheet to look at the formula which generates sine.

Note: A spreadsheet measures angles in radians not degrees.

1 radian is equivalent to $\frac{108}{\pi} = 57.3$ degrees. So 90° is equivalent to $90 \times \frac{\pi}{180} = 1.570796327$ radians.

The formula for sine is:

$$\sin x = x - \frac{x^3}{3!} + \frac{x^5}{5!} - \frac{x^7}{7!} + \frac{x^9}{9!} - \ldots$$

where for example $5! = 5 \times 4 \times 3 \times 2 \times 1 = 120$.

So there is a sequence of functions which get closer to $\sin x$.

$$f_1(x) = x, \quad f_2(x) = x - \frac{x^3}{3!} \quad f_3(x) = x - \frac{x^3}{3!} + \frac{x^5}{5!} \quad \text{etc.}$$

1) The aim is to see how closely these functions approximate sin x. Use a spreadsheet to find the values of sin x and of $f_1(x)$, $f_2(x)$ and so on up to $f_{10}(x)$. How quickly you can enter the formulas for the functions will depend on how expert you are at using a spreadsheet. It might be a good idea to have columns for $n!$ and for $x^n/n!$ Record also the error for each of the functions.

   Try different values of x. How does this affect the errors?

2) Extend your spreadsheet, so that sin x and $f_1(x)$ etc are shown for values of x between 0° and 90°. Use the graph plotting facility on the spreadsheet to show the graphs of these functions on the same diagram. What can you conclude?

3) Before the days of computers, tables of sines and cosines were often found by the method of differences. The values would be calculated for whole numbers of degrees, and values in between could be calculated from them.

Set up a spreadsheet showing the values of sine at 0°, 1°, 2° up to 10°. For the next row show the differences between these values. The row after that shows the differences between the differences and so on.

Display as many decimal places as possible. Which row is almost constant? How can you use the table to find the value of sin 11°, or of sin 8.3° ?

Miscellaneous exercises

Group A

1) It is known that 40% of the voting population is under 35, 40% is between 35 and 65, and 20% is over 65. A sample of 30 people, 10 from each group, revealed 3 people under 35 in support of a proposal, 4 from the second age range in favour, and 8 from the third range in favour. Estimate the support from the population as a whole.

2) The following figures give the weights of 20 people. Find the mean weight and the standard deviation. Find the interquartile range of the figures.

Weight in kg	55	48	73	50	48	50	52	59	43	68
	64	59	48	49	53	64	60	56	59	62

3) Two makes of tyres were tested to see how many miles they travelled before replacement was needed. Draw histograms for the two makes, and comment on the difference.

1,000's of miles	10–15	15–20	20–25	25–30	30–35
Type A Frequency	5	23	38	24	10
Type B Frequency	15	21	28	22	14

4) The daily maximum temperatures in a resort over July and August were measured. Draw a histogram to illustrate these figures.

Temperature in °F	50-60	60-70	70-75	75-80	80-85	85-90	90-100
Frequency	8	10	8	11	10	7	8

5) A marathon race was run. The women entrants came in close together, with an average time of 4 hours 43 minutes. The men were widely separated, with an average of 4 hours 5 minutes. Sketch the frequency graphs which might show the times for men and women.

6) A garage sells leaded petrol in grades **, ***, ****. The amount of petrol sold, in hundreds of gallons, during Monday and Tuesday of a certain week is given by the matrix below.

	**	***	****
Monday	5	2	16
Tuesday	3	4	18

a) Form a matrix product which will give the total petrol sold on each day.

b) Form a matrix product which will give the total of each grade sold on both days.

c) The grades of petrol cost £1.95, £1.98, £2.05 per gallon respectively. Form a matrix product which will give the total revenue from the petrol.

7) On the right is a map showing the roads between three villages. Write down the route matrix for the map.

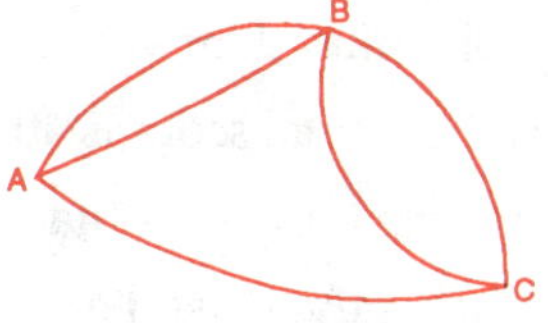

Suppose that on one of the roads connecting A to B traffic can only go from A to B. Write down the new route matrix. Square it, and find all the two stage routes from B back to B.

8) The precedence of five tasks is shown in the table on the right. Draw the corresponding network.

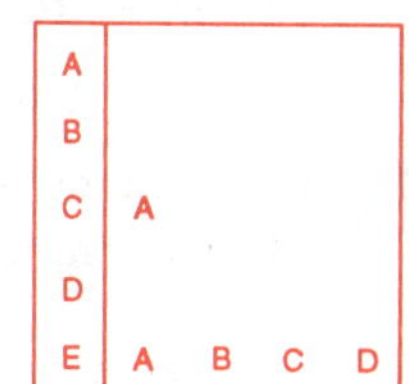

A	
B	
C	A
D	
E	A B C D

9) Suppose the tasks A, B, C, D, E of Question 8 take 5 days, 2 days, 4 days, 7 days, 2 days respectively. Find the critical path and the completion time. Find the slack time for task D.

10) A seamstress makes curtains which are either de luxe or ordinary. Each de luxe curtain uses 6 m^2 of material, and takes 96 minutes to make. Each ordinary curtain uses 4 m^2 and takes 24 minutes. She can receive at most 60 m^2 of material per day, and she will not work more than 8 hours per day.

Letting x and y be the numbers of de luxe and ordinary curtains respectively, find two inequalities in x and y. Illustrate them on a graph.

If the profits on de luxe and ordinary curtains are £16 and £8 respectively, how can she spend her time most profitably?

11) $\frac{3}{4}$ of a batch of tulip bulbs will give flowers. If I plant two, what is the probability that

a) both flower b) neither flowers?

12) A bag contains 5 red and 7 blue marbles. Two are picked out at random. What is the probability that:

a) both are red b) exactly one is red?

13) The diagram on the right shows the simplified map of a village. A motorist enters at A, and at every cross roads she goes straight ahead with probability $\frac{1}{2}$, and turns right or left with equal probability $\frac{1}{4}$. Find the probability that:

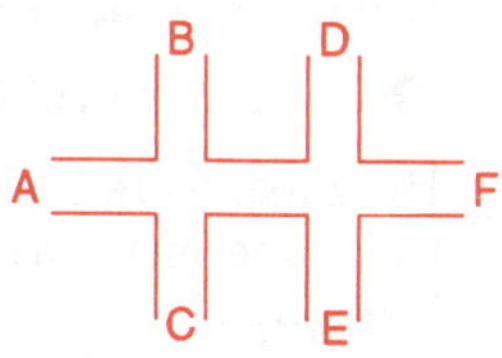

a) She goes to B b) she goes to D c) she goes to F.

14) Two cards are drawn from a pack. What is the probability that:

a) both are Aces b) neither is an Ace

c) exactly one is an Ace.

Group B. Challenge questions

15) The scores of 20 golfers are shown in the table below. The average score was 88.7. Find x and y.

Score	86	87	88	89	90	91
Frequency	1	x	5	3	y	3

16) Two cards are drawn from a pack. What is the probability that the first is an Ace and the second is a Heart?

17) A floor is covered with tiles which are 10 cm square. A disc of radius 4 cm is thrown onto the floor. What is the probability that it doesn't cross any of the gaps between the tiles?

18) An icosahedral (20 sided) die has the numbers 1 to 20 on its faces. It is rolled twice. Find the probability that:

   a) the total score is 40 b) the total is more than 4

   c) the numbers obtained are different.

   What is the most likely total score? What is its probability?

19) Four coins are spun. How many possible outcomes are there? What is the probability that:

   a) all the coins show Heads b) at least one coin shows Heads?

20) In how many ways can the letters A B C D be ordered? List the possible orderings. If the letters are ordered at random what is the probability that B and C will be next to each other?

Group C. Longer exercises

21) **Embarrassing questions**

   Suppose you want to conduct a survey, but do not trust the people questioned to give an honest answer, because it might be embarrassing or even incriminating. You can use probability to get round this problem.

   You might want to investigate the extent of drug-taking among athletes. If you ask the question "Have you ever taken anabolic steroids?" you could not rely on the answers. Instead give each person a die, and ask them to roll it, without showing you the result. They are to respond A if the die shows 1 or 2 and they have taken steroids, or if the die shows 3, 4, 5 or 6 and they haven't taken steroids. Otherwise they reply B.

   Suppose that the proportion of athletes who have taken steroids is k. Show that the proportion of them who will respond A is $\frac{2}{3}-\frac{1}{3}k$.

   Suppose that in your survey you found that 45% of the people questioned responded A. What proportion of them have taken steroids?

   Use this technique to obtain an honest response to an embarrassing question of your own.

22) **The birthday problem**

   How many are there in your class? Do you all have different birthdays, or is there a pair of you with the same birthday? In fact, with a class of 25 or so it is likely that two people have the same birthday.

   a) We shall find the probability that a group of people all have different birthdays. It doesn't matter what the first person's birthday is. If the second person's birthday is different, then it must be one of the other 364 days.

With 2 people, the probability of different birthdays is $\frac{364}{365}$.

The third person must have have a birthday different from the previous two.

With 3 people, P(different birthdays) = $\frac{364}{365} \times \frac{363}{365}$.

Continue, with 4, 5, 6 people. Don't bother to write down all the terms, but keep them on your calculator as you go along. Fill in the table below:

Number of people	2	3	4	5	10	15	20	25	30
P(different birthdays)	.997	.992							

b) Have you ever collected sets of cards which appear in cereal packets? Were you annoyed when after only a few packets you got a card which you already had?

Suppose there are 20 different cards to be obtained. By the method above fill in the table below:

Number of packets	2	3	4	5	10	15	20
P(all cards different)	.95						

23) **Crown and Anchor**

A gambling game is as follows. You can bet on any one of the numbers 1 to 6. Three dice are rolled, and if your number comes up on one of the dice your money is doubled. If it comes up on two of the dice your money is tripled, and if it comes up on all three dice your money is quadrupled.

What is the probability that you win with this game? If you play it 216 times, betting £1 each time, how much would you expect to win or lose?

Revision exercises

1) Devise a survey sheet to find out which television channel is most popular.

2) The table below shows the ages of 10 employees of a firm and their annual salaries (in £1,000's). Plot the points on a scatter diagram. Draw a line of best fit. From your line estimate the age of someone earning £19,000.

Age	21	25	31	35	36	39	42	48	56	61
Salary	12	11	16	22	25	23	21	36	32	23

3) List some of the qualities people want in a compact-disc player. Devise a questionnaire to find which of these qualities are thought to be most important.

4) Below are the inflation rates for 10 industrialized countries. Find the mean, median and range.

% Rate: 5, 6, 11, 2, 8, 2, 3, 4, 3, 4

5) Two fish and chip shops were investigated: in each shop eight 50 p portions of chips were bought and weighed. The results in grams are shown below. What conclusions can you reach?

Nice Plaice: 95, 105, 99, 110, 115, 98, 89, 101

Rock of Ages: 96, 125, 81, 92, 130, 75, 150, 71

6) The weights of 40 eggs were found. Arrange the data in a frequency table, choosing a suitable interval. Use your table to find the mean weight.

Weight in grams: 65 69 71 55 51 77 63 57 72 45

65 74 56 49 55 54 59 61 64 60

57 72 74 69 61 49 68 65 50 62

78 52 46 62 69 73 47 50 81 66

7) The former pupils of a school were contacted 20 years after they had left, to find out what salary they were earning. The results of the 100 ex-pupils who replied are below:

Salary in £1,000	10-15	15-20	20-25	25-30	30-35	35-40
Frequency	8	12	27	35	12	6

Draw a frequency diagram to show these figures. Find the mean salary.

8) Find the cumulative frequencies for the figures of Question 7. Plot a cumulative frequency graph, and find the median and the interquartile range.

9) Will the results of the survey described in Question 7 provide a fair picture of the salaries of the ex-pupils of the school?

10) a) Write a flow-chart which will take x to $2x - 3$.

b) Write a flow chart which will take $2x - 3$ back to x.

11) Write a flow-chart to find the first n for which $2^n > 10{,}000$.

12) Write a flow chart to solve the equation $2^x = 100$ to an accuracy of 2 decimal places.

13) The diagram on the near right shows the sales of two brands of toothpaste. Is it fair? If not how should it be changed?

14) The bar-chart on the far right shows the monthly sales of a brand of washing powder after an expensive advertising campaign. Does it give a fair picture of the situation?

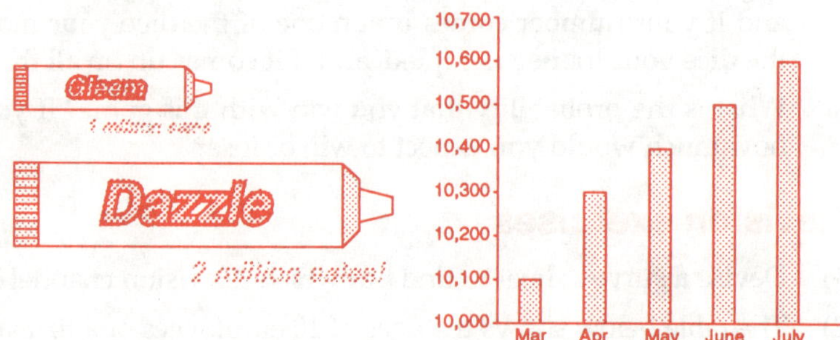

15) A roulette wheel has holes numbered 1 to 36. What is the probability that the ball lands in a hole whose number is:

a) 23 b) divisible by 7 c) at least 7?

16) In the roulette wheel of Question 12, what is the probability that the ball lands in a hole whose number is:

a) under 7 or over 30 b) even or divisible by 5.

17) Three coins are spun. List all the possible outcomes. What is the probability that there will be three Tails?

18) There are 2 white beads and 5 black beads. They are to be strung on a circular necklace: one arrangement is shown – list all the other arrangements. What is the probability that the white beads are next to each other?

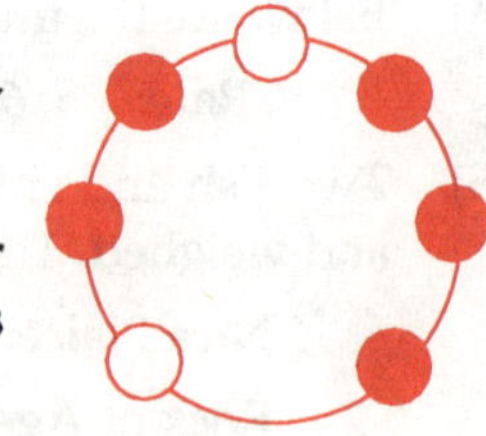

Puzzles and paradoxes

1) The most famous paradox in probability is the St Petersburg paradox. As so often in probability, it involves gambling.

In the casino, a coin is tossed until Heads first appears. If it appears on the first toss, you win 1 rouble. If it first appears on the second toss, i.e. Tails then Heads, you win 2 roubles. If it first appears on the third toss, you win 4 roubles. And so on – the winnings double at each spin of the coin. The question is, if the game is fair, how much should you pay to play it?

Your chance of winning 1 rouble is the chance of Heads on the first toss, i.e. $\frac{1}{2}$. Your chance of winning 2 roubles is the chance of Tails then Heads, i.e. $\frac{1}{4}$. Your chance of winning 4 roubles is the chance of Tails, Tails, Heads, i.e. $\frac{1}{8}$. Add up all the amounts you expect to gain:

$$\text{Amount expected} = \frac{1}{2}\times 1 + \frac{1}{4}\times 2 + \frac{1}{8}\times 4 + \frac{1}{16}\times 8 + \ldots$$
$$= \frac{1}{2} + \frac{1}{2} + \frac{1}{2} + \frac{1}{2} + \ldots.$$

So you expect an infinite amount of roubles. So you should pay the bank an infinite amount of money to be allowed to play the game. Does this seem wise?

2) In a gaol there are three prisoners under sentence of death. The dictator of the country announces that one of the three will be spared. So each prisoner thinks that the probability that he will be spared is $\frac{1}{3}$.

Prisoner A goes to the gaoler and says: "I know that at least one of B and C will be executed. You aren't giving anything away if you tell me which one."

The gaoler tells him that B will be executed. Prisoner A is now happier. Either he or C will not be executed, and so his chances of survival have gone up to $\frac{1}{2}$.

Is A's reasoning correct, if the gaoler hasn't really given him any information about his own fate?

3) (**Prisoner's Dilemma.**) Two men are arrested on suspicion of a burglary. The detective investigating the case keeps them separate, and visits each in turn. He says to each: "If you confess that you both did the burglary, I'll see that you get off with 2 years in prison. If you don't confess but your confederate does, then you'll get 7 years in prison."

What should the prisoner do, confess to the crime or continue to deny it? Remember, the prisoners cannot talk to each other.

Mental test 1

1) How much change from a £20 note is there after spending £9.46?

2) Convert $\frac{1}{3}$ to a percentage, to 2 decimal places.

3) Add 1.92 to 2.36.

4) Three consecutive numbers add to 66. What are they?

5) Convert 20 feet to yards and feet.

6) What is the date and time 100 hours after 5 p.m. on 2nd January?

7) Find the square root of 0.01.

8) The average income of 12 people is £15,000. What is their total income?

9) What is $\frac{1}{4}$ to the power -2?

10) Express the ratio $\frac{1}{3}:\frac{1}{4}$ as a ratio of integers.

11) Express two millionths in standard form.

12) Add a fifth to a seventh.

13) A train leaves at 9 a.m., give or take 1 minute. I take 10 minutes to walk to the station, give or take 2 minutes. When should I set off to be sure of catching the train?

14) A rectangle is $3x$ cm by $4y$ cm. What is its perimeter?

15) List the cells on a spreadsheet which are adjacent to C3.

16) A triangle has base 3 and height 6. What is the side of a square with the same area?

17) The shorter sides of a right-angled triangle are 30 cm and 40 cm. What is the hypotenuse?

18) You know the three sides of a triangle. What do you use to calculate the angles of the triangle?

19) Cos x and sin x are both negative. Where between 0° and 360° must x be?

20) A card is drawn from a pack. What is the probability it is either a Jack or a Diamond?

Mental test 2

1) In a computer game you get 700 for each goblin destroyed and 1,000 for each ghost. How could you get a total of 4,800?

2) What is the least number which 2, 5 and 15 will divide into?

3) What is 27 to the power $\frac{1}{3}$?

4) 200 kg is divided in the ratio 1:3:6. What is the smallest part?

5) What is the date 40 days after July 1st?

6) How much does Marsha earn for a 38 hour week at £6 per hour?

7) At an acceleration of $\frac{1}{10}$ m/sec^2, how long will a train take to reach a speed of 20 m/sec from rest?

8) A width is given as 10.0 cm, to 1 decimal place. What is the least possible width?

9) The area of a square is 49 sq. feet. What is its perimeter?

10) A grapefruit weighs $\frac{2}{3}$ of a pound. How many are there in 6 lb.?

11) What is the square root of x^2y^4?

12) Convert x grams to kilograms.

13) 4 is added to x, and this is doubled. What is the result?

14) The rule for converting Reaumur temperatures to Fahrenheit is: divide by 4, multiply by 9, add 32. Write down the rule for converting from Fahrenheit to Reaumur.

15) What is the bearing of a place which is 10 miles north and 10 miles east?

16) An area of 5 cm^2 is enlarged by a scale factor of 2. What is the new area?

17) What angle between 0° and 360° has the same cosine as 60°?

18) You know the shorter sides of a right-angled triangle. What function do you use to find the angles?

19) An octahedron is made by glueing together the square bases of two pyramids. How many edges does the octahedron have?

20) With each dart, I have probability $\frac{1}{10}$ of hitting the bull's-eye. What is the probability that my first dart hits the bull's-eye and my second misses?

Revision test 1

1) Use a calculator to evaluate the following without writing anything down except the final answers:

   a) $(3.15 + 2.79) \times (9.43 - 5.37)$ b) $\dfrac{3.27}{2.97 + 3.82 - 9.25}$

2) Round the figures of Question 1 to the nearest whole number. Hence find the approximate answers to the calculations without the use of a calculator.

3) Evaluate $\frac{2}{3} + \frac{4}{5} - \frac{3}{7}$, leaving your answer as a fraction.

4) How many inches are there in a distance of x yards and y feet?

5) Find the value of $12x - 24y$ when $x = \frac{1}{4}$ and $y = -\frac{1}{3}$.

6) Solve the inequality $3x + 4 < 12 - x$.

7) Let $\mathbf{a} = \begin{pmatrix} 1 \\ 3 \end{pmatrix}$ and $\mathbf{b} = \begin{pmatrix} -2 \\ 3 \end{pmatrix}$. Find $3\mathbf{a} - 2\mathbf{b}$.

8) A room is a rectangle of sides 5 m and 6 m. What angle does the diagonal of the room make with the longer side?

9) In ten opinion polls the support for a party was as below. Find the average of these figures.

   41% 42% 39% 36% 40% 41% 38% 40% 44% 43%

10) I have an ordinary six-sided die and a four-sided die with the numbers 1 to 4 on its faces. If both are rolled what is the probability that the total score is 10?

Revision test 2

1) A form has two entrants for the 100 m sprint. It is reckoned that Fiona has probability $\frac{1}{3}$ of winning, and that Harriet's probability is $\frac{1}{5}$. What is the probability that either will win? Give your answer as a fraction.

2) A grandmother is inviting her grandchildren to tea. She is not sure whether 4, 5 or 6 of them will come. What is the least number of cakes she can bake to ensure that they will be shared equally between the children, however many turn up?

3) Find as fractions:

a) The square of $\frac{2}{3}$ b) the reciprocal of $2\frac{3}{7}$

4) Solve the equations:

$$2x + y = 7$$
$$3x - 2y = 14$$

5) Factorize: $2x^2y^2 + 8xy^3 - 12x^3y$

6) The bottom of a drawer is a rectangle which is 63 cm by 47 cm. What is the longest stick which can lie on the bottom of the drawer?

7) A painting is a 8 cm by 10 cm rectangle. It is framed within a mount, surrounding it by 3 cm on all sides. What is the area of the mount?

8) Two cog wheels are connected. One wheel has 60 teeth, and rotates at 120 r.p.m. The other wheel rotates at 40 r.p.m. How many teeth does the second wheel have?

9) Express in terms of inequalities the shaded region shown on the right.

10) The performances of 8 athletes in the high jump and the long jump are shown below. Draw a straight line through the points.

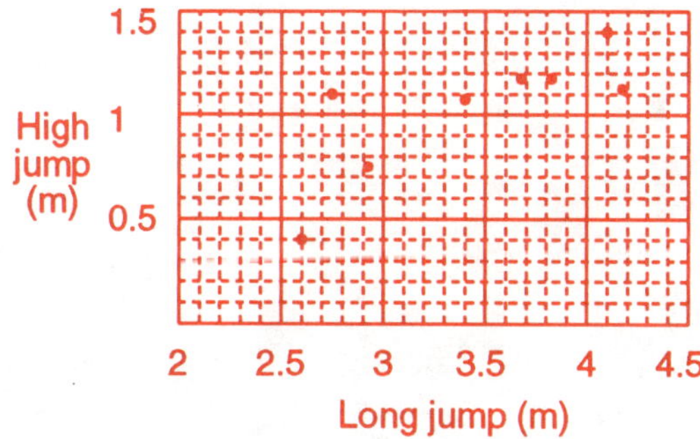

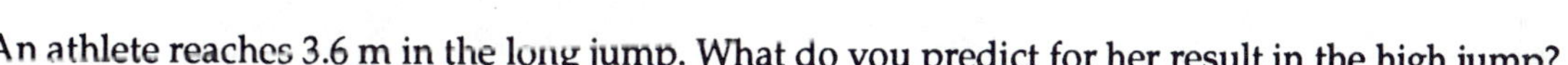
An athlete reaches 3.6 m in the long jump. What do you predict for her result in the high jump?

Revision test 3

1) Construct a triangle with sides 7 cm, 11 cm, 13 cm. Measure the angles of the triangle.

   Use Pythagoras's Theorem to tell whether or not the triangle is right-angled.

2) 30 people enrolled for an evening class. The full price of the class was £55, and the concessionary price was £24. The total amount of money received was £1,495.

   If x people paid the full price, and y the concessionary price, form two equations in x and y and solve them.

3) By Trial and Improvement solve the equation $x^3 + 7x = 29$, accurate to 1 decimal place.

4) A cylindrical can has height 8 cm and the circumference of its rim is 20 cm. Find the volume of the can.

5) In a certain country there are two political parties, the Yellows and the Browns. There are 200 seats to be contested in the general election. The frequency table below gives the majority of the Brown Party in the 200 constituencies, in 1,000's of votes. (Negative values correspond to Yellow majorities).

Brown majority	–25 to –15	–15 to –5	–5 to 5	5 to 15	15 to 25
Frequency	32	51	67	42	8

   Find the cumulative frequencies, and plot a cumulative frequency chart. What is the median majority? Who do you think won the election?

Revision test 4

1) The first term of a sequence of fractions is $\frac{1}{5}$. Subsequent terms are found by adding 1 and finding the reciprocal. So the second term is:

$$\frac{1}{1+\frac{1}{5}} = \frac{5}{6}$$

Find the next four terms of the sequence, expressed as fractions.

There are rules by which the numerator and denominator of each fraction are found from the numerator and denominator of the fraction before it. Explain these rules.

2) A company offers its sales staff two salary schemes.

Scheme A. Fixed salary of £8,000, commission of £200 per sale.

Scheme B. Fixed salary of £6,000, commission of £300 per sale.

A saleswoman expects to make 25 sales. Which scheme should she choose?

If a saleman expects to make x sales. Find expressions in terms of x for his incomes under the two schemes. For what values of x will he be better off under Scheme A?

3) An observer stands on top of a 200 m cliff. A boat is out to sea, 1,000 m due North of the cliff. Taking the x-axis to be Eastwards, the y-axis Northwards, and the z-axis vertically upwards, find the coordinates of the boat from the observer.

The boat sails due East at 4 m/sec. Find its coordinates after 1 minute.

When will the boat be on a bearing of 045°?

4) Work through the flow diagram below, with inputs of (a) $n = 2$ (b) $n = 4$. Each time you pass X write down the values of i and P.

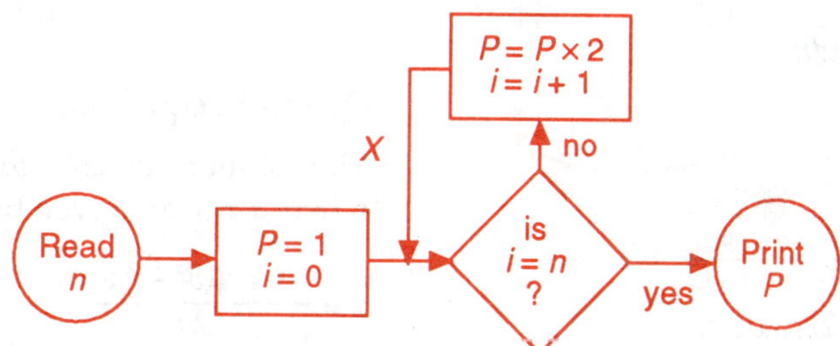

What function does the flow diagram evaluate?

Formula sheet

When you sit the GCSE exam, you will be given a sheet of formulas similar to this one, to refer to when answering the questions.

Area of triangle = $\dfrac{\text{base} \times \text{height}}{2}$

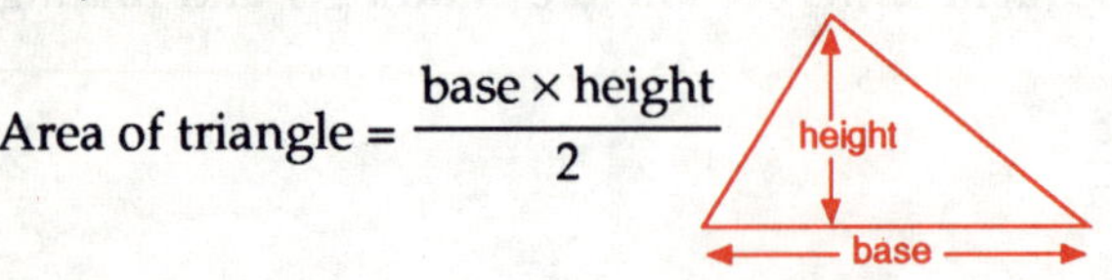
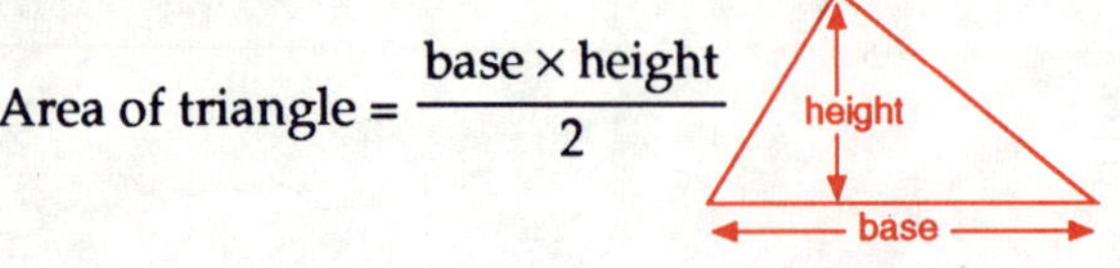

Volume of sphere = $\frac{4}{3}\pi r^3$

Surface area of sphere = $4\pi r^2$

Volume of cuboid = height × width × length

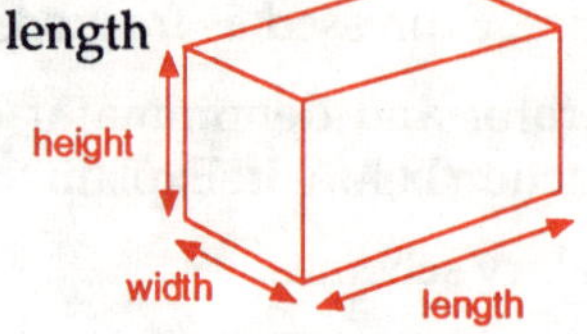

Area of trapezium = $\frac{1}{2}(a + b)h$

Volume of cone = $\frac{1}{3}\pi r^2 h$

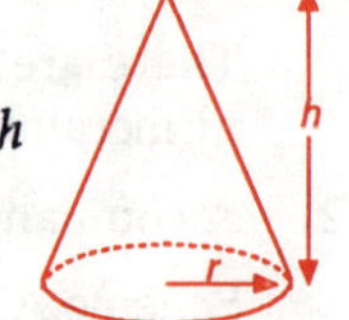

adj = hyp × cos θ
opp = hyp × sin θ
opp = adj × tan θ

or $\sin\theta = \dfrac{\text{opp}}{\text{hyp}}$

$\cos\theta = \dfrac{\text{adj}}{\text{hyp}}$

$\tan\theta = \dfrac{\text{opp}}{\text{adj}}$

Volume of cylinder = $\pi r^2 h$

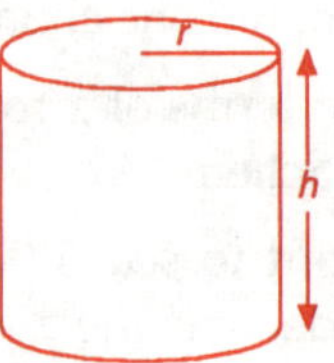

Area of parallelogram = base × height

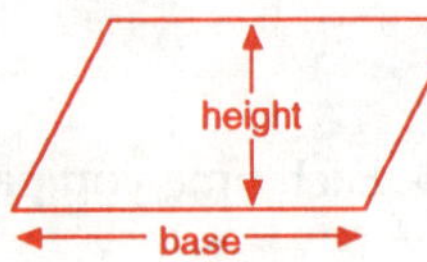

Pythagoras' Theorem

$a^2 + b^2 = c^2$

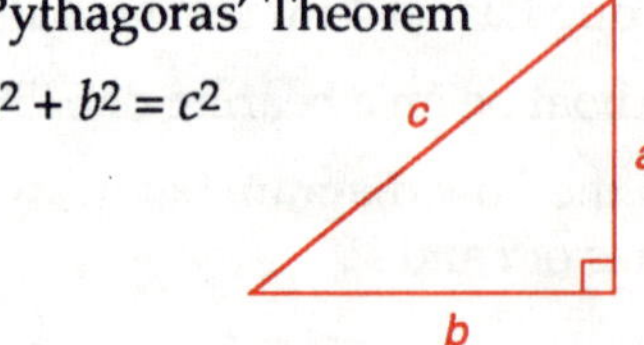

Curved area of cylinder = πdh

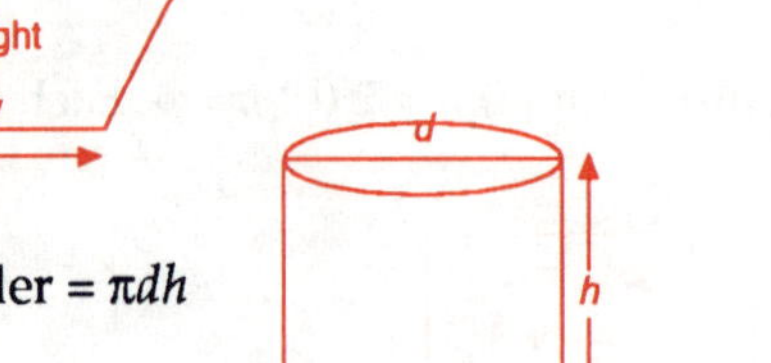

Quadratic equations

The solutions of $ax^2 + bx + c = 0$ where $a \neq 0$, are given by

$$x = \frac{-b \pm \sqrt{(b^2 - 4ac)}}{2a}$$

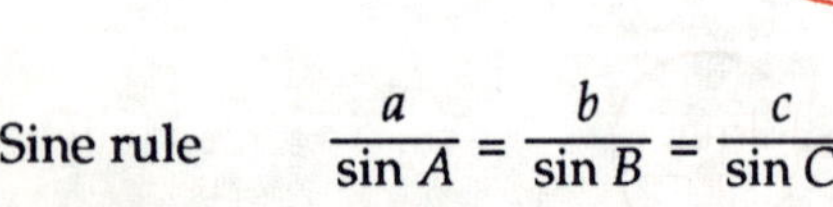

Sine rule $\dfrac{a}{\sin A} = \dfrac{b}{\sin B} = \dfrac{c}{\sin C}$

Cosine rule $a^2 = b^2 + c^2 - 2bc \cos A$

$$\cos A = \frac{b^2 + c^2 - a^2}{2bc}$$

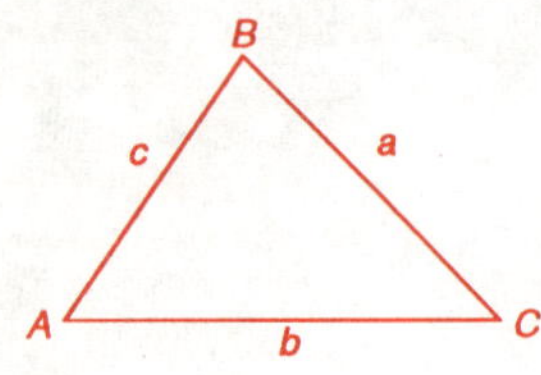

Standard deviation $s = \sqrt{\dfrac{\Sigma x^2}{n} - \left\{\dfrac{\Sigma x}{n}\right\}^2}$

Volume = area of base × height

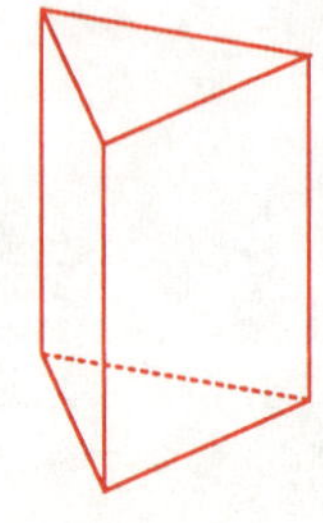

Area = length × width

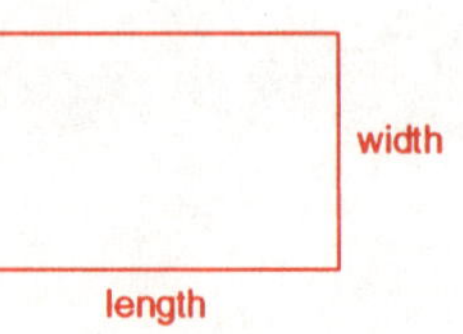

Exam 1

Answer all the questions.
Time: 2 hours

1) Make u the subject of the formula $v^2 = u^2 - 2as$. (2) [2]

2) A soft-drinks firm announces that annual consumption of its product SWILL is 11.34 cans per person. It predicts that consumption will rise by 10% next year. What will then be the annual consumption? (2)

The figure of 11.34 represents a rise of 8% compared with last year. What used to be the consumption? (4) [6]

3) In the diagram shown DT is a tangent to the circle. CDT = 48° and BAC = 27°.

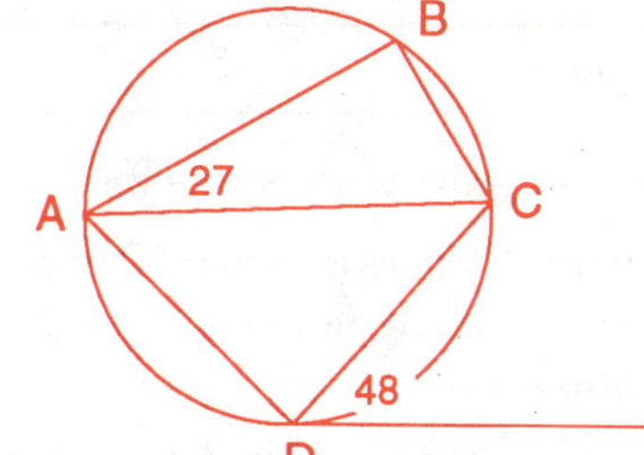

Find $C\hat{A}D$ and $B\hat{C}D$, giving short explanations for your calculations. (4) [4]

4) a) Find an obtuse angle x for which $\sin x = 0.3$. (2)

b) y is an angle between 0° and 360°, for which $\sin y = -\frac{4}{5}$ and $\cos y = -\frac{3}{5}$. Find y. (2) [4]

5) Mr Suleiman needs to get a bridging loan of £40,000 from a bank. The Bristol Bank will charge 1% of the loan, plus 1.2% per month while the loan is outstanding. The Cardiff Bank charges 0.1% of the loan plus 1.4% per month. Find the amount of interest charged by each bank if the loan will be outstanding for 2.3 months. (3)

Up to how many months would it be advantageous to borrow from the Cardiff Bank rather than from the Bristol? (4) [7]

6) ABCDEF is a regular hexagon with centre O. $\underline{OA} = \mathbf{a}$ and $\underline{OB} = \mathbf{b}$. Express in terms of $\mathbf{a}$ and $\mathbf{b}$:

$\underline{AB}$, $\underline{BC}$, $\underline{AC}$, $\underline{FC}$, $\underline{AE}$ (5)

Find on the figure (a) a rhombus, (b) a rectangle, (c) a trapezium that is not a parallelogram. (3) [8]

7) A bent coin has probability x of coming up Heads. It is spun twice. Complete the tree diagram shown. (2)

Find in terms of x the probabilities of (a) two Heads, (b) one Head and one Tail, in either order. (3)

This experiment is repeated many times. It is found that the situation of (b), 1 Head and 1 Tail, occurs one time in three. Form an equation in x. (3)

Solve this equation, to 3 decimal places. (4) [12]

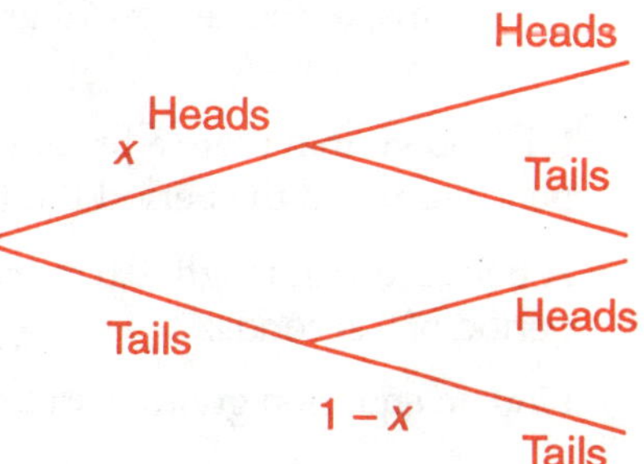

8) For the numbers below, the second row consists of the squares of the numbers in the top row.

1	2	3	4	5
1	4	9	16	25

Find the mean and median of the numbers in the top row. (2)

Find the mean and median of the numbers in the second row. (2)

Is the square of the mean the mean of the squares? (1)
Is the square of the median the median of the squares? (1) [6]

9) The Hamburger Harriers ran a cross-country race of 5 miles. Their times are given below.

Time (minutes)	30-32	32-34	34-35	35-36	36-38	38-40	40-50
Frequency	5	8	6	5	7	4	15

Draw a histogram to illustrate these figures. What was the modal time? (6)

The Ravioli Runners also had 50 entrants for the race. Their average time was 33 minutes, and they finished much more closely together. On your histogram sketch a possible histogram for the Ravioli Runners. (4) [10]

10) A cliff is 50 m high. A ship A is due north, and its angle of depression from the top of the cliff is 5°. Find the distance of A from the base of the cliff. (3)

A second ship B is on a bearing of 045°, and its angle of depression from the base of the cliff is 3°. Find the distance between the ships. (8) [11]

11) ABC is a triangle, in which AB = 16, BC = 8, B = 90°. A rectangle BXYZ is drawn inside the triangle as shown.

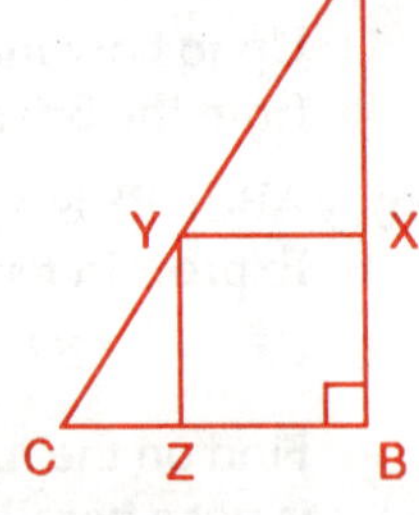

a) Write down three similar triangles. (3)

b) Let BZ = x and BX = y. Show that $y = 16 - 2x$. (4)

c) Show that the area of the rectangle is $A = 16x - 2x^2$. (1)

d) Either plot a graph of A against x, taking values of x between 0 and 8, or complete the square of the expression for A. Find the greatest possible area of the rectangle. (8) [16]

12) a) A rectangular field has length 120 m and width 90 metres, both figures being given to the nearest 10 m. What is the greatest possible area of the field? (2)

b) Certain coins weigh 5.2 grams each, to 1 decimal place. A stack of these coins weighs 520 grams, to the nearest 10 grams. What is the least and greatest number of coins there could be in the stack? (4) [6]

13) It is known that there a proportionality relationship of some sort between the length L of a pendulum and the period P it takes to swing to and fro.

A pendulum of length 0.6 m had a period of 1.5 seconds, and a pendulum of length 2.4 m had a period of 3 seconds.

Find an equation giving L in terms of P. (5) (5)

14) a) Define what is meant by an *irrational* number. (2)

b) Which of the following are irrational?

i) 2 (ii) $\sqrt{2}$ (iii) 1.414 (iv) $\sqrt{2} \times \sqrt{2}$ (2)

c) Write $\frac{53}{101}$ as a recurring decimal. (1)

d) Find the fraction corresponding to 0.63636363.... (3) [8]

15) The marks obtained by 10 pupils in an exam were as follows:

43 55 38 41 53 67 39 61 65 47

Find the mean and standard deviation of these marks. (3)

It is decided to award an extra 10 marks to each candidate, for turning up to the exam.

Write down the new mean and standard deviation, explaining how they were obtained from the old mean and standard deviation. (3) [6]

16) Express $\frac{1}{x+7} - \frac{1}{x+8}$ as a single fraction. (3)

Express $x^2 + 3x - 4$ in the form $(x + a)^2 + b$, where a and b are to be found. Hence find the least value of $x^2 + 3x - 4$. (3) [6]

17) The GNP of a country is given as 1.3×10^{10} dollars. Three years ago it was 9.3×10^9 dollars.

a) What is the percentage increase in GNP over these three years? (1)

b) What is the actual increase over these ten years? (2) [3]

Exam 2

Answer all the questions.
Time: 2 hours

1) a) By rounding each term to 1 significant figure, obtain a rough estimate of the following expression. Show all your working.

$$\frac{3.17 + 4.89}{2.24}$$ (3)

b) Evaluate the expression of part (a), giving your answer to three significant figures. (1) [4]

2) A tax system is such that the first £4,000 is tax free. Then tax is charged at 30% of the taxable income, up to an income of £20,000. Income over that is taxed at 50%.

How much tax is paid by someone earning £25,000? (2)

Ms Rogers pays £8,300 tax. What is her income? (2)

Mr Jackson pays 30% of his income in tax. What is his income? (3) [7]

3) Solve the equation $3.2x + 7.1 = 23.5$, giving your answer to 1 decimal place. (2)

The three numbers in the equation above are accurate to 1 decimal place. Find the range of values within which the solution x must lie. (4) [6]

4) Find the square roots of the following, giving your answers to three significant figures where appropriate.

a) 4

b) 40

c) 4×10^{18}

d) 0.0000004 (2)

Which of the square roots above are rational? (2)

For what values of n is $\sqrt{4 \times 10^n}$ a rational number? (2)

Find a number, bigger than 1, whose square root and cube root are both rational. (2) [8]

5) A gardener charges a call-out fee, and then a constant rate per hour. Work lasting 3 hours costs £16.50, and work lasting 5 hours costs £23.50

Find the hourly rate and the call-out fee. (2)

What is the charge for h hours work? (2)

How many hours work do you get for £P? (2) [6]

6) On the right is a graph showing the speed of a runner in the first 20 seconds of a race.

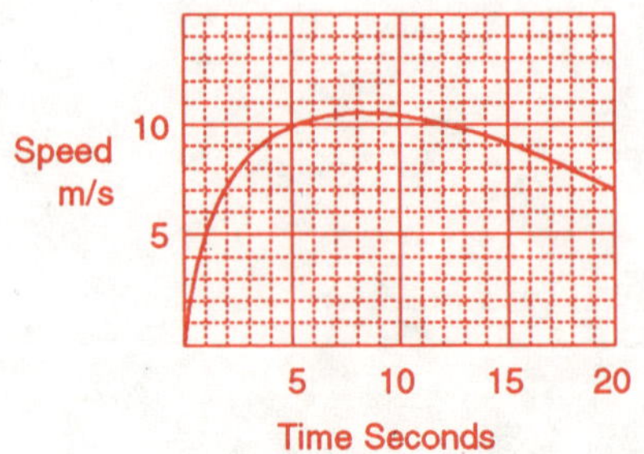

Estimate the total distance run during these 20 seconds. (4)

Briefly describe the runner's performance during the race. (3) [7]

7) Find two pairs of values of x and y which satisfy the equation $4x + 3y = 11$. Plot these pairs on a graph, and hence draw the straight line with equation $4x + 3y = 11$.(2)

Similarly, plot the graph of the line with equation $3x - 4y = 2$ on the same graph paper. Read off the coordinates of the crossing point.(2)

What can you say about these lines?(1)

Write down the equation of a line which is parallel to

$$4x + 3y = 11.$$(1) [6]

8) (a) below is the graph of $y = \sin x$ for x between 0° and 180°. On (b), (c) and (d) sketch the graphs of $y = 2 \sin x$, $\sin (x + 90°)$, $\sin 2x$ respectively.(6) [6]

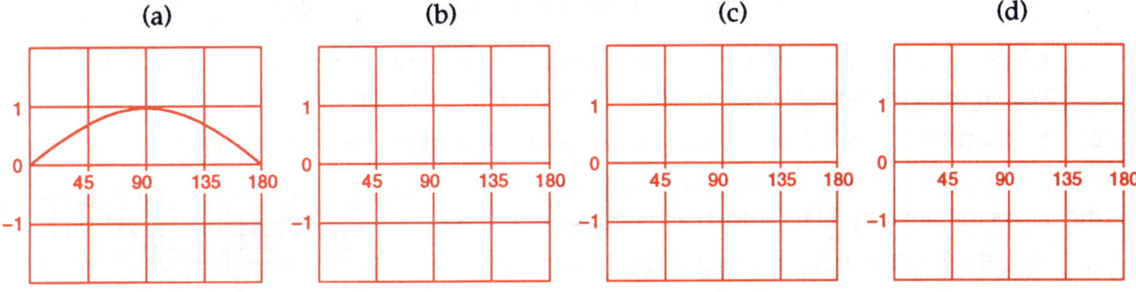

9) In a three dimensional coordinate system, a point (x,y,z) is x miles north of the origin, y miles east of it and z miles vertically above it.

Find the distance from the origin to (3, 5, 1).(2)

Find the angle of elevation of this point from the origin.(2) [4]

10) Write down the inverses of the following transformations:

a) An enlargement of scale factor 2 about (1,1).(1)

b) A rotation of 45° clockwise about (0,0).(1)

c) A reflection in the line $y = 3x - 7$.(1)

d) A translation given by the vector $\begin{pmatrix} 3 \\ 4 \end{pmatrix}$.(1) [4]

11) Triangle ABC has vertices at (1,1), (1,–3), (–2,1). It is enlarged to triangle PQR, with vertices at (–2,–2), (–2,6), (4,–2). Plot these triangles on graph paper and find the scale factor and centre of the enlargement.(3)

Write down the matrix which performs this enlargement.(3)

On certain graph paper ABC has area 2.3 cm². Find the area of triangle PQR.(3) [9]

12) The diagram shows the net of a pyramid, formed out of a square of side 6 cm and four triangles with base 6 cm and height 5 cm.

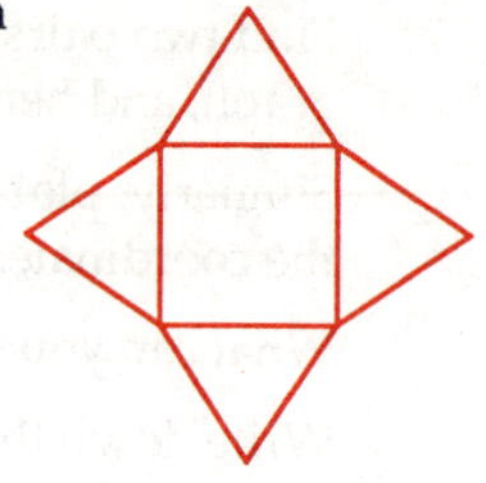

Find the surface area of the net. (3)

Find the height of the pyramid after it has been assembled. (3)

Find the volume of the pyramid. (2) [8]

13) The matrix P below gives the prices of honey and jam in three shops A, B and C.

$$\begin{array}{l} \\ \text{Honey} \\ \text{Jam} \end{array} \begin{array}{c} \text{A}\quad\text{B}\quad\text{C} \\ \begin{pmatrix} 89 & 95 & 85 \\ 43 & 52 & 41 \end{pmatrix} \end{array} = \text{P}$$

a) Mr Smith wishes to buy 2 jars of honey and 3 of jam. Write down a matrix product which will show how much he would have to pay in each shop. (2)

b) Find a matrix product which gives the average price of the two items. (2) [4]

14) On the right is a cumulative frequency curve for the marks obtained by 1,000 students in an exam.

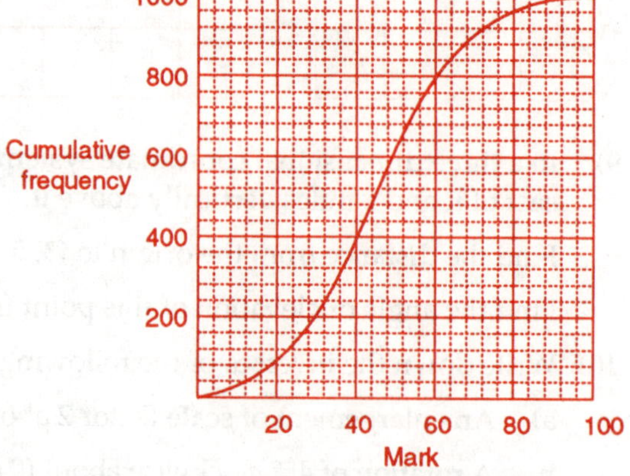

a) Find the median and the quartiles. (3)

b) If the pass mark is 45%, what percentage of the students will pass? (2)

In another exam, taken by a large number of students, the lower quartile is 35%. If two students are picked at random find the probabilities that:

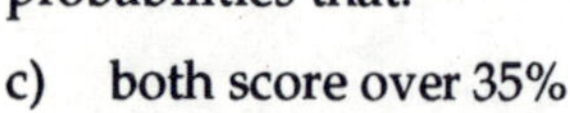
c) both score over 35%

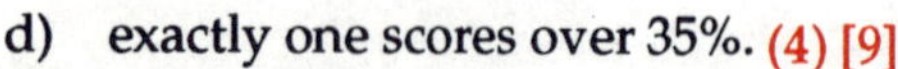
d) exactly one scores over 35%. (4) [9]

15) An electric power station can use either oil or coal. It has a contract with a nearby mine to use at least 100 tons of coal per week. Each ton of coal provides 6 units of energy, and each ton of oil produces 10 units. The station must produce at least 1500 units per week.

The pollution produced by coal and oil is 5 and 2 units per ton respectively. Local regulations restrict pollution to 1,000 units per week.

Let x and y be the numbers of hundreds of tons of coal and oil respectively used per week. Write down inequalities in x and y which describe the above restrictions. (4)

Illustrate the inequalities on graph paper, leaving unshaded the region of possible options. (4)

The cost of coal is £250 per ton, and of oil £350 per ton. What is the cheapest permissible way to supply the power? (4) [12]

Exam 3

Answer all the questions in both sections
Time: 2 hours 30 minutes

Section A

1) Solve the equation $\frac{1}{x} = \frac{3}{x+3}$. (2)

   Check your answer by substituting it back into the original equation. (2) [4]

2) In a certain county the cost of land is £3 per square metre. What is the cost of 2 km^2? Give your answer in standard form. (4) [4]

3) Two shopping areas were investigated, by visiting 10 stores in each area and finding the prices of a standard basket of goods. The results rounded to the nearest £ were:

A:	32	28	25	36	34	30	31	24	27	33
B:	28	27	29	30	28	26	27	29	27	29

   Find the mean and standard deviation for each set of figures. (4)

   What do your results tell you about the areas? (3) [7]

4) The probability that Tom and Robin will play squash on Saturday is $\frac{1}{3}$. The probability that Tom will win is $\frac{1}{4}$.

   Find the probability that Tom and Robin will play squash next Saturday and that Tom will lose. (2)

   Find the probability that they will play on two successive Saturdays and that Tom will beat Robin once and lose to Robin once. (5) [7]

5) When I started my holiday I had £250, to the nearest £10. During the journey to France I spent £20, to the nearest £5. The exchange rate is 9.5 French Francs per £, to 1 decimal place.

   What is the greatest amount of FF I can change my money to? [7]

6) An object is pulled by two forces as shown. One force is of 10 N due north, the other of 8 N north-east. No other forces act on the object. By a diagram or otherwise find the direction in which it will move. (4)

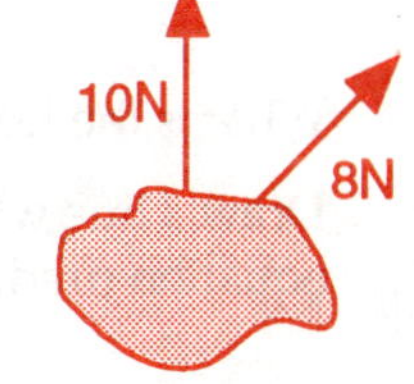

   What is the magnitude of the force that will counteract the effect of the two original forces? (4) [8]

7) Draw axes on graph paper, taking 1 cm per unit and placing the origin near the centre of the page. Plot the triangle T with vertices at A(1,2), B(3,–1), C(–1,–2). (1)

   Let Q be the transformation of reflection in the x-axis. Let P be the transformation of reflection in the line $y = x$. Apply Q to T and then P to the result, plotting the transformed triangles. (3)

   What single transformation is equivalent to this combination of transformations? (3)

   Without doing any plotting, write down the transformation equivalent to doing P and then Q. (3) [10]

8) The street map shows part of a town which is built on the block system. Let N represent walking a block north, and E represent walking a block east. One way of going from A to B could be written NNEE.

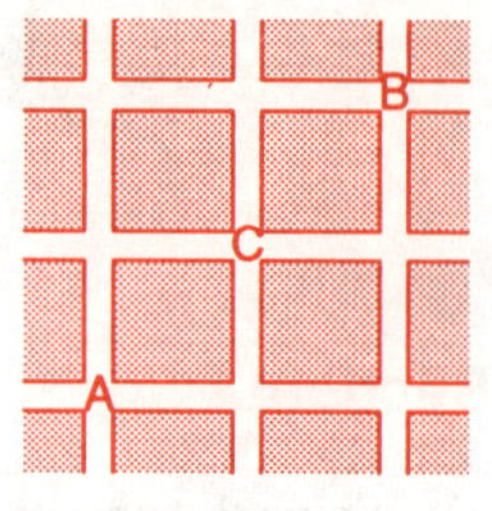

Write down all the other ways of going from A to B, without ever going out of your way. (4)

Assuming that all the ways are equally likely, what is the probability that you will pass through C? (3) [7]

9) Stephanie bought 1160 shares at 253p each. The commission was £48.42 and the transfer stamp was £15. What was the total cost? (2)

Later the price reached 308 p per share, and she sold them at this price, paying a commission of £66.10. What was (a) her actual profit (b) her percentage profit? (4)

The proceeds of the sale were invested in a building society at 8% compound interest. How much will it have amounted to after 5 years? (4) [10]

10) Three sides of a field are straight, and make 90° with each other. The third side is bounded by a stream. A scale diagram of the field is drawn on graph paper as shown, to a scale of 1 unit per 10 m.

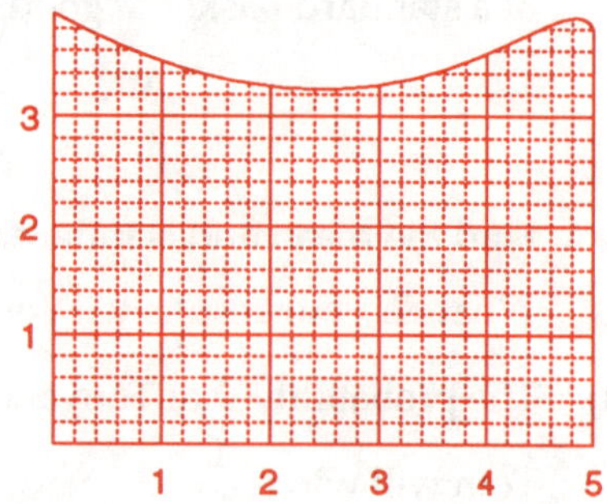

Use the trapezium rule with 5 intervals to estimate the area of the field. [8]

11) Let $f(x) = \left(1 + \frac{1}{x}\right)^x$

Evaluate f(1), f(2), f(3), f(4). What can you say about this sequence? (5)

As x gets bigger, f(x) tends to a fixed value called e. Evaluate f(10), f(100), etc. until you have found e to 5 decimal places. (4)

What does $g(x) = \left(1 - \frac{1}{x}\right)^x$ tend to when x becomes bigger?

What is the connection between this value and e? (5) [14]

12) Plot the following points on graph paper:

(0.5,1.5) (2,2.5) (3,4) (4,5.5) (5,7) (7,7.5) (1)

What is the least possible gradient of a line joining a pair of points? Draw this line. (3)

Draw a line which goes through the plotted points. Find the equation of your line. From your equation predict the y value of a point whose x value is 6. (5) [9]

13) A lampshade is to be made by cutting a sector of angle 120° from a circle of radius 24 cm, and then removing a sector of a circle of radius 12 cm. The shape is then folded round to make a truncated cone.

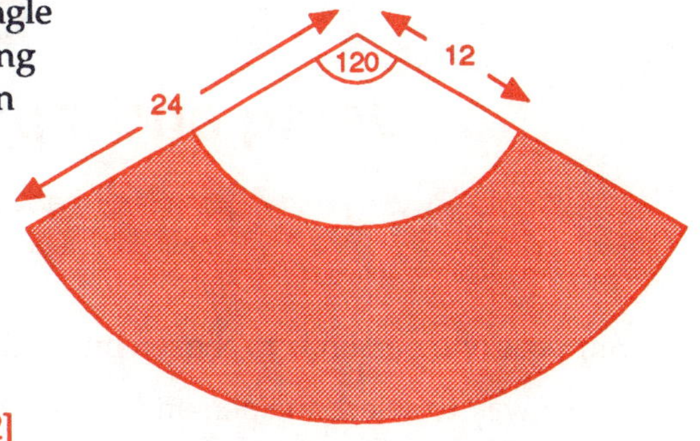

Find the lengths of the two arcs. (2)

Find the radii of the circles at top and bottom of the lampshade. (2)

Find the height of the lampshade. (5)

Find the volume enclosed by the lampshade. (3) [12]

14) Plot the graph of $y = x + \frac{1}{x^2}$, taking $\frac{1}{2}, \frac{2}{3}, 1, 1\frac{1}{2}, 2, 3, 4$ as your values of x. (5)

By drawing a tangent, find the gradient of the curve at $x = 1$. (2)

What is the least value of y? (2)

On the same graph draw the line $y = 2x + 1$. Show that where they cross $x^3 + x^2 - 1 = 0$. Write down the solution to this equation. (4) [13]

Section B

Using and Applying Mathematics

15) If n is a whole number, let f(n) be the number of positive integers less than n which do not have a common factor with n. For example, the numbers less than 9 are 1, 2, 3, 4, 5, 6, 7 and 8. Of these, 1, 2, 4, 5, 7 and 8 do not have a common factor with 9. There are six of these numbers, so f(9) = 6.

1) Show that f(6) = 2. Evaluate f(3), f(4), f(10), f(12). (2)
2) What is common to the values you have found so far? Does it hold true for all numbers? (3)
3) Investigate f(p), where p is a prime number. (4)
4) Find f(2), f(4), f(8), f(16). Find a formula for f(2^n). (6) [15]

16) Starting from a false statement, any other statement can be deduced. For example, from 0 = 1 we can deduce that 1 = 2 by adding 1 to both sides.

You are to deduce the following from 0 = 1, using ordinary mathematics and ordinary arguments.

1) 3 = 5 (2)
2) There are 10 member states of the EC. (3)
3) For any x, $x = 90$. (4)
4) Every rhombus is a square. (3)
5) You are the Pope. (3) [15]

Exam 4
Using and Applying Mathematics

Attempt as many of the questions as you can.
Time: 1 hour 30 minutes

1) Suppose one person is to chosen out of three. (As the one not to play squash, for example.)

   A fair way to select one person is for each person to spin a coin. If the coins are the same they are spun again. If one is different from the others the person with the odd one is chosen.

   Suppose one person is to be chosen out of five. (As the one not to play tennis, for example.) Describe a fair way to choose that person using coins. (4) [4]

2) The inhabitants of the planet Xurgon count using their seven tentacles. So they count 1, 2, 3, 4, 5, 6, 10, 11, 12, ...

   a) Change 22 from Xurgon numerals to Earth numerals. (2)

   b) Convert 86 to Xurgon numerals. (2)

   c) A Xurgon calculator display shows 5 ^{03}. What number is it registering? (2)

   d) A Xurgon calculator display shows 5.32. What fraction does this represent? (2) [8]

3) A sequence of fractions obeys the rule $\frac{x}{y} \to \frac{y}{x+y}$

   i.e. at each stage the new numerator is the old denominator, and the new denominator is the sum of the old numerator and denominator.

   Investigate this sequence. (8) [8]

4) How could you find the radius of the Earth, using only elementary instruments to measure angles and distances? (8) [8]

5) In a wind-tunnel experiment, the speed of the wind and the force on an object in the tunnel were measured. The result are below.

Speed v	2	4	6	8
Force F	3	24	64	124

   Dr Noakes thinks that F is proportional to a power of v. Using the first two values only, i.e. for $v = 2$ and $v = 4$, find the power and the formula giving F in terms of v. (4)

   Professor Moakes thinks that the relationship is of the form $F = av + bv^2$. Use the first two values to find two equations in a and b, and solve them. (4)

   Which formula gives a better fit to the actual values? (4) [12]

6) On the first fine Saturday of the year you and a group of friends decide to have a barbecue. List the tasks that are necessary before you can start eating. They might include:

Get barbecue set out of shed and clean it.

Buy food.

Prepare food for being cooked.

Light barbecue.

Buy charcoal.

Estimate the time needed for all the tasks. Arrange the tasks in a critical path diagram to find the shortest time for completion. (10) [10]

Solutions to multiple choice questions

The references are to the 'Points to note' at the end of each chapter.

Chapter 1

The correct answer is (a).

If your answer was (b), then you have wrongly multiplied the base numbers 3 and 9. Refer to (2)
If your answer was (c), then you have multiplied the powers instead of adding them. Refer to (2).
If your answer was (d), then you have confused taking powers and multiplying. Refer to (1).
If your answer was (e), then you have squared the power of 9 instead of doubling it.

Chapter 2

The correct answer is (b).

If your answer was (a), then you converted 5% to 0.5, instead of 0.05. Refer to (2).
If your answer was (c), then you added 5% to the new price, instead of taking 5% off the original price. Refer to (3).
If your answer was (d), then you divided by 1.05 instead of 0.95. The sale price must be less than the original price.
If your answer was (e), then you found 50% of the sale price.

Chapter 3

The correct answer is (c).

If your answer was (a), then you have direct proportion, not inverse proportion.
If your answer was (b), then you have got x and y the wrong way round.
If your answer was (d), then you have forgotten the constant of proportionality.
If your answer was (e), then you have not expressed the relationship in the best way. Refer to (2).

Chapter 4

The correct answer is (a).

If your answer was (b), then you subtracted the errors instead of adding them. Refer to (2).
If your answer was (c), then you gave the error in the first number as 0.01, not 0.005. Refer to (1).
If your answer was (d), then you added the expressions instead of subtracting them.

Chapter 5

The correct answer is (d).

If your answer was (a), then you have multiplied by 0.8 one time too many. Refer to (2a).
If your answer was (b), then you are increasing by 20% each time instead of decreasing.
If your answer was (c), then you are decreasing by 80% each time instead of by 20%.
If your answer was (e), then you are taking powers of the whole expression not just of the decreasing factor. Refer to (2b).

Chapter 7

The correct answer is (b).

If your answer was (a) then you have not factorized fully. Refer to (1a).
If your answer was (c) then there are too many x's in your brackets. Refer to (1b).
If your answer was (d) or (e) then you have got the signs wrong. Refer to (1d).

Chapter 8

The correct answer is (e).

If your answer was (a), then x occurs on both sides of the equation. Refer to (2).
If your answer was (b), then you have added bx instead of subtracting it. Refer to (1).
If your answer was (c), then your fraction is the wrong way up. Refer to (1).
If your answer was (d), then when you factorized $ax - bx$ you introduced an unnecessary factor of 2.

Chapter 9

The correct answer is (e).

If your answer was (a) then you have multiplied by $\pm\sqrt{113}$, instead of adding and subtracting it. Refer to (4b).
If your answer was (b) then you forgot that the c term is negative. Refer to (4c).
If your answer was (c) then you did not press the = button before dividing by 2a. Refer to (4d).
If your answer was (d), then you forgot that the b term is negative. Refer to (4c).

Chapter 10

The correct answer is (d).

If your answer was (a), then you have given only one of the solutions. Refer to (2b).
If your answer was (b), then you have given the y values as well as the x values. Refer to (2a).
If your answer was (c), then you have found where $x^2 + \frac{1}{x}$ equals 3, not where it equals $3 - x$.
If your answer was (e), then you have probably drawn the wrong line. The line $y = 3 - x$ should go through (0, 3) and (3, 0).

Chapter 11

The correct answer is (b).

If your answer was (a), then you have got the gradient the wrong way up. Refer to (1b).
If your answer was (c), then you have not noticed that the y-change is negative.
If your answer was (d) or (e), then you have taken the line from the origin to one of the points. Refer to (1c).

Chapter 12

The correct answer is (a).

If your answer was (b), then you have found the area instead of the gradient. Refer to (2).
If your answer was (c), then you have the gradient of the line from the origin to the point. Refer to (1b).
If your answer was (d), then you found the distance after 2 secs. Refer to (2).
If your answer was (e), then you probably drew an inaccurate tangent.

Chapter 13

The correct answer is (e).

If your answer was (a), then you have found the diameter instead of the radius. Refer to (1b).
If your answer was (b), then you have confused the arc AB with the chord AB. Refer to (1a).
If your answer was (c), then you have multiplied by π instead of dividing.
If your answer was (d), then you took the arc length to be the circumference of the whole circle.

Chapter 14

The correct answer is (d).

If your answer was (a), then you assumed that X is the centre of the circle. Refer to (1a).
If your answer was (b), then you assumed that AB and CD were parallel.
If your answer was (c), then you assumed that AXD is a straight line.
If your answer was (e), then you are making opposite angles of a cyclic quadrilateral equal.

Chapter 15

The correct answer is (d).

If your answer was (a) or (c), then you gave only one of the solutions. Refer to (2a).
If your answer was (b), then you ignored the minus sign. Refer to (1).
If your answer was (e), then one of your values of x is less than 0°. Refer to (2b).

Chapter 16

The correct answer is (b).

If your answer was (a), then you used $\sin^{-1}$ instead of $\tan^{-1}$, Refer to (4).
If your answer was (c), then you thought that BXY was right-angled at Y. Refer to (2).
If your answer was (d), then you did not have BX as the hypoteneuse of your triangle. Refer to (4).
If your answer was (e), then you thought that BXY was right-angled at X. Refer to (2).

Chapter 17

The correct answer is (b).

If your answer was (a), then you have not squared the ratios. Refer to (1c).
If your answer was (c), then you have multiplied by the ratio instead of dividing by it.
If your answer was (d), then you have taken the ratio between the sides to be 1:2, not 1:3. Refer to (1b).
If your answer was (e), then you have found the area of ΔAXY.

Chapter 18

The correct answer is (e).

If your answer was (a), then your use of the sine rule was the wrong way up.

If your answer was (b), then you have found $\hat{C}$ instead of $\hat{B}$. Refer to (1a).
If your answer was (c), then you have used the sine rule when you should have used the cosine rule. Refer to (1b).
If your answer was (d), then you have made a calculator error in your use of the cosine rule. You did not press = after the top line. Refer to (2a).

Chapter 19

The correct answer is (d).

If your answer was (a), then you have found the modulus of **a** + **b**. Refer to (3c).
If your answer was (b), then you have found the modulus of **b**. Refer to (3c).
If your answer was (c), then you have found |**a**| - |**b**|. Refer to (2).

If your answer was (e), then you have assumed that $\sqrt{a^2+b^2}=a+b$. Refer to (2).

Chapter 20

The correct answer is (a).

If your answer was (d), then you did the reflections in the wrong order. Refer to (1).
If your answer was (b), (c) or (e), then you may have transformed the square correctly, but you have not seen that the letters of the square have been rotated. Hence the square was not reflected, enlarged or translated.

Chapter 21

The correct answer is (e).

If your answer was (a), then you found the mean deviation. Refer to (2a).
If your answer was (b), then you forgot to take the square root.
If your answer was (c), then probably you averaged the differences before squaring, instead of the other way round. Refer to (2c).
If your answer was (d), then you found the mean.

Chapter 22

The correct answer is (c).

If your answer was (a), then you haven't shown that B's times were all about the same.
If your answer was (b), then you make B's average time better than A's.
If your answer was (d), then you make B's times more widely spread than A's.

Chapter 23

The correct answer is (a).

If your answer was (b), then you have multiplied the matrices in the wrong order. Refer to (1b).
If your answer was (c), then you have the rows and columns the wrong way round. Refer to (1a).
If your answer was (d), then the matrix is jumbled up.
If your answer was (e), then you have written the right hand matrix horizontally instead of vertically.

Chapter 24

The correct answer is (c).

If your answer was (a), then you have did not notice that one boundary was dotted. Refer to (1c).
If your answer was (b), then you have the first inequality the wrong way round. Refer to (1b).
If your answer was (d), then you have labelled the shaded region.
If your answer was (e), then you have the second inequality the wrong way round. Refer to (1b).

Chapter 25

The correct answer is (a).

If your answer was (b), then you found the probability that both were red.
If your answer was (c), then you found the probability that either was red but not both. Refer to (3).
If your answer was (d), then you added the probabilities, even though the events were not exclusive. Refer to (4).
If your answer was (e), then you found the probability that neither marble was red.

Solutions

Chapter 1

1.1.2 Page 2

1) (a) 81 (b) 256 (c) 1 (d) 1024
   (e) $\frac{1}{8}$ (f) 0.027 (g) 3.375 (h) −8

2) (a) $\frac{1}{2}$ (b) $\frac{1}{27}$ (c) $\frac{1}{125}$ (d) $\frac{1}{64}$
   (e) 1 (f) 2 (g) 9

3) (a) 3^6 (b) 2^7 (c) 4^5 (d) 3 (e) 7^3

4) (a) 4^4 (b) 3^2 (c) 4^7 (d) 5^{-4} (e) 5^{-5} (f) $\left(\frac{1}{2}\right)^9$

5) 2^1 6) 3^{-3}

7) (a) 6.19 (b) 3,190,000 (c) 103,000 (d) 0.0678 (e) 486,000

8) (a) 2 (b) 3 (c) 4 (d) 5 (e) −1
   (f) −1 (g) −1 (h) −3 (i) 0

1.2.2 Page 4

1) (a) 3 (b) 10 (c) 2 (d) $\frac{1}{7}$ (e) $\frac{1}{4}$ (f) 10

2) (a) 4 (b) 27 (c) 100 (d) 16 (e) 2 (f) 10

3) (a) 2^3 (b) 3^3 (c) 10

4) (a) x (b) y (c) 1

5) (a) 1.96 (b) 1.58 (c) 0.0838 (d) 1.10 (e) 0.785

1.3.2 Page 5

1) (a) $0.666.. = 0.\dot{6}$ (b) $0.555.. = 0.\dot{5}$ (c) $0.6363... = 0.\dot{6}\dot{3}$
   (d) $0.12612... = 0.\dot{1}2\dot{6}$ (e) $0.285... = 0.\dot{2}8571\dot{4}$

2) (a) 0.7777777 (b) 0.1212121 (c) 0.1351351 (d) 0.2072072

3) (a) $\frac{2}{3}$ (b) $\frac{4}{9}$ (c) $\frac{3}{11}$ (d) $\frac{5}{37}$

Chapter 2

2.1.2 Page 9

1) (a) 4.5×10^4 (b) 1.001×10^5 (c) 3×10^{-5} (d) 2.7×10^6
   (e) 4.321×10^9 (f) 4×10^{11} (g) 5.3×10^{-3} (h) 3×10^{-9}
   (i) 5×10^{-15}

2) (a) 27,000 (b) 4,973.2 (c) 0.000018

3) (a) 3×10^{12} (b) 1.28×10^6 (c) 2×10^{-10} (d) 1.357×10

4) (a) 1.6×10^8 (b) 2×10^{-10} (c) 8.75×10^1 (d) 7×10^3

5) (a) 6.76×10^{10} (b) 2.7×10^{25} (c) 2.5×10^{-5} (d) 7.4088×10^{-20}

6) 1.52×10^9 7) 1.1×10^{21} m^3 8) 5.87×10^{13} miles

9) 1.752×10^{-3} 10) 5.9×10^{27} 11) 65,000

2.2.2 Page 10

1) (a) 4.67×10^4 (b) 4.95×10^9 (c) 8.09×10^{12} (d) 4.3×10^{-6} (e) 1.05×10^9
   (f) 1.017×10^{-5}

2) (a) 5.83×10^4 (b) 9.92×10^{12} (c) 8.31×10^{32} (d) 5.32×10^{-4}
   (e) 8.623×10^{-16} (f) -5.71×10^5 (g) -1.6915×10^{16} (h) -3.28×10^{-5}

3) 1.22×10^9
4) (a) 1.58×10^9 km (b) 1.28×10^9 km
5) 3.04×10^{-26} kg

2.3.2 Page 11

1) (a) 1.05 (b) 1.3 (c) 0.93 (d) 0.25
2) (a) 6% increase (b) 10% increase (c) 70% increase
(d) 9% decrease (e) 60% decrease (f) 97% decrease
3) £5,036 4) £11,511 5) 44.6 million 6) £103,600
7) 0.599 kg 8) £2,621 9) 146,000 square miles

2.4.2 Page 12

1) £15,000 2) £2,400 3) £120 4) £2,000
5) 15,500,000 6) £500 7) 120,000 8) £8,000
9) 2.5 kg

Chapter 3

3.1.2 Page 16

1) 272 miles 2) 90 grams 3) £6 4) 2 days
5) 2 hours 6) $y = 3x$. 15
7) (a) 72 (b) 30
8) (a) $3\frac{1}{2}$ amps (b) 120 volts
9) 100 km 10) $q = \dfrac{70}{p}$. 5
11) (a) 4 (b) 16
12) $V = \dfrac{200}{P}$. 5 m^3
13) (a) 50,000 cps (b) 250 m

3.2.2 Page 17

1) (a) $y = 4x^2$ (b) 36 (c) 1
2) (a) $T = 2S^2$ (b) 72 (c) 4
3) 62.5 4) $P = 2Q^3$. 6 5) $M = 4L^3$.108 g. 1.5 cm 6) $E = 2V^2$. 10 m/sec
7) $E \propto e^2$ $E = 5e^2$. 20 8) $B = \dfrac{2}{C^2}$. 8. $\frac{1}{4}$ 9) 4 candle–power
10) $R = \dfrac{3}{r^2}$. 48 ohms. 2 mm

3.3.2 Page 19

1) $y = x^2$ 2) $y = \dfrac{36}{x}$ 3) $y = 5x^3$ 4) $y = \dfrac{240}{x^2}$
5) $y = \dfrac{576}{x^2}$ 6) square. 108 7) cube. 27
8) inversely proportional 9) proportional

Chapter 4

4.1.2 Page 23

1) (a) 14,8 (b) 3.58, 3.54 (c) –0.009, –0.021

2) (a) 35 ± 2 (b) 22.15 ± 0.05 (c) 0.3 ± 0.4
3) 905 kg 4) 75,000 – 85,000 5) 0.535 – 0.545 6) 315 – 325
7) 600 ± 5 grams 8) -32.4 ± 0.05
9) (a) Not necessarily (b) yes

4.2.2 Page 24

1) (a) 12 ± 3 (b) -1.6 ± 0.2 (c) 3 ± 3
2) 600 ± 10 grams 3) 18.3 ± 0.1 4) 90 ± 10 feet 5) 44.17 ± 0.02 secs

4.3.2 Page 25

1) (a) 8 – 24 (b) 6.9 – 8 (c) 3.6 – 7.33
2) (a) 15 ± 9 (b) 7.44 ± 0.6 (c) 5 ± 2.4
3) (a) 13 ± 0.4 (b) 30 ± 0.6 (c) 4.84 ± 0.3
(d) 250 ± 40 (e) 20 ± 3.4 (f) 0.064 ± 0.03
4) 276 ± 30 cm^2 5) 55.4 ± 1.4 6) 336 ± 3 grams 7) 300 ± 1 gram
8) 2.7 ± 0.25 hours 9) 3.08 ± 0.008 10) £95 ± 3 11) £221.4 ± 4 12) 7.28

Chapter 5

5.1.2 Page 28

1) (a) $3n - 2$ (b) $5n + 8$ (c) $\frac{1}{2}n + 1\frac{1}{2}$ (d) $9 - 2n$
2) $10{,}000 + 1{,}000n$ 3) £80. $1{,}000 + 80n$ 4) $6{,}000 + 200n$ 5) 6, 7
6) (a) 6, 5 (b) $1\frac{1}{2}, \frac{1}{2}$ (c) 5, –2
7) (a) $\frac{1}{2}$ (d) –1

5.2.2 Page 30

1) (a) 2^{n-1} (b) $5 \times 3^{n-1}$ (c) $2 \times \left(\frac{1}{2}\right)^{n-1}$ (d) $2 \times (-3)^{n-1}$
2) (a) 2, 2 (b) 15, 3 (c) $2, \frac{1}{3}$
3) 1.02. 12×1.02^x million. 35 years 4) $10{,}000 \times 1.09^x$. 13 years
5) $6{,}000 \times 0.75^x$. 6.2 years 6) 4×0.5^n. 4×2^n 7) $2 \times \left(\frac{1}{2}\right)^{n/4}, 2 \times 2^{n/4}$ 8) $10{,}000 \times 2^{n/6}$

5.3.2 Page 32

1) 1.732 2) 3.162 3) 24, 720 5) 1.221
6) (a) 1.33 (b) –5.19 (c) 56.0
7) (a) 1.618 (d) –1.32

Chapter 6

6.1.2 Page 37

2) (a) 1 (b) 0 (c) 1 (d) 1 (e) 2.718282 (f) 0.367879

6.2.2 Page 38

1) (a) 2.33375 (b) 6.7625 (c) 1.443

6.3.2 Page 39

1) (a) $x=1, y=2$ (b) $x=6, y=2$ (c) $x=13, y=-1$
2) (a) $x=1, y=3, z=-1$ (b) $w=2, x=-1, y=3, z=4$

6.4.2 Page 40

1) 0.688, 0.6752 2) 0.6, 0.56, 0.556 3) 0.45, 0.465, 0.4605
4) (a) $\frac{2}{3}$ (b) $0.5555 = \frac{5}{9}$ (c) $0.461538 = \frac{6}{13}$
5) $0.4285714 = \frac{3}{7}$

Chapter 7

7.1.2 Page 55

1) $x^2 + x - 6$ 2) $x^2 - 8x - 9$ 3) $x^2 - 12x + 32$ 4) $p^2 - q^2$
5) $x^2 - 9$ 6) $4x^2 - 1$ 7) $x^2 + 2x + 1$ 8) $x^2 + 14x + 49$
9) $4x^2 - 4x + 1$ 10) $6x^2 + x - 1$ 11) $8x^2 - 6x - 9$ 12) $2x^2 - 5xy - 12y^2$
13) $mr + ms + nr + ns$ 14) $pr - ps - qr + qs$ 15) $6xw - 2xz + 3yw - yz$

7.2.2 Page 57

1) $(x + 1)(x + 2)$ 2) $(x + 2)^2$ 3) $(x + 3)(x + 4)$ 4) $(x - 3)(x - 8)$
5) $(x + 3)(x - 2)$ 6) $(y - 4)(y + 3)$ 7) $(z + 6)(z - 1)$ 8) $(w - 6)(w + 2)$
9) $(x - 8)(x + 3)$ 10) $(p + 10)(p - 3)$ 11) $(p + q)(p - q)$ 12) $(t + 1)(t - 1)$
13) $(2 + n)(2 - n)$ 14) $(q + 3)(q - 3)$ 15) $(3 + s)(3 - s)$ 16) $7(1 + s)(1 - s)$
17) $2(1 + 2x)(1 - 2x)$ 18) $9(1 + 3a)(1 - 3a)$ 19) $(7t + 3s)(7t - 3s)$ 20) $(4m + 5n)(4m - 5n)$
21) $(y + \frac{1}{2})(y - \frac{1}{2})$ 22) $(\frac{1}{3} + z)(\frac{1}{3} - z)$ 23) $(2x - 1)(x + 3)$ 24) $(3x + 2)(x - 4)$
25) $(5y + 4)(y + 1)$ 26) $(6x - 1)(x + 6)$ 27) $(6a + 5)(a + 1)$ 28) $(3p + 2)(2p - 3)$
29) $(s + r)(t - q)$ 30) $(a - b)(x - y)$ 31) $(3t - 2)(2s + 1)$ 32) $(x + 2)(y + 3)$
33) $(2z + 1)(w - 3)$

7.3.2 Page 57

1) 2, 1 2) 3, 2 3) 15, 4 4) −1, −5 5) −5, −6 6) 3, −2
7) 3, −5 8) 3, 3 9) −2, −2 10) $2, \frac{1}{2}$ 11) $3, -\frac{2}{3}$ 12) $\frac{1}{2}, \frac{1}{2}$

7.4.2 Page 58

1) (a) $(x + 2)^2 + 2$ (b) $(x - 4)^2 - 25$ (c) $(x + 2)^2 + 4$
(d) $(x - 5)^2 - 24$ (e) $(x - 1.5)^2 + 2.75$ (f) $(x + 0.5)^2 - 3.25$
2) (a) $2, x = -2$ (b) $-25, x = 4$ (c) $4, x = -2$
(d) $-24, x = 5$ (e) $2.75, x = 1.5$ (f) $-3.25, x = -0.5$
4) $2((x - 1)^2 + 5)$. 10
5) (a) $2((x + 1)^2 + 3)$, 6 (b) $3((x - 1)^2 + 3)$.9 (c) $5((x + 2)^2 - 10)$, −50
6) 9
7) (a) $6, x = 2$ (b) $15, x = -3$ (c) $1.25, x = 0.5$ (d) $2, x = 1$
8) $-5((t - 3)^2 - 9.4)$, 47 metres

Chapter 8

8.1.2 Page 62

1) $\frac{A - B}{3}$ 2) $\frac{z + 2}{4}$ 3) $\frac{b}{a} - 3$ 4) $\frac{3}{m + n}$
5) $\sqrt{\frac{A}{4\pi}}$ 6) $\sqrt{\frac{s - u}{a}}$ 7) $\frac{T}{a + c}$ 8) $\frac{b}{a - 1}$

9) $\frac{T}{g-a}$ 10) $\frac{-5a-2b}{2}$ 11) $\frac{cp-ap}{b-d}$ 12) $\frac{7b-3a}{a+b}$

13) $\frac{mr}{1-m}$ 14) $\frac{1+3y}{y-1}$ 15) $\frac{3}{a+b-c}$ 16) $\frac{-a+3b+8c}{a+b+c}$

8.2.2 Page 63

1) $\frac{x}{y}$ 2) $\frac{2x}{z}$ 3) $x+2$ 4) $\frac{2x+1}{3y+4}$

5) $\frac{p}{q}$ 6) $\frac{ay}{b}$ 7) $2y+3$ 8) $\frac{1}{5}$

9) $\frac{1}{b+c}$ 10) $\frac{1}{a}$ 11) $\frac{x+1}{x-1}$ 12) $\frac{x+5}{x+7}$

13) $2y-5$ 14) $\frac{x-5}{x-2}$ 15) $2x$ 16) $\frac{y}{x}$

17) $\frac{1}{a}$ 18) $\frac{1}{xy}$ 19) $\frac{ac}{bd}$ 20) $\frac{2x^2}{5}$

21) $\frac{4x^2}{3y^2}$ 22) $\frac{xw}{yz}$ 23) $\frac{7}{2}$ 24) $\frac{q^2}{2}$

25) $\frac{1}{3x(x-1)}$ 26) $\frac{6z^2}{z^2-1}$ 27) $\frac{2(x+2)}{3(x-1)}$

8.3.2 Page 65

1) $\frac{11x}{15}$ 2) $\frac{5a}{4}$ 3) $\frac{7r-4}{12}$ 4) $\frac{-11x-18}{12}$

5) $\frac{27b-1}{6}$ 6) $\frac{7c-25}{12}$ 7) $\frac{2y+3}{xy}$ (8) $\frac{3bc+4a}{abc}$

9) $\frac{7x+3}{x(x+1)}$ 10) $\frac{-7z+5}{z(1-z)}$ 11) $\frac{z^2+z+6}{3(z+1)}$ 12) $\frac{17y+8}{y(3y+2)}$

13) $\frac{3y+5}{(y-1)(y+3)}$ 14) $\frac{-2w+1}{(3w+1)(w+2)}$ 15) $\frac{16p+4}{(2p-1)(2p+3)}$ 16) $\frac{-3q+1}{(3-2q)(1-q)}$

Chapter 9

9.1.2 Page 69

1) 3 2) 2 3) 1 4) 1 5) 5 6) 1
7) 147 8) 3 9) –4 10) 23 11) 28 12) 16
13) 2 14) 70 15) –6 16) –16 17) 8 18) 24
19) 11 20) –60 21) 8 22) –17 23) 3 24) –32
25) 17 26) 16 27) 50 28) 40 29) $6x-3=11(x-3)$, 36
30) n+1, n+2. 146 31) 8 32) $3x$, $6x$. £180, £540, £1,080
33) £($9x$+50), 87 34) 260 35) 90 36) 84

9.2.2 Page 71

1) –0.349, –2.15 2) 4.56, 0.438 3) 1.19, –4.19 4) 2.30, –1.30
5) 2.46, –4.46 6) 1.47, –1.14 7) 1.30, –2.30 8) 3.82, –6.82
9) 4.24, –0.236 10) 1.30, –2.30 11) 0.618, –1.62 12) 7.11, –2.11
13) 10.5 14) 3.45 15) 0.513 16) 21.3, 4.69
17) 0.587 18) 4.86 cm

9.3.2 Page 72

1) 4 2) 2 3) 2 4) 6 5) 6 6) 3 7) 4 8) $\frac{7}{3}$ 9) 9

Chapter 10

10.1.2 Page 77

1) $x = 1, y = 2$ 2) 0 3) $-2, x = -1$ 4) 2, 0
5) (a) -1 min. $x = 0$ (b) 2 min. $x = -1$ (c) -4.25 min. $x = -1.5$
(d) 1.25 max. $x = 0.5$
6) $x = \frac{-b}{2}$ 7) Min. if $a > 0$. Max. if $a < 0$
8) (a) $x = 0$ (b) $x = 0$ (c) $x = 2$ (d) $x = -3$
9) $x = -a$

10.2.2 Page 79

1) 0.4 & 2.6. 0.3 & 3.7 2) -1.4 & 1.4. 1 & -2 3) -1.6 & 0.6 & 1
4) -1 & 1 & 2 5) 1.2 6) -0.6, 0.6
7) -1.6

10.3.2 Page 81

3) $k = 1, m = -2$ 4) $p = -2, q = -1, r = -1, s = -1$

Chapter 11

11.1.2 Page 85

1) (a) 1 (b) 2 (c) $\frac{1}{3}$ (d) $-\frac{3}{4}$
2) 3 3) $\frac{1}{2}$, $x = 1, y = 4$
4) (a) 4 (b) 1 (c) $\frac{1}{2}$ (d) $-\frac{3}{4}$
5) (a) $x = 3, y = 4$ (b) $x = 3, y = 2$ (c) $x = 2, y = 3$
(d) $x = 4, y = 1$
7) (a) $y = 3x$ (b) $y = x + 1$ (c) $y = -3x + 7$
(d) $y = \frac{1}{2}x + \frac{1}{2}$ (e) $y = 2x$ (f) $y = -2x - 1$
8) (a) $y = 2x - 1$ (b) $y = \frac{1}{2}x + 1$ (c) $y = 3 - x$
9) £14, £12. £$(14 + 12x)$ 10) 5, \$1.6 per £1. \$$(1.6x - 8)$

11.2.2 Page 87

1) -2, 4 2) 1.4, 2.8 3) 0.75, 0.9
4) -4, -1 5) 0.006, 0.01

11.3.2 Page 87

1) (a) 8 (b) 10.5 (c) 16
2) (a) 6 (b) 4 (c) 3 (d) 6 (e) 1 (f) 4
(g) 8 (h) 12
3) 6 4) 11

11.4.2 Page 89

1) 21 2) 4.7 3) -1.25 4) 4.4
5) 13.7 6) 0.7 7) 4050 m^2

Chapter 12

12.1.2 Page 93

1) (a) 3 m.p.h. (b) 7 m.p.h.
2) 24 m.p.h., 32 m.p.h. 3) 60 m.p.h., 20 m.p.h.
4) Both 8 m/sec 5) 3 m/sec, 5 m/sec
6) (a) 10 m/sec (b) 3.6 secs
7) 1,000 cm/sec 8) (a) 20 m/sec, 10 m/sec (b) 22 m, 2 secs
9) (a) 15 m/sec (b) 26 m/sec
10) (a) 1 cm/sec (b) 0.5 cm/sec

12.2.2 Page 95

1) (a) both $\frac{1}{3}$ m s^{-2} (b) 1,200 m
2) (a) 1 m s^{-2} (b) 9 m
3) (a) 5 m s^{-2} (b) 90 m
4) (a) 10 m s^{-2}, 20 m s^{-2} (b) 5 m (c) 2.5 m
5) (a) 1.8 m s^{-2} (b) 46 m
6) (a) 5 m s^{-2} (b) 33 m
7) (a) 1.2 m s^{-2} (b) 360 m
8) −10 m s^{-2}, 80 m 9) 0.8 m s^{-2}. 14 m. 10) 140 m

Chapter 13

13.1.2 Page 111

1) (a) 10.9 (b) 28.3 (c) 44.7
2) (a) 4.36 (b) 23.2 (c) 8.73
3) 4.36 cm^2 4) 5.09° 5) 15.1 cm 6) 85.9°
7) 31.8 cm 8) 92 m 9) 191°

13.2.2 Page 113

1) (a) 7.85 cm^3 (b) 80 m^3 (c) 205 cm^3 (d) 268 cm^3
2) 72 cm^3 3) 1.19 cm 4) 1.13 m 5) 6 m 6) 3 cm 7) 264 cm^3
8) 2.05 m 9) 1.69 cm
10) (a) 524 cm^3 (b) 7240 m^3 (c) 14.1 cubic feet
11) (a) 2.22 cm (b) 1.42 in. (c) 1.10 mm
12) (a) 314 cm^2 (b) 1810 m^2 (c) 28.3 sq ft
13) 11.0 cm^2 14) 50.4 mm^3
15) (a) 402 cm^3 (b) 26.4 m^2 (c) 232 mm^2 (d) 69.0 m^2
16) 1.18 cm, 14.9 cm^3.

13.3.2 Page 114

1) (a) 14 (b) 14 (c) 14 (d) 10
2) (a) 5 (b) 6 (c) 6 (d) 10
3) 163 m, 1314 m^2 4) 3028 cm^2
5) 20.9 cm^3, 44.0 cm^2 6) 8.38 cm^2
7) 6.28 cu. in. 8) 512 m^3

13.4.2 Page 115

1) (a) 0.425 (b) 18.3 (c) 12.0
2) 11.5 in 3) 1636 cm^3
4) (a) 7.07 cm^2 (b) 28,300 cm^3
5) (a) 17,700 cm^3 (b) 31,400 cm^3 (c) 13,700 cm^3

6) 35,200 cm
7) (a) 61.3 cm^3 (b) 3060 cm
8) 0.196

Chapter 14

14.1.2 Page 120

1) (a) 25° (b) 35° (c) 70° (d) 40°
2) 90°, 50°
3) (a) 60° (b) 63°
4) (a) 44° (b) CDB (c) DXC & AXB, AXD & BXC
5) (a) 124° (b) 106°, 74°
7) 68°, 184°
8) (a) 35°, 35°, 70° (b) 44°, 44°
9) 70°, 110°, 70°. Parallel

14.2.2 Page 122

1) (a) 15° (b) 76° (c) 30°
2) 35° 3) 108° 6) 60°, 57°, 63° 7) 70°, 54°, 56° 8) 98°, 83°, 82°, 97°

14.3.2 Page 124

1) (a) 4 (b) 2 (c) 6
2) 7.5 3) 22 4) 12 5) 8
6) 6.5 m 7) 5 8) 22,600 m

Chapter 15

15.1.2 Page 128

1) (a) sin 42° (b) –cos 81° (c) –tan 4° (d) sin 62° (e) –cos 77° (f) –tan 89°
2) (a) 150° (b) 139° (c) 156° (d) 168° (e) 133° (f) 110°
3) 37°, 143° 4) –0.6 5) $-\frac{4}{3}$ 6) 0.714, –0.714
7) 0.6, –0.8, –0.75 8) –34 miles, 94 miles 9) –5.2 m, 3 m

15.2.2 Page 130

1) (a) –sin 42° (b) –cos 65° (c) tan 77° (d) –sin 35° (e) cos 20°
(f) –tan 71° (g) sin 58° (h) cos 38° (i) tan 58°
2) (a) 64°, 116° (b) 73°, 287° (c) 45°, 225° (d) 197°, 343° (e) 127°, 233° (f) 104° 284°
3) (a) 143° (b) 337° (c) 217°
4) (a) 140° (b) 230° (c) 45°
5) (a) 0.75, –0.75 (b) 1, –1 (c) 0.8, –0.8
6) –178 miles, –91 miles 7) 4.9 m, –3.4

15.3.2 Page 132

1) (a) sin 140° (b) cos 240° (c) tan 340°
2) (a) sin 40° (b) –cos 60° (c) –tan 20°
3) (a) 60°, 300° (b) 120°, 240° (c) 130°, 230°
4) (a) $90° < x < 270°$ (b) $180° < x < 360°$
(c) $30° < x < 150°$ (d) $120° < x < 240°$
5) (a) 5 (b) 103°, 330°
6) (a) 1.4 (b) shifted by 90°
8) 3 m, –5.2 m 9) $x = 90°$

Chapter 16

16.1.2 Page 136

1) (a) 10.5 (b) 9.75 (c) 4.94 (d) 28.8
2) (a) 73° (b) 22°
3) 2.75 4) 25.9 5) 33° 6) 2.66 m 7) 11.5 cm. 34°
8) 187 m. 54° 9) 572 m 10) 113 m 11) 955 m
12) (a) 6.43 (b) 18.4 (c) 51.7
13) (a) 45° (b) 283 cm^2

16.2.2 Page 138

1) 13.9, 40°, 55°, 60° 2) 24, 65, 64.6, 84°, 67°
3) 5.66 cm, 5.29 cm. 62°, 71°
4) 10.4 cm. 73° 5) 3.54 ft. 34°, 25°, 45°
6) (a) 141 m (b) 86.6 m (c) 70.7 m (d) 35.3° (e) 45°
7) (a) both 6.93 cm (b) 71° (c) 2.31 cm, 4.62 cm (d) 55°
8) 8.19 cm^2, 98.3 cm^3 9) 23 cm^2, 230 cm^3 10) 3.22 km, 10.7°
11) 1.69 km 12) 1063 m, 10.8° 13) 58 m 15) 48°, 60°, 56°

Chapter 17

17.1.2 Page 143

1) a & b, c&e 2) 1:4. 2, 30 3) FAE & FCD. 1:9 4) AXY & ABC. 2:5. 42
5) 1:4. 1:8 6) 0.6 m^3 7) 4,000 m^3 8) 22.5 cm^2
9) (a) 4 m (b) 40 cm^2 (c) 10 m^3
10) (a) 0.2 m (b) 12.8 m^2 (c) 0.15625 kg
11) 1:20 (b) 20 cm^2 (c) 10
12) 1:8. $x^3 = 2$. 1.26

17.2.2 Page 146

1) a. 2) a & b & e. c & g. d & f 3) BDE & BCA. SAS
4) BAC & BDE. BAE & BDC. SAS 5) XPQ & XRS. ASA

Chapter 18

18.1.2 Page 151

1) (a) 10.6 (b) 4.19 (c) 15.8
2) (a) 37° (b) 44° (c) 44°
3) 5.19, 2.19 4) 43°, 75° 5) 18.6 m, 7.27 m
6) 1010 m 7) 76°, 2.01 m 8) 148 km

18.2.2 Page 153

1) (a) 6.50 (b) 20.2 (c) 13.3
2) (a) 58° (b) 108° (c) 89.6°
3) 15.7 4) 31° 5) 121 miles 6) 40.7 cm
7) 101°, 79°, 12.7 cm 8) 218°, 330°
9) (a) negative, obtuse (b) $c = a - b$ (c) $c = a + b$

18.3.2 Page 155

1) (a) 7.24 (b) 15.0 (c) 15.1
2) (a) 80° (b) 51° (c) 86°
3) 83° (4) 65° 5) 33°, 99°, 30.6
6) 47°, 8.3°, 0.790 7) 103.4° 8) 14 ft

Chapter 19

19.1.2 Page 158

1) (a) $\begin{pmatrix}3\\3\end{pmatrix}$ (b) $\begin{pmatrix}3\\-1\end{pmatrix}$ (c) $\begin{pmatrix}-4\\-1\end{pmatrix}$
2) (a) 4.24 (b) 3.16 (c) 4.12
3) $\begin{pmatrix}4\\-1\end{pmatrix}$
4) (a) $\begin{pmatrix}7\\-6\end{pmatrix}$ (b) $\begin{pmatrix}29\\-9\end{pmatrix}$ (c) $\begin{pmatrix}-11\\-17\end{pmatrix}$ (d) $\begin{pmatrix}3\\8\end{pmatrix}$
5) (a) 7.28 (b) 5.10 (c) 9.22 (d) 22.0 (e) 12.4
6) $x = 4, y = 7$ (7) $x = 1, y = 2$
8) (a) $\begin{pmatrix}3\\8\end{pmatrix}$ (b) $\begin{pmatrix}9\\-13\end{pmatrix}$ (c) $x = 1, y = 4$ (d) $x = 2, y = 1$

19.2.2 Page 160

1) $\begin{pmatrix}1\\2\end{pmatrix}, \begin{pmatrix}1\\-6\end{pmatrix}, \begin{pmatrix}2\\4\end{pmatrix}, \begin{pmatrix}2\\-4\end{pmatrix}, \begin{pmatrix}-3\\2\end{pmatrix}$. $\underline{AB}$ & $\underline{CD}$.
2) $\begin{pmatrix}2\\5\end{pmatrix}, \begin{pmatrix}1\\-3\end{pmatrix}, \begin{pmatrix}-3\\9\end{pmatrix}, \begin{pmatrix}-4\\1\end{pmatrix}, \begin{pmatrix}-5\\4\end{pmatrix}$. $\underline{JK}$ & $\underline{ML}$.
3) 3:1. no 4) no 5) $\sqrt{13}, \sqrt{2}$. no
8) A, B, D 9) (0,0) 10) (5,–1)
11) 3 12) (a) 2**i** – **j** (b) –**i** + 1.5**j** (c) **i** – 1.5**j**
13) $\mathbf{c} - \mathbf{b}, \frac{1}{4}\mathbf{b}, \frac{1}{4}\mathbf{c}, \frac{1}{4}(\mathbf{c} - \mathbf{b}), \mathbf{c} - \frac{1}{4}\mathbf{b}$. $\underline{BC}$ & DE. 30
14) **c**, **b**, 2**b**, –**b** + **c** 15) **e**, –**a**, 2**a**, **e** + 2**a**
16) **a**, **a** + **b**, **a** – **b**. 17) $\mathbf{b} = \mathbf{a} + \mathbf{c}, \mathbf{c} - \mathbf{a}, \frac{1}{2}\mathbf{b}, \frac{1}{2}(\mathbf{a} + \mathbf{c})$. Same.
18) $\frac{1}{2}\mathbf{c}, \frac{3}{4}\mathbf{b}, \frac{3}{4}\mathbf{b} - \mathbf{c}, \frac{3}{8}\mathbf{b} - \frac{1}{2}\mathbf{c}, \frac{3}{8}\mathbf{b} + \frac{1}{2}\mathbf{c}, -\frac{3}{8}\mathbf{b}$.

19.3.2 Page 163

2) 5.83 km.p.h. 31° to line across river.
3) 37°to line across river. 3 minutes.
4) 097°. 403 m.p.h. 5) 83°. 397 m.p.h.
6) 8.60 N. 54°. 7) 9.22 N. 184°
8) $\begin{pmatrix}5\\12\end{pmatrix}$. 8.25, 5, 13. 9) $\begin{pmatrix}-12\\-32\end{pmatrix}$
10) Swim at 30° to line across river.

Chapter 20

20.1.2 Page 167

1) (a) 180° (2,3) (b) 90° cw (9,1) (c) 90° cw (14,2)
2) (1,2) 180° 3) (2,0) 90° acw 4) (0,1) 90° cw 5) (2.5,1) 180°

20.2.2 Page 168

1) Translation, 4 to left 2) Rotation, 180° about (3,1) 3) Translation, 2 to right
4) Translation, 4 down 5) Rotation, 180° about (1,1) 6) Rotation, 180° about (2,–1)

7) Translation, 2 down 2 to left 8) Translation, 6 down 2 to left
9) 180° about (3,1), 180° about (5,1). (Many other answers).

20.3.2 Page 169

1) (a) Translation of $\begin{pmatrix} -2 \\ -3 \end{pmatrix}$ (b) Translation of $\begin{pmatrix} 3 \\ -1 \end{pmatrix}$
(c) Rot. 90° acw about (1,0) (d) Rot. 120° cw about (3,2)
(e) Rot. 180° about (0,0) (f) Enl. sf. $\frac{1}{2}$ about (2,3)
(g) Enl. sf. 2 about (1,2) (h) Enl. sf. –1 about (0,0)
(i) Refl. in $x = 3$ (j) Refl. in $y = 2x$

2) Trans. 2 left 1 down Reflection Enl. sf. $\frac{1}{2}$
3) $(PQ)^{-1} = Q^{-1}P^{-1}$

20.4.2 Page 171

1) (a) (1,–2), (3,–2), (2,–1) (b) (–1,2), (–3,2), (–2,1)
(c) (2,–1), (2,–3), (1,–2) (d) (–2,1), (–2,3), (–1,2)
(e) (–2,–1), (–2,–3), (–1,–2)
2) (a) (1,–1) (1,–3) (2,–3) (2,–1) (b) (–1,1) (–1,3) (–2,3) (–2,1)
(c) (1,–1) (3,–1) (3,–2) (1,–2) (d) (–1,1) (–3,1) (–3,2) (–1,2)
(e) (–1,–1) (–3,–1) (–3,–2) (–1,–2)
3) (a) Refl. in x–axis (b) Refl. in y–axis
(c) 90°cw rot. (d) 90° acw rot.
(e) Refl. in $y = -x$
4) (f) (0,0) (3,0) (3,3) (0,3) (g) (0,0) $(\frac{1}{2},0)$ $(\frac{1}{2},\frac{1}{2})$ $(0,\frac{1}{2})$ (h) (0,0) $(\frac{1}{2},0)$ $(\frac{1}{2},1)$ (0,1)
(j) (0,0) (1,0) (1,2) (0,2) (k) (0,0) (–2,0) (–2,–2) (0,–2)
5) (f) enl. sf. 3 (g) enl. sf. $\frac{1}{2}$ (h) 'squash' along x–axis (j) 'stretch' along y–axis
(k) enl. sf. –2
6) $\begin{pmatrix} 4 & 2 \\ -2 & -1 \end{pmatrix}$ 7) $\begin{pmatrix} 2 & 3 \\ 3 & 2 \end{pmatrix}$ 8) $\begin{pmatrix} 2/3 & 4/3 \\ 5/3 & 2/3 \end{pmatrix}$

20.5.2 Page 173

1) (a) $\begin{pmatrix} 5 & 6 \\ 1 & 1 \end{pmatrix}$ (b) $\begin{pmatrix} 0 & 6 \\ -1 & -9 \end{pmatrix}$ (c) $\begin{pmatrix} -8 & 7 \\ -7 & 8 \end{pmatrix}$
2) BA = $\begin{pmatrix} 0 & -1 \\ -1 & 0 \end{pmatrix}$ 3) DC = $\begin{pmatrix} 1 & 2 \\ 0 & -1 \end{pmatrix}$

Chapter 21

21.1.2 Page 189

1) (a) 0.35, 0.35, 0.5, 0.45, 0.75 (b) 0.48
2) (a) 0.39 (b) 0.455 (c) 0.494
6) 37.5% 7) 2.03 8) £9.325 9) 5.175

21.2.2 Page 191

1) 14.5, 7.5, 8.34 2) 4, 2, 2.35 3) 7, 4.22, 4.85
4) 0.9, 1, 1.45 5) C: 0.45 D: 34.1 6) B: 13, 3.6 G: 14, 1.4
7) A: 23, 2.55 B: 23.5, 8.65

Chapter 22

22.1.2 Page 195

1) (b) 30–35 (c) $\frac{191}{500}$

2) (b) 20–30 (c) $\frac{3}{5}$

22.2.2 Page 197

8) (a) 25, 5 (b) 2, 0.6

Chapter 23

23.1.2 Page 202

1) (a) (64.5,72,62). Average for each subject. $\begin{pmatrix}203\\205\\161\\225\end{pmatrix}$ Total for each pupil.

(b) $M = \begin{pmatrix}0.4\\0.4\\0.2\end{pmatrix}$

2) (a) $T = \begin{pmatrix}1\\1\\1\end{pmatrix} . \begin{pmatrix}74\\76\end{pmatrix}$ (b) R = (1,1). (66,53,31) (c) $P = \begin{pmatrix}25\\30\\40\end{pmatrix} . 4480$

3) (a,c) $P = R = \begin{pmatrix}1\\1\\1\\1\\1\end{pmatrix}$ (b,c) S = Q = (1 1 1)

4) $\begin{matrix} & A & B \\ \text{But.} & \frac{1}{2} & \frac{2}{5} \\ \text{Flo.} & \frac{1}{2} & \frac{3}{5}\end{matrix}$ $\begin{pmatrix}\frac{1}{2} & \frac{2}{5}\\ \frac{1}{2} & \frac{3}{5}\end{pmatrix} . \begin{pmatrix}15\\30\end{pmatrix}$

23.2.2 Page 204

1) (a) $\begin{pmatrix}0 & 1 & 1\\1 & 0 & 1\\1 & 1 & 0\end{pmatrix} . \begin{pmatrix}2 & 1 & 1\\1 & 2 & 1\\1 & 1 & 2\end{pmatrix}$ (b) $\begin{pmatrix}0 & 2 & 0\\2 & 0 & 1\\0 & 1 & 0\end{pmatrix} , \begin{pmatrix}4 & 0 & 2\\0 & 5 & 0\\2 & 0 & 1\end{pmatrix}$

(c) $\begin{pmatrix}0 & 2 & 1\\2 & 0 & 2\\1 & 2 & 0\end{pmatrix} . \begin{pmatrix}5 & 2 & 4\\2 & 8 & 2\\4 & 2 & 5\end{pmatrix}$

2) (a) $\begin{pmatrix}0 & 0 & 1\\1 & 0 & 1\\0 & 1 & 0\end{pmatrix}$ (b) $\begin{pmatrix}0 & 1 & 0\\1 & 0 & 1\\0 & 1 & 0\end{pmatrix}$ (c) $\begin{pmatrix}0 & 1 & 1\\1 & 0 & 1\\1 & 1 & 0\end{pmatrix}$

23.4.2 Page 207

1) (a) 18. ABD (b) 21. CDE (c) 23. CEF
2) (a) C, 2 (b) A, 1. B, 1 (c) A, 9. B, 2. D, 6
3) 39 minutes. BADEFGIH 4) 41, EFABIH

Chapter 24

24.1.2 Page 211

3) (a) $x + y \leq 4$ (b) $x > 1, y > 1, 4x + 3y \leq 12, 3x + 4y \leq 12$
(c) $x + y < 4, y \leq x$
4) (a) 6, 6 (b) 7, 8 (c) $\frac{1}{2}, \frac{1}{3}$
(d) 5, 3 (e) 6, 2.6 (f) 5.5, 3.5
5) (c) (0,0) (d) (1,1) (2,1) (3,1) (4,1) (1,2) (2,2) (3,2)
(e) (4,0) (5,0) (6,0) (3,1) (4,1) (2,2) (3,2) (f) (4,2)
6) $10x + 15y \leq 100$ 7) $x + y \leq 8$ 8) $3x + 4y \geq 15$
9) $9x + 3y \geq 64$. $x + y \leq 16$. $42x + 6y \leq 210$. $x = 3, y = 13$.

24.2.2 Page 213

1) 10 type 1, 5 type 2 2) 300 car, 50 lorries
3) $x + y \leq 5$. $200x + 300y \leq 1200$. £280
4) $4X + 6Y \geq 16$. $5X + 3Y \geq 11$. $X = 1, Y = 2$
5) $x \leq y$. $5x + 4y \leq 44$. $150x + 80y \geq 900$. $x = y = 4$
6) $3x + 4y \leq 600$. $20x + 50y \leq 5000$. $x \geq 50$. £10,000

Chapter 25

25.1.2 Page 217

1) (a) $\frac{1}{17}$ (b) $\frac{4}{51}$ (c) $\frac{13}{51}$ (d) $\frac{25}{51}$
2) (a) $\frac{1}{6}$ (b) $\frac{1}{6}$ (c) 0
3) (a) $\frac{2}{3}$ (b) $\frac{5}{9}$
4) (a) $\frac{1}{4}$ (b) $\frac{1}{13}$ (c) $\frac{1}{4}$ (d) $\frac{1}{13}$ (e) $\frac{1}{2}$

25.2.2 Page 219

1) $\frac{81}{100}$ 2) $\frac{2}{7}$ 3) $\frac{1}{21}$ 4) $\frac{1}{6}$ 5) $\frac{14}{57}$
6) (a) $\frac{66}{325}$ (b) $\frac{84}{325}$
7) $\frac{1}{125}$ 8) $\frac{1}{6}$
9) (a) $\frac{1}{36}$ (b) $\frac{1}{6}$
10) (a) $\frac{1}{36}$ (b) $\frac{1}{36}$ (c) $\frac{1}{4}$
11) (a) $\frac{1}{20}$ (b) $\frac{7}{16}$
12) (a) $\frac{2}{5}$ (b) $\frac{1}{3}$
13) (a) $\frac{1}{17}$ (b) $\frac{1}{221}$ (c) $\frac{1}{52}$

25.3.2 Page 221

1) $\frac{8}{11}$ 2) $\frac{33}{221}$ 3) $\frac{11}{36}$ 4) $\frac{99}{100}$ 5) $\frac{9}{14}$ 6) $\frac{175}{256}$

7) 0.518 8) 0.651 9) 0.570 10) $\frac{29}{120}$ 11) $\frac{17}{60}$

12) (a) $\frac{1}{18}$ (b) $\frac{5}{36}$

13) (a) $\frac{3}{8}$ (b) $\frac{11}{24}$

14) (a) $\frac{1}{15}$ (b) $\frac{3}{25}$

15) $\frac{8}{27} \cdot \frac{19}{27}$

Mental tests

Test 1 Page 236

1) £10.54 2) 33.33% 3) 4.28 4) 21, 22, 23

5) 6 yd 2 ft 6) 9 p.m., 6th Jan. 7) 0.1 8) £180,000

9) 16 10) 4:3 11) 2×10^{-6} 12) $\frac{12}{35}$

13) 8.47 14) $6x + 8y$ 15) C2 D2 D3 D4 C4 B4 B3 B2

16) 3 17) 50 cm 18) cosine rule 19) 180°, 270°

20) $\frac{4}{13}$

Test 2 Page 237

1) 4 goblins, 2 ghosts 2) 30 3) 3 4) 20 kg

5) August 10th 6) 228 7) 200 secs 8) 9.95 cm

9) 28 ft. 10) 9 11) xy^2 12) $\frac{x}{1000}$ kg

13) $2x + 8$ 14) subtract 32, divide by 9, multiply by 4 15) 045°

16) 20 cm^2 17) 300° 18) tan 19) 12

20) $\frac{9}{100}$

Index